Dial M for Murdoch

TOM WATSON

and

MARTIN HICKMAN

Dial M for Murdoch

News Corporation and the Corruption of Britain

ALLEN LANE
an imprint of
PENGUIN BOOKS

ALLEN LANE

Published by the Penguin Group
Penguin Books Ltd, 80 Strand, London WC2R ORL, England
Penguin Group (USA) Inc., 375 Hudson Street, New York, New York 10014, USA
Penguin Group (Canada), 90 Eglinton Avenue East, Suite 700, Toronto, Ontario,
Canada M4P 2Y3 (a division of Pearson Canada Inc.)
Penguin Ireland, 25 St Stephen's Green, Dublin 2, Ireland (a division of Penguin Books Ltd)
Penguin Group (Australia), 250 Camberwell Road, Camberwell, Victoria 3124,
Australia (a division of Pearson Australia Group Pty Ltd)
Penguin Books India Pvt Ltd, 11 Community Centre,
Panchsheel Park, New Delhi – 110 017, India
Penguin Group (NZ), 67 Apollo Drive, Rosedale, Auckland 0632, New Zealand
(a division of Pearson New Zealand Ltd)
Penguin Books (South Africa) (Pty) Ltd, Block D, Rosebank Office Park,
181 Jan Smuts Avenue, Parktown North, Gauteng 2193, South Africa

Penguin Books Ltd, Registered Offices: 80 Strand, London WC2R ORL, England

www.penguin.com

First published 2012
001

Set in 10.5/14 pt Sabon LT Std
Typeset by Jouve (UK), Milton Keynes
Printed in Great Britain by Clays Ltd, St Ives plc

Hardback ISBN: 978–1–846–14603–9
Trade paperback ISBN: 978–1–846–14604–6

www.greenpenguin.co.uk

ALWAYS LEARNING   PEARSON

For
Saoirse and Malachy
and
Rachel, Kate and Finlay

Really what Rupert Murdoch managed to do was break the civil compact of this country through achieving a degree of control over the essential institutions of a free society: the press, the police and the politicians.

I've been one who has never accepted any of this 'gate' stuff and all the parallels – that are usually made by the Murdoch press – to some sex scandal ... but this is for real. And the parallels are remarkable.

– Carl Bernstein, asked how the hacking scandal compares to
Watergate, 29 September 2011

Power tends to corrupt, and absolute power corrupts absolutely. Great men are almost always bad men.

– Lord Acton, 1887

Contents

List of Illustrations   xi

Dramatis Personae   xv

Preface   xvii

1 The Wrong Headlines   1

2 Wapping's News Factory   13

3 The Dark Arts   27

4 First Heads Roll   36

5 Rogue Defence   53

6 The Manchester Lawyers   68

7 One Determined Reporter   81

8 Intimidating Parliament   96

9 A Murder   107

10 Our Man in Downing Street   121

11 Losing a Battle   135

12 Out of Control   149

13 U-turn at Wapping   167

14 Summer's Lease   183

15 A Missing Girl   189

16 Sky Plus   210

17 'We Are Sorry'   228

18 Democracy Day   238

19 Assault on the Establishment   255

20 The Ghosts of Wapping   269

CONTENTS

21 The Press on Trial   289

22 Darker and Darker   305

Appendix 1: Individuals in Glenn
    Mulcaire's Notes   319

Appendix 2: Arrests   323

Acknowledgements   326

Notes   329

Index   341

List of Illustrations

Section One

1. Rupert Murdoch in London in 1969, the year he took over the *News of the World* © Sydney O'Meara / Getty Images

2. Rupert Murdoch in London in 2011, the day after his appearance before the Commons Cultural Committee © Press Association Images

3. Piers Morgan, Rebekah Brooks and Andy Coulson, at a party hosted by Elisabeth Murdoch and Matthew Freud in 2004 © Dave M Bennett / Getty Images

4. Rebekah Brooks and Tony Blair at the Newspaper Press Fund reception in 2004 © Fiona Hanson / Press Association Images

5. James Murdoch, David Cameron and George Osborne at a summit on social responsibility in 2007 © Stephen Lock / Rex Features

6. Tommy and Gail Sheridan celebrate their libel victory over the *News of the World* in 2006 © Jeff J Mitchell / Getty Images

7. Glenn Mulcaire, the private investigator convicted of hacking phones for News International © Bloomberg / Getty Images

8. Clive Goodman, the *News of the World*'s royal editor, jailed in 2007 © Chris Jackson / Getty Images

9. Les Hinton, Rupert Murdoch's loyal man for five decades © Bloomberg / Getty Images

10. Max Mosley, Formula I motor-racing chief, who triumphed over the *News of the World* in 2008 © Michael Cooper / Getty Images

11. Gordon Taylor, chief executive of the PFA and the first phone-hacking victim to mount a legal challenge to News International (pictured with the footballer Cristiano Ronaldo) © John Peters / Man Utd / Getty Images

12. Charlotte Harris, one of the first lawyers to take on the *News of the World* © Nick Harvey / WireImage / Getty Images

13. Nick Davies, the Guardian journalist who unpicked News Corp's defence © Guardian News & Media Ltd 2011

14. Neville Thurlbeck, the *News of the World*'s chief reporter © Yui Mok / Press Association Images

15. John Yates, Assistant Commissioner of the Metropolitan Police, who declared his faith in Operation Caryatid © Dan Kitwood / Getty Images

16. Neil 'Wolfman' Wallis, deputy editor of the *News of the World*, later hired by Scotland Yard (with friends) © Dennis Stone / Rex Features

17. David Cameron and Andy Coulson: Coulson helped the Conservative Leader acquire the 'tabloid touch' © Tom Stoddart Archive / Getty Images

18. Cameron and Murdoch in bed: in 2010, the Conservatives backed News Corp's takeover bid for BSkyB © Sang Tan / AP / Press Association Images

Section Two

19. The Golden Lion, the site of Daniel Morgan's murder in 1987 © Rex Features

20. Jonathan Rees, the private detective re-employed by Coulson's *News of the World*, after he was jailed for conspiracy to pervert the course of justice © Rex Features

21. Daniel Morgan, Rees's murdered business partner © Press Association Images

22. 'The world's greatest newspaper 1843–2011' Colin Myler and *News of the World* staff outside the office as the paper closes down © Yui Mok / Press Association Images

23. Sir Paul Stephenson resigned as Commissioner of the Metropolitan Police in July 2011 © Leon Neal / AFP / Getty Images

24. Rebekah Brooks and Rupert Murdoch after the closure of the *News of the World* – and shortly before she resigned © Ian Nicholson / Press Association Images

25. Detectives raid Andy Coulson's home in July 2011, on suspicion of phone hacking and corruption © Paul Hackett / Reuters

26. 'I Regret Hiring Coulson' © Ray Tang / Rex Features

27. Protesters outside the Houses of Parliament in July 2011 © Paula Bronstein / Getty Images

28. James and Rupert Murdoch appear before MPs – and the world watches © Press Association Images

29. Steve Coogan, Hugh Grant and Max Mosley at Parliament's joint committee on privacy in December 2011 © Press Association Images

30. J. K. Rowling felt as though she was being 'blackmailed' by the *Sun* over a leak of the fifth Harry Potter book © David Miller / Empics / Press Association Images

31. Charlotte Church, harassed by News International papers from an early age © NBC via Getty Images

32. Sienna Miller began a High Court case against News International in 2010 © Reuters

33. Bob and Sally Dowler, Milly Dowler's parents, arrive at the Leveson Inquiry with Mark Lewis © Rex Features

The Cotswold Triangle

Cartographer: Michael Hill / Maps Illustrated

1. Rebekah and Charlie Brooks © Alan Crowhurst / Getty Images

2. The Brooks Residence © Rui Vieira / Press Association Images

3. Hackers Lane © INS News Agency

4. Burford Priory © Prixnews / Alamy

5. Elisabeth Murdoch and Matthew Freud © Dave M Bennett / Getty Images

6. David Cameron's constituency home
© INS News Agency Cartoon
© Howard McWilliam / *The Daily Telegraph*

Dramatis Personae

NEWS CORPORATION

Rupert Murdoch, chairman and chief executive

James Murdoch, chief executive, News Corp Asia and Europe; Chairman, BSkyB

Les Hinton, chief executive, News International

News of the World:

Rebekah Brooks (nee Wade), editor

 (Later editor of the *Sun* and chief executive, News International)

Andy Coulson, editor

 (Later, communications director, Conservative Party)

Colin Myler, editor

Tom Crone, legal director

Neville Thurlbeck, chief reporter

Clive Goodman, royal editor

METROPOLITAN POLICE

Sir Paul Stephenson, Commissioner

Andy Hayman, Assistant Commissioner

John Yates, Assistant Commissioner

Sue Akers, Deputy Assistant Commissioner

PRIVATE DETECTIVES

Steve Whittamore

Glenn Mulcaire

Jonathan Rees

LAWYERS
Mark Lewis

Charlotte Harris

Mark Thomson

POLITICIANS
John Prescott

Tom Watson

Chris Bryant

LITIGANTS
Gordon Taylor

Max Clifford

Sienna Miller

Steve Coogan

Hugh Grant

Max Mosley

Charlotte Church

JOURNALISTS
Guardian:

Nick Davies

Amelia Hill

New York Times:

Don van Natta Jr

Jo Becker

Graham Bowley

BBC:

Glenn Campbell

Independent:

Martin Hickman

Cahal Milmo

Preface

This book tries to explain how a particular global media company works: how it came to exert a poisonous, secretive influence on public life in Britain, how it used its huge power to bully, intimidate and to cover up, and how its exposure has changed the way we look at our politicians, our police service and our press. Some political 'friends' have tried to portray the hacking and bribery which has exposed the workings of News Corporation as part of the price you pay for good tabloid journalism. They're wrong. Of course, tabloids sometimes get out of hand, but this is not (at least, not much) a story of harmless mischief, of reporters in false moustaches and rollicking exposés of hypocrites. It is not just the famous and wealthy who have been damaged, but ordinary decent people who happened to be in the wrong place at the wrong time.

The legendary Fleet Street names whose reputations have been tarnished could almost (but not quite) be considered tiny pawns. This is a power game played out in the boardrooms and dining salons of the elite, and every political party, mine included, has had an inner circle of people on the Murdoch invitation list. Ultimately this scandal is about the failure of politicians to act in the interests of the powerless rather than themselves. As the book shows, I hope beyond any doubt, prime ministers, ministers, Parliament, the police, the justice system and the 'free' press became collectively defective when it came to investigating the activities of NewsCorp. Now that Murdoch's corrupt grip on our national institutions is loosening, and thanks to the laser-beam focus of Lord Justice Leveson, who leads the public inquiry into this affair, these individuals and public bodies are belatedly starting to clean up their acts.

I know from personal experience what it's like to be attacked by Rupert Murdoch's organization. In the book, I give a first-hand account of some of the worst moments – though they were infinitely less bad, of course, than others have suffered. Sometimes, now, I can laugh at my former situation: a well connected ex-minister in parliament, altering his route home at night, fearful of someone who might be in pursuit. But the affair has taken its toll: the failure of my marriage, the loss of friends and intense stress over many years. Even though the mechanisms of intimidation have now been exposed, I still obsessively memorize the number plates of unfamiliar vehicles parked outside my house. That's what it does to you when you're at the receiving end of the Murdoch fear-machine – the threats, bullying, covert surveillance, hacking, aggressive reporting and personal abuse make you permanently wary.

That was the state I was in – suspicious and paranoid – when Martin Hickman called me in October 2010, for the first time in ten years. I was distrustful of most reporters and at a low ebb, but Martin was an old friend: we had known each other well at Hull University, where he'd set up a newspaper and I'd become president of the Students' Union, my first elected position. At that stage, a trusted journalist seeking to investigate a media cover-up was rare. Regularly from then on, we would meet quietly at the Fire Station bar next to Waterloo station in South London, often for black coffee and breakfast before work, or occasionally late at night over a beer. Whilst the commuters tapped into their laptops and the revellers partied, we would sit in the corner, away from prying MPs and journalists, talking about developments as they happened. Martin was always a great person to bounce things off.

Of course, I wasn't working in isolation. Many individuals, most notably the *Guardian*'s Nick Davies, the BBC's Glenn Campbell and lawyers Mark Lewis and Charlotte Harris, played critical parts in unravelling this complex scandal. Even so, in the early days, it was a lonely pursuit. We became close in the face of opposition from Murdoch's UK executives, the Metropolitan Police, the Crown Prosecution Service, the Press Complaints Commission and many of my fellow politicians. We were all helped by the brave whistleblowers who summoned the courage to share key information with us. Though still too frightened to go public, they know who they are, and believe me, they are heroes.

Because I was involved, I come into the book myself from time to time, as Martin does occasionally too. But though the story is inevitably coloured by personal experiences, we didn't want to over-emphasize our roles, and for that reason it is written in the third person: I am not 'me' or 'Tom' but 'Tom Watson'; similarly Martin is 'Martin Hickman'.

Martin is calm and cautious. I am not. I hope our contrasting char-acters have created an accurate and informative account, albeit one which leaves you in no doubt as to what we think of the events and organization we are writing about. Many of the events are public knowledge, but they have become so in fits and starts and the connec-tions between them have not been made. We believe that seeing the story whole, as it is presented here for the first time, allows the char-acter of the organization to emerge unmistakably. Please tell us what *you* think. We're on Twitter at @tom_watson and @Martin_Hick-man.

This story is not yet over, but it extends deeper into the past than some may realize. For most, it really began when a newspaper story about the hacking of a missing girl's phone prompted a national wail of outrage so loud it was heard in the lofty world of Rupert Murdoch, and the mighty proprietor had to account for his actions to repre-sentatives of the people for the first time. So this is where our story begins – in the middle of those tumultuous days.

Tom Watson
April 2012

I

The Wrong Headlines

They caught us with dirty hands
　　　　　　　　　　　　－ Rupert Murdoch, 19 July 2011

On a clear summer's day in July 2011, a black chauffeur-driven Range Rover weaved its way through the streets of London towards the House of Commons. As it stopped at a red light diagonally opposite Big Ben, photographers crowded round the rear window and snapped its eighty-year-old VIP passenger. His thickly lined jowly face offered up a weak smile. Rupert Murdoch was three hours early for his first appointment with British democracy.

For decades, the most powerful media mogul in the world had orchestrated public life from the shadows, hugely influential but hidden. Now he had been hauled before a parliamentary committee to do something peculiar for him: explain himself. In a single tumultuous fortnight, the global business he had accumulated over sixty bustling years had fallen into a deep crisis. His moralizing tabloid newspaper, the *News of the World,* had been caught systematically and illegally spying on the rich, the powerful and the famous. For years, his British executives had covered up its crimes. They had destroyed evidence, run smear campaigns, lied to Parliament and threatened and intimidated journalists, lawyers and politicians. Despite their efforts, the truth about the 'dark arts' of newsgathering at Murdoch's UK newspaper empire, News International, had slowly surfaced.

Trawling for scandal, a private detective working for the *News of the World,* Glenn Mulcaire, had been hacking into the mobile phone messages of princes, pop stars, TV presenters, Hollywood actors,

Premiership footballers, cabinet ministers and their friends, relatives, agents and advisers. News International's lawbreaking involved not just phones, but everything electronic, including personal computers and state archives. Through a network of corrupt police officers and public officials, Murdoch's muckrakers could obtain private phone numbers, emails, vehicle registrations, and tax, income, employment and medical records. But their targets were not just the wealthy and famous. If misfortune called, the grieving and even the dead could be swept into the sights of his clandestine news-gatherers. On 4 July 2011, the *News of the World* created a scandal bigger than any it had ever investigated – when the public learned it had hacked into the voicemails of a missing thirteen-year-old schoolgirl, and shortly after-wards, those of parents of murdered children and survivors of terrorist bombings. There was national revulsion; gutter journalism had sunk into the sewer.

Amid the outrage, Murdoch tried to manoeuvre himself out of trouble, but such was the outpouring of disgust that Britain's political leaders, for so long servile to the Australian tycoon who took US citizenship in 1985, rose up against him and opposed his biggest ever business deal, the intended takeover of the BSkyB TV network, from which he was forced to withdraw.

As the scandal swirled around Britain and the world, it cost Murdoch tens of millions of pounds, ruined the reputations of several of his most trusted lieutenants, and damaged the wider press, police, prosecutors and UK government. In London, the Prime Minister, David Cameron, announced a judge-led inquiry to investigate the delinquency of British newspapers. In the United States, the Federal Bureau of Investigation launched an investigation into the possible hacking of the victims of the 9/11 terrorist attacks. Shares in Murdoch's multimedia conglomerate, moored in a black skyscraper in New York, fell 19 per cent, wiping $10 billion from its value. Commentators began whispering that the octogenarian billionaire might be deposed and his quick-tempered son James might never inherit the crown. Shareholders might even force the sale of his British papers. In all his years in business – mostly of breakneck expansion – these were the heaviest blows to rain down upon Rupert Murdoch.

Yet at first, increasingly remote and with his powers failing, he had not realized the seriousness of his predicament. While his troubled news empire dominated the radio and TV bulletins, he had stayed in the US and tried to shrug off the fuss, as he had done in the past whenever touched by controversy, which was often. When he had arrived in London on 10 July, he had smiled for the cameras. As if to underline his position in an elite space above democracy, he had refused an invitation to appear before the House of Commons Culture, Media and Sport Committee, which had – along with a few journalists and lawyers – unpicked the connections between his executives and the politicians and police who had protected his interests. The committee's MPs then did something unimaginable two weeks before: they dispatched one of Parliament's ancient-office holders, the Deputy Serjeant-at-Arms, to Murdoch's newspaper headquarters in Wapping, east London, where he delivered the order to testify. Theoretically the Australian-born chief executive* could have been thrown into jail if he had disobeyed the summons, but its true significance was that Parliament was asserting its will against a figure it had never dared to challenge before. In an instant, Murdoch's four-decade spell over British public life was broken.

On the morning of 19 July, the public queued round the block for seats at the inquisition in Portcullis House, a modern annexe to the House of Commons, as Murdoch, looking pale and diminished, arrived on the white upholstery of his four-wheel drive. A global audience of millions watched on TV as he and his 38-year-old son took their seats in front of the MPs shortly after 2.30 p.m. After four days of preparation, the Murdochs had a plan to minimize the bad publicity by reading out a prepared statement apologizing for the wrongdoing, but the MPs barred James from reading it. His eyes flashed with barely suppressed anger. As he blustered, his father touched his arm and said: 'I would just like to say one sentence . . .' and his lips uncurled a headline: 'This is the most humble day of my life.'

One of the nine Parliamentarians facing the Murdochs was Tom Watson, MP for West Bromwich East. He had spent two years excavating what had been going on in their business, during which time

---

* A variety of US laws restrict ownership or control of US media companies to US citizens. Rupert Murdoch took on US citizenship in 1985.

his marriage had disintegrated and he had constantly shuffled between London, his constituency, his family and friends' homes. He had had whispered conversations with shadowy contacts who spoke of collusion between Murdoch's news-gatherers and the government, the security services and London's police force. At one stage he had melodramatically (but not entirely unreasonably) feared for his life. At others he was astonished as evidence of widespread criminality exposed the bullying reality of an out-of-control organization whose family controllers had escaped accounting for their behaviour.

In the oak-panelled Wilson Room, Rupert Murdoch came across not as a modern-day Citizen Kane, but as a deaf, doddery, proud old man, his son as being trapped in a Master of Business Administration presentation, deploying a strangulated American-British accent and tortuously phrased sentences. They were humble and apologetic, but also defiant. They insisted they had not known about the criminality in their midst: they stressed what a tiny part the *News of the World* played in their multimedia empire. 'My company has 52,000 employees,' Rupert Murdoch explained. 'I have led it for fifty-seven years and I have made my share of mistakes. I have lived in many countries, employed thousands of honest and hard-working journalists, owned nearly 200 newspapers.'

So who, wondered the veteran Scottish MP Jim Sheridan, did he blame for his tabloid's excesses and the loss of the BSkyB bid? Murdoch's reply was clear – his rivals: 'They caught us with dirty hands and they built the hysteria around it.'

Just before 5 p.m., the proprietor who had eaten humble pie two hours earlier at the start of the session, received another helping. A 'comedian' called Jonathan May-Bowles rose from his seat and, to the shock of MPs and police, strode over to the global entrepreneur and shoved a paper plate loaded with shaving foam into his face. May-Bowles was met by a firm slap from Murdoch's Chinese-born wife Wendi Deng. The proceedings were called to a halt for ten minutes, and Watson strolled over to father and son. As he did so, he heard one of the Murdoch aides say: 'Don't worry, this will play well.' Watson poured the mogul a glass of water and told him, 'Your wife's got quite a right hook.' He asked James if he would like some water too. 'No, Mr Watson,' James replied. Watson poured him a glass anyway. At 5.08 p.m. the hearing resumed.

As the three-hour session drew to a close, Watson had a question for the young heir. He wanted to know about an incriminating document about an extraordinarily large payment to a hacking victim, whose silence was bought. 'James – sorry, if I may call you James, to differentiate,' Watson said. 'When you signed off the Taylor payment, did you see or were you made aware of the "For Neville" email, the transcript of the hacked voicemail messages?' James Murdoch looked straight at Watson and replied: 'No, I was not aware of that at the time.' The future of the Murdoch dynasty would turn out to hang on the truthfulness of those ten words.

As he entered his ninth decade, Rupert Murdoch ruled over a media business mightier than any other in history. He was, as the title of a recent biography put it, *The Man Who Owns the News*.[1] At the start of 2011, 1 billion people daily digested his products – books, newspapers, magazines, TV shows and films – and News Corporation, his holding company, had annual sales of $33 billion.

His passion was not money, though, but business itself. He loved the piratical thrill of takeovers – the brinkmanship, the deal-making, the constant expansion – and the power. Both came most intoxicatingly in ink. In Britain, he had come to control 40 per cent of national newspaper circulation – making him the most important proprietor in politics – through his ownership of the best-selling Sunday paper the *News of the World* and the daily *Sun*, and their quality stablemates *The Times* and *The Sunday Times*. In his native Australia his dominance was greater still: 70 per cent of the newspaper market; while in his adopted United States, through the *New York Post*, the *Wall Street Journal* and the most-watched cable news outlet, Fox News, Murdoch exerted a strong pull on American politics.

All this he had accrued from a single newspaper in Adelaide, the *News*, which he inherited from his domineering father in 1952 and where he learned the uncompromising tactics that made him the news baron of the twenty-first century. In his Australian apprenticeship, Murdoch did not overly bother with journalistic ethics or notions of media responsibility, but identified and published what sold. His newspapers plumbed the commonest denominators of sex, celebrity, crime, scandal and sport – ideally, all together. After moving to the UK in the 1970s, he promoted the naked page 3 girl, published the fraudulent 'Hitler Diaries', and backed the *Sun*'s hot-headed editor Kelvin Mackenzie despite the printing of false stories, such as the front page claiming that Liverpool football fans had pickpocketed the dead during the 1989 Hillsborough Disaster. The 'Dirty Digger', as he was named by *Private Eye*, operated with guile, charm, tenacity and ruthlessness. As soon as he took over a newspaper, he broke his promises. After buying the *News of the World* in 1969 he swiftly eased out the chairman Sir William Carr despite promising to keep him; at the *Sun* he abandoned his assurance that he would maintain its support of Labour, when it backed the Conservatives in 1979; and at *The Times* and *The Sunday Times* he broke all of his guarantees of editorial independence in his first year of ownership. Harry Evans, *The Times*'s erstwhile editor, recalled: 'He put his point of view very simply to the home editor of *The Times*, Fred Emery, when he summoned him from holiday on 4 March to his office shortly before asking for my resignation: "I give instructions to my editors all round the world, why shouldn't I in London?" He was reminded of his undertakings to the Secretary of State. "They're not worth the paper they're written on," Murdoch replied.'[2]

Most importantly, Murdoch courted and cajoled politicians. He started with a bust of Lenin in his room at Oxford University, but soon espoused the hard-right-wing views common among the super-rich: for strong leadership, low taxation and light regulation, and against trade unions, the European Union and global-warming science. His newspapers undermined disobedient politicians and wholeheartedly supported challengers who would advance his political and commercial agenda, particularly by granting him favours in the heavily regulated TV industry.

He championed the Conservative leader Margaret Thatcher, whose government approved his purchase of the *Times* titles, ordered the police to help him fight the print unions at Wapping (where he installed industry-changing new technology – an achievement which transformed the finances of newspapers), and exempted his Luxembourg-based Sky satellite business from rules on foreign ownership. Aware that no political party stayed in power for ever, Murdoch changed political horses in the mid-1990s, when he began wooing Labour's youthful leader Tony Blair. Desperate to end Labour's electoral drubbings, in 1995 Blair made a transcontinental pilgrimage to a News Corp conference on Hayman Island off Australia, where he spoke to the assembled executives of News Corporation and held talks with the kingmaker. In his book *Where Power Lies*, the former Labour spin doctor Lance Price wrote: 'A deal had been done, although with nothing in writing. If Murdoch were left to pursue his business interests in peace he would give Labour a fair wind.'[3] According to the diaries of Piers Morgan, the former *News of the World* editor, an apologetic Blair told him: 'Piers, I had to court him . . . It is better to be riding the tiger's back than let it rip your throat out. Look what Murdoch did to Kinnock.'*[4]

Murdoch's newspapers endorsed Tony Blair at three general elections. In return, Blair's Labour Party opposed plans to impose tougher cross-media ownership rules in 1996, rejected calls for a ban on predatory pricing of newspapers in 1998, the same year lobbied for Murdoch's television interests – asking the Italian Prime Minister Romano Prodi whether the tycoon could acquire Silvio Berlusconi's Mediaset TV network – and frequently gave interviews and important announcements to his papers, such as the date of the 2001 general election.

As Murdoch jetted around the world overseeing his business interests, his favoured editors became his *de facto* powerbrokers in his absence. He became particularly enamoured of one of them, Rebekah Wade, a mischievous, red-haired tabloid queen, a 'larrikin' in Murdoch's Australian vernacular, who inspired fatherly feelings in the ageing patriarch. As a grammar-school girl in Warrington in England's industrial north, her father a tugboat worker, Wade hankered for a career in journalism. She turned up on the *News of the World* at Wapping as a 21-year-old secretary in 1989 and eleven years later, after working, scheming and networking her way to the top, had become

---

* During the 1992 general election campaign, the *Sun* campaigned vigorously against Labour leader Neil Kinnock. On polling day it superimposed his head on a front-page picture of a lightbulb with the warning: 'If Kinnock wins today will the last person to leave Britain please turn out the lights.' How far such attacks (or endorsements) actually affect the behaviour of voters is uncertain, but politicians of all parties believe that they do.

its editor. A *News of the World* reporter recalled that her 'charisma' matched her ambition. 'She was very tactile, touching you on the arm, looking straight into your eyes as though there was no one more important in the room. From the way she acted, you would think she wanted to sleep with you [but] she was way too up the scale for that.'[5]

The coquettish Wade enjoyed Murdoch's full support, despite making blunders such as (having been promoted to edit the *Sun* in 2003) admitting to a parliamentary committee that his newspapers had bribed police.* He even forgave her two years later when she spent eight hours in police cells for attacking her then husband, the *East Enders* star Ross Kemp.

Usefully, Wade was very friendly with senior politicians, notably Tony Blair. During his ten years at 10 Downing Street, she was a frequent kisser of the prime ministerial cheek and one of the keepers of the Blairite flame. Those who crossed Tony Blair often saw themselves attacked by the papers under Rebekah Wade's sway – as Tom Watson found out.

On becoming an MP in 2001, Tom Watson was oblivious to the scale of the influence wielded behind the scenes in politics by Rupert Murdoch. Within months of being elected to Parliament, the 34-year-old former backroom Labour strategist was identified as a person of interest by News International's head of corporate affairs, Alison Clark; he accepted a tour of the company's Wapping HQ and drank

---

* On 1 March 2003, giving evidence to a media inquiry by the House of Commons Culture, Media and Sport Committee, Wade painted a picture of a responsible news-gathering operation that abided by the law and journalism's code of practice. But a glimpse of the truth slipped from her lips when Chris Bryant, a committee member, asked her whether News International paid police for information. A fellow back-bencher in a Commons tearoom had told Bryant that after losing his wallet at a London restaurant, the *News of the World* had run an innuendo-laden piece about an MP losing money late at night in Soho, a red-light district. To the surprise of the Committee members, Wade replied: 'We have paid the police for information in the past.' In his diaries, the editor of the rival *Mirror*, Piers Morgan, remarked: 'Rebekah excelled herself by virtually admitting she's been illegally paying police for information. I called her to thank her for dropping the tabloid baton. She said: "That's why I should never be seen or heard in public."'[6]

champagne aboard its yacht on the Solent. As he moved up the career ladder, becoming a minister in the whips' office in 2004 and a junior Defence Minister in May 2006, Watson began to realize the close relationship between the Prime Minister and News Corp's chief executive. When ministers formulated policy they often had an eye on Murdoch's response; he was a constant invisible presence in Downing Street.

Not long after joining the government, Watson became disenchanted with Blair. As a defence minister, his nightly papers described the mounting number of soldiers killed in Iraq and Afghanistan (name, rank, religion, family). The floundering military campaigns in Iraq and Afghanistan had undermined Blair's political authority and diminished the trust between him and the voters. Watson had doubts about Tony Blair's leadership of the country, but it was two trivial matters which convinced him that the Prime Minister had lost touch: reports that Blair had billed the Labour Party for his wife Cherie's haircuts during the 2005 general election campaign, and that he had ordered the redecoration of the nuclear bunker at public expense.

On Thursday 31 August, during the summer recess, Watson was pushed into outright rebellion while sinking pints of real ale with two fellow MPs in Ye Olde Robin Hood pub on the banks of the river Severn at Ironbridge, Shropshire. A political journalist had tipped off Siôn Simon, one of Watson's companions, that Blair had given an interview to the next day's *Times* in which he refused to timetable his departure, declaring: 'I've said I'm not going to go on and on, and I said I'll leave ample time for my successor. Now at some point people have to accept that as a reasonable proposition and let me get on with the job.'

That night Watson and a few friends ate in the Bilash Indian restaurant in Wolverhampton. Contrary to subsequent reports, the ensuing mutiny against Blair was not hatched there, but the following day. As Watson recovered from a hangover, MPs' phones buzzed and the Labour backbencher Chris Bryant, who had been infuriated by Blair's comments, drafted a letter urging him to set a term to his premiership. Watson agreed to sign it if Bryant and Simon moderated its language. Seventeen backbenchers, seven ministerial aides and Watson signed the private letter to the Prime Minister calling for him to set a departure date. It was leaked to the press on 6 September. Watson resigned as a minister, followed by the seven ministerial aides.

In an angry statement, Blair called Watson 'disloyal, discourteous and wrong', adding that he had planned to sack him anyway. A few miles east of Downing Street, in another centre of power, Rebekah Wade was fuming that her close friend had been undermined.

Watson now experienced what it was like to get on the wrong side of the Murdoch empire. On 7 September, the *Sun* called him the ringleader of the 'plotting gang of weasels', reported fury at him 'for playing grubby politics at a time when soldiers are dying in Afghanistan' and condemned him for 'shamefully' walking out of his job. But as a result of the growing pressure, Blair announced that day that he would step down within a year. At the Labour Party conference the following month, Watson was told by the *Sun*'s political editor George Pascoe-Watson: 'My editor will pursue you for the rest of your life. She will never forgive you for what you did to her Tony.'

Gordon Brown succeeded Tony Blair as Prime Minister in June 2007 and made Watson a Cabinet Office minister the following year. Watson soon experienced the wrath of News International's newspapers again. Murdoch, his son James and Rebekah Wade were moving against Brown and anointing the new Opposition leader, David Cameron. In April 2009, the political blogger Iain Dale erroneously implicated Watson in a plan by Brown's special adviser, Damian McBride, to smear Cameron and his close ally George Osborne. In an email to a former Labour special adviser, Derek Draper, McBride had rekindled rumours that the Conservative leader had an embarrassing medical condition and Osborne had taken drugs with a prostitute, which he suggested could be circulated on a new left-wing website, Red Rag. The right-wing 'Guido Fawkes' blogger, Paul Staines, somehow obtained McBride's emails, and passed the story to *The Sunday Times* and the *News of the World*. Shortly afterwards, Staines destroyed his computer hard drives.

The 'Damian-gate' plot marked a new low in Brown's faltering government and undermined his publicly stated ambition to move beyond the 'spin' of Blair's administration. McBride resigned, but one of the emails had mentioned Watson in passing. Watson issued a statement denying he was involved, but for some political journalists the story was too good to drop and on 12 April the *Mail on Sunday* ran it. As he and his wife Siobhan travelled to Cornwall, where his brother-in-law was about to undergo a double organ transplant, Watson issued a second statement again denying any complicity. While he was away from his constituency home neighbours chased off three men – one with a camera – who had scaled a 6ft gate to rifle through paperwork in his garage. Then, on 14 April, the knives came out: the *Sun*'s columnist Fergus Shanahan informed its 7 million readers: 'There is another unsavoury creature lurking in the shadows who should join McBride on the dole – and he's not a civil servant like McBride but a minister appointed by Brown. Treacherous Tom Watson – a tub of lard who is known without affection at Westminster as 'Two Dinners' Tommy – is suspected of being in this up to his bloated and bulging neck.' Under the headline 'Mad Dog was trained to maul', the *Sun*'s political writer Trevor Kavanagh accused 'hatchet man Tom Watson' of being among the plotters, writing: 'This was the motley crew who dreamed up grisly lies about David Cameron and George Osborne.' The paper urged Brown to sack the 'poisonous' minister, whose continued employment was 'a stain on the Prime Minister's judgement and the government's credibility'. George Pascoe-Watson later told Brown's spokesman Michael Dugher that Wade had forced him to write knocking stories about Watson that he knew were 'bollocks'. Wade also texted someone very close to Brown personally urging him to sack Watson. The Prime Minister refused to do so but, stung by the coverage, he called Watson and asked: 'I have to ask you this: do you know anything about the registration of the Red Rag website?' If Watson had set up Red Rag, Brown would have faced calls for his resignation.

As he lay in bed in the Ship Inn in Perranporth on 15 April, Watson could not sleep; his mind was abuzz and he constantly replayed events. He had hired a researcher on a temporary contract for three months. She was a blogger. What if she had set up Red Rag without his knowledge? At 3 a.m., he went to the bathroom and rang her. In a frantic, whispered conversation, he asked if she had been responsible. She had not, but she became anxious about Watson's state of mind. Shortly before dawn, Watson crept out of bed and bought the papers. His picture was at the top of yet another story in the *Sun* – this time on the front page – about pressure building on Gordon Brown. That day *The Times* mocked up McBride, Watson, Nick Brown, Ian Austin, Charlie Wheelan and Ed Balls as characters from *Reservoir Dogs*. As Watson walked along the beach, he was in tears.

The following morning, Siôn Simon took a call from Watson that he remembers as unlike any other:

> At first I thought something really cataclysmic had happened, like someone had died or got arrested. He's been one of my closest friends for a long time, and I've never heard him sound like that before or since. He was literally raving. Struggling to choke back tears most of the time, his voice was broken and distorted, and he was just talking crazy. Usually the most hard-headed hyper-rationalist you'll come across, he was just saying ridiculous things: 'I'm going to resign, today or tomorrow; I'm completely innocent of everything they're saying. It's all just lies and bile, but I'm going to resign anyway, just to show them. I'll resign with a hard-hitting statement of exactly what they are like, all the lies, all the things they do, the way they just do what they want.'
>
> I told him that it would have no impact, that in any other circumstances, he wouldn't even be thinking like that, not for a second, but he was massively upset and just looking for a way out of the pressure, to make it go away. I told him he had to keep going. He held it together and didn't resign. We talked it all through again a few days later, and he was still just saying: 'Yes, yes I know. Yes, you're right. Yes I know. I know.' But he didn't sound like he really knew anything any more.[7]

At the next reshuffle, in June 2009, Watson returned to the backbenches, hoping to stabilize his family life. He had had enough; most political commentators thought he was a Brown toady and a thug. By coincidence, five weeks later, he found himself investigating a scandal rooted in Rupert Murdoch's sprawling empire.

2

Wapping's News Factory

Our motto is the truth
      – *News of the World*, 1 October 1843

The *News of the World* started with a moral purpose. Founded in 1843 as a digest of news for 'respectable tradesmen', its first edition proclaimed: 'Our motto is the truth; our practice is the fearless advocacy of the truth.' Circulation rose steadily from a few thousand at launch to 4 million by 1939. By the 1950s, with sales at a high of 8.5 million, the paper was best known for its salacious chronicling of fallen women, adulterous vicars and deviant scoutmasters. After Rupert Murdoch bought it in 1969 with circulation at 6 million, the 'carnal business' moved steadily from the inside pages to the front, aided by its proprietor's grasp of newsstand success. Attacked for buying the memoirs of the Profumo scandal call-girl Christine Keeler in the first months of his ownership, Murdoch responded: 'People can sneer as much as they like, but I'll take the 150,000 extra copies we're going to sell.'[1]

By the mid-1990s onwards, the *News of the World* newsroom, in a converted rum warehouse in London's docklands, was extreme, even by Murdoch's standards. Exhorted by him to smash its closest competitors, the *People* and the *Sunday Mirror*, its management fostered an ultra-competitive atmosphere. Reporter was set against reporter and executive against executive. Two competing teams of journalists – the news desk and the features desk – connived and backstabbed to land the front-page story, or 'splash'. Fearful about the consequences of carrying out their orders, reporters sometimes illictly taped the briefings they received from news editors.[2] Management regularly totted up the numbers of bylines and those who failed to provide an adequate dose of sex and scandal were sacked.

How the newspaper landed its circulation-boosting scoops was not of the utmost importance. While Rupert Murdoch disliked receiving unfavourable judgements from the industry-financed watchdog, the Press Complaints Commission (PCC), he cared more about grinding his rivals into the dust. What mattered most was the proprietor's opinion: 'When you work for Rupert Murdoch you do not work for a company chairman or chief executive: you work for a Sun King,' recalled Andrew Neil, editor of *The Sunday Times* between 1983 and 1994. 'You are not a director or a manager or an editor: you are a courtier at the court of the Sun King – rewarded with money and status by a grateful King as long as you serve his purpose, dismissed outright or demoted to a remote corner of the empire when you have ceased to please him or outlived your usefulness.'[3]

Although Murdoch sometimes left Neil alone for weeks, he regularly made menacing calls peppered with expletives during Neil's eleven years as editor: 'Since nobody is ever sure when the next autocratic intervention will take place (or on what subject), they live in fear of it and try to second-guess what he would want, even in the most unimportant of matters.' After one of his many talks with Neil, Murdoch did not expect to see his particular views immediately reflected in the next edition of *The Sunday Times*: 'But he had a quiet, remorseless, sometimes threatening way of laying down the parameters within which you were expected to operate ... stray too far too often from his general outlook and you will be looking for a new job.'[4]

Rather than bring in senior people with experience outside News International to edit his titles, Murdoch generally preferred to appoint young journalists whose outlook had been shaped by his business and who would forever be grateful to him, the Sun King. In particular he promoted ruthless showbusiness hacks whose speciality was becoming ever more important in shifting copies – journalists such as Piers Morgan, Rebekah Wade and Andy Coulson. In their late twenties and early thirties, they were pitched into a lucrative, adrenaline-charged whirl, the backseat of chauffeur-driven limousines and – to their delight and surprise – the dining chairs of Downing Street.

In 1994, Murdoch plucked the 28-year-old Piers Morgan from the *Sun*'s celebrity gossip column, 'Bizarre', to edit the *News of the World*, then the highest-selling newspaper in the English-speaking world. The proprietor would regularly enthuse, berate and gossip with his young protégé. In his rumbustious account of his own tabloid capers, *The Insider*, Morgan described one of the many calls Murdoch made to him one Saturday. On 1 April 1995, Morgan had obtained a picture of the gangster Ronnie Kray in his coffin. Murdoch roared: 'What? You're splashing on a dead body?' 'Erm, yes, Mr Murdoch,' Morgan replied. The grizzled tycoon paused. 'Look, it's not my job to edit the papers,' he said, 'but one thing I can tell you is that stiffs don't sell papers.' Instead, Morgan ran a picture of Earl Spencer's wife Victoria at an alcohol and bulimia clinic, earning him a public rebuke from the PCC and soon after from Murdoch too. On 22 May, after delivering the slapdown to his 'young editor', Murdoch called again. Morgan realized there was no point complaining because Murdoch was not interested in whining: 'He just wants to hear precisely how you intend to smash the opposition into oblivion.' 'I'm sorry about all that press complaining thingamajig,' Murdoch explained. 'We had to deal with it the way we did or they'd all have been banging on about a privacy law again and we don't need that right now. Anyway, it's done now. How are you going to sell me more papers?'[5]

Under Morgan, the paper bribed staff on the rival *Sunday Mirror* and the *People* to obtain their newslists.[6] He happily stole other papers' exclusives – including those of other News Corp titles. On 15 October 1994, he sent his cunning new features editor, Rebekah Wade, to hide in a toilet dressed as a cleaner so she could run back to the *News of the World* from Wapping's printworks with a copy of *The Sunday Times*'s serialization of Jonathan Dimbleby's new book on Prince Charles. On another occasion he laughed at a letter from the *Mail on Sunday* warning him not to lift a copyrighted interview to be published that night with the rugby player Will Carling and his wife Julia. Morgan consulted Tom Crone ('superbright, fearless and cunning'), the *News of the World*'s veteran lawyer. He wrote:

> To save time I just shouted to our lawyer across the room: 'Hey Tom, how many fingers will this cost if we nick it all?' Tom flicked five fingers

at me: £50,000 maximum damages. Well worth a front page and two spreads inside. We got the *Mail* at about 7 p.m. and set about excavating every word . . . At about 9 p.m. we got another fax from the *Mail* legal team, issuing dire warnings about our 'flagrant breach of copyright'. . . We laughed again.[7]

Paul McMullan, the deputy features editor between 1994 and 2001, swindled the source of a story about the actor Robert de Niro. 'Yeah, I did a story about two girls in a bubblebath,' he recalled casually in 2011, 'and one of them was foolish to tell me all about it and give me all the pictures without signing a contract. So, you know – the normal thing is you promise ten grand [£10,000] for a splash or twenty, ten maybe for a spread . . . and that made a spread . . . And we didn't pay her. She was on my back for ages, but because we didn't pay her, as I recall, I got a 750 quid bonus for ripping off the source of the story.'[8]

When McMullan found topless pictures of the models Naomi Campbell, Helena Christensen and Carla Bruni in a low-circulation French magazine, he told Piers Morgan: '"Here's Naomi Campbell topless, and Helena Christensen and [French President Nicolas] Sarkozy's now wife, but we'll never get them in a million years because the French are precious about that kind of thing." And he said: "It's okay, we'll just nick them."' On another occasion, McMullan was asked to find the woman in France who had supposedly taken John Major's virginity: 'We found her but couldn't get the picture of her with her new boyfriend. I think the cleaner was in so I blagged my way in and pinched it off the mantelpiece. Rebekah [Wade] said: "No, put it back, we're not allowed to nick stuff", but Piers said: "Well done."'[9]

Sex was an obsession at the *News of the World,* so much so that the paper was nicknamed the *News of the Screws.* In the late 1990s, more than 10 million readers – including 4 million from the ABC1 social classes – eagerly consumed its titillating diet of sizzling, lust-filled celebrity romps, 'kiss and tells', spanking and perversion. A dedicated team winkled out unusual sexual habits across the UK, infiltrating swingers' parties to chronicle their deviance. Typically the investigators would obtain sufficient documentary evidence to 'make their excuses and leave', but in 1998, under Morgan's successor as editor, Phil Hall, a senior reporter, Neville Thurlbeck, failed to follow that tradition when visiting a naturists' guesthouse in Dorset. Suspicious at his voyeuristic demands, the guesthouse's owners, Sue and Bob Firth had secretly videoed him watching them have sex and recorded him masturbating. Thurlbeck naturally made no mention of his own behaviour in his report, 'The Guesthouse Where All Rooms Come with En-Suite Pervert'. In retaliation, the Firths posted the pictures to the *NoW* with a request for £250,000 for lost earnings and distress, prompting the paper to hit back with another story that Sunday: 'The Nudists, Our Naked Reporter and £1/4m Hush Money', in which Thurlbeck was quoted as saying: 'If you're pursuing rats, you some-times have to go into the sewer.' The video of his exploits subsequently appeared on the Internet, to the amusement of colleagues in the *News of the World*'s newsroom. An investigation by the Press Com-plaints Commission and the paper's management cleared Thurlbeck of wrongdoing and he kept his job. The Firths were not paid off.

After her stint as Piers Morgan's deputy in the mid-1990s, aged twenty-seven, Rebekah Wade's charm and ruthlessness were being recognized by Rupert Murdoch. With her burningly ambitious eyes and extravagantly curled red hair tumbling over her shoulders, she cut an enchanting figure and had demonstrated her willingness to suc-ceed at every instance. Her *modus operandi*, explained one former executive, was 'to solve your problem'.[10] She became friends with Elisabeth Murdoch and learned to sail – because the Murdochs sailed. Rupert Murdoch promoted her to deputy editor of the *Sun* in 1998 and in May 2000 to editor of the *News of the World,* a heady position for a 32-year-old with no journalism training.

Wade's notoriously hard-bitten executive news editor was Greg Miskiw, a portly middle-aged man of Ukrainian descent. Neville Thurlbeck, the reporter who had exposed the Firths and himself, was promoted to news editor.

Wade immediately set about repaying Murdoch's confidence by raising the paper's profile and sales. On 23 July, she launched a cam-paign against paedophiles, named after Sarah Payne, an eight-year-old abducted in West Sussex 22 days ealier. The 'For Sarah' campaign called for the government to allow parents access to police records identifying local paedophiles. Under the headline 'NAMED SHAMED' and the subheading: 'Everyone in Britain has a child sex offender living within one mile of their home . . .', the *Screws* published forty-nine pictures of paedophiles and announced its intention to publish the identities of all of the UK's 110,000 child sex offenders in following weeks. The campaign provoked a wave of reprisals, most notably in Portsmouth, where more than 100 vigilantes holding up placards saying 'Kill Paedophiles' marched through the streets nightly and rioted outside the home of a local taxi driver named by the paper. Another child sex offender, James White, a father of five, committed suicide after a mob surrounded his home in Oldham, Greater Manchester. While White's case may not have elicited much public sympathy, there were several instances of mistaken identity, such as in Portsmouth, where four innocent families were forced out of their homes; in Plymouth, where a family had to flee their home after the father was mis-identified as a paedophile, and in Manchester, where an innocent man was attacked because he was wearing a neck brace similar to that of an offender pictured in the *News of the World*. In Newport, Gwent, protestors daubed graffiti on the front door of a paediatrician, Yvette Cloete, because of confusion about her job. Police, probation officers and children's charities warned the campaign would push offenders underground and, amid government unease, Wade suspended it after two weeks, saying the government had agreed to back its demands. The Home Office minister Paul Boateng contradicted that – but Wade's profile had been raised and the paper had put on 95,000 sales.

Wade's *News of the World*, which prided itself on going harder and further than other titles, also devoted its extensive resources to investigating the disappearance of another child, Milly Dowler, in Surrey in 2002. Through its newsgathering network, it was convinced the thirteen-year-old had been employed by a recruitment agency in the Midlands, or that she was working at a factory in the north of England. Its leads were wrong and responding to them had wasted police time: Milly Dowler had been murdered by a local man.

Wade's style with her staff could be dictatorial and, sometimes, abusive. For her amusement, in 2001, a year after she became editor, she instructed a reporter, Charles Begley, to change his name to Harry

Potter and dress up as the fictional wizard at news conferences. A few hours after the September 11 attacks on the Twin Towers, Begley was rebuked for not wearing his robes and being 'in character'.*

In January 2003, following the drive-by shooting of two teenagers in Birmingham, Miskiw sent the investigations editor, Mazher Mahmood, to show how easy it was to buy a gun. Mahmood was no stranger to tricky situations: he had hurriedly resigned from *The Sunday Times* in 1989, shortly before he was about to be sacked, for entering the newspaper's IT system to make it look as if a news agency was responsible for a mistake he had made in a story about a police inspector's drink-driving. When Mahmood arrived in a car park to buy two handguns, he was mugged by a machete-wielding gang for the £1,500 he had obtained from petty cash. He reported the incident to Miskiw. 'Greg asked me if I was all right and, as soon as I'd shakily said "Yes, I think, I'm okay," continued: "OK, don't worry about the money, but you have got to get me a gun for this week. The editor really wants the story." '11

Mahmood later became the paper's 'Fake Sheikh', a bogus Arab prince who would spend tens of thousands of pounds hiring helicopters, Rolls-Royces, five-star penthouse suites and first-class

---

* Begley went home and later rang in sick with stress. After a couple of days to-ing and fro-ing with executives, Miskiw came on the line at Begley's home. Begley taped and transcribed the conversation, as reported in the *Daily Telegraph*:

'I don't think I can make a final decision on my future right now,' Begley told Miskiw.

'I'm not forcing you into a decision,' Miskiw said. 'I'm telling you something that will benefit you.'

'I'm so wound up about this.'

'Charles, Charles, Charles, let me tell you something. This is not a business for prima donnas. You know that and I know that.'

'I'm disillusioned,' Begley said.

'I've told you that this isn't going to be held against you. Charles, you should think very seriously about coming in on Tuesday.'

'Well, to be frank Greg, as far as my future at News International is concerned, I haven't toed the line for the editor's pet project. I didn't prance around while the World Trade Center was being bombed for her personal amusement. I can't just stroll in.'

'Why not?' Greg urged him. 'Charles, this is what we do – we go out and destroy other people's lives.'

flights to gull minor celebrities, sportsmen and royals into committing indiscretions, often persuading them to offer him cocaine and then exposing them for doing so.

Despite its tawdry reputation, the *News of the World* lauded itself as a bastion of investigative journalism and cultivated contacts in high places. As well as schmoozing leading politicians – many of whom were persuaded to write columns for a fee several times their MP's salary – senior journalists were friendly with police officers. Mahmood worked closely with Scotland Yard,* which often nabbed the criminals he had exposed after publication, so that his stories would not be foiled by the law of contempt of court, which forbids prejudicial media coverage after arrests have been made. In the late 1990s, Neville Thurlbeck was receiving records of criminal convictions from a detective constable, Richard Farmer, on the National Criminal Intelligence Service, which liaised between Scotland Yard and the domestic security service MI5. Access to the Police National Computer allowed Thurlbeck to write thirty-six stories, including one about a Labour MP committing an obscene act. In return, he had passed tips about criminals back to Farmer. In 2000, the pair stood trial for corruption, but there was no hard evidence of payment and a judge at Luton Crown Court, Justice McKinnon, said the information Thurlbeck had received from Farmer was not especially 'confidential or sensitive'; both men were acquitted.

There were more exalted links too. Among the paper's senior police contacts was Sir John Stevens, the Commissioner of the Metropolitan Police with whom Rebekah Wade dined regularly, three times at London's top theatreland restaurant, the Ivy, in August 2002, June 2003 and December 2004 – the last after she had admitted at the Culture Committee that News International bribed police. After he left the force in 2005, Sir John wrote for the *News of the World*, receiving £5,000 a column, and the *NoW* and *The Times* serialized his autobiography, *Not for the Faint-hearted*.

---

* In this book, Scotland Yard is used synonymously for the Metropolitan Police; similarly, Fleet Street stands, somewhat anachronistically, for the national newspaper industry, and Wapping for News International.

Flush with cash* and comforted by the company's friendliness with senior politicians and police officers, a sleazy, drink-fuelled atmosphere prevailed inside the *News of the World*'s newsroom; one senior Wapping executive remarked that after walking through it he 'felt like taking a shower'.[12] A former reporter, Sharon Marshall, gave what she said was a frank account of the alcohol-fuelled shenanigans at the paper in *Tabloid Girl: A True Story*, straplined 'Sex. Scandal. Celebrities. All in a Day's Work'. Published in 2010, the book purported to be an amalgam of newspaper newsrooms, but was often a thinly disguised account of the *Screws*, where she worked between 2002 and 2004 (between 1998 and 2002 she was at the *People*). Marshall's tabloid days were a blast of infiltrated 'vice dens', exaggerated kiss and tells, marathon drinking sessions, fiddled expenses and dodgy stories. Discussing whether reporters made up stories, Marshall wrote: 'Yes. Sometimes the quotes were written before we ever left the office. Before we knew who we were interviewing.' Asked to write an article that 'sounded' as if it had been written by the glamour model Jordan, she went home, drank two bottles of white wine and fabricated 1,000 words. The drinking was 'harsh': often a 9.a.m. whisky in the pub as the executives departed for the morning news conference, followed by a bottle of wine at lunch, followed by more drinking with contacts in the afternoon, 'slipping casually into an evening's absolute bender'.

'My career was kick-started with booze and it carried on that way for the ten years I worked on tabloids.' It was expected and, in times of need when you'd overdone it, your colleagues would rally round to help. We had a small glass box – about four foot square – next to the newsdesk, with soundproofed walls. It contained an armchair and a TV. If someone was so supremely drunk they could no longer be relied on to stay conscious at their desk, or ran the risk of disrobing and hurling obscenities at the editor at a moment's notice, we'd throw them into the chair, stick on a DVD of some footage from an undercover job and lock the door . . .

---

* Although slowly losing sales throughout the 2000s, the *Sun* and the *News of the World* were still making pre-tax profits of £93 million in 2003 and £147 million in 2004.

During Wade's tenure, the *News of the World* fleshed out its obsession with sex with another fixation: celebrity. In the early 2000s, demand soared for stories delving into the private lives of actors, pop stars and TV presenters. Paparazzi pictures which would have fetched £5,000 in 2000 made £100,000 in 2005. Getting stories about stars, however, became harder. Publicists had become cannier about maximizing commercial opportunities and arranged interviews only when their clients had a product to promote. Unpaid interviews became bland to the point where *Heat*'s editor, Mark Frith, observed, readers no longer wanted glossy PR pictures and fawning, product-shifting interviews, but 'fast, pacy and unapproved' stories. The *News of the World* and *Heat* exemplified this new proposition: celebrities in the raw; too skinny, too fat, too plain, too gaudy, too slovenly, too much Botox, taking drink, drugs, lovers, becoming mentally ill. In February 2003 *NOW* magazine (unconnected to the *Screws*) experimented with the new approach by running a cover with unflattering pictures of the actress Lisa Kudrow, TV host Fiona Phillips and the actress Nicole Kidman with the headline: 'ROUGH! Even the stars have bad days'. It worked: the magazine sold 730,000 copies, up 150,000. The advent of reality TV shows, starting with Channel 4's *Big Brother* in 2000, manufactured a stream of manipulable young new stars without agents or experience. Reporters became inured to the idea that 'slebs' might have feelings.

After he handed Rebekah Wade the editorship of the *Sun* in January 2003, Rupert Murdoch made her friend and deputy, Andy Coulson, thirty-two, editor of the *News of the World*. The bespectacled Coulson did not look like a stereotypical tabloid hack: he was neat, calm and polite, but had cold eyes and hard edges. Educated at a comprehensive school in Wickford, Essex, Coulson had shone on the *Sun*'s showbusiness column, landing story after story about the lives of celebrities.

Coulson had an instinctive feel for what made tabloids edgy and fun. He sent a reporter to find the 'family' of a whale stranded in the Thames and suspended a showbusiness reporter in a perspex box in the newsroom for twenty-four hours to emulate a stunt by the illusionist David Blaine. He recruited powerful columnists, including the former Conservative leader William Hague in December 2003 (for an annual fee of around £200,000). He also poached executives from other papers, most notably the editor of the rival *People*, Neil 'Wolfman' Wallis. A legend in tabloid newsrooms, the 52-year-old Wallis had acquired his 'Wolfman' tag on account of his pinched facial features and his theory that the Yorkshire Ripper struck only during full moons. A grinning chancer, Wallis had a volcanic temper and a gift for innovation. His false story that the pop star Elton John had visited a rent boy led to the *Sun* paying record libel damages of £1 million in 1988. At the *Sun*, where he had been deputy editor and Coulson's mentor, he had launched the Police Bravery Awards in 1996 and become friendly with senior officers, including Sir John Stevens. Appointed in Coulson's first month, Wallis the following year recruited to the *Screws* two of his news editors at the *People*, Ian Edmondson and James Weatherup.

With these new signings, the *News of the World* led the tabloid pack, breaking a string of circulation-boosting stories about the private lives of the famous and powerful, such as the kiss and tell on David Beckham ('Beckham's Secret Affair') in April 2004, for which Beckham's personal assistant Rebecca Loos was paid £300,000, and 'Blunkett's Affair with a Married Woman' in August 2004, which prompted Home Secretary David Blunkett's resignation. In October 2004, the paper made damaging allegations about the sex life of the founder of the Scottish Socialist Party, Tommy Sheridan, marking the start of an epic legal battle between Sheridan and News International.

On a Tuesday night in March 2005, Coulson's *News of the World* won Newspaper of the Year at the British Press Awards, whose judges said it had shown vitality and originality and, in the Beckham and Blunkett exposés, had broken 'important stories with far-reaching consequences'. In keeping with the heady atmosphere in newspapers at the time, the event at the Hilton Hotel in London's Park Lane was a raucous affair. Journalists booed and jeered the handing of gongs to rivals. As the *Sun* accepted the Cudlipp Award for Popular Journalism, the Live Aid founder Sir Bob Geldof stormed the stage and swore at papers whose coverage of his charity work had displeased him. He told the guests that a visit to the lavatory had confirmed that rock stars 'have bigger knobs than journalists'. Jeremy Clarkson, the motoring writer and TV presenter who at the previous year's awards had punched Piers Morgan (who had left the *Screws* in 1995 to edit the *Daily Mirror*), renewed the feud onstage, announcing: 'Piers Morgan, you are an arsehole.'

'Even by its normal debased standards it was a remarkable event,' noted the *Independent*'s media commentator, Stephen Glover.[13] The *New York Times* said the awards less resembled a mutually respectful celebration of the British newspaper industry than a football match attended by 'a club of misanthropic inebriates'. Editors of quality papers had their sensibilities upset by the *News of the World*'s triumph. Soon after, the editors of ten non-Murdoch national newspapers agreed to boycott the awards. In a rare celebratory interview with the *Evening Standard*, Coulson shrugged off criticism, pointing out that Britain's best-selling paper was not all about sex. He had a simple answer to those questioning his paper's conduct: 'If we'd done anything wrong, there's a pretty well-established set of Press Complaints Commission rules, and there's the law. We know the law, we know the PCC code, and we work within it.'[14]

Media pundits wondered how the *News of the World* ferreted out its agenda-setting stories. A *News of the World* 'source' explained the mystery to the journalist Tim Luckhurst for an article in the *Independent*, saying that while luck played a part, 'it's mainly down to good old-fashioned journalism and a reputation for paying well for good news, pictures and information'.[15]

But all the while, the *News of the World* was having a secret affair of its own. As well as opening its large chequebook for celebrity kiss and tells, the paper was short-circuiting the usual journalistic methods. One technique in particular transformed the newsroom: phone hacking. Eavesdropping on the trivia of people's lives unearthed, message by message, political intrigue, illicit love and showbusiness secrets.

Listening to other people's mobile phone messages was a trick discovered by tabloid showbusiness reporters in the late 1990s. A reporter called the mobile number of a celebrity and, if the line was engaged, the call would go through to their inbox. Inboxes also had their own number, and, if that was known, it could be rung directly. Either way, once the inbox had been accessed, the voicemails could be unlocked by inputting a personal identification number, or PIN code.

Usually the manufacturer's default code worked because people tended not to bother setting their own code, but if PINs had been changed, private investigators could obtain them from corrupt phone company employees.

Another technique was 'blagging' confidential records, or paying corrupt police, tax or other officials for private data. At the *News of the World*, a sports reporter, Matt Driscoll, stumbled across the practice after he received a tip that Sir Alex Ferguson, the manager of Manchester United, had a health problem. He went about the story the old way, calling his contacts; it was clear it might be true.

> But then I couldn't get any further forward on it because I hit a brick
> wall in terms of getting anyone to go on record . . . and in the end I had
> to go to my sports desk and say: 'I really don't think I can get any fur-
> ther forward with this.' And then my sports editor said: 'Leave it with
> me. We'll see what we can come up with.'

Later that day his sports editor said: 'You're absolutely right. The story is true. I have his medical records with me at the moment.'

Driscoll said: 'I was told that sometimes you'd get a situation where if an investigator sent a fax to a GP or a hospital saying: "I'm his specialist, I need these details," it was incredible how many times they would just get sent straight back.'[16]

The *Screws* used another technique, 'leverage', with Sir Alex. The paper offered to keep his health problem secret 'and because of that, he then started cooperating with the paper . . . a few months later he gave us some stories.'*

Driscoll said:

> It seemed to me that any method that could stand a story up was fair
> game. It was also clear that there was massive pressure from the top
> to break stories. It was largely accepted that this pressure came from
> the proprietors and editors on the basis that big, sensational stories
> sell papers and therefore make more money. There were times when
> I would return from interviewing a prominent Premier League foot-
> ball manager only to find the paper using material from a months old

---

* In 2011, when Driscoll made his comments, Sir Alex declined to respond to them.

interview in order to obtain a better headline. I didn't consider this to be true journalism or true live reporting – and I often voiced my disapproval. But all of this was simply a reflection of the growing pressures being placed on editors to try and combat the decline of sales. There was an ever growing trend to get the big story or headline by any means possible.'[17]

The paper bullied staff who failed to perform or who questioned its methods. Driscoll became a marked man when he failed to stand up a tip from Andy Coulson that Arsenal would play in purple shirts to mark their last season at Highbury. Arsenal told Driscoll the story was not true, but a few months later it surfaced in the *Screws* daily sister and rival, the *Sun*. The reporter recalled: 'I got a phone call from my sports editor at the time saying: "We're dead. Coulson's going to go absolutely crazy over this and will want to know why we got this wrong and why this appeared in the *Sun*." '[18]

After being disciplined for failing to tape an interview with the footballer Kolo Toure (taking a shorthand note instead), Driscoll wrote to Coulson saying he would take the warning but still did not feel he had done anything wrong. On 11 November 2005, Coulson replied: 'In my view your actions on this matter merited dismissal.'[19]

In 2005, another long-standing reporter, Sean Hoare, fell foul of Coulson – his old friend and former boss on the *Sun*'s 'Bizarre' column in the late 1990s. As a showbusiness reporter during the cash-rich glory years of redtops, Hoare had lived a rock and roll lifestyle with the pop stars he was covering, but when he became addicted to drink and drugs and struggled at work, he was sacked.

The *News of the World* was vicious, but Driscoll and Hoare knew secrets about its workings that would one day return to haunt Andy Coulson.

3

The Dark Arts

Oliver Twist to the press's Fagin
– private investigator Steve Whittamore on his relationship
with newspapers, 21 September 2010

Fleet Street was never innocent. Newspapers had always paid dubious characters for tip-offs and exclusives, and deployed sweet-talking reporters to the doorsteps of the bereaved and badly behaved to extract confessions and heartache. In the analogue age, reporters traced individuals by flicking through phone books, checking the electoral roll and Companies House register and calling friends, neighbours and colleagues. But, while entirely legal, these methods were time-consuming and did not always produce results. By the late 1990s, many reporters were relying on private investigators who could instantly and illegally access the growing volume of information stored on computer databases. Private detectives knew people inside the police, vehicle and tax offices – and blaggers who could extract health records from GPs' receptionists and phone numbers from phone companies.

One of the first signs to the outside world of the existence of this shadowy network emerged not in London, the powerhouse of Britain's national media, but in rural Devon, after David Welsh, a former nightclub owner who wanted to develop an outdoor swimming pool in Plymouth, complained to the police in 2001 that he was being blackmailed about his criminal record. In January 2002, Devon and Cornwall Police launched Operation Re-proof into the sale of confidential data and discovered that a serving detective constable in

Exeter, Philip Diss, had been checking criminal records on the Police National Computer and passing them on to his former boss, Alan Stidwill, a retired police inspector who ran a company called SAS Investigations in the seaside town of Exmouth. As they began to unpick his network, in autumn 2002, Devon and Cornwall asked the Information Commissioner's Office, which polices confidential databases, for one of its officers to accompany its detectives on a raid of a private investigator – just in case it found any data protection breaches in addition to those of the Police National Computer. Alec Owens, the ICO's senior investigating officer and former police detective inspector, accompanied Devon and Cornwall's officers when they raided a private detective agency in Surrey, Data Research Ltd, in November 2002. As he wandered around the agency's office, Owens saw a sheaf of car registration numbers on a desk, picked them up and contacted the Driver and Vehicle Licensing Agency in Cardiff. The DVLA checked the numbers and found they had been checked by a now deceased manager at a regional branch, and, after his death in March 2002, by a junior employee. In the diary of the dead manager, the DVLA found one number marked 'Protected', which Owens, a former Special Branch officer, knew was either an unmarked undercover police vehicle or the car of a senior police officer. That check had been ordered by another private detective, who turned out to be one of the most important figures in the phone hacking scandal: Steve Whittamore.

While Devon and Cornwall carried on its investigation for another two years, the ICO began an investigation into Whittamore: Operation Motorman. On 8 March 2003 – two years before Andy Coulson stepped on stage at the Hilton Hotel – Owens and four other investigators from the Information Commissioner's Office raided Whittamore's house in Orchard Grove, New Milton, a market town on the edge of the New Forest in Hampshire. 'We went there not knowing what the hell we would find,' Owens recalled later.[1] They were amazed at what they discovered: Britain's best-selling newspapers and magazines were driving a thriving black market in illegal data, requesting (and receiving) ex-directory numbers, car registration numbers, health records and criminal records. The targets ranged from glamorous actresses such as Elizabeth Hurley to the families of victims of newsworthy crimes, such as the parents of Holly Wells, a child murdered by the paedophile Ian Huntley at Soham, Cambridge- shire, in 2002.

From an office in his three-bed bungalow Whittamore had been running a network of corrupt officials and blaggers who conned data out of unsuspecting office workers or bribed them into handing it over. Among them were a civilian worker at Tooting police station in London who invented reasons for checking criminal records on the National Police Computer; DVLA workers who sold names and number plates; and a Hell's Angel who blagged ex-directory and Friends & Family numbers from British Telecom.

Unfortunately for his Fleet Street customers, Whittamore had kept detailed notes of his work, recording thousands of orders from some of the best-known publications. His best customers were the *Daily Mail*, the *People*, *Daily Mirror*, *Mail on Sunday* and *News of the World* – and some of the individual journalists requesting searches were very senior: they included the *News of the World*'s executive news editor, Greg Miskiw, and its editor, Rebekah Wade. Wade had asked Whittamore to 'convert' a mobile phone number to find its reg- istered owner. Whittamore recorded each request with a code – 'XD' for an ex-directory number, 'CRO' for a criminal records check and 'Veh Reg' for tracing the owner of a number plate: all of which broke the law on data protection, fraud or bribery, depending on the method.

The trade was highly lucrative. Whittamore's company, JJ Services Ltd, charged £75 to find the address of the owner of a mobile phone, £150 to £500 for a DVLA check and £750 for mobile phone records. Between 2001 and 2003 he had received 17,489 orders and made £1.8 million, though some of that went to his corrupt contacts. Owens recalled: 'He was living the high life. He had just come back from a fort- night in Goa. There was an extensive wine cellar in his garage.'[2]

But despite facing a jail term, he would not snitch on his paymasters. Owens said: 'Whittamore made it very [clear] that whilst he would admit to his own wrongdoing, under no circumstances would he say anything which would incriminate any member of the press. I was undecided as to whether this was because he feared the press or whether he anticipated some financial recompense in return for his silence.'[3]

Whittamore's records showed clear breaches of Section 55 of the

Data Protection Act, which made it a criminal offence to obtain, disclose or 'procure the disclosure' of personal information 'knowingly or recklessly' – punishable by a fine of up to £5,000 in the magistrates' court and an unlimited fine in the Crown Court. In the Information Commissioner's Office in Wilmslow, Cheshire, Owens and his fellow investigators started working through the material with a view to prosecuting the journalists who had commissioned the private detective. What happened next is still a matter of controversy. According to Owens in 2011, a week after the raid:

> An informal meeting was arranged with Richard Thomas, the Commissioner, and Francis Aldhouse, Deputy Commissioner and Head of Operations, to update them. It was at this meeting that I was able, by using examples of the paperwork seized, to show ICO were in a position to prove that a paper chain existed right through from identified journalists working for named newspaper groups requesting information be obtained from a private detective who in turn used corrupt sources or 'blaggers' to obtain such information. We could also prove by way of the seized bills for payment and numbered invoices for payments settled by the newspaper groups exactly how much money had been paid for each transaction and by and to whom it had been paid. Where the information involved such requests as Criminal Record Checks, VRM details, ex-directory numbers, conversions and family and friends without any claim of 'public interest' we were in a position to prosecute everyone in the chain from the 'blagger' right up to the journalists and possibly even the newspaper groups.
>
> It was at this point Francis Aldhouse with a shocked look on his face said: 'We can't take the press on, they are too big for us.' Richard Thomas did not respond, he merely looked straight ahead appearing to be somewhat bemused by the course of action I was recommending. For my own part I remember thinking 'It's our job to take them or indeed anyone else on, that's what we are paid to do. If we do not do it then who does?' At this point Richard Thomas thanked me for updating him and at the same time congratulated me and the team for a job well done.[4]

Owens and his investigators started to prepare twenty-five to thirty prosecution cases, but within weeks 'were informed that we were not to make contact with any of the newspapers identified and we were not to speak to, let alone interview any journalists. Despite our protests we were told that this was the decision of Richard Thomas and that he would deal with the press involvement by way of the Press Complaints Commission. We were now instructed to restrict our investigation solely to the bottom of the pyramid, those involved with correctly supplying information or "blagging" information.'

On 4 November 2003, Richard Thomas wrote to Sir Christopher Meyer, the new chairman of the Press Complaints Commission, indicating that the matter could be dealt with by rewriting the PCC's code of practice to warn against breaching data protection laws, rather than by prosecuting journalists. He told Meyer:

> I am considering whether to take action under the Data Protection Act against individual journalists and/or newspapers. My provisional conclusion, however, is that it would be appropriate first to give the Press Complaints Commission and its Code Committee the prior opportunity to deal with the issue in a way which would put an end to these unacceptable practices across the media as a whole ... Following your review of any such material, I anticipate that this would at least lead to revision of the code. The approach I have in mind ... could provide a more satisfactory outcome than legal proceedings.[5]

Meyer's PCC failed to change its code until four years later, in 2007.

Over the following months the Information Commissioner's investigators interviewed around seventy 'victims' of Whittamore's, including the actor Hugh Grant, the singer Charlotte Church and TV presecuter Chris Tarrant. In February 2004, it handed over all evidence to the ICO's Legal Department.

In the meantime, the Metropolitan Police had begun Operation Glade into the procurement of criminal records from the Police National Computer. Fortunately for the crooked information-gatherers, they were to have a stroke of luck. When, in August 2003, as a result of the Whittamore raid, police arrested Paul Marshall, the civilian police worker who had been accessing the PNC at Tooting police station, they also found he had stolen a truncheon, handcuffs and other equipment for sex games with his partner. He was dying, and at a court hearing for the thefts, a judge gave him a conditional discharge.

On 15 April 2005, the prosecution at Blackfriars Crown Court – quoting from articles in the *Sunday Mirror*, *Mail on Sunday* and the *News of the World* – said Whittamore had provided journalists with 'very personal and confidential details' about high-profile figures, including the general secretary of the Rail, Maritime and Transport Union, Bob Crow, the *EastEnders* actors Jessie Wallace and Clifton Tomlinson, and the troubled son of the actor Ricky Tomlinson. Whittamore and a fellow private detective with whom he had worked, John Boyall, pleaded guilty to breaching the Data Protection Act, while Paul Marshall and Alan King, a recently retired police detective, pleaded guilty to conspiracy to commit misconduct in public office. But because Marshall had been given a conditional discharge for the more serious offence of the theft of police equipment, Judge John Samuels QC felt unable to give him and his fellow conspirators a higher sentence for the lesser data offence. The four men received two-year conditional discharges and walked triumphantly out of court. None of the 305 journalists who had requested information from Whittamore was put in the dock by the ICO.

In 2010, Whittamore would complain about the failure to call the newspapers to account. 'I suppose you could view it as my Oliver Twist to the press's Fagin,' he said. 'Requests were asked of me by people whom I viewed as really being above reproach. They were huge corporations.'[6] Alec Owens said: 'I was disappointed and somewhat disillusioned with senior management because I felt as though they were burying their heads in the sand. It was like being on an ostrich farm.'[7] He believed the ICO was 'frightened' of the press.[8] The Information Commissioner, Richard Thomas, claimed there was no clear evidence Whittamore's journalistic customers knew he was breaking the law, and that the disappointing outcome of the Blackfriars Crown Court case made further prosecutions impracticable. Thomas told Lord Leveson*: 'We were subsequently advised by external counsel that the

---

* The Leveson Inquiry into the Culture, Practices and Ethics of the press was set up by the government in July 2011. Presided over by Lord Justice Leveson, an Appeal Court judge, its assessors were: Sir David Bell, non-executive director of the *Economist* and former chairman of the *Fnancial Times*; Shami Chakrabarti, director of Liberty; Lord Currie, founding chairman of the media regulator Ofcom; Elinor Goodman, former Channel 4 political editor; George Jones, former political editor of the *Daily Telegraph*; and Sir Paul Scott-Lee, former Chief Constable of the West Midlands.

leniency of the sentence meant that it would not be in the public interest to continue or pursue parallel and further prosecutions.' The ICO dropped its prosecution of Steve Whittamore, Taff Jones, the Hell's Angel in Sussex who had been blagging phone numbers, another private detective, John Gunning, who denied any wrongdoing, and the surviving corrupt DVLA worker, who has never been named.

During its three-year investigation, Devon and Cornwall Police had identified its own shadowy data network. It discovered that the retired police inspector in Exmouth, Alan Stidwill, had been supplying criminal records checks on Labour politicians to Glen Lawson, a private detective in Newcastle upon Tyne. In February 2003 Devon and Cornwall had raided Lawson's firm, Abbey Investigations, and found that in late 2000 Lawson had supplied a national newspaper with checks of the criminal records of Gordon Brown, then Chancellor of the Exchequer, his close ally Nick Brown, the Agriculture Minister, and another Labour MP, Martin Salter. The newspaper which bought the checks (which came back blank) has never been named but, in 2000 and 2001, News International was siding with Tony Blair in his frequent rows with Gordon Brown, and Rebekah Wade's *News of the World* had placed Salter on a 'naming and shaming' list for criticising the 'For Sarah' campaign.

During their operation, Devon and Cornwall had investigated thirty-seven people and had evidence of checks on ninety-three individuals, including Gordon Brown and Nick Brown. In order not to over-complicate the prosecution, Glen Lawson had not been charged, but six others stood in the dock: Philip Diss; Alan Stidwill; a serving CID officer; a council investigations officer with access to the Department for Work and Pensions system; and two others. But at Gloucester Crown Court in March 2006, Judge Paul Darlow threw out the case, saying: 'In my judgment it is not a proportionate use of valuable resources to prosecute these matters.' Stidwill, the retired policeman who ran SAS Investigations, said: 'It's been a dreadful waste of taxpayers' money.' Devon and Cornwall's investigation, like that of the ICO, had ended in failure. The trade in illegal newsgathering techniques continued to flourish.

A former Devon and Cornwall detective was quoted in the *Western Morning News* in July 2011 as saying: 'Between 2002 and 2006,

Devon and Cornwall Police were right at the heart of what we now know was going on at the *News of the World*. It was a very thorough and professional investigation. The question is why it was kicked out of the courts and why, particularly, the Metropolitan Police didn't follow up on it.'

For the moment, the 'dark arts' had stayed hidden.

In November 2005, courtiers at Clarence House, Prince Charles's official residence in London, became alarmed when they read stories about his sons, Princes William and Harry, in the *News of the World*. These were not the usual royal stories about the death of Princess Diana, Prince Charles meddling in politics, or whether his wife, Camilla, would become queen. They were tittle-tattle. The first appeared on page 32 on 6 November, at the top of the 'Blackadder' gossip column ('Your snake in the grass of the rich and powerful'). Although only six paragraphs, it became one of the most infamous stories in Fleet Street's history. It began: 'Royal action man Prince William has had to postpone a mountain rescue course – after being crocked by a ten-year-old during football training.' The Prince, it explained, had pulled a tendon in his knee after a kickabout and was having physiotherapy near Highgrove, Prince Charles's country home in Gloucestershire.

On the Richter scale of royal revelations, this was barely a tremor, but it caused a shock at St James's Palace because nobody there could understand how it had appeared in print. The following Sunday, Blackadder reported that Prince William had borrowed some television equipment from a journalist: 'If ITN do a stock take on their portable editing suites this week, they might notice they're one down. That's because their pin-up political editor Tom Bradby has lent it to close pal Prince William so he can edit together all his gap year videos and DVDs into one very posh home movie.' Neither William nor Tom Bradby had leaked the story; together they worked out that it had been known only by themselves and two people 'incredibly close' to the prince. Bradby explained to William and his brother Harry that during his time as a royal correspondent, redtop reporters sometimes hacked voicemail messages. Later, Bradby recalled: 'They felt – rightly, as it turned out – that the tabloids were invading every aspect of their lives and the question who might be betraying them and how was a preoccupation, bordering on an obsession. So I told them what I thought was going on and suggested it might be a good idea to talk to the police.'[9] St James's Palace called in the Metropolitan Police's Anti-Terrorist Branch, responsible for royal security, and on 21 December began one of the most controversial inquiries in Scotland Yard's 183-year history, Operation Caryatid.

4

First Heads Roll

Undoubtedly the newspaper business is a tough business
– John Kelsey-Fry QC, Old Bailey, 26 January 2007

For Scotland Yard, the investigation could not have come at a worse time. Six months before, on 7 July 2005, Islamic extremists had detonated four bombs on London's transport system, killing fifty-two people and injuring 700 – the first suicide bombing in Britain after the September 11 attack in the US. Across the country in 2005 and 2006, the Met's Counter-Terrorist Branch was investigating the attacks and hunting down Al Qaeda cells. London's police force, which had national responsibility for counter-terrorism, had drafted in hundreds of officers from other constabularies to help the dragnet.

Still, the suspected interception of royal voicemails was a concern, since anyone accessing them might have knowledge of the movements of members of the royal family. Six members of the counter-terrorism unit assigned the job, SO13, began Operation Caryatid in great secrecy. Within days, SO13 had advised members of the royal household to continue leaving messages for each other and not to let their friends or relatives know that they suspected that, somewhere, the *News of the World* was listening. Britain's elite counter-terrorism officers, skilled at penetrating terrorist cells, did not have far to look for a suspect.

The 'Blackadder' column was written by the *News of the World*'s royal editor, Clive Goodman. In the late 1990s, Goodman had been one of the paper's stars, landing 'splash' after 'splash' about the troubles of Charles and Diana, and her death. He had cultivated a network of royal informants and some of their rarefied airs, wearing Savile Row suits, tweeds and occasionally a fob chain and monocle. But now he was forty-eight and the Royal story had moved on, St James's Palace had rooted out leaks by staff and his pre-eminence on the royal beat was being challenged by a young reporter, Ryan Sabey. Under the dynamic regime of Andy Coulson, Goodman turned to a trick to unearth stories without leaving his home or his office: phone hacking. He was nicknamed 'the eternal flame' because, it was said, he never went out.

Inside New Scotland Yard, the office block which headquartered the Met, SO13 began checking Blackadder's work each Sunday and the numbers calling the voicemails of those inside St James's Palace. By the end of January, SO13 had established from Vodafone that nine 'rogue' numbers were calling the inboxes of two royal aides with intimate knowledge of William and Harry's lives: Jamie Lowther-Pinkerton, the princes' private secretary, and another aide, Helen Asprey, their personal secretary. One of the numbers was that of Goodman's home in Putney, south-west London. The princes' phones were being accessed too.

While the detectives continued their covert inquiries, slowly uncovering ever more victims, Goodman continued chronicling the minutiae of the princes' lives. In April 2006, one of his stories – co-authored by Neville Thurlbeck – was based on a phone call made by Prince William to Prince Harry. Headlined 'Fury After He Ogled Lapdancer's Boobs', it read:

> Shame-faced Prince Harry has been given a furious dressing-down by Chelsy Davy over his late-night antics in a lapdancing bar. His loyal girlfriend discovered how strippers perched on the edge of his chair as he partied with a string of naked dancers and ogled their boobs. Yesterday the repentant prince took an ear-bashing call as news broke.
>
> 'It's Chelsy. How could you? I see you had a lovely time without me. But I miss you so much, you big ginger, and I want you to know I love you,' said a hysterical voice.
>
> Luckily the caller was joker brother, Prince William. He thought the whole episode was hilarious and decided to take the mickey by putting on a high-pitched South African accent like Chelsy's.[1]

Police had identified 'five or six potential victims' and had rumbled an embarrassing security problem. Not only were the targets very high-profile, but continuing the monitoring operation increased the security risk. At the same time, Detective Superintendent Philip Williams, who was leading the operation, was concerned that it was taking resources away from counter-terrorism and that 'the media might seek to criticize the [Metropolitan Police] and SO13 for the use of anti-terrorist resources against what, albeit [with] far wider security implications of the voicemail networks, appears to be a non-terrorist-motivated intrusion on the privacy of a member of the royal family where non-terrorist-related criminal offences have been committed'.[2]

In April, SO13* held a case conference with the Crown Prosecution Service to discuss what charges might be laid against Goodman. The CPS advised that one reading of one of three relevant laws, the Regulation of Investigatory Powers Act, suggested that a crime was committed only if the intended recipient had not listened to a message before it was intercepted – but added that that interpretation was 'untested'. In essence, the provisional advice from the CPS was that if someone had already heard a message in their inbox, someone else – such as a reporter – hacking into that message would not have committed a crime. This was an odd interpretation of the law and would become important, because the police would later claim that it significantly limited their investigation.

While SO13 continued monitoring Goodman's calls, Scotland Yard was keen, as always, to maintain its good relationship with the press – and in particular the country's biggest newspaper group, News International. Dick Fedorcio, the director of the Met's Public Affairs Directorate, had forged close relationships with editors since the days of the former Commissioner Sir John Stevens. One of the officers most friendly with Fleet Street papers was the country's top counter-terrorism officer, 46-year-old Andy Hayman, who wanted to ensure they understood the gravity of the growing terrorism threat. Assistant Commissioner Hayman, who had enterprisingly combined his early career in uniform in Essex with running a mobile disco, was also the

---

* By April, SO13 had been merged with another unit to form SO15. For continuity, we will continue to refer to it as SO13.

Association of Chief Police Officers' 'media lead', a duty he carried out with enthusiasm. He was in close touch with the *News of the World*'s crime editor, Lucy Panton, herself married to a serving Scotland Yard officer, and was also on good terms with its editors. On 25 April, in the middle of Operation Caryatid – on which he had been briefed – he and the Director of Public Affairs, Dick Fedorcio, dined at the Soho House private members' club in central London with the *News of the World*'s editor, Andy Coulson, and his deputy, Neil 'Wolfman' Wallis, the executives running the newspaper his junior officers were investigating.

By early May, officers on Operation Caryatid had made another discovery. The phone company O2 alerted Scotland Yard of some 'suspicious activity': a man posing as a member of staff, 'John Jenkin from credit control', was calling its operatives and asking them to change the PIN codes of Helen Asprey and a second royal aide, Paddy Harverson, Prince Charles's communications secretary, to the default number. O2's recordings of the calls showed that he had the current password which allowed him to change the PINs, even though it was itself changed regularly – suggesting he was, somehow, receiving inside information from O2. The police tracked back through the phone system to discover the real identity of 'John Jenkin'. Their inquiries led them to the Kimpton industrial estate in Sutton, south London, where the calls had originated from phone lines registered to a 'Paul Williams'. The police soon discovered that 'Paul Williams' was an alias used by a private investigator, Glenn Mulcaire, a former part-time footballer with AFC Wimbledon. In 1998 Mulcaire had been taken on by News International as a 'researcher'. By 2006, his company, Nine Consultancy UK Ltd, was being paid £104,988 a year by NI, ostensibly for performing electoral roll and other legal checks. He was also receiving £500 cash a week from Clive Goodman, who listed him on his expenses as a confidential royal source, 'Alexander'. The detectives soon realized that Mulcaire was not a legitimate researcher or a legitimate royal source, but an industrial-scale hacker of voicemails. His specialist skill was blagging phone companies into switching PINs back to the manufacturer's default number.

By monitoring Mulcaire's phone lines, officers discovered he was also accessing the voicemails of the publicist Max Clifford, who had fallen out with the *News of the World* the previous year over Andy Coulson's treatment of one of his clients, the singer Kerry Katona. Part of Clifford's pitch was that he could keep stories out of the papers as well as place them; Coulson had ignored Clifford's pleas not to run a story in 2005 about Katona's cocaine habit. Detectives discovered that the voicemails of another person, known as HJK, the friend of an MP, were also being accessed: the intrusion clearly extended well beyond the royals. They started to match calls to the voicemails of more than a dozen potential victims with stories in the *News of the World*, and began to realize that they would soon have to take dramatic action.

While the police secretly tracked Goodman and Mulcaire's calls, the Information Commissioner's Office gave the first public hint of the illegal data trade underpinning many newspaper stories. On 13 May 2006, it published a report to Parliament, 'What Price Privacy? The Unlawful Trade in Confidential Personal Information', which complained that confidential data was being bought by finance companies, local authorities and criminals intent on witness or juror intimidation, and also mentioned a 'major case' where a private detective had supplied private information to '305 named journalists working for a range of newspapers'. Though it did not name Steve Whittamore, the report outlined the type of records found in his house three years earlier, published his tariff of charges and pointedly mentioned Rebekah Wade's comments to Parliament about paying police for information, explaining that the disappointing outcome of the case at Blackfriars Crown Court had frustrated its own attempts to seek justice. It did not mention that it had ample evidence to prosecute journalists in March 2003, three years previously, and had chosen not to do so, instead lobbying the Press Complaints Commission. Nor did it state the number of requests (17,489), nor name any of the newspapers or newspaper groups which had made the requests. But in the absence of any prosecutions of journalists by his own office and any action by the PCC, the Information Commissioner, Richard Thomas, used the report to launch a campaign for a two-year custodial sentence for breaches of Section 55 of the Data Protection Act. In November 2011, Alec Owens, the ICO's frustrated senior investigator, complained:

The publication in May 2006 of 'What Price Privacy?' was no more than an attempt to lock the stable door after the horse had bolted in an effort to cover up the fact that the ICO had failed in its duty to conduct a full and proper investigation into the conduct of journalists at the time when they could and should have. Throughout the whole of the time Motorman investigation was going on there was never any mention or suggestion of any report being commissioned for Parliament. I felt it was no coincidence that this report was not published until May 2006, only a few weeks before the Mulcaire scandal broke. It is my belief that when ICO became aware that the Metropolitan Police were conducting yet another investigation involving more wrongdoing by the press, they decided to pre-empt and deflect any criticism which was bound to be directed towards them in relation to their lack of action against the press in Operation Motorman. All the evidence published in this report had been gathered and had been available since March 2003 ... why did it take over three years to prepare it, and [then] not publish it until thirteen months after the prosecution against Whittamore had concluded?[3]

News International was not greatly concerned by the ICO's report. On 16 May 2006, three days after it was published, Andy Coulson walked on to the stage at Claridge's hotel in London to accept the Sunday Newspaper of the Year Award for the third year running. The judges at the London Press Club described the *News of the World* as the paper they would least like to be without, 'an incredible sledge-hammer of a production'.

On Sunday 21 May, the *Screws* headlined its triumph: 'We're Crowned Triple Champs', stressing: 'No other paper has ever achieved this hat-trick.' That day its front page was: 'Hugh and Jemima on Rocks: Hugh Grant and Jemima Khan's love is on the rocks, the *News of the World* can reveal. The glamour couple, who have been together nearly two years, are close to splitting after a string of furious rows.' On page 7, the first line read: 'Distraught Jemima Khan phoned Hugh Grant and sobbed: "I can't go on like this."' Both Grant and Khan were later informed by Scotland Yard that the paper had intercepted their voicemails.

Applauded by his peers and his bosses at Wapping, Coulson set about victimizing the sportswriter Matt Driscoll. After a complaint from

Charlton Football Club in March 2006 about a small story (which turned out to be true), Driscoll faced a trumped-up disciplinary hearing. In July 2006, Coulson emailed his deputy, Neil Wallis, saying he wanted Driscoll 'out as quickly and cheaply as possible'.[4] That month, Driscoll went on sick leave, suffering from severe depression. Despite being informed of his GP's advice that he should distance himself from work, the paper bombarded him with daily phone calls and sent multiple recorded letters to his home, then stopped his pay.

On 4 August 2006, Andy Coulson suffered a rare setback. After a five-week trial in Glasgow, a court ruled that the *News of the World*'s swinger story had defamed the Scottish politician Tommy Sheridan and awarded him £200,000 damages. On the steps of the court, Sheridan likened his win to the equivalent of football minnows Gretna beating Real Madrid on penalties, adding: 'They are liars and they have proved they are liars.'[5]

By now Scotland Yard, still conducting its operation in secrecy, became aware that the *News of the World* was hacking not just the phones of the princes and their aides but a growing number of high-profile figures. Mindful of the seriousness of the terrorist threat – and perhaps also of its close relationship with Rupert Murdoch's newspapers – the force decided to limit the scope of the investigation. A Crown Prosecution Service file note dated 14 July 2006 stated 'the police have requested initial advice about the data produced and whether the case as it stands could be ring-fenced to ensure that extraneous matters will not be dragged into the prosecution area'. By 25 July, the CPS had agreed privately with the police that the case should be 'deliberately limited' to 'less sensitive' witnesses. A senior Crown Prosecution Service lawyer wrote: 'It was recognized early in this case that the investigation was likely to reveal a vast array of offending behaviour. However the CPS and the police concluded that aspects of the investigation could be focused on a discrete area of offending relating to JLP and HA [the royal aides] and the suspects Goodman and Mulcaire.'[6] For a long time neither the Crown Prosecution Service nor Scotland Yard admitted the existence of this strategy in their subsequent testimony to Parliament, nor in their public announcements.

With their horizons sufficiently narrowed and with sufficient call data and corresponding newspaper stories based on intercepted messages, the police finally struck. Clive Goodman's career as one of Britain's most senior journalists came to a noisy end at 6 a.m. on 8 August 2006 when officers burst into the house he shared with his wife and eighteen-month-old daughter in Putney, arrested him and took him to a police station while they searched his home – where they found an important internal memo in a chest of drawers in his bedroom.

Later that morning, officers executed a search warrant at the *News of the World* in Wapping with the intention of seizing material from Goodman's desk and financial records. In the absence of the *NoW*'s holidaying lawyer Tom Crone, the company called Julian Pike, a partner at News International's solicitors, Farrer & Co (ironically, also the Queen's lawyers), and asked him 'to assist' in the search. The four officers who gained access to the *News of the World* received a hostile reception – as Detective Chief Inspector Keith Surtees later explained:

> We got to the desk of Goodman, we seized some material from the desk of Goodman. There was a safe on his desk, which was unopened. My officers were confronted with photographers, who were summoned from other parts of News International, and they were taking photographs of the officers. A number of night or news editors challenged the officers around the illegality of their entry into News International. They were asked to go to a conference room until lawyers could arrive to challenge the illegality of the section 8 (1) and 18 (5) and section 8 PACE authorities, and it was described to me as a tense stand-off by the officer leading that search. The officer tried to get our forensic management team, our search officers into the building. They were refused entry, they were left outside. Our officers were effectively surrounded and photographed and not assisted in any way, shape or form. That search was curtailed. Some items were taken. The search did not go to the extent I wanted it to.[7]

At the time the officer leading the search, Detective Inspector Pearce, feared that the *News of the World*'s staff 'may offer some form of violence against the small police team in the building', though none occurred because the police soon left. They did not return because, as Detective Chief Inspector Surtees explained, the 'moment had been lost with regard to the information we sought. It, I think, had gone, quite frankly.'[8] Details of News International's obstruction and intimidation of the police were made public only six years later.

At the same time as they raided Goodman, detectives raided the home and offices of Glenn Mulcaire, from which they took away an extensive array of paperwork, CD-roms, audio cassettes and white-boards on which were written PIN numbers, security codes and bank details of his targets. Mulcaire and Goodman stayed silent in their interviews with detectives and, after a night in the cells, were released on police bail. That day, 9 August, the Counter-Terrorism Branch arrested twenty-five people for a conspiracy to blow up nine transat-lantic airliners – which quickly became its biggest investigation.

Police resources were again under strain. Detective Chief Inspector Surtees ordered a team of Special Branch officers to work day and night to draw up a list of potential victims from Mulcaire's notes. What they found astonished them: Mulcaire had scrawled down thousands of names, phone numbers and PIN codes onto sheaf after sheaf of loose A4 notes. In all, there were 11,000 pages. Crucially, in the top left-hand corners of each page – where Mulcaire noted down which journalist commissioned him – there were twenty-eight differ-ent first names, such as 'Clive'.

Just as the Information Commissioner's Office had at the home of Fleet Street's data thief Steve Whittamore two years before, the police had stumbled onto an industrial-scale intrusion into the private lives of newsworthy individuals. In all, the Special Branch officers inputted the names of 418 'potential victims' into a computer spreadsheet. Here was evidence that Mulcaire, at least, had targeted not just the princes and their aides and a few others but hundreds upon hundreds of high-profile figures. Among them were two serving cabinet minis-ters, the Deputy Prime Minister, John Prescott – the voicemail PIN of whose Chief of Staff, Joan Hammell, Mulcaire had noted – and the Culture Minister, Tessa Jowell, who had responsibility for media pol-icy and her husband, David Mills (who worked for the Italian Prime Minister Silvio Berlusconi). Also listed were a former cabinet minister, the former Home Secretary David Blunkett, whose affair with the publisher Kimberly Fortier had been one of the *News of the World*'s award-winning splashes two years earlier, the Conservative front-bencher Boris Johnson, the Respect Party leader, George Galloway, and at least three senior Metropolitan Police officers, including Sir Ian Blair, the current Commissioner, Assistant Commissioner John Yates and his fellow Assistant Commissioner (who was overseeing the investigation) Andy Hayman. There was also evidence that Mulcaire had somehow obtained details of members of the public who had been given new identities by the Met under its witness protection scheme.

Despite the huge haul and clear circumstantial evidence that other *News of the World* journalists had commissioned Mulcaire, Scotland Yard made only a cursory attempt to identify wrongdoers other than Goodman and Mulcaire. Crown Prosecution Service records suggest that the police did not disclose to it the true scale of the evidence seized from Mulcaire. At a case conference on 21 August, the officer in overall charge of the operation, Detective Superintendent Philip Williams, told the CPS that there were potentially around 180 victims.* When the row over Operation Caryatid exploded later, the CPS said: 'We enquired whether there was any evidence connecting Mulcaire to other *News of the World* journalists. Again we were told that there was not, and we never saw any such evidence.'[10]

On 7 September, in an attempt to ascertain whether other journalists had commissioned the hacking, Scotland Yard wrote to News International explaining its intention to find 'co-conspirators' and asked for its notes and files on Mulcaire together with the records of phone calls made from its offices to him. Burton Copeland, a firm of lawyers contracted by News International to 'assist' the police, replied on 14 September that its client could find only one document (which has not been publicly disclosed) and refused to hand over the phone records, to protect 'sources'. Under the 1984 Police and Criminal Evidence Act, officers could only obtain a search warrant for 'journalistic premises' if the company was not cooperating. The police decided that News International was not cooperating, but nevertheless did not request a search warrant.

Then they did something strange. Someone inside Scotland Yard –

---

* He later told the Leveson Inquiry this was meant only as 'an indicative number'.[9]

it is not known who – approached Rebekah Wade, the *Sun*'s editor, and apparently gave her details of the operation. The rationale for this seems to have been that Wade was herself in Mulcaire's notes. She was thus, as *Sun* editor, potentially a victim of the *News of the World*'s newsgathering operation – which was also used to spy on other journalists, such as four at the *Mail on Sunday*. The police intended to approach her to ask whether she wished to pursue a case against her own employers, News International. The briefing she received was captured in an internal email sent by the *News of the World*'s lawyer to its editor, Andy Coulson:

From: Tom Crone
Sent: 15 September 2006 10.34
To: Andy Coulson
Subject: Strictly private and confidential

Andy,

Here's [what] Rebekah told me about info relayed to her by cops:

1. They are confident they have Clive [Goodman, former royal editor] and GM [Mulcaire] bang to rights on the Palace intercepts;

2. [on Mulcaire's] . . . accesses to voicemails. From these they have a list of 100–110 'victims';

3. The only payment records they found were from News Int, ie the NoW retainer and other invoices; they said that over the period they looked at (going way back) there seemed to be over £1m of payments.

4. The recordings and notes demonstrate a pattern of 'victims'. . . replaced by the next one who becomes flavour of the week/month;

5. They are visiting the bigger victims, ie where there are lots of intercepts;

6. Their purpose is to insure that when GM comes up in court the full case against him is there for the court to see (rather than just the present palace charges);

7. All they are asking victims is 'did you give anyone permission to access your voicemail?' and if not 'do you wish to make a formal complaint?'

8. They are confident that . . . they can then charge Glenn Mulcaire in relation to those victims . . . they are keen that the charges should demonstrate the scale of GM's activities . . . so they would feature victims from different areas of public life, politics, showbiz, etc

In terms of *NoW*:

(a) They suggested [this part of the email is unclear] *News of the World* journalists directly accessing the voicemails (this is what did for Clive).

(b) But they have got hold of *NoW* back numbers to 2004 and are trying to marry CG accesses to specific stories,

(c) In one case they seem to have a phrase from an NoW story which is identical to the tape or note of GM's access,

(d) They have no recordings of NoW people speaking to GM or accessing voicemails,

(e) They do have GM's phone records which show sequences of contacts with *News of the World* before and after accesses . . . obviously they don't have the content of the calls . . . so this is at best circumstantial.

10. They are going to contact RW today to see if she wishes to take it further.[11]

Unsurprisingly, Wade did not wish to submit a formal complaint against her employers. Scotland Yard showed a similar lack of enthusiasm for widening Operation Caryatid. At the time, the Met was engaged in seventy live operations, some of which were not being fully staffed for lack of resources. At the end of September, Deputy Assistant Commissioner Peter Clarke, Andy Hayman's deputy, made the decision to limit the investigation to Goodman and Mulcaire.

Speaking six years later at the Leveson Inquiry, he stood by his decision:

> Invasions of privacy are odious, obviously. They can be extraordinarily distressing and at times they can be illegal, but, to put it bluntly, they don't kill you. Terrorists do.[12]

He expressed disappointment, however, at the execution of the police's strategy to inform victims. Officers told thirty-six individuals in the government, military, police and royal household who they deemed needed to know their phones had been compromised for reasons of national security. Strangely, these did not include John Prescott, the Deputy Prime Minister, who was known to have been distrustful of Rupert Murdoch's political meddling.

Police later said that they understood that the mobile phone companies would alert affected customers. O2 warned forty straight away; the others waited for a staggering five years. Citing a concern that doing so would prejudice police inquiries, Orange and T-Mobile only notified their forty-five and seventy-one subscribers respectively in July 2011, while Vodafone waited until January 2012 to contact its forty affected customers. This meant that until then all those individuals were unaware they could change their PIN codes or sue News International. The overwhelming majority of Mulcaire's victims did not find out for years that they had been targeted.

Police had found a thoroughly detailed haul of incriminating evidence indicating that Mulcaire had hacked hundreds of news-worthy targets. But they had misled prosecutors about the number of victims and the involvement of other *NoW* journalists, failed to inform directly the vast majority of people who were likely to have been eavesdropped on, and rejected the options of selecting a wider sample of wrongdoing, pursuing a limited number of heavy users of Mulcaire at the *News of the World* or farming out the investigation to a less stretched unit. So the prosecution would be very narrow indeed.

This was a relief to the obstructive authorities at Wapping. Journalists there had been expecting the police to be knocking on their doors early in the morning, but the knocks never came. Faced with the on-going threat to their reputations from the continuing, albeit limited, fallout from Goodman and Mulcaire's arrests, Rupert Murdoch's executives considered how best to respond to the steadily escalating crisis. They then did what they thought was proper in the circumstances: for the next five years they mounted a sustained and deliberate cover-up, threatened, followed and attacked their critics, and lied to the public, media and Parliament.

The first pressing problem was how to minimize the impending prosecution of Clive Goodman. According to Lawrence Abramson, a senior lawyer at Harbottle & Co, which later worked for News International, internal emails at Wapping in 2006 'revealed quite an active involvement' in Clive Goodman's prosecution: 'They showed [the company] trying to influence the way the prosecution was being conducted or the defence was being conducted.'[13]

Naturally News International did not want its royal editor to suggest that phone hacking was rife at the *News of the World,* nor that he had only been doing what was expected of him. To demonstrate to Goodman that he was still valued, despite the shame he had brought, Tom Crone relayed to him Andy Coulson's repeated assurance that he could come back to the *News of the World* once he had served his sentence. News International continued to pay Goodman's full salary while he stayed at home, and even called him occasionally for help on royal stories. It also continued to pay Glenn Mulcaire his full salary.

While the Crown Prosecution Service put together the limited case against Clive Goodman and Glenn Mulcaire, News International had become concerned about an attack from another direction – the campaign by the Information Commissioner, Richard Thomas, to introduce a prison term for breaches of the Data Protection Act. On 24 July 2006, the Department for Constitutional Affairs issued a consultation paper agreeing with his proposal. In an attempt to lobby support for it, on 27 October Thomas met the chairman of the Press Complaints Commission's powerful Code Committee, which set its code of conduct and who happened to be Les Hinton, News International's executive chairman and one of Rupert Murdoch's closest allies. Since joining the *News* in Adelaide as a copy boy in 1960, Hinton had worked his way up to head Murdoch's British newspapers, where he had stewarded the promotions of Rebekah Wade and Andy Coulson. Although NI was implacably opposed to jail terms, Thomas said the meeting was 'civilized and reasonably constructive' and that Hinton 'talked a lot about the efforts which would be made to tackle misconduct'.[14] Thomas was extremely surprised a few days later to see a 'personalized and hostile leading editorial' on him and the ICO in *The Sunday Times* on 29 October 2011:

> Where someone lives, who they are, who their friends and family may be is hardly confidential information. It is common currency that is easily discovered by talking to neighbours, looking at the electoral register or searching the Land Registry, as anyone is entitled to do. To propose imprisonment for reporters – and insurers, solicitors and private investigators – who obtain such deals would be laughable, if it were not so sinister.

A further hostile leader appeared in *The Times* three days later, on 1 November:

> It [the proposal] could all too easily prevent investigative journalists looking at personal data in pursuit of a public-interest story; deter whistleblowers from revealing malpractice; and blow wide open the confidentiality that protects the journalist and his source.

Thomas told the Leveson Inquiry: 'At that time, nothing else was appearing in the mainstream press about 'What Price Privacy?' to prompt these attacks. The episode raised questions in my mind about proprietorial influence on editorial independence and freedom.'*

---

* At the inquiry, News International denied that Hinton had required its editors to write the editorials. Under close questioning from its counsel, Rhodri Davies, Thomas appeared to distance himself from his earlier comments. Asked about the supposed proprietorial influence, he told Davies: 'That is absolutely how I saw it at the time. I thought: "Gosh, this is very surprising and strange." Just forty-eight hours or less than that after I'd met the most senior person person at News International, here suddenly I'm appearing in a leading article, the lead editorial in *The Sunday Times*, on something which is not part of the public debate at the moment.' He added: 'I've now seen the witness statements from the editor at the time and also from [News International's lawyer] Mr Linklater, and they say categorically they were not directed by Mr Hinton. I have absolutely no reason to challenge or disagree with that. All I've said was at the time to me, and to others around me, it looked strange.'

At a pleas hearing at the Old Bailey in London in November 2006, the limited nature of the prosecution of Clive Goodman and Glenn Mulcaire became apparent. Under the Criminal Law Act 1977, the men pleaded guilty to conspiracy to intercept the communications of the royal aides Jamie Lowther-Pinkerton, Helen Asprey and Paddy Harverson. In the eight months leading up to their arrests, they had made 609 calls to the direct dial inboxes of the trio (Goodman making the most, 487). Under the 2000 Regulation of Investigatory Powers Act, Mulcaire also pleaded guilty to hacking the phones of five other individuals whose voicemail inboxes he had called a total of sixty-six times. He had ransacked the messages of Max Clifford, who had negotiated Rebecca Loos's £300,000 kiss and tell on David Beckham, but who had refused to deal with Andy Coulson again after the *Screws* turned over Kerry Katona. Two of the other figures came from the football world, which Mulcaire knew well: Gordon Taylor, chief executive of the Professional Footballers' Association, and Sky Andrew, a sports agent whose most famous client was the Arsenal footballer Sol Campbell. The other two were the supermodel Elle Macpherson and the Liberal Democrat MP Simon Hughes, who had recently admitted he was bisexual after being confronted by the *Sun* with evidence that he had called gay chatlines. All five would have been of interest to the *News of the World*, but probably not to its royal editor – which indicated the involvement of others at Wapping.

Even though the charges represented only a fraction of the *Screws'* true criminality, they were highly embarrassing for News International: one of its most senior journalists had been caught burgling the secrets of the royal family. As an act of contrition, Andy Coulson wrote to Sir Michael Peat, Prince Charles's Private Secretary, apologizing and offering to make a substantial donation to charities of the prince's choosing.

Despite the seriousness of the offences, News International still desperately hoped Clive Goodman would be spared jail, and hired one of the country's most expensive criminal barristers, John Kelsey-Fry QC, to represent him. At sentencing on 26 January 2007, Kelsey-Fry painted a sorry picture of the royal editor: 'He was demoted, sidelined, and another younger reporter was appointed to cover the royal family. Undoubtedly the newspaper business is a tough business. It is a ruthless business. It was while under that pressure that he departed from those high standards by which he had lived his entire life.' Seeking to minimize the extent of Goodman's wrongdoing, Kelsey-Fry made plain that his client had not been embroiled in Mulcaire's non-royal hacking, saying very briefly: 'Whoever else may be involved at the *News of the World*, his involvement is so limited.' Kelsey-Fry argued that his client should be spared the 'clang' of the prison gates because of the relative unimportance of the stories he had written, prison overcrowding and his public disgrace. On 26 January 2007, the judge, Mr Justice Gross, jailed Goodman for four months and Mulcaire for six for the 'grave, inexcusable and illegal invasion of privacy'.

Neither the judge, nor the prosecution, nor the hundreds of victims, nor the wider public had any idea of the scale of the lawbreaking at Wapping. That knowledge was confined, for the moment, to News International and Scotland Yard.

5

Rogue Defence

*Goodman's hacking was aberrational, a rogue exception, an
exceptionally unhappy event in the 163-year history of the
News of the World involving one journalist*
— Colin Myler, 22 February 2007

If Clive Goodman had been given a suspended sentence or community service, Andy Coulson might have been able to maintain his
position, but that was now impossible. His glorious career at Wapping ended in ignominy at the age of thirty-five. In a statement to the
media, Coulson said that although he had not known about hacking, he 'ultimately' bore responsibility as editor. In a bad-tempered
farewell speech to staff that evening, he remarked that the Home
Secretary had recently recommended only the most dangerous criminals be imprisoned, to relieve overcrowding, and that only that day
a downloader of child pornography had been spared jail. Terribly
unjust it may have been, but the award-winning editor was now out
of work.

Rupert Murdoch quickly replaced him with an old tabloid hand,
Colin Myler, executive editor of his aggressive *New York Post,* who
was hurriedly flown over from New York. Until then Myler had been
best known in Britain as the editor of the *Sunday Mirror* who, in
1992, published intimate pictures of Princess Diana working out in a
private gym.

Despite Goodman and Mulcaire's hacking representing a serious
invasion of privacy, the newspaper industry was seemingly relaxed
about the case – only the *Daily Telegraph* put the sentencing on its

front page. But the wrongdoing was regarded as so serious by the Press Complaints Commission that it began an investigation, as did separately the Commons Culture, Media and Sport Committee, which had also been concerned by the ICO's 'What Price Privacy?' report and the harassment by photographers of Prince William's girlfriend, Kate Middleton.

Surprisingly, as Clive Goodman paced his cell at the maximum security HMP Belmarsh, News International carried on paying his wages. The situation was too embarrassing to continue and on 5 February 2007, a week after sentencing, Les Hinton sacked Goodman: the *News of the World* would not, after all, be honouring Andy Coulson's promise to give him his old job back. But there was a sweetener – a year's salary, £90,502. 'I recognize this episode followed many unblemished, and frequently distinguished, years of service to the *News of the World*,' Hinton informed Goodman. 'In view of this, and in recognition of the pressures on your family, it has been decided that upon your termination you will receive one year's salary. In all the circumstances, we would of course be entitled to make no payment whatever . . . You will be paid, through payroll, on 6 February 2007, twelve months' base salary, subject to normal deductions of tax and national insurance.' Goodman was fuming: he believed he had taken the rap and kept his mouth shut, yet he was now being cast into the cold by his employers.

After firing Goodman, the *News of the World* had to fight off the two external inquiries. The PCC, under its chairman Sir Christopher Meyer, decided that because Andy Coulson had 'left the industry', he need not be interviewed, but it wanted to hear from his successor, Colin Myler. On 22 February Myler explained that Goodman had concealed the identity of his mysterious royal source, 'Alexander'; no one else at the paper had known that he was hacking phones and all of the paper's journalists understood fully the 'necessity of total compliance' with the PCC's code of practice. Myler wrote: 'Goodman's hacking was aberrational, a rogue exception, an exceptionally unhappy event in the 163-year history of the *News of the World* involving one journalist.' The abandonment of Clive Goodman was complete.

But Goodman was not finished. On 2 March, he wrote to News International's director of human resources, Daniel Cloke, giving notice of his intention to request an internal appeal against his dismissal, despite being jailed for serious professional misconduct. The letter left News International in no doubt that he could still open his mouth.

Dear Mr Cloke

I refer to Les Hinton's letter of February 5, 2007, informing me of my dismissal for alleged gross misconduct.

The letter identifies the reason for the dismissal as 'recent events'. I take this to mean my plea of guilty to conspiracy to intercept the voicemail messages of three employees of the royal family.

I am appealing against this decision on the following grounds:

I) The decision is perverse in that the actions leading to this criminal charge were carried out with the full knowledge and support of [*]. Payment for Glenn Mulcaire's services was arranged by [**].

II) The decision is inconsistent, because [*] and other members of staff were carrying out the same illegal procedures. The prosecution counsel, the counsel for Glenn Mulcaire, and the Judge at the sentencing hearing agreed that other News of the World employees were the clients for Mulcaire's five solo substantive charges. This practice was widely discussed in the daily editorial conference, until explicit reference to it was banned by the Editor. As far as I am aware, no other member of staff has faced disciplinary action, much less dismissal.

III) My conviction and imprisonment cannot be the real reason for my dismissal. The legal manager, Tom Crone, attended virtually every meeting of my legal team and was given full access to the Crown Prosecution Service's evidence files. He, and other staff on the paper, had long advance knowledge that I would plead guilty. Despite this, the paper continued to employ me. Throughout my suspension I was given book serialisations to write and was consulted on several occasions about royal stories they needed to check. The paper continued to employ me for a substantial part of my custodial sentence.

IV) Tom Crone and the Editor promised me on many occasions that I could come back to a job at the newspaper if I did not implicate

---

* Names have been redacted at the request of the Metropolitan Police to avoid prejudicing criminal trials.

*the paper or any of its staff in my mitigation plea. I did not, and
I expect the paper to honour its promise to me.*

*V) The dismissal is automatically unfair as the company failed to go
through the minimum required statutory dismissal procedures.*

Yours sincerely
Clive Goodman

cc *Stuart Kuttner, Managing Editor, News of the World*
  Les Hinton, Executive Chairman, News International Ltd

In 360 precise words, Goodman was threatening to explode the
company's defence: he was claiming phone hacking had been carried
out routinely, with management's 'full knowledge'.

Four days after the letter was sent, Les Hinton gave evidence to the
House of Commons Culture, Media and Sport Committee into press
standards. Hinton had to be careful, since the last time a senior News
International executive had appeared before the committee she had
admitted that the company bribed police. But he would never make
that mistake. On 6 March 2007, the urbane, silver-haired executive
chairman assured the MPs that phone hacking had been a one-off
case, the result of lax controls on payments, which had been exploited
by Goodman. The police had carried out 'pretty thorough investigations', with the result that two men had gone to prison, the *News of
the World* had paid a substantial sum to charity and the editor had
resigned. Hinton looked them in the eye and said: 'I believe absolutely
that Andy did not have knowledge of what was going on.'

Asked by John Whittingdale, the committee's Conservative chairman, who had authorized the 'cheques' that Goodman had spent,
Hinton put him right: these were cash payments. 'There were actually
two issues involved in the Goodman case,' he said:

> There had been a contract with Glenn Mulcaire, during which he was
> carrying out activities which the prosecution and the judge accepted
> were legitimate investigative work. There was a second situation where
> Clive had been allowed a pool of cash to pay to a contact in relation to
> investigations into royal stories. That, the court was told, was where
> the money came from and the detail of how he was using that money

was not known to the editor. That is not unusual for a contact, when you have a trusted reporter – which Clive was ...

At the end of the session, Whittingdale checked: 'You carried out a full, rigorous internal inquiry, and you are absolutely convinced that Clive Goodman was the only person who knew what was going on?' 'Yes, we have,' Hinton replied, 'and I believe he was the only person, but that investigation, under the new editor, continues.'

A week later, on 14 March, Goodman decided to appeal his sacking and wrote to Daniel Cloke asking him for a long list of documents for the internal hearing, including emails between himself and several executives at the *News of the World* and, tellingly, a transcript of Les Hinton's evidence to the Culture Committee. News International denied Goodman's request for the emails. Instead, Cloke and NI's legal director Jonathan Chapman (who had previously worked at Enron) reviewed 2,500 emails between Goodman and the executives. They were looking for anything which demonstrated that Goodman was right to claim that others had known about phone hacking and that other journalists at the paper were also engaged in the lawbreaking.

In April, the company's problems intensified when Glenn Mulcaire launched an employment tribunal case claiming that he was due a pay-off on the grounds that he was an employee. As they considered Mulcaire's claim, Chapman and Cloke found evidence of police corruption in the internal emails requested by Goodman – which they ignored since they were civil lawyers engaged in an employment law case and had no professional obligation to inform the police. They determined that there was no 'reasonable evidence' in the emails to support Goodman's case that management had known about his criminality and that consequently he had been unfairly dismissed. As they pondered what to do with their jailed royal editor, who had already been paid £90,502, the *News of the World* finally took action against another reporter, though one who had always conducted himself legally. On 26 April 2007, the paper sacked Matt Driscoll, still on sick leave with depression. He began an employment tribunal case.

By now News International had another problem: Gordon Taylor, the footballers' union leader whose phone Mulcaire had admitted hacking in court. More particularly, News International was having a problem with Taylor's dogged lawyer, 42-year-old Mark Lewis, a combative figure who prided himself on lateral thinking. By the time Lewis had become head of litigation at the Manchester law firm George Davies, he had overcome a difficult childhood, been the first from his working-class family to go to university and, aged twenty-six, been diagnosed with multiple sclerosis, which disabled his right hand and affected his speech.

As he watched the BBC's *Ten O'Clock News* report of the sentencing of Goodman and Mulcaire on 26 January 2007, Lewis remembered a curious incident a year and a half before. In July 2005, the *News of the World*'s chief reporter, Neville Thurlbeck, had turned up on the doorstep of Jo Armstrong, a lawyer at the Manchester-based Professional Footballers' Association, hoping to ask questions about the private life of its chief executive, Gordon Taylor. A passerby had spotted a photographer taking pictures of the pair lunching and had alerted Taylor, who chased after the snapper and discovered he was working for the *News of the World*. Lewis had written to the newspaper on Taylor's behalf denying the story. In its response, the *News of the Screws* explained it had obtained the story through 'proper journalistic inquiry'; the phrase stuck in Lewis's memory, and he was suspicious of it.

Lewis reasoned that because Mulcaire had admitted intercepting the voicemails of five individuals outside the orbit of the royal family, those individuals would have a civil claim against News International for breach of privacy – and, given that Goodman was a royal reporter and other victims came from sport, showbusiness and politics, other News International journalists were likely too to have been hacking phones. In early 2007, Lewis wrote to each of the non-royal hacking victims (Max Clifford, Taylor, Sky Andrew, Simon Hughes and Elle Macpherson). Only Taylor wanted to pursue a case; Lewis wrote to News International making a civil claim for invasion of privacy.

At that stage, had News International offered £20,000 damages under a legal manoeuvre known as a Part 36 offer (which puts pressure on a litigant to settle or risk paying the other side's costs if a case goes to court and a judge awards a lower amount), Lewis would have advised Taylor to settle, since he had no evidence other than Mulcaire's court admission – which was not itself proof that he had acted on behalf of the *News of the World*. Instead, to his surprise, the *NoW*'s legendary Tom Crone asked if he could visit him in person in Manchester, which he did at the offices of George Davies on 3 May 2007. 'That was their big mistake,' Lewis said later. 'Crone never went outside London. It flagged up they thought they had a really big problem. His starting point was: "We thought this had all gone away, let's settle."'[1] Lewis asked for £200,000 damages. Crone rejected the request, grabbed his coat and left.

News International was now facing trouble on five fronts: the PCC and Culture Committee investigations, which did not know about the use of the dark arts; Clive Goodman and Glenn Mulcaire, who did; and Gordon Taylor, who suspected but had no proof.

The PCC was easily dispatched. On 18 May 2007, the commission – which had not been told of Goodman's letter of 2 March, nor of Gordon Taylor's legal complaint – ruled that while Goodman's behaviour had been appalling, there was 'no evidence' to challenge the *Screws*' insistence that he was a rogue reporter. Praising the 'numerous examples' of good practice throughout the industry towards data privacy, the watchdog issued six new technical recommendations on covert newsgathering, such as inserting its code of practice into staff contracts and introducing stricter controls on cash payments. With that it let the matter drop.

With one problem gone, News International tried again to get rid of Clive Goodman. News International's legal director, Jonathan Chapman, asked an external firm of lawyers, Harbottle & Lewis, to confirm its decision to reject his employment appeal. In a delicately phrased letter to Harbottle's senior partner Lawrence Abramson on 9 May, Chapman wrote that News International's own review had determined there was no reasonable evidence to support Goodman's contention that phone hacking had been widespread. However, he continued: 'Because of the bad publicity that could result from an allegation in an employment tribunal that we had covered up potentially damaging evidence found on our email trawl, I would ask that you or a colleague carry out an independent review of the emails in question and report back to me with any findings of material that could possibly tend to support either of Goodman's contentions.'[2] Abramson

and junior colleagues were given electronic access to the same emails
Chapman and Cloke had reviewed, though some were strangely blank
and others cut off halfway through. Because Abramson could not
access some of them electronically he requested paper copies, which
were sent to his offices. Abramson agreed with his client: there was no
reasonable evidence in the emails to support Goodman's case (again
overlooking police corruption, which he was under no professional
obligation to report to the police). After some haggling, on 29 May
Abramson agreed with Chapman the following wording of the results
of the independent review of Goodman's emails:

Re: Clive Goodman

We have on your instructions reviewed the emails to which you
have provided access from the accounts of:

Andy Coulson
Stuart Kuttner
Ian Edmondson
Clive Goodman
Neil Wallis
Jules Stenson*

I can confirm that we did not find anything in those emails which
appeared to us to be reasonable evidence that Clive Goodman's
illegal actions were known about and supported by both or either
of Andy Coulson, the editor, and Neil Wallis, the Deputy Editor,
and/or that Ian Edmondson, the News Editor, and others were
carrying out similar illegal procedures.

After completing the exercise, Harbottle and Lewis filed away its
report, together with the paper copies of the emails, where they lay
until they re-emerged with devastating impact four years later. For
now, nothing was publicly known about corruption at News International, nor of the attempts to influence the outcome of Goodman's

* Jules Stenson was features editor of the *News of the World*.

prosecution, nor of his legal action, nor of the ill-treatment of the sports reporter Matt Driscoll. What happened next, though, would dramatically raise the stakes when these things resurfaced.

In the spring of 2007, David Cameron was looking for a new press secretary. On becoming leader of the Conservative Party in 2005, aged thirty-nine, he faced two personal electoral difficulties: his privileged background and his lack of experience. Educated at Eton and Oxford, where he was a member of the boisterous Bullingdon dining club of rich young men, Cameron's only jobs prior to entering Parliament had been as a Tory Party worker, ministerial aide and public relations executive at Carlton Television. After three successive general election defeats to the Murdoch-backed Tony Blair, Cameron wanted to reposition the Conservatives as kinder and concerned about public services, poverty and the environment. Cameron's closest aides espoused a more mature politics and believed that newspaper proprietors were enjoying political power without accountability; they sought to curb the power of the press barons. Speaking in 2011, Cameron's press chief at the time, George Eustice, said: 'Part of David Cameron's whole prescription of where Blair had gone wrong was that it was all about headlines and endless initiatives and nothing being done, so part of his argument was ... we're not going to deviate things just to get a headline in a Sunday paper.'[3] Cameron's team decided they would cultivate political reporters rather than their proprietors and would politely decline invitations to address News Corp conferences. Eustice recalled: 'We didn't want to say to them [proprietors]: "We're going to put you in your box." We didn't want it to be like that. We just wanted them to get used to it.'[4]

Launching a mission to soften the Conservative brand, in February 2006 Cameron made a speech saying that youths who wore hooded tops were misunderstood rather than dangerous (the perception of many voters), and in April 2006 posed on a husky sled on a Norwegian glacier to vaunt his credentials on climate change. Despite successfully reshaping attitudes towards his party, the approach alienated some traditional supporters. Rupert Murdoch was particularly unimpressed. In an interview on US television on 20 July 2006, he described Cameron as 'charming', but when asked what he thought of him replied: 'Not much. He's bright. He's quick. He's totally inexperi-enced.'[5] With Blair having already announced he would not stand for another term, Murdoch hoped Gordon Brown would become prime minister a year or two before the next general election due in 2010 to allow a 'match up between Brown and the new Conservative leader-ship.'[6] In effect, Murdoch was giving notice to the leaders that his endorsement was winnable.

By early 2007, Cameron began to fear his aloofness towards editors and proprietors risked a backlash at election time, partly because Blair's likely successor, Gordon Brown, was courting the media so much. According to Eustice: 'The media wouldn't say: "We respect what David Cameron is doing," they would react to the game. They would literally say: "Gordon Brown came over for dinner and David Cameron won't speak at our conference, why should we back him?"'[7]

Cameron and his closest political ally George Osborne, the shadow Chancellor and fellow Bullingdonian, began looking for a new press chief to replace Eustice, who wanted in any case to become an MP.

Osborne thought particularly warmly of Andy Coulson, who a year earlier had taken the sting out of a highly controversial story that could have wrecked his career. When he was twenty-two, Osborne had known a dominatrix, Natalie Rowe, who was expecting the baby of one of his friends, William Sinclair, who had developed a drug habit. In 2005, Rowe (professional name Mistress Pain), had been hawking around a picture of herself with the rising star of Her Maj-esty's Loyal Opposition just out of university. In the picture, Osborne was putting his arm around Rowe, with a line of white powder in the background which she claimed was cocaine.

Rowe had contracted Max Clifford, who sold the story to the *Sunday Mirror*, which published it on 16 October 2005 under the headline: 'Vice Girl: I Snorted Cocaine with Top Tory Boy'. Despite not agreeing a deal with Rowe, Andy Coulson's *News of the World* had also somehow obtained the picture and splashed the story. It was noticeably gentler on Osborne and included sympathetic quotes from him, such as: 'It was a stark lesson to me at a young age of the destruc-tion which drugs bring to so many people's lives.' Coulson's editorial suggested that Osborne had been a young man caught up in a shadowy world, pointing out that he robustly condemned drugs.

Rebekah Wade also reportedly recommended Coulson to David Cameron.[8] Aware that the *News of the World*'s former editor had resigned over a scandal, Cameron asked Coulson whether there was anything in his past that could embarrass them. Coulson gave the necessary assurances, and on 31 May 2007 was appointed as the new director of communications to the Leader of Her Majesty's Loyal Opposition. With his working-class background and redtop newspaper experience, Coulson provided an earthy counter-weight to the upper-class Cameron and Osborne, and could 'tabloid proof' policies. In his new role, Coulson started reaching out to right-wing journalists and proprietors, particularly Rupert Murdoch, and almost simultaneously the Conservatives began to roll out policies designed to hit the sweet spots of right-wing voters and editors. At the party conference in October 2007, George Osborne launched a plan to raise the threshold for inheritance tax from £300,000 to £1 million, which would benefit thousands of homeowners in the South-East and in his leader's address David Cameron vaunted traditional values and backed a cap on migrants from outside the European Union. The BBC's political reporter Brian Wheeler noted that Cameron had reprised his optimism and sincerity. 'But there was none of the New Age rhetoric of last year's "let the sun shine in" speech. He spoke at length about education, calling for a return to traditional standards in the classroom, more discipline and "setting by ability". He set out policies to strengthen the family, including removing incentives in the benefit system for couples to live apart.'[9]

Under Coulson, Cameron quickly adopted the *Sun*'s 'Broken Britain' campaign against social breakdown, at odds with his earlier message of understanding. On 10 January 2008, for instance, in a 'time to reclaim our streets' speech in Salford, he said: 'Today, I want to speak about the senseless, barbaric and seemingly remorseless prevalance of violence in our country. A violence that takes our families, torments them with suffering and tears them apart.' Rebekah Wade's *Sun* backed the hard line and on 30 January blazoned Cameron's tough talking on the police on a front page headlined 'Police

Cameron Action'. Its helpful political editor George Pascoe-Watson wrote: 'David Cameron yesterday unveiled his plans to mend broken Britain ... and give power back to the police. In an exclusive interview he said officers could be given free rein to stop and search youngsters on the street.'[10]

For Rupert Murdoch, the hacking scandal was now in the past and he returned to his quest to dominate the world's media. While an enthusiast for the new medium of television in the 1950s and 60s, the septuagenarian tycoon had been caught out by the sudden and disruptive arrival of the Internet. Setting aside his initial scepticism, he had embraced the information age in July 2005, buying the social networking site MySpace for $580 million. Under News Corp's management, MySpace initially prospered, and two years after its acquisition had become the world's largest social networking site, with 110 million subscribers. Murdoch's true love, though, remained his first – print – and, in May 2007, he sought to acquire one of the grand American newspapers he had long coveted, the *Wall Street Journal*. There was just one problem: its parent company, Dow Jones, was owned by the Bancroft family, who saw themselves as responsible custodians of independent journalism. Murdoch offered $60 a share, a 67 per cent premium to Dow Jones's recent price, but the Bancrofts raised the phone hacking prosecutions and allegations that Murdoch interfered in his newspapers. In a swooning 1,200-word letter to the Bancrofts published by the *Wall Street Journal* on 14 May 2007, Murdoch praised the family's 'record of journalistic independence', while attesting to his own virtues: 'Any interference – or even a hint of interference – would break the trust that exists between the paper and its readers, something I am unwilling to countenance ... I don't apologize for the fact that I've always had strong opinions and strong ideas about newspapers, but I have always respected the independence and integrity of the news organizations with which I am associated.'

Inside News Corp, Murdoch, now seventy-six, was also dealing with a fraught question: his succession. Originally the presumption had been that his eldest son, Lachlan, would take over the chairmanship, but Lachlan had resigned as its deputy chief operating officer the previous summer, August 2005, reportedly after a row with his father, and moved back to Australia (though he remained a director). Elisabeth, the most independently ambitious of Murdoch's three children by his second wife, Anna Torv, had shunned the family business since 2000, concentrating on growing her TV production company, Shine. She and her husband, Matthew Freud, the PR specialist behind Freud Communications, were among the most powerful and glittering figures in London's medialand.

By contrast, Murdoch's youngest son, James, had long been a rebel. At the prestigious Horace Mann High School in New York he dyed his hair blond, got a tattoo and pierced his ears and an eyebrow. Subsequently he dropped out of Harvard to found a hip-hop label, Rawkus, keeping a gun under his table to deal with some of its Uzi-carrying stars. After a succession of business flops, in 2000 he had come back into the fold, turning around News Corp's loss-making Asian TV operation Star, before three years later becoming the chief executive of BSkyB, where he successfully increased the number of subscribers and promoted its environmental credentials. He was aggressively bright and impetuous, and conducted business meetings standing up behind his desk. He would soon take centre stage in the phone hacking affair.

Three thousand miles from New York, in Wapping, News International still faced the problems of what to do with Clive Goodman, the 'rogue reporter' who was threatening to take his case to a public employment tribunal; a similar claim from Glenn Mulcaire; the Gordon Taylor legal action; and, more immediately, the parliamentary investigation by the Commons Culture Committee. On 3 July, the Culture Committee published its report. Though it was more sharply worded than the PCC's complacent findings, executives at Wapping who knew the truth must have read it with relief. The MPs described Goodman's hacking of the royal household as a serious breach of journalistic ethics but appeared to accept the company's excuse that it had been the result of lax controls on cash payments. Nonetheless the MPs said it was 'extraordinary' that the Press Complaints Commission had failed to question Andy Coulson, and criticized Fleet Street's 'complacency' towards the Information Commissioner's disclosure in 'What Price Privacy?' that many reporters had bought illegal data from Steve Whittamore. It warned the press that, unless it improved its behaviour, it would undermine its unique ability to regulate itself outside of the law.

In June, News International's executive chairman, Murdoch's right-hand man Les Hinton, sanctioned a payment of £80,000 to Glenn Mulcaire to settle his employment case, with a further £5,000 for legal fees: Mulcaire had admitted making over 200 calls to hack phones and had been jailed for six months. In July, Hinton authorized the payment of a further £153,000 to Clive Goodman to settle his claim. Goodman's appeal against his sacking had been dismissed internally and externally, but News International's problem was that both he and Mulcaire could open their mouths and make accusations at employment tribunals, which would be heard in public. In total, in the six months since being jailed, Goodman had been paid £243,000; his settlement naturally included a stringent confidentiality clause. A year later, Goodman began freelancing at the *Daily Star Sunday*, a paper owned by Murdoch's fellow proprietor Richard Desmond. Remarkably, on being released from prison, Glenn Mulcaire was contracted to give security advice to a private security company, Quest, whose chairman was Sir John Stevens, the former Met Police Commissioner.

Rupert Murdoch's power and influence continued to rise unabated. On 1 August 2007, he finally won his battle for Dow Jones in a $5.7 billion deal, giving him control of the *Wall Street Journal*, whose publisher (editor, in British terms) soon left. Despite being the most important figure in British media, Murdoch had only ever been called to give evidence to parliament once, on 17 September 2007, at a private session of unelected peers on the Lords Communications Committee in New York, when – in direct contradiction of his statement to the Bancrofts just four months earlier – he had confirmed that he set the political policy of the *Sun*. An appendix to the committee's report summarized his evidence:

> Mr Murdoch did not disguise the fact that he is hands on both econom-ically and editorially. He says that 'the law' prevents him from instructing the editors of The Times and The Sunday Times. The inde-pendent board is there to make sure he cannot interfere and he never

says 'do this or do that' although he often asks 'what are you doing?' He explained that he 'nominates' the editors of these two papers but that the nominations are subject to the approval of the independent board. His first appointment of an editor of *The Times* split the board but was not rejected.

He distinguishes between *The Times* and *The Sunday Times* and the *Sun* and the *News of the World* (and makes the same distinction between the *New York Post* and the *Wall Street Journal*). For the *Sun* and *News of the World* he explained that he is a 'traditional proprietor'. He exercises editorial control on major issues – like the party to back in a general election or policy on Europe.

In December 2007, Murdoch reshuffled his leading lieutenants, sending his most trusted executive, Les Hinton, who had approved the secret pay-offs to Clive Goodman and Glenn Mulcaire, to New York to take charge of Dow Jones. Murdoch promoted his son James to chief executive of News Corp Europe and Asia, making him responsible for News International in the UK. Business was good: in the six months to 31 December, News Corp's sales were up by 13 per cent to $15.6 billion.

The cover-up was working. News International had brushed off the Press Complaints Commission and the Commons Culture Committee and paid off both Goodman and Mulcaire. A journalist and a private detective had been jailed. Their crimes had exposed the ease with which the security of mobile phones – increasingly widely used over the previous decade – could be breached, but despite a substantial body of evidence, the police had not followed up many leads, the watchdog had been asleep, and the newspaper industry had refrained from embarking on a period of soul-searching. After a brief period of unemployment, the editor who had resigned had found another, weightier job – as one of the most important and trusted confidants of the next prime minister.

The only outstanding issue was Gordon Taylor.

6

The Manchester Lawyers

*In the light of these facts there is a powerful case that there is
(or was) a culture of illegal information access*
– Michael Silverleaf, QC for News International, 3 June 2008

In his offices in Manchester, Mark Lewis's difficulty was that he still
had no evidence that the *News of the World* had ordered the hacking
of Gordon Taylor's phone. Nevertheless, he put together a team to
fight the case, bringing in Charlotte Harris, a media lawyer in George
Davies's sports department, and Jeremy Reed, a barrister at Hogarth
Chambers in Lincoln's Inn, London. Together they built an 'inferen-
tial' case: Mulcaire had admitted hacking Taylor's phone; he worked
for the *News of the World*; therefore the *News of the World* must
have hacked Taylor's phone; therefore it had breached his privacy and
must pay him damages. News International responded with derision
to the case, reserving the right to have it struck out. It continued to
frustrate and obstruct Taylor's lawyers. Under the legal process of
discovery, which compels parties to court cases to disclose relevant
information, Lewis and Harris had sought from News International
internal documents about phone hacking. But, as Harris explained:
'The initial disclosure from the *News of the World* was almost nothing. It was just a load of articles about the princes and they said they
had nothing to disclose.'[1]

Lewis, a cussed individual, did not give up. He demanded Scotland
Yard hand over its evidence about the hacking of Taylor's phone
accrued during its investigation into Goodman and Mulcaire in 2006.
The Metropolitan Police, which had thousands of pages of Mulcaire's

notes and other material, resisted disclosure, but in December 2007 a High Court judge, Nicholas Bragge, ordered its cooperation. At that hearing, according to Lewis, Mark Maberly, a detective sergeant in the Metropolitan Police, told him: 'You're not having everything, but we will give you enough on Taylor to hang them.' Maberly denies saying this.

When Taylor's legal team finally received the police evidence in January 2008, it astounded them. Reed phoned Harris at home and said: 'I've got the disclosure in. It's dynamite.' Scotland Yard handed over three items seized from Mulcaire's home in August 2006: one was an audio recording of Mulcaire discussing phone hacking with an unnamed sports reporter; the second a contract from February 2005 signed by the *News of the World*'s news editor, Greg Miskiw, promising to pay Paul Williams (Mulcaire's pseudonym) £7,000 for a story about Gordon Taylor; and the third an email dated 29 June 2005 from the *News of the World* to Mulcaire's address (shadowmenuk@yahoo.co.uk) 'Hello, this is a transcript for Neville.' The 'For Neville' email, as it became known, was devastating. It had been sent by a *News of the World* reporter, Ross Hindley, to Mulcaire on 29 June 2005 and contained the transcripts of thirty-five voicemail messages, including seventeen left by Taylor on Armstrong's phone and thirteen vice versa. The messages were simply casual exchanges between two colleagues, but the significance was that they had clearly been hacked – and had now been disclosed to their victim. On one, Armstrong had told Taylor: 'Thank you for yesterday. You were great.'* At the same time Lewis had obtained from the Information Commissioner News International's orders for illegal searches from Steve Whittamore.

In April, News International's executives received copies of the police disclosures. They were alarmed. The 'For Neville' email – sent by one *News of the World* journalist, Ross Hindley, with a title referring to another, Neville Thurlbeck – was clear proof that Goodman was not the only *Screws* reporter who knew about Mulcaire's

---

* The incident in July 2005 when Taylor had caught a *News of the World* photographer taking pictures of him and Jo Armstrong now made sense. Lewis explained that Armstrong had been thanking Taylor for delivering the eulogy at her father's funeral.

hacking, while the Whittamore material showed its journalists had requested illegal searches.

On 24 May, Tom Crone, the *News of the World*'s lawyer, emailed Colin Myler with the bad news: the 'For Neville' email, though Crone did not refer to it by that name, contained a large number of transcripts of voicemails from Taylor's telephone, while the Information Commissioner's material included a 'list of named *News of the World* journalists and a detailed table of Data Protection Infringements between 2001 and 2003 . . .' Crone pointed out: 'A number of those names are still with us and some of them have moved to prominent positions on *NoW* and the *Sun*. Typical infringements are "turning round" car reg, and mobile phone numbers (illegal).'[2] The executives Crone was referring to included the *Sun*'s Rebekah Wade, who at the *News of the World* had ordered a 'mobile conversion' (finding a mobile phone number's registered owner) from Whittamore. Having to make this point must have been difficult for Crone since by this time Wade had a close working relationship with the Murdochs.

Under the heading 'Where we go', Crone stressed:

> This evidence, particularly the email from the *News of the World*, is fatal to our case. Our position is very perilous. The damning email is genuine and proves we actively made use of a large number of extremely private voicemails from Taylor's telephone in June/July 2005 and that this was pursuant to a February 2005 contract, i.e. a 5/6 month operation. He [Taylor] has no evidence that the *News of the World* continued to act illegally after that but he can prove Mulcaire continued to access his mobile until May 2006 (because Mulcaire pleaded guilty to it). We will be getting guidance from a senior QC next week about our next step. Inevitably this will be at the very least an admission of liability to a large part of the claim and an attempt to put Taylor under costs pressure by making a formal offer of substantial damages and his costs. He is claiming both ordinary damages and exemplary (punitive) damages and will succeed on both claims. His case will be expensive.

Mark Lewis told Julian Pike, partner at News International's law firm Farrer & Co, that his client wanted to be 'vindicated [in court] or made rich'. Taylor was effectively demanding a massive payment in return for silence, and such a big pay-off would have to be approved by News International's new chairman, James Murdoch. News International asked a leading QC, Michael Silverleaf, for an opinion. At Wapping on 27 May, Pike recorded Myler's position: 'Spoke to James Murdoch – not any options – wait for silk's view.'

On 3 June, the legal opinion arrived – and it was horrendous for the company. Silverleaf said the 'For Neville' email, the Greg Miskiw contract and the illegal searches ordered from Steve Whittamore were 'overwhelming evidence' that a number of News International journalists had broken the law to write stories. Silverleaf wrote:

> In the light of these facts there is a powerful case that there is (or was) a culture of illegal information access used at NGN [the News International subsidiary which owned the *News of the World*] in order to produce stories for publication. Not only does this mean that NGN is virtually certain to be held liable to Mr Taylor, to have this paraded at a public trial would, I imagine, be extremely damaging to NGN's public reputation.[3]

Silverleaf estimated that if the case went to court a judge could award up to £250,000 damages – off the scale for a privacy case. (At that stage the highest privacy payout had been the £14,600 a court had ordered *Hello!* to pay Michael Douglas and Catherine Zeta-Jones in 2000 for publishing unauthorized photographs of their wedding.) The trouble for News International was that Gordon Taylor was furious that he had been illegally targeted and that Hinton had misled Parliament by suggesting that Clive Goodman was a rogue reporter when, Taylor knew, phone hacking had been more widespread.

On 3 June, News International offered Taylor an extraordinary £350,000 plus his costs, a total of about £550,000, in a Part 36 offer, which meant that Taylor could be left with a bill of hundreds of thousands of pounds even if he won the case in court. News International probably thought its offer, and the risks of not accepting it, were high enough.

On 6 June, Mark Lewis phoned Julian Pike and demanded a jawdropping figure of no less than £1 million damages and £200,000 costs. In his file notes, Pike noted down the rationale of Lewis's client:

'I [Taylor] want to carry on because of issues because NGN is wrong then carry on – one way or another this is going to hurt. Want to show NoW stories – NoW doing this – rife in organization – Palt [Parliament] inquiries told this not happening when it was. I want to speak out on this.'

At 2.31 p.m. on Saturday 7 June, Colin Myler informed his chairman James Murdoch in an email, which neither of them could ever have expected to be made public four years later:

> James
>
> Update on the Gordon Taylor (Professional Football Association) case.
>
> Unfortunately it is as bad as we feared.
>
> The note from Julian Pike of Farrer's is extremely telling regarding Taylor's vindictiveness.
>
> It would be helpful if Tom Crone and I could have five minutes with you on Tuesday.
>
> Colin[4]

He forwarded Pike's account to Crone of his conversation with Mark Lewis the night before, 6 June, which referred to Taylor's belief that hacking had been 'rife' at the *News of the World*. Pike wrote: 'He [Taylor] wishes to see NGN suffer: one way or another he wants this to hurt NGN. He wants to demonstrate that what happened to him is/was rife throughout the organization.'[5]

Three minutes after receiving the email chain at 2.34 p.m., Murdoch replied: 'No worries. I am in during the afternoon. If you want to talk before I'll be home tonight after seven and most of the day tomorrow.' He later said he did not 'review the full e-mail chain at the time or afterwards'.[6]

Whether Myler and Murdoch discussed the case that weekend is not known. What was clear was that Gordon Taylor and James Murdoch were engaging in a high-stakes game of bluff and counter-bluff. If Taylor insisted on humbling News International in court he risked losing hundreds of thousands of pounds, but Taylor also knew that News International desperately did not want the case to reach court because a public hearing would be hugely embarrassing and sink its 'rogue reporter' defence. Other victims of hacking would also realize that they too could sue and the costs of those cases would far outweigh the amount that Taylor was demanding.

Colin Myler, Tom Crone and James Murdoch had a half-hour meeting at Wapping on Tuesday 10 June to discuss the case. What happened would be hotly disputed three years later: Tom Crone said that he had taken in the 'For Neville' email and the Silverleaf opinion to show Murdoch – but Murdoch insisted he saw neither. What is indisputable is that James Murdoch agreed to pay Gordon Taylor £425,000 plus his legal fees of £220,000. Taylor had wanted to expose News International's lies but he was prepared to stay silent if he was paid enough. For him the balance was tipped at £425,000 – almost thirty times the record payout to Michael Douglas and Catherine Zeta-Jones by *Hello!* magazine. How and why such an extraordinarily high settlement came to be made would be one of the greatest controversies in the phone hacking affair.

After the wrangling was over, Tom Crone invited Mark Lewis to a conciliatory lunch at the Fleet Street wine bar El Vino's in November 2008. The atmosphere was jovial until Crone settled the bill, at which point Lewis announced that he had two other clients whose phones had been hacked by News International. Crone quickly left the bar.

In early 2009, Lewis's team won further payouts of around £100,000 damages for Jo Armstrong, who had left messages on Gordon Taylor's phone, and another sports lawyer who had dealt with Taylor, John Hewison, a partner at George Davies, who received £10,000. At the insistence of News International, the settlements remained confidential: there was a risk that if the other four non-royal victims found out, they too would start legal actions.

This was a disappointment to Lewis and Harris, who had been hoping that publicity about the cases would trigger new claims, which would dismantle what they suspected was a cover-up. But because the deals were private they received no coverage in the media. Signing a confidentiality agreement also meant that Gordon Taylor could not relay his experience of phone hacking to members of the Professional

Footballers' Association, several of whom later turned out to have been victims too.

Gordon Taylor had not been vindicated in court, but he had been made rich.

While News International battled Mark Lewis, the Information Commissioner, Richard Thomas, was becoming ever more insistent about the need for stiffer penalties for information misuse. On 13 December 2006 he had made good on his promise in 'What Price Privacy?' to publish a six-monthly update on his campaign to secure an option of a prison term for breaches of data protection. In the foreword to his new report, 'What Price Privacy Now?', he wrote: 'Progress has been significant and encouraging.' Underlining the need for action, he published a league table of Steve Whittamore's customers, naming for the first time thirty-two national newspapers and women's magazines which had ordered searches from him – and the number of journalists ordering searches at each publication, showing that, for the five most prolific titles, Whittamore had dealt with fifty-eight journalists at the *Daily Mail*, fifty at the *People*, forty-five at the *Daily Mirror*, thirty-three at the *Mail on Sunday* and twenty-three at the *News of the World*. The table put the number of transactions at 3,757 rather than the 17,489 calculated by Alec Owens. With the support of Lord Falconer's Department for Constitutional Affairs, the Ministry of Justice had incorporated a custodial sentence for breaches of the Data Protection Act into the Criminal Justice and Immigration Bill which, by October 2007, had received its second reading in Parliament and was heading towards the statute book.

In early 2008, Richard Thomas became aware that several newspaper groups were applying pressure on ministers to scrap the new custodial term, or, as he put it, 'press organizations were engaged in a powerful campaign against the proposal'.[7] On 11 February 2008, the Justice Secretary, Jack Straw, who like most cabinet ministers sought to maintain a warm relationship with the press, informed Thomas that the clause introducing the option of a custodial sentence was likely to be withdrawn. On 5 March, Thomas met Gordon Brown in Downing Street, afterwards emailing colleagues in Wilmslow to report back on a disappointment. While the Prime Minister considered the trade in personal information to be 'entirely unacceptable' and had been a victim of it himself in the past, 'he is concerned to strike the right balance with protecting freedom of expression, especially in relation to legitimate investigative journalism. Now that some time has been bought, he wants a compromise position to be achieved to minimize media concerns.'[8]

On 3 April, the government dropped Clause 129.* Instead, ministers would be given a reserve power to introduce custodial terms at a later, unspecified date. At the time of writing, this power has not been activated. The press had killed off tougher penalties for data theft. In 2011, Richard Thomas told Lord Leveson: 'Whatever was precisely known about the nature and extent of misconduct across the industry as a whole, it became increasingly clear that the press were able to assert very substantial influence on public policy and the political processes.'

With the Taylor settlement going unreported, it was business as usual at the *News of the World* – especially for Neville Thurlbeck. In March 2008, the paper's sex specialist was investigating the private life of motor racing executive Max Mosley, the son of the fascist politician Oswald Mosley. After reading physics at Oxford, Mosley had been called to the bar, but his passion had been motor racing and in 1993 he had become president of the world governing body for motorsport in Paris, the Fédération Internationale de l'Automobile. In his own time, he occasionally participated in sado-masochistic orgies. Although not ashamed of this activity, he was aware that many people would disapprove of it and kept it from his wife, family and colleagues. While the world of S&M usually carefully guarded its secrets, a forthcoming participant at one of Mosley's parties, known as 'Michelle', had mentioned his name to her husband, an MI5 agent,

---

* In a speech to the Society of Editors in Bristol on 10 November 2008, Paul Dacre, editor of the *Daily Mail*, welcomed the end of the proposal – which he described as 'truly frightening' – and disclosed that he, Les Hinton, and Murdoch MacLennan, chief executive of the *Daily Telegraph*, had raised concerns about it at a lunch with Gordon Brown the previous year. Dacre said: 'This legislation would have made Britain the only country in the free world to jail journalists and could have had a considerable chilling effect on good journalism. The Prime Minister – I don't think it is breaking any confidences to reveal – was hugely sympathetic to the industry's case.'

who realized Mosley might make a valuable story and contacted the *News of the World*. Thurlbeck offered 'Michelle' £25,000 and coached her how to record what he hoped would be Mosley performing a Sieg Heil salute. The orgy, themed on a correctional camp, duly took place at an apartment in Chelsea on Friday 28 March. After it was all over, Mosley and the women had a chat and a cup of tea.

Two days later, the *News of the World*'s front page screamed: 'F1 Boss in Sick Nazi Orgy with Five Hookers', with the strapline 'Son of Hitler-loving fascist in sex shame'. When Mosley showed the paper to his wife she thought her mischievous husband had mocked it up, but it was not a joke. Publication alerted Mosley's wife, his family, his friends, his colleagues at the FIA and tens of millions of people to his secret sexual behaviour, which he had been lawfully practising in private at private premises. The *Screws* had also posted a ninety-second video clip online, where it was watched 1.4 million times.

Mosley, a genial but flinty character, set about getting his revenge. To ensure he was not being eavesdropped by the *News of the World*, he hired the Quest security consultancy, whose operatives stood watch over a walled garden in Chelsea while he met the arranger of the session, 'Woman A', as she was later known in court. Together they worked out he must have been betrayed by 'Michelle'. MI5 sacked her husband after learning he had sold a story to the newspapers.

As Mosley battled to restore his reputation, the *News of the World* sought to gather more material about him for another story the following Sunday. On Wednesday 2 April, Thurlbeck emailed one of the female participants, threatening that unless she and the other women involved agreed to cooperate in the writing of a follow-up story, the paper would publish unpixilated pictures of them at the orgy and thus identify them. The women, some of whom had professional jobs, were horrified, but they did not give in to the threats.

On Friday 4 April 2008, Mosley sued the *News of the World* for breach of privacy. Tabloids usually bargained that anyone whose sex life had been exposed would not sue because a court case allowed embarrassing details to be reported by all papers and TV stations without fear of legal action. During the three-week trial in the High Court in July, the *News of the World*'s QC, Mark Warby, subjected Mosley to an extensive cross-examination on his sex life, but he stood firm: he explained that the paper had conflated two scenes, one of an English prison camp and a second where he had happened to speak German, which, he explained, he had done as a favour to one of the women, whose fantasy was to be ordered about in a foreign language. The *News of the World* admitted it had not bothered to translate Mosley's German remarks to check whether they contained Nazi references. 'Michelle' did not turn up to testify for the *NoW* because she was 'feeling unwell'. (The paper had 'renegotiated' her fee down to £12,500 because Mosley had not in the event performed a Sieg Heil.) To the surprise of the *News of the World*, the other dominatrices gave evidence for Mosley.

Delivering judgment on 24 July 2008, Mr Justice Eady described Thurlbeck's testimony as 'erratic and changeable' and remarked that the *News of the World*'s failure to discipline him for sending an email verging on blackmail was 'a remarkable state of affairs'. He ruled there had been no Nazi element to the orgy nor any public interest in publishing the story. On Mosley's use of German, he noted: 'It contained a certain amount of explicit sexual language about what the claimant [Mosley] and Woman B were planning to do to those women in the submissive role, but nothing specifically Nazi, and certainly nothing to do with concentration camps.' He awarded Mosley £60,000 damages and his costs. However, the court later taxed down* Mosley's costs, meaning that despite winning the case he lost £30,000.

News International's redtops, which had long decried judgments arising from the 1998 Human Rights Act, which enshrined a right to privacy in British law, were furious. The *Sun* described the ruling as a 'dark day for British freedom' and a step towards 'a dangerous European-style privacy law'. The *News of the World* complained that the powerful should not be able to run to the courts to gag papers from publishing 'true' stories, adding: 'This is all about the public's right to know.'

Mosley began suing the *News of the World* in other European countries where the paper had been sold. Just as significantly, from his

---

* Courts assess the reasonableness of the victor's costs and sometimes reduce them. In this case, the High Court reduced the portion of Mosley's legal bill of £510,000 which News International had to pay to £420,000, leaving Mosley to find the remaining £90,000.

home in Monaco he started to take an interest in the phone hacking affair. News International had made an intelligent, tenacious and wealthy enemy.

Meanwhile, David Cameron was making friends – or, rather, one big friend: Rupert Murdoch. Socially, the Conservative leader was becoming ever closer to the American's British newspaper editors, including his old Eton contemporary James Harding (a friend of James Murdoch appointed editor of *The Times* in December 2007) and Rebekah Wade, the *Sun*'s editor, who lived a few miles from Cameron's wisteria-clad farmhouse in the Cotswolds hamlet of Dean. Cameron had been friends for thirty years with Wade's new beau, another Eton contemporary, the former racehorse owner Charlie Brooks, and regularly went hacking with him in the Oxfordshire countryside, sometimes on a retired police horse, Raisa, which Wade had borrowed from the Metropolitan Police in 2008 after a lunch with the Commissioner, Sir Ian Blair.

Cameron and Wade were among the most important members of a network of influential media, political and showbusiness friends living around the Cotswolds town of Chipping Norton. Other members of the Chipping Norton Set included Liz Murdoch and her PR guru husband, Matthew Freud, who owned the opulent Elizabethan manor house Burford Priory, and the celebrity BBC *Top Gear* presenter and *Sunday Times* columnist Jeremy Clarkson, who lived in the village of Churchill.

With Rebekah Wade and James Harding among his personal friends and Andy Coulson leading his media team, Cameron began to reach out to the Murdochs. On 16 August 2008, in a journey redolent of Tony Blair's homage to Australia in 1995, the Conservative leader boarded Matthew Freud's Gulfstream jet for Santorini in Greece, where he joined Freud's father-in-law, Rupert Murdoch, for drinks on his yacht, *Rosehearty*. What they discussed remains a mystery, but from that point on the media policy of the Conservatives and the interests of the Murdochs began to converge. Three months after the meeting, in November 2008, Cameron penned a comment piece for the *Sun* headlined 'Bloated BBC out of touch with the viewers' protesting at rises in the licence fee.[9] In January 2009, his shadow Culture

Minister Ed Vaizey promised the party would force the BBC to publish the salaries of its highest-paid performers;[10] in July that year, Cameron said he intended to remove the policy-making powers of Ofcom, the media regulator;[11] and in October, Jeremy Hunt, his shadow Culture Secretary, said the Tories would abolish the BBC Trust, the governing body of the corporation.[12]

These policies coincided with the demands of the Murdochs, explicitly outlined by James Murdoch in his MacTaggart lecture to the Edinburgh Television Festival in August 2009. Openly and uncompromisingly, the heir apparent to the Murdoch dynasty identified the BBC as the enemy of free and dynamic programming offered by the likes of BSkyB. 'The scale and scope of its current activities and future ambitions is chilling,' he protested. 'Being funded by a universal hypothecated tax, the BBC feels empowered and obliged to try and offer something for everyone, even in areas well served by the market.' The BBC was lavishing large salaries on entertainers such as Jonathan Ross that no commercial broadcaster could afford, its news website was unfairly competing with national papers, and the BBC Trust had an 'abysmal record' in limiting the corporation's creep. As to Ofcom – which two months before had ordered BSkyB to cut its rates for selling sport and films to rivals – Murdoch complained that it was placing 'astonishing' burdens on commercial broadcasters. In the most significant portion of his remarks, he said: 'There is an inescapable conclusion that we must reach if we are to have a better society. The only reliable, durable, and perpetual guarantor of independence is profit.'

The demand was clear: the government should hobble the BBC and Ofcom and give a freer run to commercial broadcasters, such as BSkyB. The Conservatives' announcements between the meeting on the yacht and James Murdoch's broadside in Edinburgh showed how much Cameron and Murdoch were beginning to appreciate one another.

Rebekah Wade, who with James Murdoch had encouraged the *rapprochement*, was the powerbroker. In the summer of 2009, Wade was at the height of her power. She had been told by Rupert Murdoch that she would shortly become NI's chief executive, responsible not just for the *Sun,* but also the *News of the World, The Times* and *Sunday*

Times; and in June, her marriage to Charlie Brooks had confirmed her position at the centre of political and media power. Guests at the reception at Clarkson's home included Gordon Brown, the Prime Minister, David Cameron, George Osborne, the Chancellor of the Exchequer, Will Lewis, editor of the *Daily Telegraph*, her pop star neighbour, Blur bassist Alex James, and all the most powerful Murdochs – Rupert, James, Elisabeth and Matthew Freud.

But as they partied, a reporter on a rival newspaper was preparing an explosive story.

7

One Determined Reporter

Very relaxed
    – a spokesman for David Cameron, giving his response to
      Nick Davies's story on Gordon Taylor, July 2009

Nick Davies, a 56-year-old investigative reporter with a swirl of reced-ing white hair, eschewed regular contact with executives at the *Guardian*. His contract stipulated he had to write only twenty-four substantial features a year 'or the equivalent in time and effort' – which meant that unlike the vast majority of journalists he could stay on one story. Working from his home in Lewes, East Sussex, he responded by exploring the hidden sides of British life: poverty, failing schools, drug addiction and child prostitution. Frustrated by the mis-reporting of the Iraq War, in 2007 he wrote a book about falsehood and distortion in the media, *Flat Earth News*, which contained a chapter on Steve Whittamore – and described how Fleet Street news-papers illegally obtained criminal records, car registration details, ex-directory numbers, mobile phone records and bank statements.

Davies then had two strokes of luck which led him towards a big-ger scandal. The first was that Stuart Kuttner, the *News of the World*'s managing editor, appeared alongside him on BBC Radio 4's *Today* programme in February 2008 and dismissed his newly published book as 'sour and gloomy'. He went on: 'If you read Nick's book you get a view of British journalism as a corrupt profession but I think it's the finest in the world. It is admired throughout the world and rightly so. My *News of the World* reporters wouldn't recognize that descrip-tion at all,' adding that hacking 'happened once' at the *News of the*

World. 'The reporter was fired, he went to prison. The editor resigned.' After the programme a *News of the World* insider contacted Davies and told him the scale of illegality at the paper. Davies said: 'I felt it was the sheer, brazen dishonesty of Kuttner that made that person get in touch.'[1]

The second piece of good luck was that soon afterwards Davies found himself at a social function sitting 'next to somebody very senior from the Met', who casually referred to the extent of material in Glenn Mulcaire's notes: 'Oh, yeah, thousands of names.'[2] ('Scotland Yard is a snakepit of people who hate each other and that's very helpful,' Davies said later.) By now Scotland Yard had put the thousands of pages of Mulcaire's notes in storage. That they were opened again owed much to what Davies did next. Throughout 2008 and early 2009, while working on other projects, he scanned back copies of the *News of the World* to identify 'interesting' stories and began contacting their authors. Many former *NoW* journalists willingly spoke to him because of bullying at the paper, and would refer him to others who felt similarly: 'They would say: "I know such and such hated that boss."' But they wanted to stay anonymous because Rupert Murdoch was so powerful, or because they were freelancing or in PR and were trying to sell stories to News International.[3]

Eventually, Davies gathered enough material. The *Guardian*'s editor, Alan Rusbridger, recalled: 'In early 2009 he came in and closed the door and said: "I've got this amazing story" and he told me about the Gordon Taylor settlement, and it was immediately obvious that this was a story that would cause enormous trouble.'[4] At 5.33 p.m. on 8 July 2009, the *Guardian* website (and the newspaper the following day) published the story: 'Murdoch papers paid £1m to gag phone-hacking victims':

> Rupert Murdoch's News Group Newspapers has paid out more than £1 million to settle legal cases that threatened to reveal evidence of his journalists' repeated involvement in the use of criminal methods to get stories.

For the first time Davies referred publicly to the existence of the 'For Neville' email (though he omitted its title) and revealed that Wapping had settled with Taylor for around £400,000 damages plus costs – while the company had paid out £300,000 in damages and legal costs to two 'other football figures' [Taylor's two lawyers]. Davies quoted a police source as saying News International journalists had hacked into 'thousands' of mobile phones, and suggested that the targets included John Prescott while he was Deputy Prime Minister. He also mentioned the *Screws'* use of Steve Whittamore searches to obtain tax records, social security files, bank statements and itemized phone bills. It was the single most important story in the phone hacking scandal.* While many journalists and politicians had been sceptical that Clive Goodman had been the only *News of the World* reporter to hack phones, until then the proof had been missing. Now it was clear that the *NoW* had paid out a vast sum to secure the silence of a union leader who was unlikely to have been eavesdropped by its jailed royal editor. The Press Complaints Commission, which had fallen for the *News of the World*'s explanation of the hacking in 2007, launched a new inquiry. From the G8 summit in Italy, Gordon Brown said the story raised serious questions that 'have to be answered'. John Prescott urged the Leader of the Opposition to sack Andy Coulson, during whose editorship the hacking had taken place. Geoff Hoon, the Labour former cabinet minister, said: 'It is hard to see how in these circumstances Andy Coulson can continue as David Cameron's communications chief.' However, David Cameron's office batted off the demands, telling the *Daily Telegraph* that the Conservative leader was 'very relaxed about the story'. Asked that evening by Bloomberg news wire about the payment to Gordon Taylor, Rupert Murdoch replied: 'If that had happened, I would have known about it.'[5]

Shortly after 9 a.m. the following day, 9 July, the Metropolitan Police's new Commissioner, Sir Paul Stephenson, a Lancastrian former shoe salesman with a reputation for straight-talking, announced that he was asking a senior officer to look into the allegations. Educated at Marlborough College and a history graduate of King's College London, Assistant Commissioner John Yates was no ordinary copper; he was one of a new breed of graduate, politically astute senior officers. Like his forerunner Andy Hayman, he was the country's

---

* Davies has never disclosed his 'multiple sources' for the Gordon Taylor story.

top counter-terrorism officer and, like Hayman, he took his media duties seriously. He regularly dined with journalists, including the *News of the World*'s deputy editor, Neil Wallis, a long-standing friend, with whom he would have regular lunches and dinners that were not declared in the Met's Register of Hospitality because, according to Yates, they were 'private engagements'. Yates had taken on some high-profile cases, investigating allegations that Labour had sold peerages and that Princess Diana's former butler Paul Burrell had stolen her possessions. Neither resulted in a conviction, but they established him in the minds of his friends in Fleet Street as a fearless investigator: 'Yates of the Yard'.

That day, Keir Starmer, the new Director of Public Prosecutions, launched an 'urgent' examination of the evidence the police had supplied to the Crown Prosecution Service during the investigation in 2006. The CPS examined the case for a week, but despite the intense political heat, Yates's review was over in hours. At 11 a.m. he convened a 'gold meeting' in Room 556 of the Victoria Block of Scotland Yard with eight senior staff, including the now-promoted Detective Chief Inspector, Philip Williams, the senior investigating officer on Operation Caryatid. The minutes of the meeting gave a curious account of the inquiry:

> Why was there not a more wide-ranging investigation?
> There was no evidence to expand the investigation under which if had done, then this would have been an ineffective use of police resources.
> Did we alert others?
> Yes ... No evidence to support wider phones had been intercepted. Wider people were not informed as there was no evidence to suggest any criminal activities on their phones.
> What other journalists were involved?
> There was no evidence at that time to implicate the involvement of any other journalists.'[6]

On John Prescott, the minutes recorded: 'PW [Detective Chief Superintendent Philip Williams] confirmed that he had no knowledge of John Prescott's phone being intercepted. If he had been subject to interception and evidence supported this then he would have been informed.'[7]

At 5.40 that evening, 'Yates of the Yard' announced that there was nothing new in the story; the police had been in possession of the 'For Neville' email during Operation Caryatid in 2006 – and that inquiry had been a success. Yates said: 'Their potential targets may have run into hundreds of people, but our inquiries showed that they only used the tactic against a far smaller number of individuals . . . in the majority of cases there was insufficient evidence to show that tapping had actually been achieved.' Where there was 'clear evidence' of hacking, all those individuals had been informed, Yates said, adding: 'I therefore consider that no further investigation is required.'

On 10 July, other papers followed up the *Guardian*'s allegations but focused on Yates's refusal to reopen the inquiry. The *Daily Telegraph* quoted a Conservative Party spokesman as saying: 'Labour have made themselves look stupid by following a story that fell apart within twenty-four hours.'

That afternoon News International, which privately knew the 'For Neville' email was a 'fatal' document, poured scorn on the story. In a statement, the company 'stated with confidence' that there was not and never had been any evidence to suggest that, apart from Goodman's royal hacking and the Taylor case, journalists at the *News of the World* had accessed anyone's voicemails: 'All of these irresponsible and unsubstantiated allegations against the *News of the World* and other News International titles and its journalists are false.' News International's senior executives knew this was untrue.

Despite Yates's public backing of the original inquiry, behind the scenes there was some concern that perhaps not all of the potential victims had been informed. At 7.36 p.m. on Friday 10 July (after most newspaper deadlines), Scotland Yard slipped out another statement saying that it would contact anyone where there was 'any suspicion' they may have been hacked, adding: 'The process of contacting people is currently underway and we expect this to take some time to complete.' Yates ordered a small team to start typing the names in Mulcaire's notes into the Home Office Large Major Enquiry System, so that the information would be searchable. If the original police investigation had indeed been complete, as the Yard claimed, the need to contact new victims was puzzling.

The following day, News International's newspapers launched an offensive against the *Guardian,* starting with *The Times*, whose then media editor Dan Sabbagh* trotted out the company line:

> News International last night criticized 'selective and misleading journalism' by the *Guardian* newspaper and rebutted allegations that reporters on the *News of the World* engaged in widespread hacking into celebrities' mobile phones.

The publisher said that it had been a victim of irresponsible and unsubstantiated allegations made by the *Guardian*.

The *News of the World* joined the attack the following day, 12 July, describing the *Guardian*'s reporting as 'inaccurate, selective and purposely misleading' and reminding readers that despite purporting to represent the highest standards of journalism the paper had in 1983 handed back to the government leaked documents that led to the jailing of the civil servant Sarah Tisdall and in 1993 had forged the signature of the cabinet minister Jonathan Aitken.

Both *The Times* and the *NoW* carried an article by a new columnist who explained that while there had been several hundred names in Mulcaire's notes, only 'perhaps a handful' had actually been hacked. He wrote: 'Had there been evidence of tampering in the other cases, that would have been investigated, as would the slightest hint that others were involved.' The columnist was Andy Hayman, the Scotland Yard chief who had overseen Operation Caryatid. In December 2007, eleven months after the jailing of Goodman and Mulcaire and a month after an internal inquiry was begun into his expenses,† Hayman announced his resignation from the Met. Seven months later, in July 2008, he had become a columnist on *The Times*. As well as

---

* At the time, *The Times* was covering up its own newsgathering scandal. Its reporter Patrick Foster had hacked into the emails of a Lancashire Detective Constable, Richard Horton, to identify him as the anonymous police blogger 'Nightjack', but it had misled the High Court by giving the false impression that it had obtained the story honestly. *The Times* stayed quiet about the incident for two years. In 2010 its editor, James Harding, promoted Foster to media editor (see Chapter 22).

† Hayman, who enjoyed champagne dinners with *News of the World* journalists, had racked up £19,000 on his Scotland Yard Amex credit card in two years. He strenuously denied he had misused his expenses. In April 2008, an independent report by Gwent's Chief Constable Mike Tongue, overseen by the Independent Police Complaints Commission, cleared Hayman of any misconduct.

having an insider right next to the Conservative leader, Wapping now had a former Scotland Yard chief on its payroll.

Some media commentators pointed to the significance of the Taylor story: Andrew Neil, a former editor of *The Sunday Times*, said he was 'shocked' by the allegations of such widespread lawbreaking; others such as the *Independent*'s Stephen Glover condemned the 'hysteria'. On Monday 13 July he wrote:

> Mr Davies is a journalist who dislikes much journalism, especially of the tabloid variety. He recently published a book which suggests that the press is wildly dysfunctional. I've never had the pleasure of meeting him, but he seems to me to be a misanthropic, apocalyptic sort of fellow – the sort of journalist who can find a scandal in a jar of tadpoles.

On Thursday 16 July, a week after launching his internal inquiry, the Director of Public Prosecutions, Keir Starmer, announced there was no need to reopen the case. After speaking to his predecessor as DPP, Ken Macdonald, and the then Attorney General, Lord Goldsmith, Starmer deemed the original prosecution to have been 'proper and appropriate'. He explained that under the law on phone hacking, the Regulation of Investigatory Powers Act (see p. 38), intercepting a phone communication was illegal only 'in the course of its transmission', and so did not apply when it had been heard by the owner of the phone. Even if there were many names in Mulcaire's notes, Starmer was saying, they were not necessarily victims. What was striking about this interpretation is that it had not been the one used at the trial of Goodman and Mulcaire by the CPS barrister David Perry, who had explicitly stated that RIPA covered saved messages.

Despite the lack of concern from police and prosecutors, the Gordon Taylor story prompted action from Max Clifford, the publicist whom Mulcaire had in court admitted hacking in 2006. Clifford phoned George Davies and asked to meet the lawyers who had fought Taylor's case, Mark Lewis and Charlotte Harris. George Davies was reluctant to take on another phone hacking case (Taylor had complained about the appearance of the *Guardian* story) and Harris had moved to another law firm in Manchester, JMW. Clifford instructed Harris to sue.

Now a Foreign Office minister, Chris Bryant was also reflecting on his treatment by the *NoW*. On 30 November 2003, eight months after he had asked Rebekah Wade in Parliament about payments to police, the *News of the World* and the *Mail on Sunday* had published a picture of him in his underpants on the Gaydar website. There was more to come. The following Sunday, the *NoW* reported that the former vicar was facing the sack. In an unusually abusive profile *The Sunday Times* described him as a 'bumptious little berk' and a 'pillock'. 'Short, fair-haired and with his eyes set wide apart, Bryant has used the sanctimonious tones of his former vocation to lecture MPs on morality.' More characteristically the *Sun* urged voters to give the Rhondda MP 'a Rhondda Rogering'. Humiliated, Bryant received hate mail, acquired a stalker and feared his political career was over. He said: 'It's the closest I've ever been to suicidal.'[8] As he read more about the behaviour of News International, he remembered that his London flat had been broken into in 2003 and began to fear his phone had been hacked and perhaps his computer too. After reading Davies's article, he wrote to Scotland Yard asking whether he was in the Mulcaire files. It took eight months to reply.

A third individual, the actress Sienna Miller, was becoming increasingly convinced that her phone had been hacked after her engagement to the Hollywood actor Jude Law in 2004. With astonishing accuracy, the *News of the World* had chronicled their lives under punning headlines: 'How Jude do that?' in August 2005 (about an argument); 'It's on and off' in October 2005 (about an alleged fling with another actor); and 'Jude's not Sien her any more' in July 2006 (recording the end of their relationship). During that period calls Miller answered quickly went dead, voicemails she had not listened to appeared in her inbox as 'old', and messages from friends and family never arrived. She changed her mobile phone three times in late 2005 but the stories kept appearing. She began to suspect that she was being betrayed by someone close to her, and started to experiment, leaving messages for friends with bogus snippets of information which would duly appear in print. She accused her friends and family of betraying her: 'I sat down in a room with my mother, my best friend, my sister, my boyfriend and said: "Someone in this room is lying and selling stories and one of you has got to admit it." '[9] Mark Thomson, Miller's silver-haired, occasionally irascible lawyer, wrote to the Met asking whether she featured in Glenn Mulcaire's notes. As with Bryant, the letter went unanswered for months.

While the authorities stonewalled, the MPs on the cross-party Culture Committee decided to look afresh at the *News of the World*. The Committee was just concluding another inquiry into the press, prompted by Fleet Street's repeated libelling of Kate and Gerry McCann, whose three-year-old daughter Madeleine had gone missing in Portugal. During that inquiry, phone hacking had been so forgotten that Colin Myler and Tom Crone were not even asked about it when they gave evidence in May, and the focus had been on the *NoW*'s treatment of Max Mosley. Now the MPs summoned Myler and Crone back.

On the eve of their reappearance on 21 July, News International wrote to the committee demanding the removal from the hearing of its newest member, Tom Watson. While still at the Cabinet Office, Watson had taken the unusual step of suing the *Sun* for its hounding of him during the Damien McBride affair. NI had asked Number 10 aides to pressure Watson into dropping the claim, and he was called by the Attorney General, Baroness Scotland, who advised him it would be 'unwise' to proceed with the case while a minister. Watson did not drop the case, but returned to the backbenches in June (see p. 12). Looking for a new beginning, in July he had joined the Culture, Media and Sport Committee, where he hoped to pursue his interest in the digital economy.

News International wrote to the Committee's Conservative chairman, John Whittingdale, demanding Watson's removal on the grounds that he was still in dispute with the *Sun*, even though it had accepted weeks before, on 30 June, that it had defamed him and all that remained was to reach a settlement about the damages and apology. After taking advice from parliamentary lawyers, Whittingdale rejected the request. At the start of the session, the urbane Tom Crone repeated the demand, warning Whittingdale: 'If he [Watson] remains we will be making a complaint to the Parliamentary Commissioner.' News International never made the complaint but its attempt to eject Watson was a good PR trick: it, rather than the substance of the hearing, became a breaking story on Sky News.

With its demand frustrated, News International now had to survive the session without making any embarrassing admissions. Even without public knowledge that Mulcaire's notes ran to 11,000 pages, that NI's counsel had identified a 'culture of illegal information gathering', and that sizeable pay-offs had already been made to Goodman and Mulcaire, the company's story was a mess. NI's then chairman, Les Hinton, had told the committee in March 2007 that Goodman was the only reporter who hacked voicemails; yet it had now emerged that the *News of the World* had secretly paid off another victim who was very unlikely to have been hacked by Goodman.

Myler and Crone's tactics soon emerged: confusion, obfuscation and spectacular memory loss. They could not remember who had done what, nor, they added, could the colleagues they asked. The Goodman case was very much in the past and checks for other wrongdoing had found nothing: Operation Caryatid had been very thorough. Crone said:

> The police raided Mulcaire's premises, they raided Goodman's premises, and they raided the *News of the World*'s offices. They seized every available document; they searched all the computers, all the files, the emails. Subsequent to the arrests they came to us and made various requests to us to produce documents. At no stage during their investigation or our investigation did any evidence arise that the problem of accessing by our reporters, or complicity of accessing by our reporters, went beyond the Goodman/Mulcaire situation.[10]

Not much was known, they said, about the 'For Neville' email, except that it showed the *NoW* had hacked Taylor's phone and thus the paper had settled. The MPs wanted to know if the Neville in the email was Neville Thurlbeck, the paper's chief reporter. 'I questioned Neville Thurlbeck then, and I have spoken to him about the same subject since,' Crone replied. 'His position is that he has never seen that email, nor had any knowledge of it.' He explained that Ross Hindley, the journalist who transcribed the hacked messages, had been unable to remember whether he had sent the email on to Thurlbeck.

Myler and Crone flatly denied any reporter other than Clive Goodman had been involved in phone hacking. When the Conservative MP

Philip Davies challenged that, Myler replied: 'No evidence, Mr Davies, has been produced internally or externally by the police, by any lawyers, to suggest that what you have said is the truth, is the case.' Myler failed to point out that Thurlbeck himself – not a lawyer or a police officer – had alleged the involvement of others. (See Chapter 21.)

The committee was incredulous. Despite the *News of the World* paying a convicted phone hacker more than £100,000 a year, only Goodman had colluded in his illegal work. Asked whether Mulcaire had been paid £200,000 to stay silent – a report in *Private Eye* – Myler said: 'I am not aware of any payment that has been made.' Crone said: 'I had nothing to do with that area, because if there is any sort of payment or dealings with Mulcaire it is not going to be in my area.'

Pressed on this carefully worded evasion by Davies: 'It did not take place?' Crone reluctantly agreed that Mulcaire had been paid something:

> The employment laws as they stand, as I understand it, and I am certainly no expert in this area, mean that if someone works for you for X hours a week it does not matter whether he is staff, he is freelance or is on a contract, whatever, he has certain employment rights. Given those employment rights there is a process that has to be followed when that relationship comes to an end. Because of failures, and we can possibly check it out (I do not have the information in detail) there was a sum of money paid to him. I do not know exactly what it is, but it bears no relation to the figure you have given us.

As senior executives knew, News International had paid Mulcaire £85,000 two years previously. (See Chapter 5.) The Labour MP Paul Farrelly, a former journalist on the *Observer*, asked whether Goodman, too, had received a pay-off. Initially Crone said he was not 'aware' of one, but he later added: 'I have a feeling there may have been a payment of some sort.' (Goodman had received payments totalling £243,000.)

Tom Watson had barely noticed the jailing of Goodman and Mulcaire in 2007, but he was riled by Crone's attempt to have him thrown out of the hearing. Since returning to the backbenches, he had watched every episode of the American detective TV series *The Wire* and decided to follow the advice of one of its characters, Lester Freamon, to 'follow the money' (itself Deepthroat's advice to the *Washington Post* during Watergate). Watson asked if News International's board had authorized the Taylor pay-off. The exchanges give a flavour of the extent to which its executives blustered and stalled:

WATSON: A £700,000 payment would be a decision taken at board level. Is that right?

CRONE: I am not aware of that.

WATSON: So the News International board did not agree the payment in any way?

MYLER: What do you mean by the 'board'?

WATSON: Your managing board, the directors of the company.

MYLER: Why would they need to be involved?

WATSON: Because it is a huge amount of money and they have got a responsibility to the proprietor and the shareholders, I assume?

MYLER: Yes, and as I have said, Mr Watson, the sum of money that Mr Taylor first set out to receive was significantly higher than the sum he did receive.

WATSON: I am sorry, I thought that was the easy question. So the board did not know about the payment . . .

CRONE: I do not know. I am sorry. All I do is report to the next stage up.

WATSON: So you could write to us and let us know whether the board took the decision?

CRONE: I could ask the question and give you the answer, yes.

The executives had been unable to say whether News International's board had authorized the payment, but had agreed to find out. Watson changed tack. He asked Crone: 'When did you tell Rupert Murdoch?', to which Crone fired back: 'I did not tell Rupert Murdoch.' Myler then intervened.

MYLER: The sequence of events, Mr Watson, is very simple. Mr Crone advised me, as the editor, what the legal advice was and it was to settle. Myself and Mr Crone then went to see James Murdoch and told him where we were with the situation. Mr Crone then continued with our outside lawyers the negotiation with Mr Taylor. Eventually a settlement was agreed. That was it.

WATSON: So James Murdoch took the ultimate decision?
MYLER: James Murdoch was advised of the situation and agreed with
our legal advice that we should settle.

Crone looked unhappy: Myler had just admitted that James Murdoch, the heir to the Murdoch dynasty and a News Corp director, had
authorized a hush payment to a victim of phone hacking. If James
knew that its rogue reporter defence was untrue, neither he nor anyone else at News International had corrected the company's earlier
testimony, nor alerted the police to the possibility of more widespread
criminality.

In the afternoon, Andy Coulson and Stuart Kuttner gave evidence.
Coulson was now the Opposition leader's director of communications
and his credibility was at stake. He was smooth and assured, insisting
that he had neither condoned hacking nor had any 'recollection' of it
taking place. During his four-year editorship, he said, his instructions to
staff were clear: they were to work within the Press Complaints Commission code. Alas, he recalled, Clive Goodman had deceived him.
'I have thought long and hard about this,' he told MPs. 'What could I
have done to stop this happening? But, if a rogue reporter decides to
behave in that fashion I am not sure that there is an awful lot more I
could have done.'

He denied that he had received any money from News International
while working for the Conservatives. Watson asked him: 'You have
not got any secondary income other than that have you?' 'No,' replied
Coulson. Watson double-checked: 'So your sole income was News
International and then your sole income was the Conservative Party?'
'Yes,' said Coulson. Adam Price, a Welsh Nationalist MP who had
vigorously challenged the executives, asked: 'So far as you were aware
the *News of the World* while you were editor or deputy editor never
paid a serving police officer for information?' 'Not to my knowledge,'
Coulson replied. Price checked: 'No journalist on the *News of the
World*?' Coulson: 'No.'

As managing editor, Stuart Kuttner signed off payments and was the
paper's public face, appearing in Rebekah Wade's absence in July 2000
to defend its 'For Sarah' campaign. On 8 July 2009, the day Nick Davies broke the Taylor story, NI had announced Kuttner's resignation.
Kuttner demanded that Philip Davies withdraw from the hearing for

suggesting – falsely, Kuttner insisted – that his departure was linked to the Taylor story. Again, Whittingdale rebuffed the request, but it deepened MPs' suspicions that News International was hiding something.

By the close of the session, its executives had wriggled out of trouble by flatly denying anything was wrong. This was difficult to dispute without conflicting evidence, even though their story sounded very dubious. Despite the smokescreen, there were anomalies for the MPs to probe: the company had admitted James Murdoch had authorized the Taylor payment and that Goodman and Mulcaire had been paid off after they had been jailed.

With its story faltering in public, News International began to strike back aggressively in private. Unbeknown to members of the Culture Committee, the *News of the World* established a secret team to investigate their private lives. For several days, as chief reporter Neville Thurlbeck would later tell Tom Watson, reporters searched for any secret lovers or extra-marital affairs that could be used as leverage against the MPs. Thurlbeck said:

> All I know is that, when the DCMS [Department of Culture, Media and Sport Select Committee] was formed or rather when it got onto all the hacking stuff, there was an edict came down from the editor and it was find out every single thing you can about every single member: who was gay, who had affairs, anything we can use. Each reporter was given two members and there were six reporters that went on for around ten days. I don't know who looked at you. It fell by the wayside; I think even Ian Edmondson [the news editor] realized there was something quite horrible about doing this.[11]

Separately, a *News of the World* figure tasked with talking to Watson and other committee members to glean their question plan let them know that Rebekah Brooks believed Watson and Farrelly were the inquiry's 'ringleaders'. Watson was privately told by Downing Street insiders that Wapping was using its connections to persuade senior politicians to urge him to hold back. Gordon Brown called Watson to tell him that Rupert Murdoch had phoned Tony Blair to tell him to call Watson off.*

---

* Blair has denied this.[12] Gordon Brown cannot remember the phone call to Watson.

Speaking three years later, Alastair Campbell, Tony Blair's former communications director, recalled the 'bullying culture':

> I recall Rebekah Wade telling me that so far as she was concerned, with Tom Watson it's personal, and we won't stop till we get him. In July 2009, when the *Guardian* published a story indicating phone hacking was even more widespread than had been thought, I did a number of TV interviews saying this was a story that was not going away, that News International and the police had to grip it and come clean, that David Cameron should reconsider his appointment of Andy Coulson, and that what appeared to be emerging was evidence of systematic criminal activity on a near industrial basis at the *News of the World*. I received a series of what can only be termed threatening text and phone messages from both Rebekah and the office of James Murdoch.[13]

News International's cover-up was becoming ever more desperate.

8

Intimidating Parliament

I absolutely do not know – Les Hinton, 15 September 2009

News International attacked from every direction. At the end of July, its solicitors Farrer & Co wrote to Mark Lewis threatening him with an injunction if he represented any more phone hacking victims, on the grounds that he was privy to sensitive information from earlier cases:

> *It goes without saying that our client will object to your involvement in this or any other related case against our client for the reasons set out above. We reserve our client's rights to take injunctive proceedings against you, should you choose to disregard the matters contained in this letter. However, you have an opportunity to correct matters by confirming that you will now accept that you cannot act for any individual wishing to bring a claim against News Group in respect of the voicemail accessing allegations ...*[1]

Lewis paraphrased the letter as saying: 'You know too much, please don't act against us or we will bring the whole weight of the organization down on you.' He said: 'I think it was designed to upset me, but it did not.'[2] In his reply, he threatened to pass the work to another firm, thus informing another lawyer about the prevalence of hacking at Wapping. The injunction never materialized.

Inside News International, executives would soon begin using another tactic in the cover-up – ordering the deletion of millions of emails to destroy evidence that might help victims of phone hacking in the civil courts. (See chapter 11.) Publicly, Colin Myler insisted to the Press Complaints Commission that the company's 'internal inquiries' had found no evidence aside from the 'For Neville' email that any staff beyond Goodman had intercepted messages. Allegations by the *Guardian* that thousands of phones had been hacked were, he told the regulator, 'not just unsubstantiated and irresponsible, they were wholly false'. The PCC continued its inquiry.

Separately, Myler indicated to the Culture Committee that News International's patience was wearing thin with its unceasing investigation. In August 2009, he confirmed in writing that payments had been made to Goodman and Mulcaire to settle employment law cases, but declined to disclose the amounts on the grounds that they were confidential. He told the MPs: 'We have now answered all the outstanding questions from the committee on 21 July and trust that this now brings to a close our involvement in your committee's proceedings.'

But it did not. Many members of the committee felt that they had been misled and after the summer recess, they called Scotland Yard's Assistant Commissioner, John Yates, to give evidence. On 2 September, 'Yates of the Yard' stuck rigidly to his position that the original investigation had been a success. 'As I said previously,' he maintained, 'there is essentially nothing new in the [Taylor] story other than to place in the public domain additional material which had already been considered by both the police investigation into Goodman and Mulcaire and by the CPS and the prosecution team.' Rather ludicrously, he said he could not know the identity of the Neville in the 'For Neville' email because 'It is supposition to suggest Neville Thurlbeck or indeed any other Neville within the *News of the World* or any other Neville in the journalist community.' Even if Thurlbeck had been interviewed, he added, it was '99.9 per cent certain' he would have said nothing to the police, just like Goodman and Mulcaire. Paul Farrelly protested: 'But there is a series of transcripts of phone conversations.' 'Perhaps in 2006 it ought to have been done,' Yates replied, 'I do not know – but in 2009 that is going to take us absolutely nowhere.'

The committee recalled Les Hinton, who was now running Murdoch's new acquisition in the US, Dow Jones. Like others, Hinton had tried to avoid giving evidence, but the committee agreed to conduct the hearing by live video link from New York. On 15 September 2009, Hinton could recall few details of his time running Murdoch's multibillion-pound empire, at least about the events which led to the jailing of a senior journalist. On thirty-two occasions he said: 'I don't know,' 'I did not know' or 'I just do not know.' Had Wapping paid Goodman and Mulcaire's legal fees? 'I absolutely do not know,' Hinton replied. 'I do not know whether we did or not. There were certainly some payments made afterwards, but on the matter of legal fees I honestly don't know.'

Hinton – who had been sent Goodman's letter alleging the *NoW* routinely hacked phones and authorized his pay-off – said, 'There was never any evidence delivered to me that suggested that the conduct of Clive Goodman spread beyond him.'

As the committee continued its work, News International had another assignment for a surveillance expert who had worked for the *News of the World* since 2003, Derek Webb, whose firm was called Silent Shadow. The former policeman had legally watched dozens of pop stars, footballers and royals. Among many others, in 2005 he had followed Angelina Jolie, Delia Smith, Gordon Ramsay and the Home Secretary Charles Clarke (whose responsibilities included the police); in 2006 George Michael and the comedian Rik Mayall; and in 2007, the Duke of Westminster. Typically, his work would involve him tailing a target for five days and then noting down where they had gone, who they had met and what they were wearing.

From 28 September until 2 October 2009, at the last Labour Party conference before the general election, Webb was ordered to follow the every move of Tom Watson. He had difficulty tracking the MP down. Ironically, on the first night, 28 September, Webb would have been more successful had he phoned the *News of the World*'s political editor, Ian Kirby, who had spent the night drinking with Watson, the *Sunday Mirror*'s Vincent Moss and the *Mirror* columnist Kevin Maguire in the bar of Brighton's Grand Hotel, where they sang songs round the piano until the early hours. Tight security because of the presence of the cabinet made following Watson difficult, but Webb billed the paper for seven and a half shifts, £1,125. Before and after following Watson (who was unaware of the surveillance) he tailed Alan Johnson, the Home Secretary.

As well as its covert work, News International had a public wrecking role at the conference. With the next general election less than a year away and both Labour and Conservatives vying for its approval, the company was working from a position of strength. For months under its newly-married chief executive, Rebekah Brooks, it had been moving firmly towards her friend David Cameron, who evidently agreed with its corporate agenda. The *Sun* now used Gordon Brown's leader's speech on 29 September as the moment to abandon its whole-hearted twelve-year support for Labour. Its front page yelled 'Labour's Lost It'. In his hotel suite that night with Peter Mandelson, Ed Miliband, Ed Balls and Tom Watson (still oblivious he was being followed), Gordon Brown was shocked at the brutality: Britain's best-selling daily paper had clearly intended to sabotage his last conference before polling day. The paper wrote:

> Twelve years ago, Britain was crying out for change from a divided, exhausted government. Today we are there again.
>
> In 1997, 'New Labour', shorn of its destructive hard-left doctrines and with an energetic and charismatic leader, seemed the answer. Tony Blair said things could only get better, and few doubted him. But did they get better? Well, you could point to investment in schools and shorter hospital waiting lists and say yes, some things did – a little.
>
> But the real story of the Labour years is one of under-achievement, rank failure and a vast expansion of wasteful government interference in everyone's lives.

If Labour ministers had any doubt about what was to come, it was now dispelled. Over the coming months, the *Sun* harried and goaded Brown, deriding him in the same way it had the Conservative Prime Minister John Major before switching its support to Tony Blair in 1997. In October the *Sun*'s front page screamed 'Bloody Shameless', denouncing the blind-in-one-eye Prime Minister's alleged misspelling of the name of a young soldier killed in Afghanistan in a handwritten letter to his mother.

Back in the House of Commons, Tom Watson suspected hacking had been widespread at the *News of the World*, but it was only at the beginning of the new parliamentary session in October that he learned just how rampant the 'dark arts' were at Wapping. The Liberal Democrat MP Lembit Opik, a friend for years since they had competed against each other on TV's *Ready Steady Cook*, had brought Charlotte Harris, his lawyer, along for a drink in the Strangers' Bar, where he bumped into Watson. Watson and Harris arranged to have lunch the following day at the Adjournment restaurant in Portcullis House, where during a five-hour conversation, Watson realized many victims of the *NoW* had not been informed by police, and Harris (who could not understand why Parliament was so supine) was left in no doubt about the extent of Rupert Murdoch's political reach. On Harris's advice, Watson went to Brown, the Prime Minister, urging him to contact the Metropolitan Police to establish whether his own phone had been hacked. He also started to work more closely with politicians who feared they were in a similar position. First he patched up an argument he had had with Chris Bryant two years earlier and then mended his relationship with John Prescott, which had been strained since the latter had described Watson's resignation in 2006 as the 'corporal's revolt'; they began to meet over fried breakfasts in the House of Lords canteen.

Politically, Labour MPs and ministers started to be less charitable towards News International. In November, Brown's government published a review by the former Football Association executive David Davies into which of the 'crown jewels' of sport should be aired on terrestrial TV, which recommended that BSkyB be stripped of its exclusive live rights to screen cricket's most important fixture, the Ashes. The Culture Secretary, Ben Bradshaw, said he 'welcomed' the report. In the relationship between Brown's administration and Murdoch's company, the gloves were off.

Under Andy Coulson's gimlet eye, David Cameron had secured the support of Britain's best-selling daily paper, but Coulson had done more than that. During the summer of 2009, with his help, Cameron had consistently outplayed Gordon Brown in his handling of the MPs' expenses row – exposed by the *Daily Telegraph* – when the Conservative leader grasped much more quickly than the Prime Minister how outraged voters would be at the greed of politicians. But as he was moving the Conservatives into power, the past was beginning to catch up with Coulson. First, he had been forced to appear before the Commons Culture Committee; then, on 23 November, Matt Driscoll, the sacked sportswriter, won his employment case against the *News of the World*. A tribunal in east London ordered News International to pay Driscoll the rast sum of £792,736 in compensation for what it very specifically ruled had been a campaign of bullying orchestrated by Coulson, the director of communications for the Conservative Party. It found Driscoll had been disgracefully victimized when he was under strain mentally, stating: 'The original source of the hostility towards the claimant was Mr Coulson, the editor; although other senior managers either took their lead from Mr Coulson and continued with his motivation after Mr Coulson's departure; or shared his views themselves.'[3]

News International, which was pleased to have Coulson ensconced with Cameron, had refused to settle with Driscoll or include him in any redundancy rounds and had fought his case every inch of the way. Driscoll said bitterly:

> Ignoring the medical warnings as to the possible effect on my health, they chose to fight me for two years. They insisted, despite my health situation, on forcing me into a two-week tribunal. Having hired one of the country's top employment barristers they called no fewer than ten witnesses … they remained relentless toward me. Three times they appealed against my successful claim for unfair dismissal. Though each appeal was thrown out, the ordeal cost me my health, my career, my life savings and £150,000 in legal costs.[4]

Cameron refused to sack Coulson. He may have been bad in the past, but he was too good to lose.

On 9 November, the Press Complaints Commission, now being chaired by Baroness Buscombe, a 55-year-old former Conservative frontbencher from Oxfordshire, humiliated itself further by again exonerating the *News of the World*. Showing little scepticism or insight, the PCC accepted the police's and News International's explanations about the extent of illegality at Wapping, despite the 'For Neville' email, the size of the Gordon Taylor settlement and NI's pay-offs to Goodman and Mulcaire. Its second report into phone hacking (so flawed it was withdrawn two years later) stated:

> The PCC has seen no new evidence to suggest that the practice of phone message tapping was undertaken by others beyond Goodman and Mulcaire, or evidence that the *News of the World* knew about Goodman and Mulcaire's activities. It follows that there is nothing to suggest that the PCC was materially misled during its 2007 inquiry.
>
> Indeed, having reviewed the matter, the Commission could not help but conclude that the *Guardian*'s stories did not quite live up to the dramatic billing they were initially given. Perhaps this was because the sources could not be tested; or because Nick Davies was unable to shed further light on the suggestions of a broader conspiracy at the newspaper; or because there was significant evidence to the contrary from the police; or because so much of the information was old and had already appeared in the public domain (or a combination of these factors). Whatever the reason, there did not seem to be anything concrete to support the implication that there had been a hitherto concealed criminal conspiracy at the *News of the World* to intrude into people's privacy.

The verdict was a hammer blow to the *Guardian*; not only had the watchdog dismissed its front-page exclusive, it effectively accused it of sensationalism. Alan Rusbridger resigned from the PCC's code committee in disgust.

Scotland Yard seized the opportunity to lobby the *Guardian* to drop its hostile coverage. On 10 December 2009, the Commissioner, Sir Paul Stephenson, accompanied by his head of public affairs, Dick Fedorcio, visited Rusbridger in the paper's glass and steel office in King's Cross and told him that Nick Davies's coverage was 'over-egged' and had wrongly implied the force was 'party to a conspiracy'. Rusbridger, who had joined the paper on the same day as Davies in 1979, kept his faith in his old friend. That evening, Stephenson and Fedorcio dined with John Yates and Neil Wallis at what Stephenson later called 'a pub/restaurant that I frequented socially'. The occasion was listed in his office diary as a private event.

Undeterred by Colin Myler's letter in August, the Culture Committee requested further details of News International's internal inquiries and the pay-offs to Goodman and Mulcaire. In November, Rebekah Brooks wrote back enclosing an explanation from the legal director Jonathan Chapman confirming NI had settled Goodman and Mulcaire's claims for unfair dismissal, but only because of technicalities, and again declined to disclose the 'confidential' sums. Asked how many Nevilles the company employed, Brooks replied: 'One.'

In answer to the queries about the internal inquiries, she enclosed the letter of 29 May 2007 from Lawrence Abramson, at Harbottle & Lewis, detailing its review of the emails for Clive Goodman's employment case (see p. 60). Set in the context of an internal inquiry into widespread wrongdoing at the *News of the World*, Abramson's words looked reassuring. The letter – which would be the subject of controversy later – appeared to indicate that an external law firm had made a thorough check and found no evidence of a wider problem at Wapping. But Harbottle & Lewis had reviewed only a limited number of emails for the employment case and had not given permission for the letter to be sent to the committee.

The MPs decided they should hear from Brooks herself and asked her to give evidence. In a letter to John Whittingdale on 4 January 2010, she contemptuously dismissed the invitation to answer questions about the 'supposed incongruity' between the treatment of Clive Goodman and Matt Driscoll, the 'For Neville' email and misbehaviour by News International journalists, which, she said, related to the *News of the World*, not to other News International newspapers 'any more than they do to any other national newspapers'. She asked whether the committee intended to call chief executives of other newspaper groups, said that the *News of the World*'s editor had outlined the measures to end improper behaviour and that as chief executive she would 'ensure the proper journalistic standards continue to be applied across all our titles'. She concluded:

> Given the above, I hope you and your colleagues agree that my attendance before the committee to face questions on the three areas to which you refer would be pointless and a waste of the committee's time. As I have said before, if there are other matters being investigated by yourselves and on which you and your colleagues feel I may have direct knowledge, I remain very happy to be of assistance.

I should conclude that, given my clear commitment to assisting the committee, I am very surprised at the threat of coercion made in your letter which, I am sure you must agree, is inappropriate.

Although the committee wanted Brooks to give evidence, its members, whose private lives News International had pored over, capitulated and decided not to summons her. On the day the committee met to discuss the issue, two Labour MPs close to Tony Blair, Janet Anderson and Rosemary McKenna, were absent. The gay Plaid Cymru MP Adam Price – who in September unexpectedly announced that he would leave Parliament at the next general election to take up a Fulbright scholarship in the US – claimed that the committee's members had been warned that if they had called Brooks, their private lives would be raked over. He said later: 'I was told by a senior Conservative member of the committee, who I knew was in direct contact with executives at News International, that if we went for her, they would go for us – effectively they would delve into our personal lives in order to punish [us].'[5]

At the *Guardian*, Nick Davies came ever closer to the truth, disclosing on 1 February 2010 that the mobile phone companies Orange, O2, and Vodafone had discovered that more than 100 customers had their inboxes accessed by Mulcaire. He also divulged that the Met had finally answered the paper's Freedom of Information request, revealing that it had found ninety-two PIN codes in Glenn Mulcaire's notes. Dick Fedorcio, Scotland Yard's director of public affairs, wrote to Alan Rusbridger complaining about the article, saying that Davies 'once again presents an inaccurate position from our perspective and continues to imply this case has not been handled properly and we are a party to a conspiracy'. At a follow-up meeting with Rusbridger on 19 February, John Yates, accompanied by Fedorcio, sought to persuade Rusbridger – in Rusbridger's words – that 'Nick's doggedness and persistence in pursuing the story was misplaced.'[6]

Despite the insistence of Scotland Yard, News International and the Press Complaints Commission that nothing was wrong, the Culture Committee was not duped and on 23 February published a report, 'Press Standards, Privacy and Libel', which was highly critical of them all. The PCC, the committee said, should have been 'more assertive in its inquiries rather than accepting submissions from the *News of the*

World once again at face value', adding that its November report was 'simplistic and surprising. It has certainly not fully, or forensically, considered all the evidence to this inquiry.' The Metropolitan Police had failed to investigate properly the Greg Miskiw contract or the 'For Neville' email, which was strong evidence of additional law-breaking and the possible involvement of others. 'These matters merited thorough police investigation, and the first steps to be taken seem to us to have been obvious. The Metropolitan Police's reasons for not doing so seem to us to be inadequate.'

About News International itself, the report could hardly have been more barbed. Although the committee had seen no evidence that Andy Coulson had known about phone hacking, it was 'inconceivable' that no one else at the *News of the World* bar Clive Goodman had known about the practice. The MPs stopped just short of accusing Britain's biggest newspaper group of lying, writing:

> Throughout our inquiry, we have been struck by the collective amnesia afflicting witnesses from the *News of the World*. Throughout, we have repeatedly encountered an unwillingness to provide the detailed information that we sought, claims of ignorance or lack of recall, and deliberate obfuscation. We strongly condemn this behaviour which reinforces the widely held impression that the press generally regard themselves as unaccountable and that News International in particular has sought to conceal the truth about what really occurred.

Press coverage was muted. The *Guardian* reported the committee's acerbic verdict on its front page and the *Independent* across pages 6 and 7, but the other papers marginalized the criticism. The *Daily Mail* ran a 154-word story headed: 'Tory spin chief cleared'. The *Sun*'s political editor, Tom Newton Dunn, managed to help both the Conservative Party and his employers by writing a small piece on page 2 which claimed that the report had been hijacked: 'Labour MPs wanted to smear Tory communications boss Andy Coulson, an ex-*News of the World* editor. But the report found 'no evidence' he knew phone hacking was taking place.' *The Times* ran a small story on page 15 on the criticism of its stablemate.

The *News of the World* was apoplectic. In an editorial on 28 February, Colin Myler's paper protested that the report had been 'shamefully hijacked' by Tom Watson and Paul Farrelly. It thundered: 'We'll take no lessons in standards from MPs – nor from self-serving pygmies who run the circulation-challenged *Guardian*.' To add insult to injury, the *NoW* ran a commentary from one of the committee's Tory MPs, Philip Davies, who complained that its work on press freedom should not be overshadowed 'by pathetic and petty Labour politicians who have tried to hijack the report to settle a score with News International for supporting the Conservative Party at the next election'.[7] In a statement, News International said the select committee system had been damaged and diminished by the report, which, it protested, was laden with 'innuendo, unwarranted inference and exaggeration'.[8]

9

A Murder

No one pays like the News of the World *do*

           – Jonathan Rees

Despite the underwhelming response to the Culture Committee's report, News International and the Conservative Party knew that another dark story about the *News of the World* and Andy Coulson was lurking in the background, about to surface. On 25 February, the *Guardian's* deputy editor, Ian Katz, phoned Steve Hilton, David Cameron's director of strategy. He wanted him to know that Coulson had worked with a notorious private investigator at the *News of the World* after the man's release from a long prison term for conspiring to pervert the course of justice. The *Guardian* could not publicly report Jonathan Rees's conviction to avoid prejudicing a new court case: the man taken on by Coulson's *Screws* was now on trial for murder, accused of killing his former business partner. The case, which revealed close links between tabloid newspapers and corrupt police, dated back three decades to the late 1980s, when Scotland Yard was awash with bent coppers – and Rees, a Freemason, co-owned a detective agency in Thornton Heath, south London.

His business partner at Southern Investigations was Daniel Morgan, a gregarious 37-year-old who had become concerned about Rees's close links with corrupt police. On 10 March 1987, Morgan had been having a drink with Rees at the Golden Lion pub in Sydenham. One of the topics for discussion that night was the theft of £18,000 in cash Rees had been transporting for a client, Belmont Car Auctions. Belmont and Morgan suspected that Rees and his associates – some of whom were moonlighting police officers – had stolen the money.

A few minutes after Rees left the Golden Lion, Morgan walked into the car park towards his BMW. He never drove away. His body was discovered at 9.30 p.m., with a hatchet buried so deep in his face that the only part of it showing was the haft, which had been covered with sticking plaster to destroy fingerprints. Morgan's £900 Rolex watch had been taken but not £1,100 in cash from his pocket.

Daniel's brother, Alastair Morgan, spoke to Jonathan Rees about what had happened but was unconvinced by his explanation. He went to the police incident room at Sydenham, where he was interviewed by a CID officer, Sid Fillery, one of the detectives who had moonlighted for Rees. The murdered man's brother was surprised by Fillery's casual manner. At Morgan's inquest in 1988, Kevin Lennon, Southern Investigation's bookkeeper, testified that six months before the murder, Rees said he was planning a contract hit: 'My mates are going to arrange it. Those police officers are friends of mine and will either murder Danny or will arrange it.' Asked if he had murdered Morgan, Rees replied: 'I did not.'[1] The inquest returned a verdict of unlawful killing. The coroner said there was no forensic evidence to link anyone to the murder.

A second murder inquiry failed in 1989, by which time Fillery, who had omitted to disclose his work for Southern Investigations during the first one, had left the Metropolitan Police on medical grounds and stepped into Morgan's shoes as Rees's new business partner at Southern Investigations. Business boomed. The most lucrative work was selling confidential data to the media, much of it from bent detectives at Scotland Yard, though Rees and Fillery also developed contacts in other forces. In the late 1990s, their best customers were the *News of the World*, the *Sunday Mirror* and the *Daily Mirror*.

In 1997, following pressure from Alastair Morgan, Scotland Yard launched a third murder inquiry, Operation Nigeria. An elite anti-corruption squad, CIB3, planted a listening device in Southern Investigations' office in the hope of recording Rees and Fillery talking about Morgan's killing. Stressing the need to place the bug with great delicacy, a CIB3 report warned: 'They are alert, cunning and devious individuals who have current knowledge of investigative methods

1. Rupert Murdoch in London in 1969, the year the 38-year-old Australian took over his first British newspaper, the *News of the World*. He dominated Fleet Street for four decades.

2. The 80-year-old tycoon under pressure the day after defending his company's conduct in front of the Commons Culture Committee. Most rival papers' front pages screamed 'Humble pie', but *The Times* came out for its proprietor.

3. Young tabloid editors Piers Morgan, Rebekah Wade and Andy Coulson partying at the home of Elisabeth Murdoch and Matthew Freud in 2004, when the *News of the World* was systematically hacking phones.

4. Flirtatious and charming, at least with the powerful, Wade made sure she was friendly with senior politicians – including Tony Blair, the Labour Prime Minister, who was endorsed by News International papers at three successive general elections.

5. BSkyB's chief executive, James Murdoch, Rupert's son and heir, wooed the new Conservative leader, David Cameron, and his close ally George Osborne, the Shadow Chancellor. In 2007, they enjoyed each other's company at a summit on social responsibility.

6. Tommy Sheridan and his wife Gail celebrate their libel victory over the *News of the World* in 2006, beginning an epic legal struggle between the socialist politician and the Murdochs' British newspaper group.

7. Police found thousands of names and PIN codes in the notes of Glenn Mulcaire. The Crown Prosecution Service charged the private detective with hacking the phones of eight individuals. After his release from prison, News International settled his claim against them for £85,000. He has since remained silent.

8. Clive Goodman, the *News of the World*'s royal editor, was jailed in January 2007 for eavesdropping royal phone calls. He subsequently received settlements totalling £243,000 from News International. Like Mulcaire, has since remained silent.

9. Rupert Murdoch's right-hand man, Les Hinton, authorized the payments to Goodman and Mulcaire in 2007, before leaving the UK to take charge of News Corp's new acquisition, Dow Jones.

10. By splashing the private life of the Formula 1 motor-racing chief Max Mosley over its front page, the *News of the World* made an intelligent, wealthy and tenacious enemy.

11. Gordon Taylor, chief executive of the Professional Footballers' Association, was the first phone-hacking victim to mount a legal challenge to News International. In June 2008 he accepted an out-of-court settlement of £425,000.

12. With her fellow Manchester lawyer Mark Lewis (plate 33), Charlotte Harris took on the *News of the World*. In a failed bid to discredit her, the newspaper placed her under surveillance.

13. From his home in Lewes, East Sussex, the *Guardian*'s Nick Davies was one of the indefatigable individuals who unpicked the 'rogue reporter' defence and humbled Murdoch's $60 billion News Corp.

14. The *News of the World*'s chief reporter, Neville Thurlbeck, for whom the infamous 'for Neville' email was intended.

15. 'Yates of the Yard': John Yates, Assistant Commissioner of the Metropolitan Police, who in 2009 declared his faith in the original police investigation, Operation Caryatid, after a review lasting several hours.

16. John Yates's good friend Neil 'Wolfman' Wallis, deputy editor of the *News of the World*. In 2009, Scotland Yard gave him a job. In 2011 it arrested him.

17. Despite being warned about Andy Coulson's past, the Conservative leader's director of communications was too useful to lose. With the former *News of the World* editor by his side, David Cameron found the 'tabloid touch'.

18. Within months of winning most seats at the May 2010 general election with Murdoch's support, the Conservatives backed News Corp's £7bn takeover bid for Britain's richest TV network, BSkyB.

and techniques which may be used against them. Such is their level of access to individuals within the police, through professional and social contacts, that the threat of compromise to any conventional investigation against them is constant and very real.'[2]

The bug, which was active between April and September 1999, unintentionally picked up the chatter between Jonathan Rees and his Fleet Street customers. The Metropolitan Police gave a briefing on the conversations to journalist Graham McLagan, who published them in an article in the *Guardian* on 21 September 2002. Through their corrupt contacts in the police, Rees had sold a string of juicy stories about ongoing investigations, obtaining information about the former Chilean dictator General Augusto Pinochet, the Yorkshire Ripper Peter Sutcliffe and the neo-Nazi nailbomber David Copeland. Before the gangster Kenneth Noye was convicted in 2000 for the M25 road-rage killing four years earlier, Rees sold the fact that GCHQ had helped track him down to Spain, from where he had been extradited, as well as the secret route by which he was being transported to court.

In April, Rees discussed the arrest by anti-corruption police of another private detective later jailed for nine years for corruption and conspiracy, Duncan Hanrahan. The bug caught Rees telling an unidentified person: 'Hanrahan said what [CIB3] want to do is fuck us all. He said they keep talking about the fucking Morgan murder every time they see me.'[3]

On 4 June, Rees showed a close interest in obtaining details of the murder of Jill Dando, the *Crimewatch* presenter who was shot dead on her doorstep in London in 1999, telling a source: 'There's big stories ... nearly every day with good information on the Jill Dando murder. We found out one of our bestest friends is also on that fucking murder squad, but he ain't told us nothing. We only found out yesterday after that torrent of abuse we initially gave him. He's going to phone us today.'

Rees also had corrupt contacts outside the police. He was in touch with a corrupt VAT inspector who could access business records, two corrupt bank employees (nicknamed Fat Bob and Rob the Bank) who could provide details of personal accounts, and two former police officers working for Customs and Excise. Two blaggers conned phone companies into handing over names and addresses of customers and itemized phone bills. One, John Gunning – later convicted – was a specialist in blagging ex-directory numbers from BT. On one occasion Rees was asked by an unnamed journalist to trace the owner of a Porsche whose registration number he had been given. He had the owner's name and address from the DVLA and his criminal record from the Police National Computer in thirty-four minutes.

While the *Mirror* titles were enthusiastic customers, the *News of the World* was paying Rees £150,000 a year. The bug recorded him saying: 'No one pays like the *News of the World* do.'

Police would have carried on eavesdropping had they not stumbled on a crime they were duty-bound to disrupt. With Austin Warnes, a corrupt police officer in the Met's south-east regional crime squad, Rees had hatched a plot to plant cocaine on a former model, Kim James, so that her businessman husband, Simon James, could gain custody of their child. Drugs were duly planted in Kim James's car and Warnes provided false information about her drugs activities. In September, police raided Southern Investigations. In December 2000, Rees was sentenced to six years, increased to seven on appeal, for conspiring to pervert the course of justice. Warnes was sentenced to four years. As they closed down the corruption ring, police arrested twelve suspects and raided twenty-three premises.

With Rees in jail for a long stretch, the police began a fourth inquiry into Daniel Morgan's murder in early 2002 and arranged for an appeal to be made on BBC TV's *Crimewatch*. The husband of one of the programme's presenters, Jacqui Hames, herself a former Met police officer, was Detective Superintendent David Cook, head of the Met's north London murder squad, and it was agreed that he would make the appeal. The day after it was broadcast on 26 June, Scotland Yard warned Cook that it had picked up intelligence that Rees's partner, Sid Fillery, had been in touch with Rees's handler at the *News of the World*, Alex Marunchak, now editing its Irish edition, who had agreed to 'sort Cook out'. Surrey Police, where Cook had previously worked, also told him someone purporting to be an "Inland Revenue inspector" had tried to blag his home address from its finance department.

Unbeknown to Hames and Cook, Glenn Mulcaire had started tracking data about them. Under the heading 3 July, Mulcaire recorded the date Hames had joined the Met in 1977, her payroll and warrant numbers, the name, location and phone number of her place of work and her home phone number and address. Mulcaire recorded Cook's name, phone number, rank and made a reference to his *Crimewatch* appeal.

Hames later said:

> This information could only have come from one place: the MPS [Metropolitan Police Service]. I was horrified by the realization that someone within the MPS had supplied information from my personnel file to Mr Mulcaire, and probably for money.[4]

On 10 July, Cook noticed a van parked opposite his and Hames's home. The following day there were two vans. When he took Hames's son to school, both vehicles started following them. When the vans followed them again soon after, Cook contacted the Met who asked a policeman to stop one of the vehicles on the pretext of it having a broken tail light. Both vans were leased to News International. Police mobilized a witness protection unit and counter-surveillance team to protect the couple and their children.

At a press social event at Scotland Yard in January 2003, David Cook and his superior officer, Commander Andrew Baker, decided to confront the *News of the World*'s editor, Rebekah Wade, about its surveillance. Accompanied by Dick Fedorcio, the Met's director of public affairs, they ushered Wade into a side room and told her of the sinister activity and that there was evidence that the news executive who commissioned work from Southern Investigations, Marunchak, had a corrupt relationship with Jonathan Rees. A former colleague of Rees had claimed that some of his *News of the World*'s payments were channelled back to Marunchak, who had been able to pay off his credit card bill and his child's private school fees. (Marunchak denies this allegation.) Wade lamely claimed the paper was trying to discover whether Hames and Cook were having an affair (they were married) and defended Marunchak on the grounds that he did his job well. Scotland Yard, ever eager to maintain a good relationship with Wapping, took no further action. Sir John Stevens, the Commissioner at the time, later said he had no knowledge of the meeting.[5]

Hames told the Leveson Inquiry in February 2012:

> The *News of the World* has never supplied a coherent reason for why
> we were placed under surveillance . . . I believe that the real reason for
> the *News of the World* placing us under surveillance was that suspects
> in the Daniel Morgan murder inquiry were using their association with
> a powerful and well-resourced newspaper to try to intimidate us and so
> attempt to subvert the investigation. These events left me distressed,
> anxious and needing counselling and contributed to the breakdown of
> my marriage to David in 2010.[6]

After his release from jail in 2005, Rees was re-employed by Andy
Coulson's *News of the World* until the Met charged him with murder
three years later. For in secrecy, in 2006, a fifth murder inquiry, Operation Abelard,* had begun away from Scotland Yard, led by David
Cook and supervised by Assistant Commissioner John Yates – who
had vowed to uncover the truth about what he described as 'one of
the most disgraceful episodes in the history of the Met'.[7] The squad
consisted of thirty-five officers, all of whom were asked to declare that
they were not Freemasons. Cook built a case which included testimony from career criminals who had turned 'Queen's evidence', and
whose sentences were reduced as a result of their cooperation. In
April 2008, the police charged Rees, two brothers, Glenn and Gary
Vian, and a builder, James Cook, with Morgan's murder. Sid Fillery –
who had been convicted of possessing indecent images of children in
2003 – was charged with perverting the course of justice. In October
2009, the murder trial began at the Old Bailey. The laws of contempt
of court, which forbid mention of material that could prejudice a
case, meant the *Guardian* could not report Jonathan Rees's
re-employment by Andy Coulson after his jail term – but, in February
2010, Ian Katz spoke about it in his phone call to David Cameron's
office. Cameron kept Coulson.

While Rees's lawyers sought to throw out the murder charge at the
Old Bailey, the Central Criminal Court, the hacking scandal was
developing in the civil courts. Despite the unwillingness of Murdoch's

---

* The names of operations were chosen at random; they have no particular significance.

British news operation to acknowledge there was a case to answer, Max Clifford pursued his civil claim for breach of privacy. As Mark Lewis had done in the Gordon Taylor case, Charlotte Harris asked Scotland Yard to disclose Mulcaire's notes on Max Clifford, and, just as in the Taylor case, a judge ordered disclosure. But this time, when the documents came through on 7 December 2009, the police had struck out whole sections. Harris recalled: 'The police would only provide documents under court order and when you did get the documents they would be redacted in a random way. The police would have known that journalists at the *News of the World* were named in the top left-hand corner of many of the pages and yet they blacked them out.'[8] She returned to the High Court, where, on 3 March 2010, Justice Geoffrey Vos ordered the removal of the redactions. The expected result was that there would be clear evidence that journalists* at the *News of the World* had ordered the hacking of Max Clifford's phone. Just as in the Gordon Taylor case, News International suddenly became desperate to settle.

Relishing his own negotiating skills – which had squeezed £300,000 out of the *News of the World* for Rebecca Loos's lust-filled romps with David Beckham – Clifford lunched Rebekah Brooks at a restaurant in London, and agreed a deal: he would get £220,000 a year for three years plus his legal costs of £331,112 – a total of £991,112 – in return for his silence and for re-opening the flow of exclusives to Wapping. Clifford rang Harris and trilled: 'Poppet, poppet, I've sorted it out with Rebekah. I've done the money! Now you sort the costs out between you.' Harris was devastated that the end of the case might ruin any chance of exposing the phone hacking scandal, especially when they had come so close, but Clifford had other ideas. Harris and her barrister Jeremy Reed agreed to meet with the *News of the World*'s legal team – Tom Crone and Julian Pike from Farrer & Co – at Clifford's house in the Home Counties to thrash out the small print. Clifford emerged from the swimming pool, dried off and went out – leaving the lawyers to haggle in the sitting room, underneath portraits of the coiffeured publicist with various stars. Harris said: 'We were

---

* At the time of going to press, the names of the individuals who had commissioned the hacking cannot be published, to avoid prejudicing ongoing legal cases.

being distracted by his dogs the whole time. Tom Crone would be saying things like: "Well, it's obvious you were going to win this case, so you shouldn't be getting the 'no win, no fee' uplift" and these dogs were slavering all over my feet. When Jeremy and I wanted to talk on our own, we would leave the room and go into Max's kitchen and conservatory.'[9] On a handshake, Clifford agreed to keep the deal secret, but abandoned that when, he said, 'News of the World lawyers revealed the details of my settlement.'[10] (It is not known how or when the NoW's lawyers did this.)

He spoke to the Guardian, and on 9 March Nick Davies and Rob Evans reported the settlement online (and in the next day's newspaper): 'Max Clifford drops News of the World phone hacking action in £1m deal':

> The News of the World was tonight accused of buying silence in the phone hacking scandal after it agreed to pay more than £1 million to persuade the celebrity PR agent Max Clifford to drop his legal action over the interception of his voicemail messages.

Clifford was quoted as saying: 'I'm now looking forward to continuing the successful relationship that I experienced with the News of the World for twenty years before my recent problems with them.'

The News of the World had paid an extraordinarily large sum to keep a lid on the scandal, but it had again failed to do so. Harris said: 'The difference between Gordon and Max was that while Max settled he didn't shut up. He said to them: "Please give me this amount of money." And then: "Thanks for the money, I'm telling everyone!"'[11]

Despite disclosing the payment of yet more hush money, the Guardian's story on Clifford was not followed up by any other national newspaper. Most Fleet Street titles had their own dubious dealings with Steve Whittamore: given that reporters often moved between tabloid titles, journalists did not believe that the News of the World was the only publication to have intercepted voicemails. Editors may also have thought that the Gordon Taylor story had not really led to anything except some tutting from MPs. Notwithstanding Clifford's success, in March 2010 the small band who wanted to crack open the scandal were despondent. All the political parties were focusing on the general election in May. Almost every national paper had ignored or belittled a year-long Commons inquiry, and there was a sense that the trail was going cold. At the *Guardian*'s offices in King's Cross, Alan Rusbridger decided upon another roll of the dice and called his friend Bill Keller, executive editor of the *New York Times,* and urged him to investigate hacking: after all, it was a strong story for a liberal American paper, a potent brew of Britain's muckraking tabloids, the royal family, Scotland Yard and the Manhattanite Rupert Murdoch. The *Guardian* would offer every assistance. Sharing a story went against an editor's instincts, but Rusbridger understood that the normal rules of newsgathering didn't apply to phone hacking.

Keller dispatched a team of three senior reporters – Don van Natta Jr, Jo Becker and Graham Bowley – to the UK almost immediately. Straight off the plane, on 15 March, they met Rusbridger, Nick Davies and the *Guardian* lawyer Gill Phillips in a room on the first floor of Kings Place. Davies spoke for most of the three-hour meeting, taking the American team through the story, and repeating the process at the *New York Times*'s office in Westminster two days later. Over the following months, the Americans would criss-cross Britain investigating with the help of Davies, whom they dubbed 'Nickypedia' because of his detailed knowledge of dodgy practices among redtop journalists.

Davies himself carried on digging. He contacted celebrities whom former *Screws* employees indicated had been targeted and urged them to write to Scotland Yard. He also tracked down former *News of the World* reporters, private investigators and friends of Glenn Mulcaire. By this time, he was speaking regularly to Tom Watson, and both of them were talking to the Manchester lawyers Mark Lewis, now working for the law firm Stripes, and Charlotte Harris at JMW. All were on the edge of their respective fields, away from the centre of power: Watson was a backbencher; Lewis and Harris solicitors in provincial general practice rather than big London media firms; Davies was an outlier who rarely visited the *Guardian*'s offices. But together they continued to challenge the misinformation of News International and the Metropolitan Police.

On 4 April, Davies made a startling disclosure. Only eight phone hacking victims had been named in court – Jamie Lowther-Pinkerton, Helen Asprey, Paddy Harverson, Gordon Taylor, Max Clifford, Sky Andrew, Simon Hughes and Elle Macpherson – and 'Yates of the Yard' had told the Culture Committee that offences could be proved against only a small number of individuals. Yet in an answer to a Freedom of Information request by the *Guardian*, Scotland Yard admitted that Mulcaire's notes had contained no fewer than 4,332 names or partial names of people, 2,978 numbers or partial numbers for mobile phones and thirty audio recordings of voicemail messages. It was now incontrovertible that the true number of victims might not just be eight, or even scores, but thousands – people from all walks of life, rich and poor, famous and anonymous, whose messages had been secretly tracked, hacked and retailed by the country's largest news group. He also disclosed the existence of the secret agreement between the Crown Prosecution Service and the Metropolitan Police in July 2006 (see Chapter 4) that the case presented in court should be 'deliberately limited' to 'less sensitive' witnesses, thus excluding more high-profile, newsworthy victims, such as Princes William and Harry.

Inside Wapping in spring 2010 executives were exasperated. Although Tom Crone at the *News of the World* and Julian Pike at Farrer & Co had seen off Gordon Taylor's case and the ancillary ones of the two lawyers, Jo Armstrong and John Hewison, as well as that of Max Clifford, more cases were coming forward. Just as the Goodman and Mulcaire court proceedings had prompted Taylor's action, and Taylor's had prompted Clifford's, Clifford's now set others in motion. The sports agent Sky Andrew began to sue, represented by Charlotte Harris. Mark Lewis started to act for Max Clifford's assistant Nicola Phillips, whose phone had been hacked in an attempt to steal Clifford's stories.

Sienna Miller, Chris Bryant and others had written to the Met asking whether they appeared in Glenn Mulcaire's notes. Although other lawyers represented Miller and Bryant, News International were aware that Harris and Lewis knew the most about hacking. Crone and Pike suspected they were having an affair and sharing confidential information from their respective cases. If they could prove that, they reasoned, a complaint of professional misconduct could be made against them – which might prevent them taking any more hacking cases. Pike explained in 2011:

> For a number of reasons, by the early part of 2010, I had concerns, which had accumulated over the previous months, that Ms Harris and Mr Lewis may be exchanging highly confidential information gained from acting for claimants (and Mr Taylor in particular) in cases against [NI's subsidiary] NGN in order to assist other clients in bringing further actions against NGN.
>
> I shared those concerns with NGN and in March, I suggested we should consider again whether Ms Harris and Mr Lewis were in a position to continue acting. I also mentioned surveillance.[12]

In Wapping, Tom Crone initially 'pooh-poohed' the idea, but two days later, on 24 March, he asked the *News of the World*'s news editor, Ian Edmondson, to put in place the necessary arrangements.[13] The *News of the World* again turned to Derek Webb, the former policeman who had tailed Tom Watson at the previous year's Labour Party conference. On 1 April, Webb was asked to drive north from Godalming in Surrey where he had been following Grant Bovey, the husband of TV presenter Anthea Turner, and visit an address in Manchester. From the road he videoed a woman with dark hair and followed her, Mark Lewis's ex-wife, and their fourteen-year-old daughter Orli as they travelled to a garden centre four miles away. Webb finished his work in Manchester on 3 April, billed the *News of the World* for 9.5 surveillance shifts, or £1,425 (though in keeping with his bizarre job, that invoice included some of his work on Grant Bovey), and sent his report and video to Wapping. When the film arrived in the *News of the World*, Tom Crone must have been disappointed since Charlotte Harris was blonde and the woman on Webb's video was dark-haired; Webb had gone to the wrong house. Oddly, the male lawyer he was asked to follow was not Lewis but someone else entirely – probably due to a mix-up with the names. It was a fiasco.

The *News of the World* persisted. On 12 April it sent Webb back up to Manchester, where for five days he staked out Harris's office at JMW and that of another firm of solicitors. In 2011, Webb told the Leveson Inquiry: 'This was in the hope that they would be seen together; after a week, I had failed to get a sighting of either and the assignment was terminated.' For the second batch of surveillance, which ended on 16 April, he billed £1,350.

News International was not finished with the idea of discrediting Lewis and Harris and on 5 May instructed Julian Pike to commission a private investigation firm to search publicly available databases for information. The firm, Tectrix, checked the birth records of Harris's two children – then aged two and four – to see if Lewis was their father. He was not. Later, referring to both the Webb and Tectrix surveillance, Harris said:

> There can be no justification for this conduct. The motive was to attempt to discredit solicitors who were conducting the phone hacking cases. The reports were prepared in order to find a way to stop us acting in those cases.
>
> From March 2010 to the end of May 2010 the intensity of the litigation was increasing. In my view this organization and its lawyers thought that they could still pursue a strategy that would contain their liability and deter others from pursuing them. I had many conversations with Tom Crone at the time. He was absolutely wedded to the defence that there was only one rogue journalist engaged in phone hacking. My correspondence with Julian Pike had ended when we had a telephone conversation in or around May 2010 when he said something like 'I know what you are.' I was not sure what he meant by that at all and I certainly did not know that he had put me under surveillance.[14]

Lewis described the video of his ex-wife's home and footage of her and his teenage daughter as 'sickening'.[15]

Aware that News International had extensive surveillance powers (though at the time he was oblivious to the covert operation of the Manchester lawyers), Nick Davies realized he needed to take precautions. At meetings with sources, he and they would remove the batteries from their phones to ensure the phones were not remotely and secretly recording their conversation. He bought untraceable burner phones and shredded documents rather than put them out with the rubbish. As well as being conscious of the danger to his sources, he and his editor were fearful. Davies said: 'Alan and I were both worried that the *News of the World* might come after our private lives – they don't just expose, they also distort, so it is a nasty prospect. But we calculated that as long as we kept publishing, they would not go for us, because it would be too obviously vengeful.'[16]

Rusbridger believed that Wapping was seeking to intimidate him:

> I think one way they operated was to say things that would get back to you, so they didn't lift the phone directly to you, but they would drop something menacing to your best friend and of course you would hear about it very quickly – or they would indicate that they knew about you. Occasionally Nick would come round and say: 'You've got to be very careful – they are actively going after people.' And at one point I had someone in to sweep my house [for bugs] and within two days someone from News International rang up the press office and said: 'Has Alan Rusbridger had his house swept?' And I thought: That's not a story but they're just letting me know they know. There was definitely a black box operation going on, because other reporters who went to see them would ring me up and say: 'They're really bad-mouthing you and spreading gossip about you.'[17]

Over in west London, Britain's other liberal daily newspaper, the *Independent*, had been showing less enthusiasm for the story. Under its editor Roger Alton – whose earlier editorship of the *Observer* during the Iraq War had been criticized by Nick Davies in *Flat Earth News* – there was a feeling that the *Guardian* had overplayed its hand. After the Russian billionaire and former KGB economic attaché Alexander Lebedev bought the *Independent* in late March 2010, Simon Kelner replaced Alton – who soon after took a job as executive editor of *The Times* – and the *Independent* became more prepared to challenge the power of News International. In April, in the run-up to the general election, the *Independent* had run an advertising campaign with the slogan: 'Rupert Murdoch won't decide this election. You will.' Furious at the reference to Murdoch's power (or perhaps angered by the suggestion that he would not decide the election), James Murdoch and Rebekah Brooks strode into the *Independent*'s offices in Kensington High Street on 21 April, walked briskly through the newsroom towards Kelner (who knew them socially through his second home in the Cotswolds) and shouted: 'What the fuck are you playing at?' Kelner ushered them into his office, where they had a frank discussion. Martin Hickman, the paper's consumer correspondent, was one of the many reporters who watched stunned as Brooks and Murdoch breezed cockily back out of the building.

10

Our Man in Downing Street

'Our Only Hope'
 — Sun front page about David Cameron, 6 May 2010

At the general election in May, there was no surprise as to which horse Rupert Murdoch backed. Politically, his newspapers tended to operate in unison: in 2001 they all backed Labour, in 2005 all but one backed Labour (*The Sunday Times* gave a tepid endorsement to the Conservatives) and in 2010 they all switched to the Conservatives. On polling day, 6 May, the *Sun* ran a stylized front-page picture of David Cameron with the headline: 'Our Only Hope'. Despite Murdoch's endorsement and an ailing economy, the Conservatives fell short of an overall majority and formed a Coalition with the Liberal Democrats on 11 May.

Cameron now had to decide which members of the back-office team would join him in 10 Downing Street. By now, he and his team had received several warnings about Andy Coulson's past. The former Liberal Democrat leader Paddy Ashdown, who had been briefed by Alan Rusbridger on Coulson's employment and the Morgan murder case, said in 2011: 'I warned Number 10 within days of the election that they would suffer terrible damage if they did not get rid of Coulson, when these things came out, as it was inevitable they would.'[1] Nick Clegg, the new Deputy Prime Minister — who had been briefed by the *Guardian* in March — also cautioned Cameron about Coulson's past, only to be told by the Prime Minister that he deserved a 'second chance'.[2] Cameron shrugged off all the warnings (and the verdict in Matt Driscoll's employment tribunal) and appointed Coulson his director of communications

on an annual salary of £140,000 – more than any other official including his chief of staff, Ed Llewellyn. Coulson's instincts for the tabloid
world outweighed all other considerations.*

Within days of Cameron taking power, Rupert Murdoch entered
Downing Street through a back door for a secret meeting. As a former
Cabinet Office minister, Tom Watson knew that unofficial meetings
took place between prime ministers and Murdoch at which no officials were present. He tabled a written parliamentary question asking
the new Prime Minister who attended his meeting with Murdoch,
which civil servants were present and what was discussed. On 2 June,
Cameron refused to say, replying that he met 'a wide range of organizations and individuals on a range of subjects'. On 14 June, in another
parliamentary question, Watson asked about Coulson's responsibilities and whether he had been given security clearance to view Top
Secret documents. Cameron, who presented himself as a campaigner
for open government, referred Watson to a list of special advisers and
their salaries he had published earlier on 10 June. The Prime Minister
made no comment on Coulson's security clearance.†

Weeks after Cameron walked into Number 10, Rupert Murdoch,
keen to exploit his honeymoon with the Prime Minister, launched a
bid to take sole control of BSkyB, which through aggressive management had become the country's wealthiest broadcaster, with revenues
of £5.9 billion. News Corp already owned 39 per cent of BSkyB and
was chaired by James Murdoch, but his father wanted the remaining
61 per cent – giving him total control over its sharply rising profits.
BSkyB was throwing off cash and looked likely to make far more in
future from 3DTV and digital shopping, pornography and gambling.

---

* In a meeting with Llewellyn at the Conservative Party conference in October, the
Guardian's deputy editor, Ian Katz, again directly raised Andy Coulson's record at
the *News of the World* and his employment of Jonathan Rees, whose murder trial at
the Old Bailey had become bogged down in legal argument and whose story could not
at that time be told.

† In July 2011, when the hacking scandal exploded, the reason for the non-answer
became clear: Coulson had not undergone 'Developed Vetting' (which would have
involved checks of police and security services files), which meant that, unlike his
Labour predecessors, he was forbidden from attending cabinet meetings or viewing
Top Secret government documents – an unusual position for one of the Prime Minister's
closest aides.

A wholly owned BSkyB could be fully integrated with News Corp's Sky Italia and the partially owned Sky Deutschland; News Corp's newspapers could also be cross-promoted to the broadcaster's 10 million subscribers – giving the *Sun*, *News of the World* and *Times* titles a significant advantage over other Fleet Street papers. At £7.9 billion, BSkyB and News International's combined revenues would dwarf the BBC's £3.6 billion and ITV's £1.9 billion. A prominent media analyst, Claire Enders, warned that Rupert Murdoch could match in Britain Silvio Berlusconi's dominance of the Italian media. Britain, she said, faced a 'Berlusconi moment'.[3] In a rare show of agreement, the BBC, BT and owners of the *Guardian*, *Telegraph*, *Mirror* and *Mail* newspapers objected to Murdoch's plan. BSkyB's independent directors rejected News Corp's initial bid of 700p a share on 15 June and held out for a higher offer. As he prepared to negotiate, Murdoch sought the government's permission for the bid. At £7.8 billion, the BSkyB deal was, financially, the biggest of his career.

Andy Coulson's presence at the centre of the new administration insulted the growing numbers of individuals who believed their phones had been hacked by the *News of the World* under his editorship. Among them was the Mancunian comedian Steve Coogan, whose private life had been eagerly covered by the *Screws*. In public, Coogan played the nerdy radio presenter Alan Partridge; in real life he was intelligent, stubborn and politically aware. He suspected that his phone had been hacked because he had been contacted by his phone company in 2005 to say someone posing as him had tried to obtain his personal details. He began planning to sue for breach of privacy. He knew that taking on Murdoch risked a backlash from his newspapers, but he was irritated by seeing Coulson in Downing Street:

> It bothered me that he was there [Downing Street]. I also felt a certain hubris that came with having no skeletons in my closet. It had been well and truly emptied by all the tabloids. I had a conversation with Matthew Freud whom I had counselled for advice. 'Do you really want to make enemies of these people?' he had asked – advising me that my action was unwise. It made me angry and intrigued me. I don't like bullies; playground ones or Australian ones in suits. Almost everyone in

my life cautioned me against it. The only one who said go for it was Martin Sixsmith, a friend, who said: 'You could walk away but you're a bloody-minded northerner, you like a fight.'[4]

Another case was also progressing. In March 2010, the Labour MP Chris Bryant had finally been informed by the police that his name had appeared in Glenn Mulcaire's files. At the same time the Met had told him – as it had almost all victims – that there was no evidence that his phone had actually been hacked. Bryant contacted his lawyer, Tamsin Allen at Bindmans – who in 2006 had won him £10,000 damages from the *Guardian* over a spoof diary – and asked what action he could take. By chance, Allen also had another client, the former Metropolitan Police commander Brian Paddick, who had been told by the *Guardian* in 2009 that his name and mobile phone number appeared in Mulcaire's notes. Together Allen, Bryant and Paddick began to plan a judicial review of the Metropolitan Police's failure to inform them that they had been victims of the *News of the World*.

Crucially, Sienna Miller had also decided to take action. In October 2009 Scotland Yard had finally informed her that her name was in Mulcaire's files, while again adding there was no evidence her phone had been hacked. On 1 June 2010, her lawyer, Mark Thomson, sought an order in the High Court requiring the Metropolitan Police to disclose the evidence about her in Mulcaire's files. In July, the High Court granted the order and Thomson began preparing a case.

The cover-up at Wapping was deepening. In November 2009, four months after the Gordon Taylor settlement became public, the company had drafted a framework email deletion policy. Under the heading 'Opportunity', court documents filed two years later showed its aim was, among other matters, 'to eliminate in a consistent manner across NI (subject to compliance with legal and regulatory requirements) emails that could be unhelpful in the context of future litigation in which an NI company is a defendant'.[5] However, not all had been going well. The masterplan appeared to have been dogged by incompetence. On 29 July 2010, a senior executive* at Wapping asked: 'How come we haven't done the email deletion policy discussed and

* At the time of going to press, the senior executive cannot be named for legal reasons.

approved six months ago?' By 4 August, however, the policy was back on track and the executive, in an email referring to 'email deletion', warned colleagues that 'everyone needs to know that anything before January 2010 will not be kept'. News International's emails contained a hoard of material that could have been useful to the police and to the civil courts, but NI had no intention of keeping them.*

Over the summer the visiting *New York Times* reporters tracked down more than 100 people, mostly journalists and police, and conducted on-the-record interviews with Mark Lewis, Charlotte Harris, Max Clifford, Tom Watson and Phil Hall, Brooks's predecessor as editor of the *News of the World*. The Americans also spoke to former *Screws* reporters. Many were nervous about speaking out, even off the record, but, sometimes after several face-to-face meetings, the *NYT* team won their confidence. 'I think a few may have trusted us more because we were US journalists,' Don van Natta Jr said, 'but that wasn't the case with all our sources. Some appreciated the fact that we wanted to get the story exactly right, and that we had the time to really dig into the truth.'[6]

In late June, the *New York Times* journalists flew back to the US to write up their findings. On 1 September, their damning verdict was published in 6,167 excruciating words for the Manhattan-based Murdoch, under the headline 'Tabloid Hack Attack on Royals, and Beyond'. Most significantly, two former *News of the World* staffers claimed that Andy Coulson knew about phone hacking. For the first time, one *Screws* journalist was willing to speak out in public: Sean Hoare, the showbiz reporter Coulson had put in a perspex box for twenty-four hours during the David Blaine stunt. Hoare had been angered by the abandonment of Clive Goodman and by his old boss's new berth in Downing Street. With the encouragement of the sacked football writer Matt Driscoll, Hoare claimed that at the *Sun* he had hacked messages and that his managers at the *News of the World* had 'actively encouraged' him to do so. A second, anonymous reporter

---

* In the autumn of 2010, the *News of the World* moved from its offices in St Katherine's Dock to a nearby tower block, Thomas More Square. During the move News International smashed up reporters' computers on the grounds that they had new ones at their new home. News International said it was a routine technical upgrade.

claimed phone hacking had been rife at the redtop: 'Everyone knew. The office cat knew.' The Americans also spoke to the former *NoW* journalist Sharon Marshall (author of *Tabloid Girl*), who said:

> It was an industry-wide thing. Talk to any tabloid journalist in the United Kingdom and they can tell you each phone company's four-digit codes. Every hack on every newspaper knew this was done.

The *New York Times* team shed new light on the Metropolitan Police's investigation in 2006: 'Several investigators said in interviews that Scotland Yard was reluctant to conduct a wider inquiry in part because of its close relationship with the *News of the World*.' A detective told the Americans that when Dick Fedorcio's Scotland Yard public affairs directorate realized the *News of the World* was under investigation following the raids on Goodman and Mulcaire, a police press officer started waving his arms in the air, saying: 'Wait a minute, let's talk about this' and stressed the importance of the Met's long-term relationship with the newspaper.

Don van Natta Jr and his colleagues wrote:

> Scotland Yard's narrow focus has allowed *News of the World* and its parent company, News International, to continue to assert that the hacking was limited to one reporter. During testimony before the parliamentary committee in September 2009, Les Hinton, the former executive chairman of News International who now heads Dow Jones, said: 'There was never any evidence delivered to me suggesting that the conduct of Clive Goodman spread beyond him.'
>
> But interviews with more than a dozen reporters and editors at *News of the World* present a different picture of the newsroom. They described a frantic, sometimes degrading atmosphere in which some reporters openly pursued hacking or other improper tactics to satisfy demanding editors. Andy Coulson ... had imposed a hypercompetitive ethos, even by tabloid standards ...
>
> Despite the earlier arrest of the private investigator Steve Whittamore, the dark arts were still widely in use. Former reporters said both the news and feature desks employed their own investigators to uncover medical records, unlisted addresses, phone bills and so on.

Wapping wheeled out its standard response of strenuous denial and character assassination. Privately it briefed against Sean Hoare, portraying him as an unreliable witness. In public, News International released a statement accusing the *New York Times* of carrying out a commercial vendetta because of its rivalry with the *Wall Street Journal*:

> The *News of the World* repeatedly asked the *New York Times* to provide evidence to support their allegations and they were unable to do so. Indeed, the story they published contained no new credible evidence and relied heavily on anonymous sources, contrary to the paper's own editorial guidelines. In doing so, they have undermined their own reputation and confirmed our suspicion their story was motivated by commercial rivalry. We reject absolutely any suggestion there was a widespread culture of wrongdoing at the *News of the World*.[7]

For hours after its publication, those following the scandal were elated because they thought the story would force the government to announce an inquiry. The *New York Times* had independently corroborated the work of the *Guardian* and gone even further in its depiction of an out-of-control newsroom. Rusbridger's gamble had paid off. Although the US investigation was a feat of newsgathering, any British newspaper could have found the evidence had it looked; but most British newspapers did not want to look and it had been left to an American title to tell the British about their own scandal.

Fleet Street had been doubly shamed, but the government refused to act. In Downing Street, a spokesman for Andy Coulson (by this time, the spokesman needed a spokesman) said he 'emphatically' denied any wrongdoing, adding: 'He has, however, offered to talk to officers if the need arises and would welcome the opportunity to give his view on Mr Hoare's claims.' A spokesman for David Cameron said: 'Andy has made the position clear, and there have been a number of reports over the past few days but none of those reports change anything as far as the Prime Minister is concerned . . . He has full confidence in Andy Coulson. And he continues to do his job.'

The government would continue to maintain an air of calm for months, while the pressure slowly built. In the Commons, Tom Watson and Chris Bryant were not prepared to drop the *New York Times*'s disclosures in the face of official denial. The day after the story broke, 2 September, Watson wrote the first of many articles about the affair on the Labour Uncut website run by his friend Siôn Simon, asking detailed questions of Scotland Yard, the CPS and News International. By this time, he, Nick Davies and the Manchester lawyers had decided that, while News International would never voluntarily admit its wrongdoing and the Murdoch-backed government was unlikely to budge, it would be harder for the Met to ignore new evidence: Scotland Yard was the weakest link. The following day, Friday 3 September – as the *Guardian* and the *Independent* splashed on 'Coulson under pressure' stories – Watson wrote to the Met Commissioner, Sir Paul Stephenson (publishing the letter on Labour Uncut):

Dear Sir Paul,

I write as a Member of Parliament, a former Cabinet Office minister and a member of the Culture, Media and Sport Select Committee which took evidence last year from Andy Coulson and Les Hinton about the News of the World's illegal phone hacking operations.

The Metropolitan Police's historic and continued mishandling of this affair is bringing your force, and hence our democracy, into disrepute.

Former Assistant Commissioner Brian Paddick has requested a judicial review of the Metropolitan Police's investigation (or lack of it – we do not know) into his phone being hacked by newspapers while he was a serving officer. This is extraordinary.

Indeed, it would appear that the Metropolitan Police Service (MPS) may have deliberately withheld from this serving senior officer the information that his phone had been hacked. Please confirm whether this is true.

The phone of a serving Metropolitan Police commissioner was also on a list of numbers intended to be hacked by newspapers. It has been reported that an MPS investigation established that his phone had not been hacked. Please confirm whether this is true.

If it is, please confirm whether the phone of every other name on any list found of numbers intended to be hacked was also investigated.

If not, please confirm who decided, according to what criteria and on what authority, which names to investigate and which to ignore.

Today it has emerged that another senior MPS officer, Michael Fuller, was also on Glenn Mulcaire's list. Please confirm how many

MPS officers were on lists of names to be illegally hacked, which were investigated and which were notified. Much anger and concern centres on your force's failure to inform people that their names had been found on these lists. Please confirm exactly how many names were on Mulcaire's and any other lists.

Many Members of Parliament were on these lists. The Metropolitan Police has strongly implied that all Members of Parliament so targeted had been informed. This was not true. Please confirm how many Members of Parliament were on the lists.

Please confirm who decided which Members of Parliament to notify, according to what criteria and on what authority.

Please confirm, in all other cases, who selected which victims should be notified, on what criteria, on what authority and who else had any requisite knowledge. Please confirm who went to seize the materials, where are these materials stored, and what processes the Met go through when answering letters and inquiries about these materials.

The New York Times allege key evidence was withheld from the Crown Prosecution Service. Please confirm that all evidence was provided to the Crown Prosecution Service.

Your conduct of this matter is being scrutinized all over the world. So far, it is bringing shame – as has News International – on our country.

I await your early response. *

Yours sincerely, Tom Watson MP

---

* John Yates eventually responded, on 22 October, saying blandly it was 'inappropriate' for the force to comment on the cases of Brian Paddick, Chris Bryant and Brendan Montague (a freelance journalist, whose phone had been hacked by the *News of the World* in an apparent attempt to steal his stories), since they were the subject of judicial review proceedings; that it could not comment on the cases of third parties since it owed them a duty of confidence and that the hacking of MPs was being considered by the Commons (see p. 131 this chapter). He concluded:

Finally you raise a number of other issues about the Metropolitan Police Service's (MPS) handling of this investigation. All I can say on this point is what we have said in public statements, namely that the MPS has a duty to ensure that any inquiries are lawful, proportionate and involve an appropriate use of police resources. We worked closely with both the CPS and Leading Counsel throughout and they had oversight of all aspects of the case and sight of all material. As you also know, the DPP has conducted his own review and considered that the case was handled appropriately.

Later that day, 3 September, Tessa Jowell, Labour's former Culture Secretary, added to the political pressure by disclosing that her phone had been hacked by the *News of the World* – the most senior political target to date. During the original investigation into Goodman and Mulcaire, the Met had told her that her phone had been intercepted twenty-eight times but later informed her, she said, that she was not needed as a witness. Sean Hoare also went on BBC Radio 4's *PM* programme, leaving listeners in no doubt about the methods used at Wapping: 'There is an expression called the culture of dark arts. You were given a remit: just get the story. Phone tapping hadn't just existed on the *News of the World*. It was endemic within the whole industry.' He added that reporters dared not question the technique: 'Such was the culture of intimidation and bullying that you do it.'

On the Saturday, the *Guardian* and the *Independent* both splashed on the previous day's developments, which were tucked on the inside pages of bigger papers. On Sunday, the *Independent on Sunday*'s political correspondent Matt Chorley disclosed that the phone numbers of two former Labour ministers – Tony Blair's cabinet minister Peter Mandelson and the former Defence Minister Peter Kilfoyle – had been found in Mulcaire's notes, while the *Guardian*'s sister paper, the *Observer*, disclosed that the Met possessed clear evidence suggesting that John Prescott had been hacked while he was Deputy Prime Minister. But still the government would not budge. Michael Gove, the Education Secretary and a former *Times* journalist whose wife still worked for the title, dismissed the *New York Times* article. Appearing on the BBC's *Andrew Marr Show*, Gove said its disclosures 'seem to be a recycling of allegations we have heard before', adding it may have been a product of 'circulation wars' in the US.

Despite Downing Street's support for the police's position, Assistant Commissioner John Yates, who had long insisted that the original police inquiry had been conducted properly, was under growing pressure to re-examine the case. On Monday 6 September, the day before he was due to make a prearranged appearance at the Home Affairs Select Committee, he sought to take some of the sting out of the new disclosures in an interview with BBC Radio 4's *Today* programme. Yates stuck to his line that 'this was a very, very thorough inquiry', but added that he was willing to consider the new evidence in the *New*

York Times, saying: 'We've always said if any new material, any new material comes to light, we'll consider it and that's what we are going to do in this case.'

A few hours later, the Speaker of the House of Commons, John Bercow – himself a victim of intense tabloid interest, and who consistently allowed MPs to air allegations about the scandal – granted Tom Watson an 'urgent question', forcing a statement from the Home Secretary, Theresa May. She repeated the official story that there was nothing to worry about: two men had been jailed and the investigation had been reviewed by Scotland Yard and the Director of Public Prosecutions. The prosecution of Goodman and Mulcaire, she assured MPs, had 'appropriately represented the criminality uncovered'. In the angry debate that followed, Watson and Bryant attacked the government and police's position and the shadow Home Secretary, Alan Johnson, demanded Andy Coulson's resignation. Several Conservative backbenchers, including Philip Davies – the Culture Committee member who in February had accused Labour MPs of trying to hijack its report – said: 'Everything that we have heard today has been thoroughly covered in the Select Committee report; there is absolutely nothing new.'

At the Home Affairs Select Committee hearing, John Yates again emphasized that, while he would consider Sean Hoare's evidence, there probably were very few victims of hacking. Hacking, he said, was 'very, very difficult to prove' under RIPA, which required the police to show that voicemails had been intercepted prior to being heard by the phone's user. He said: 'We can only prove a crime against a very small number of people and that number is about ten to twelve people.' Asked whether Lord Prescott, the former Deputy Prime Minister, was on the list of the victims, he replied firmly: 'He is not on that list and he has never been hacked to my knowledge and there is no evidence that he has.' After hearing Yates's evidence, the Home Affairs Committee opened an inquiry into Scotland Yard's handling of phone hacking.

The following day, Tuesday 7 September, the *Guardian* revealed that the previous summer after the Gordon Taylor story, Stephen Rimmer, the Home Office director general for crime and policing, had warned the then Labour Home Secretary, Alan Johnson, against asking Her Majesty's Inspectorate of Constabulary to investigate the Met's record on phone hacking – apparently after taking soundings from Scotland Yard. In an email to Johnson's private secretary, Richard Westlake, Rimmer wrote: 'My own advice on this remains that there are insufficient grounds to do so ... and that the Met would deeply resent what they would see as "interference" in an operational investigation which could, of course, be revived at any given time.' To his subsequent regret, Johnson heeded the advice.

The Met's position was being bombarded on a daily basis. On Wednesday 8 September, the *Guardian* disclosed that Ross Hindley, the *News of the World* reporter who had transcribed Taylor's hacked voicemails in the 'For Neville' email, offered to talk to Scotland Yard. The following day, Nick Davies finally persuaded the former *News of the World* showbusiness editor, Paul McMullan, to step out of the shadows. McMullan had been the anonymous reporter who had corroborated Sean Hoare's information to the *New York Times*. Now McMullan spoke out in public, telling Davies for a front-page story on Thursday 9 September that phone hacking was 'so routine' at the paper that its journalists didn't realize they were doing anything wrong. 'People were obsessed with getting celebs' phone numbers,' said McMullan, now a pub landlord in Kent. 'There were senior people who were really scared when the Mulcaire story came out. Everyone was surprised that Clive Goodman was the only one who went down.' Another staffer, Davies wrote, claimed that Glenn Mulcaire could hack all thirteen of David Beckham's mobile phones.

That evening, the Speaker granted Chris Bryant another debate on hacking, during which Tom Watson articulated in an eight-minute speech the all-pervasive fear of News International – and redtop newspapers more generally:

> The truth is that, in this house we are all, in our own way, scared of the Rebekah Brookses of this world. It is almost laughable that we sit here in Parliament, the central institution of our sacred democracy – among us are some of the most powerful people in the land – yet we are scared of the power that Rebekah Brooks wields without a jot of responsibility or accountability. The barons of the media, with their red-topped assassins, are the biggest beasts in the modern jungle. They have no

predators. They are untouchable. They laugh at the law; they sneer at Parliament. They have the power to hurt us, and they do, with gusto and precision, with joy and criminality. Prime Ministers quail before them, and that is how they like it.

And yet, I sense that we are at the beginning of the endgame. Things will get better because, in many senses, they cannot get worse.

That same day, 9 September, another request was made to Wapping's IT department to destroy emails. In an email later disclosed to civil claimants, an IT employee wrote: 'There is a senior NI management requirement to delete this data as quickly as possible but it needs to be done within commercial boundaries.' A month later, on 7 October, a senior executive asked – in an email – 'How are we doing with the email deletion policy?' The cover-up was still in full flow.

At Scotland Yard, John Yates's hapless inquiry was proceeding at a sober speed. Yates asked the *New York Times*'s executive editor, Bill Keller, to hand over its evidence, but Keller refused, saying that the force had declined the paper's 'repeated requests for interviews' and refused to answer a Freedom of Information request the *NYT* had submitted months earlier. Keller said: 'Our story speaks for itself and makes clear that the police already have evidence that they have chosen not to pursue.'[8] 'Yates of the Yard' – who was concentrating on 'new' evidence – would make little progress over the next three months. He interviewed Sean Hoare under caution, meaning that anything he said could incriminate him and lead to his prosecution: understandably Hoare stayed silent. Lawyers, journalists and politicians were furious. It looked as if one of Yates's first moves following the *New York Times* article had been to scare off other whistleblowers.

Boris Johnson, the Conservative mayor of London, was emphatically unconcerned about the controversy. He had been warned by the Met's inquiry in 2006 that he had been hacked by Glenn Mulcaire, but he had not sued then or later; and though he was chairman of the Metropolitan Police Authority (which oversaw London's police force) he had also failed to do anything in July 2009 on publication of the Gordon Taylor story. Like his fellow Etonian, Bullingdonian and Conservative David Cameron, Johnson was close to Rebekah

Brooks – whose new husband was an Eton contemporary – and he dined with James and Rupert Murdoch. Johnson knew he might need the full-blooded support of News International at the mayoral election in May 2012 or if he was to fulfil his long-held ambition to become Prime Minister. At the mayor's monthly question time on 15 September 2010, Johnson – who had a £250,000 column in the *Daily Telegraph* – shrugged off demands to pressure Scotland Yard, saying he could not see anything new in the *New York Times* story. He said: 'I think it's patently politically motivated and unless there are significant new facts brought into the public domain that actually change the police case and make necessary a fresh look at it, then I don't propose to change my views.' Looking at his fellow London assembly members, he laughed: 'This is a load of codswallop cooked up by the Labour Party.'[9]

11

Losing a Battle

I have declared war on Mr Murdoch and I think we're going to win

— Business Secretary Vince Cable

Two years after he had been turned over by the *News of the World,* Max Mosley was about to strike again. During the summer of 2010, from Monaco, he had been taking an ever closer interest in the phone hacking story and had become determined to ensure the police would not be able to cover up the *Screws'* seedy past.

He had started talking to Nick Davies at the *Guardian* and had also acquired a highly confidential source, Mr X, who had told him that Scotland Yard was holding extensive evidence about hacking at the *NoW.* Mosley decided the best way to intensify the pressure was through cases in the civil courts which, through disclosure, would unlock the secrets of Mulcaire's files. But there was a problem: money. Under English law, litigants could be liable for costs, which could be crippling, and were often a severe deterrent to potential litigants. Mosley agreed to underwrite the risk for several claimants, in both the emerging civil privacy cases against the *News of the World* and in the judicial review against Scotland Yard being coordinated by Tamsin Allen at Bindmans. If the cases were lost, his costs could run into hundreds of thousands of pounds, but Mosley was a multimillionaire. He had decided he would risk half his fortune, if necessary, to fight Rupert Murdoch; ordinarily that half would have gone to one of his two sons, Alexander, but he was a regular drug user and had died of cocaine intoxication in May 2009. By early 2008 Alexander had temporarily managed to come off drugs but the *News of the World*'s exposure of his father's sado-masochism had devastated him and was, his father believed, a contributory factor in his death. On 12 September, five days before Mosley returned to London at the end of his presidency of the FIA, Allen began judicial review against the Met at the High Court on behalf of Chris Bryant, Brian Paddick and Brendan Montague; they were joined a week later by John Prescott.

Sitting in his London mews house in Kensington in 2011, Mosley said: 'I saw it as a much bigger thing than giving the *News of the World* a bit of their own back, or privacy generally, because I feel the Murdoch empire is a really sinister presence undermining the whole of our democracy. They are capable of suborning the police, Parliament and the government.' He suspected that the police had been reluctant to inform the victims 'because they knew damn well there would be writs flying down to the High Court and their friends in Wapping would be upset'.[1]

In a memo to the Home Affairs Committee in October 2010, the lawyer Mark Lewis suggested several reasons why the police might not have properly investigated hacking in 2006, including a lack of resources, high-priority terrorism cases – and the closeness of the relationship between senior officers and *News of the World* executives. With the benefit of legal privilege applying to parliamentary affairs, he also speculated whether the two officers who had said there were few victims, Andy Hayman and John Yates – both of whose own phones had been hacked – had been fearful of press coverage. Lewis wrote:

> At the relevant time, Mr Hayman had reason to fear that he was a target of Glenn Mulcaire and the *News of the World*. It became public knowledge that throughout the period of the investigation into voicemail hacking, Mr Hayman was involved in a controversial relationship with a woman who worked for the Independent Police Complaints Commission and was claiming expenses which were subsequently regarded as unusually high. The same, of course, is also true of John Yates who, we now know, at the time when he responded to the *Guardian*'s stories about Gordon Taylor's settlement with News Group, was involved in a controversial relationship with a woman who worked for the Met press bureau.

Lewis offered no evidence that the officers' behaviour towards the *News of the World* had been unduly influenced by fear, and Yates and Hayman both later denied that their conduct had been compromised by their relationships.

With pressure building on the Met, News International became ever more determined to marginalize those making its life uncomfortable. At the Labour Party conference at the end of September 2010, even after turning against Labour the year before, Wapping's executives were out in force. On the night of the Labour leader's speech News International always held a lavish reception at which there was no shortage of ambitious guests; that year it provided a useful environment in which to try to destabilize Tom Watson. Referring to a planning extension to the Watson family home, a member of the *Sun*'s political staff told Kevan Jones MP: 'Tell that fat bastard of a mate that we know everything about his little planning difficulty.' At another event, within Watson's earshot, Colin Myler referred to him as a 'fat bastard'. At a BSkyB reception a *Times* journalist told the Labour MP Stephen Pound that Watson was about to check in to the Betty Ford clinic because of heavy drinking.

Stung by the comment, Watson stopped drinking for six months. He intensified his efforts to unravel the scandal, but in the absence of interest from the mainstream media, all he could do was tweet, fire off letters to the authorities and write regular articles for Labour Uncut. Despite the website's low circulation Watson knew that those implicated in the scandal would read his pieces, while the tweets fanned out among thousands of followers, some of them with much bigger followings than himself. Graham Linehan, the comedy writer, used to distribute new developments to his tens of thousands of followers, while Jonathan Ross and George Michael would tweet the occasional message of support – bringing the story to their hundreds of thousands of followers. One tweeter posted a picture of the BBC's political editor Nick Robinson – a former Sky News political journalist – meeting Andy Coulson in a café at St James's Park. With newsworthy revelations not getting reported in newspapers, the only way to get the story to a wider audience was through social media.

*

At News Corp's annual meeting in New York on 15 October 2010, Rupert Murdoch flatly dismissed the idea that wrongdoing had been rife at his newspapers, telling investors: 'We have very strict rules. There was an incident more than five years ago. The person who bought a bugged phone conversation was immediately fired and in fact he subsequently went to jail. There have been two parliamentary inquiries, which have found no further evidence of anything at all. If anything was to come to light, we challenge people to give us evidence, and no one has been able to.' Nearly every claim in that statement was incorrect.

A week later, on 21 October, delivering the inaugural Margaret Thatcher speech at Lancaster House in London, Murdoch struck a more cautious note. News Corp's chief executive defended the 'turbulent, inquiring, bustling' press required by a free society, and said he often had cause to 'celebrate editorial endeavour', but added: 'Occasionally, I have had cause for regret. Let me be clear: we will vigorously pursue the truth – and we will not tolerate wrongdoing.' His message was that no one else needed to pursue wrongdoing at Wapping, because he and his company would hunt down the facts. The billionaire was heading towards his eightieth year, dominant across three populous and wealthy nations – America, Australia and Britain – yet he knew that there were unanswered questions about the methods by which he had accrued his power and wealth.

For the meantime he had kept the scandal at bay and could push ahead with the BSkyB bid. Once in office, the Conservative-led government had remained in tune with Murdoch's media agenda. In his first Budget as Chancellor, George Osborne announced the BBC would have the licence fee frozen at £145.50 for six years, have to take over the £300 million annual cost of running the World Service and the Welsh language broadcaster S4C, and contribute £150 million a year towards the roll-out of rural broadband. The settlement was a 16 per cent real terms cut in the BBC budget. The government also deferred until 2013 Gordon Brown's intention to force Sky to give up its exclusive live rights to home Ashes tests.

But one obstacle lay in Murdoch's path towards taking over BSkyB: a Liberal Democrat not on his social circuit, whose party had long been ignored by his papers – the Business Secretary, Vince Cable.

Under the Enterprise Act, Cable would make the 'quasi-judicial' decision whether to refer the £7.8 billion takeover to Ofcom for investigation on the grounds that it might be against the public interest. Ofcom could then advise whether Cable should refer the bid to the Competition Commission, which had the legal authority to block it. Unfortunately for News Corp, Cable was decidedly unclubbable – or, more correctly, unbiddable. In an attempt to push him into making the right decision, Wapping launched a 'campaign of bullying' against LibDems: one unnamed cabinet minister was told that if the Liberal Democrats did not do as Wapping wanted, the party would be 'done over' by Murdoch's papers.[2] On 4 November, Cable refused to buckle and asked Ofcom to assess whether the deal threatened 'media plurality', bluntly, whether it would give Murdoch too much power. His decision went against the flow of pro-Murdoch decisions made by the Cameron government.

A few weeks later Cable was visited at his surgery by two female 'constituents' who were, in fact, undercover reporters from the *Daily Telegraph*. 'You may wonder what is happening with the Murdoch press,' he told the women. 'I have declared war on Mr Murdoch and I think we're going to win. I didn't politicize it, because it is a legal question, but he is trying to take over BSkyB . . . I have blocked it. His whole empire is now under attack.' The *Daily Telegraph*, a vociferous opponent of the BSkyB deal, only reported Cable's comments after they were leaked to the BBC's business editor, Robert Peston. News International issued a statement saying it was 'shocked' by the comments, which, it said, raised questions 'about fairness and due process'.

Cable had undoubtedly given the clear impression that he would not be an impartial judge: it was an own goal. On 21 December, David Cameron stripped him of the BSkyB decision and handed it to Jeremy Hunt, the Culture Secretary, a self-made publishing millionaire who had previously expressed considerable admiration for Rupert Murdoch.* Murdoch would find the ambitious, spiky-haired

---

* In an interview with him in August 2008, *Broadcast* magazine described Hunt as a 'cheerleader for Rupert Murdoch's contribution to the health of British television'. Asked if Murdoch should be allowed to own two TV news channels, Hunt told the magazine: 'Rather than worry about Rupert Murdoch owning another TV channel,

Hunt – tipped as a future Conservative leader – more amenable to his business plans than Vince Cable.

Having undermined its own corporate opposition to the BSkyB bid through its sting on Cable, the *Daily Telegraph* hired the world's biggest detective agency, Kroll, to hunt the mole who leaked his injudicious comments. Kroll's report of March 2011 to the *Telegraph* has not been made public, but according to the news agency Reuters Kroll suspected that a *Telegraph* employee had orchestrated the leak through Will Lewis, a former editor of the paper and a friend of Robert Peston. Lewis – one of the many high-powered guests at Rebekah Brooks's wedding the previous summer – had recently been appointed general manager of News International. Kroll reported: 'In the period between 9 and 21 December there was extensive telephone, text and social contact between [the former *Telegraph* employee] Lewis, and individuals within the authorized circle of knowledge.' The *Telegraph* employee, who has not been publicly identified, was later employed at Wapping. News International did not respond to Reuters' request for a comment.[3]

While the BSkyB controversy was rumbling on, the phone hacking scandal veered off northwards – to Scotland. By November, one of the longest-running legal battles in Scottish history, between the *News of the World* and Tommy Sheridan, was edging towards a conclusion. In 2006 News International had appealed its libel defeat to Sheridan, complaining that the jury had disregarded the evidence of independent witnesses. The following year, 2007, Sheridan and his wife, Gail, were charged with perjury. One of the questions of the ensuing criminal trial, which began in October 2010, was whether the *News of the*

---

what we should recognize is that he has done more to create variety and choice in British TV than any other single person because of his huge investment in setting up Sky TV which, at one point, was losing several million pounds a day.' Hunt's own website quoted *Broadcast*'s verdict: 'Like all good Conservatives Hunt is a cheerleader for Rupert Murdoch's contribution to the health of British television.' Before he knew he would be taking the decision on the bid, Hunt told the *Financial Times* on 15 June: 'It does seem to me that News Corp do control Sky already, so it isn't clear to me that in terms of media plurality there is a substantive change, but I don't want to second guess what regulators might decide.'

World had hacked Sheridan's phone and withheld information about its financial dealings with witnesses who testified against him. On 17 November, Bob Bird, the editor of the *Screws'* Scottish edition, told the court that many emails about Sheridan had been lost while being transferred for storage to India.

Tom Watson, who had been following the case closely, had knowledge of data protection laws from his spell at the Cabinet Office. Though at the time he knew nothing about the email deletion policy at Wapping, the day after Bird's testimony, 18 November, Watson wrote to the Information Commissioner, Christopher Graham, demanding an investigation into whether News International had breached Principle 7 (requiring the safe storage of data) and Principle 8 (restricting the transfer of personal information abroad) of the Data Protection Act. It was an obscure complaint, but it placed News International in a quandary: either its executives admitted that it had a full archive of emails – potentially revealing its newsgathering crimes – or it risked the Information Commissioner launching an investigation and seizing its computers, as it had in the raid on Steve Whittamore in 2003. Watson wrote an article on the complaint on Labour Uncut, while James Hanning also covered it in the *Independent on Sunday*.[4]

On 10 December, Sheridan, who was conducting his own defence, called Andy Coulson, the Prime Minister's spokesman, to give evidence. Days before, Tom Watson had briefed Sheridan's team on phone hacking. During a three-hour interrogation, Sheridan asked the Prime Minister's spokesman about Mulcaire, whose notes contained Sheridan's mobile phone number, address and PIN code. Coulson denied knowing anything about phone hacking. He told the court he had not heard of Mulcaire until he had been arrested. 'I'm saying that I had absolutely no knowledge of it,' he said. 'I certainly didn't instruct anyone to do anything at the time or anything else which was untoward.'[5] As he left the witness box, Sheridan thought he saw Coulson winking at him.[6]

One of the consequences of the Sheridan case was that the BBC's *Panorama* team began investigating phone hacking. The Corporation had so far failed to devote much – or indeed any – of its investigative resources to unpicking the scandal, but an experienced *Panorama* reporter, Glenn Campbell, now started looking into the links between News International and private investigators. From his time as the crime reporter of ITV's *London Tonight* programme in the 1990s, Campbell had excellent contacts inside the Metropolitan Police and other forces. He began delving into the relationship between News International, corrupt former police officers and the private detectives prepared to break the law by blagging or hacking bank accounts, media records and mobile phones. His disclosures would darken the scandal, but his programme was still months away.

Publicly, in December Scotland Yard was still sticking to its position that its inquiries had been complete. Following the *New York Times* investigation and a Channel 4 *Dispatches* on 4 October – which suggested that News International had too much power over ministers and police – Keir Starmer, the Director of Public Prosecutions, began to re-examine the affair more closely. On 29 October, to the surprise of parliamentarians, he completely reversed his earlier interpretation of the law on phone hacking when he told the Home Affairs Committee that the police and prosecutors should treat all interceptions of messages as crimes – regardless of whether they had already been heard. Although RIPA had been untested in the courts, Starmer wrote, 'a robust attitude needs to be taken to any unauthorized interception and investigations should not be inhibited by a narrow approach'. The change was deeply significant. Scotland Yard had been maintaining it could not bring cases on behalf of many victims because of the narrow interpretation of the law. That excuse was now swept away.

Four years after the raids on Clive Goodman and Glenn Mulcaire, on 5 November the Metropolitan Police – under pressure to take its investigation seriously – finally interviewed Andy Coulson. Unlike Sean Hoare, the Prime Minister's communications director was not interviewed under caution, but as a witness by appointment at the offices of his solicitors. The arrangements suggested that rather than believing Coulson had to explain Hoare's allegations in the *New York Times*, the police may have believed that he could give useful information that would implicate Hoare, the whistleblower. Number 10 stressed the police's conduct of the interview, telling political reporters: 'Andy Coulson voluntarily attended a meeting with Metropolitan Police Officers yesterday morning at a solicitor's office in London. Mr Coulson – who first offered to meet the police two months ago – was interviewed as a witness and was not cautioned or arrested.' Despite Downing Street's spin, a confidant of the Prime Minister undergoing a police interview was deeply embarrassing.

It is not known what, if anything, Coulson said in his interview, but John Yates was still unable to make progress. Sean Hoare had not repeated his allegations to the *New York Times* to police since he had been interviewed under caution. (Fragile after half a lifetime of drink and drugs and interviewed by the police under caution, he started drinking heavily again.) Yates also wrote to the former *News of the World* journalist Paul McMullan asking to interview him but when McMullan failed to reply, Yates took no further action.

On 10 December, Keir Starmer reluctantly announced that there was no official, admissible evidence on which to charge anyone. With a degree of frustration, he declared in a statement: 'The contents of the reports in the *New York Times* and the associated reports and coverage are not enough for criminal proceedings unless those making allegations are prepared to provide the police with admissible evidence to support their assertions.' The thrust of his remarks was that former *Screws* journalists had failed to stand by their evidence. He had not yet grasped the obvious fact that the key evidence was not new, but old – and already in the possession of the Metropolitan Police.

As 2010 drew to a close, Tom Watson realized that the prospects of charges being brought were, extraordinarily, diminishing. Nevertheless, he fired off a barrage of parliamentary questions, Freedom of Information requests and letters to the Prime Minister, ministers, select committees, the police, the DPP, the PCC and the Information Commissioner. The few replies he received tended to be bland, cursory or contemptuous. But as a former government minister, he knew where the pressure points were, and decided to contact the country's most senior civil servant. On 22 December, the Cabinet Secretary,

Sir Gus O'Donnell, had shrugged off a complaint from Labour's shadow Business Secretary, John Denham, that Jeremy Hunt's previous support for Rupert Murdoch disqualified him from ruling on the fitness of the BSkyB bid. In a succinct rebuff, O'Donnell, a loyal and genial mandarin, informed Denham that he had consulted government lawyers, whose reassuring advice was that Hunt's interview with *Broadcast,* the cheerleader reference on his website and his comments to the *Financial Times* about News Corp already controlling the broadcaster were not an impediment to him taking the decision. 'I am satisfied that those statements do not amount to a pre-judgment of the case in question; indeed the third quotation explicitly states that Mr Hunt would not want to "second guess what regulators might decide",' O'Donnell wrote.[7]

That day, the Department of Culture, Media and Sport had confirmed that Hunt had held a meeting with James Murdoch on 28 June shortly after the News Corp bid was announced, at which no civil servants had been present and no minutes had been taken, and that a second meeting had taken place between Hunt and BSkyB's chief executive, Jeremy Darroch, on 21 July. No minutes had been taken at that meeting either, despite the fact that an unnamed civil servant had warned the Culture Secretary that Darroch was likely to ask about media regulation.

On 23 December, Watson wrote to O'Donnell pointing out his concerns about impartiality – and putting to him a long list of questions:

Dear Gus,

I have written to you several times in the past few weeks about matters of propriety and the ethics of government. I am now writing to ask about such matters again . . .

Did you know about Jeremy Hunt's 28 June meeting with James Murdoch and his 21 July meeting with Jeremy Darroch when responsibility for ruling on News Corp's proposal to take full control of BSkyB was transferred from Vince Cable to Jeremy Hunt?

What was discussed during Jeremy Hunt's meeting with James Murdoch on 28 June?

Where was that meeting held, and at what time?

As no civil servants were present at the meeting, can you be entirely satisfied that this meeting will not prejudice Mr Hunt's judgement when acting in the quasi-judicial role?

Did Jeremy Hunt discuss News Corp's proposed purchase of the remaining BSkyB shares at his meeting with James Murdoch on 28 June?

In your letter to John Denham yesterday, you said that you took legal advice on the question of whether there was any legal impediment to moving ministerial responsibility for competition and policy issues relating to media, broadcasting, digital and telecoms sectors from BIS to DCMS. You did not say, though, whether you had taken legal advice on Mr Hunt's conflict of interest.

Did you take legal advice specifically about Mr Hunt's conflict of interest?

If you did, did the lawyers know about the 28 June meeting between Jeremy Hunt and James Murdoch in providing this advice?

Did they know about Mr Hunt's 21 July meeting with Jeremy Darroch?

Did they know about his several published highly prejudicial statements?

Did you know about these meetings?

Did you, and any lawyers consulted, know about Jeremy Hunt's formal meetings with News Corp on 10 June and with BSkyB on 10 July?

Did you know about [Culture Minister] Ed Vaizey's lunch with Rebekah Brooks on 12 July?

Did you know about the News Corp dinner attended by Jeremy Hunt and [his special adviser] Adam Smith on 20 May?

Did you know that DCMS had denied the existence of some of these meetings in written parliamentary answers to me?

Are you seriously going to attempt to hold the line that Jeremy Hunt has no conflict of interest? He has made unprecedentedly prejudicial public statements. And, in a short and busy time since taking office:

he has had several formal meetings with News Corp and its subsidiaries;

he has been to their dinners;

his junior minister has been to lunch;

he has had several, unminuted, private, secret, 'informal' meetings with News Corp, the existence of which DCMS ministers have then denied in written answers to Parliament.

Jeremy Hunt is neck deep in News Corp, and you know it.

Remember, nobody expects the Prime Minister to tell the truth or do the decent thing. But the Cabinet Secretary is supposed to be the government's conscience.

I look forward to hearing from you as soon as possible.

Yours sincerely

Tom Watson

Member of Parliament for West Bromwich East

From his time in Gordon Brown's Downing Street, Watson knew O'Donnell to be a tough and clever operator and had no personal animus against him, but he also realized that O'Donnell primarily saw his role as protecting the government. Watson had done enough stonewalling himself during Gordon Brown's premiership to know how that worked, but he was aware of the psychological effect of applying pressure. For one thing, he knew that O'Donnell would be making a calculated decision that there was nothing in his letter that he couldn't ignore, but that there were questions he could not answer and questions to which he probably did not want to know the answer. It was all still 'under control', but the letter and Watson's barrage of other interventions were designed to make O'Donnell feel a little nervous and a little more nervous every time. Watson wanted to make this a problem for them all.

Despite this flurry of activity, he was running out of avenues, and was growing increasingly concerned that Wapping might win. He was also struggling personally. His marriage – strained by the Damian McBride affair and his preoccupation with the hacking scandal – had collapsed and his estranged wife had moved back to Yorkshire to be closer to her family. The MP was leading an itinerant life, traversing the country to be in London for Parliament, West Bromwich for his constituents and Yorkshire for his children.

His state of mind was not helped when he began to fear he was being followed. He still did not know that he had been tailed by Derek

Webb in Brighton in 2009, but the whispering campaign of threats, the unusual characters sitting in cars and the strange motorbike rider outside his Westminster flat led to a state of constant paranoia. He had found out that the *News of the World* used a white transit van in covert surveillance operations, and, though his rational self told him that the white van outside his rented London home probably belonged to a neighbour with a plumbing business, he was wary. He kept the curtains and blinds closed; his laptop computer never left his side. No letters or personal documents were disposed of in his own bins. Friends were warned not to discuss his work injudiciously, and key contacts were never called on mobile phones. He frequently took different routes to work.

During the parliamentary Christmas break of 2010, the MP woke early – any time between 5 a.m. and 6 a.m. – and when he was in Yorkshire he had taken to walking in the hills of the Peak District from where he would phone or text his close friends, David Wild and Siôn Simon. They indulged him as he related his latest idea for the investigation, sometimes listening to him for an hour, as his breathless pounding of hilltops made it difficult for him to complete his sentences. Although they did not say so at the time, they became deeply worried about his mental health: the hillwalking and the investigation were bordering on obsessional.

On 27 December, high up in the peaks of the Yorkshire and Derbyshire border, a phone call transformed Watson's mood. Over previous weeks, a new source had been tantalizingly close to revealing important information. The source, who had very detailed knowledge of the information technology architecture of News Corp around the world, contradicted Watson's belief that data had been lost irrevocably. During Tommy Sheridan's trial, News International had declared that key emails had gone missing when being transferred to Mumbai, prompting Watson's complaint to the Information Commissioner. The insider, who had read about the complaint on Labour Uncut, patiently explained that personal data would not be archived abroad: News Corp had very strict rules about data storage after changes to American law placed draconian sanctions on firms which failed to maintain adequate records; white-collar laws in America held directors responsible for data loss. The company, he said, would archive in the UK. There were two servers at Wapping: the first was for all emails and for ordinary staff on the company's four newspapers; the second was a more secure server that allowed executives to share confidential financial information. If an email had been sent to an executive – including an editor – it would be stored on the second secure server as well as the first. Were the first server to be destroyed in some way, the second wouldn't be. As they talked for over an hour, Watson frantically wrote notes on small pieces of paper in his pockets, taking the names of the senior IT people and those that had recently left. He probed the contact while trying not to betray his increasing sense of euphoria.

Back in 2005 when Mulcaire and Goodman were conspiring to hack phones, the company bosses felt they were untouchable. They had politicians and police in their pockets, and they had no 'predators'; Watson's logic was that with that level of power you would feel invulnerable – and if you thought yourself invulnerable, you would become complacent and make mistakes. He already knew that Brooks was complacent with her digital fingerprints because of the text message about him which she had sent in April 2009 to someone close to the Prime Minister. If others shared her arrogance, there would be a rich source of information on that second server that the police could use to crack the case. He did not know at that point that data had been or was being destroyed. But just as he had been losing hope, this new discovery reinvigorated him.

12

Out of Control

It doesn't say 'Fulham', it says 'Soham'

– Charlotte Harris

While the police and prosecutors were claiming they were searching for new evidence, the civil litigants had been making progress for months using the old. In September 2010, with the benefit of the Mulcaire notes disclosed to her by the police in July, Sienna Miller had begun a High Court case against News International. For a young woman in the entertainment industry this was a brave step: she was standing up to a powerful mogul who owned a Hollywood film studio. 'Everyone was scared of Murdoch, even governments,' she said later.[1] Miller claimed that the *News of the World* had published eleven articles about her and Jude Law derived from hacking, causing her 'extreme concern about her privacy and safety as well as enormous anxiety and distress'. Whenever she had changed phones, she told the court, Mulcaire had obtained the number's PIN codes, as well as phone numbers and PINs for her friend Archie Keswick, publicist Ciara Parkes, Jude Law and Law's personal assistant, Ben Jackson. On 15 December, Miller's lawyer, Mark Thomson, played her ace card, by disclosing to the court the name of the commissioning journalist in the top left-hand corner of Mulcaire's notes: 'Ian'. On 5 January 2011, the BBC's business editor Robert Peston broke off from the Davos summit in Switzerland to announce that the *News of the World* had suspended Ian Edmondson, the paper's long-serving news editor and one of the executives Andy Coulson had hired from the *People*. In a statement, News International said: 'The *News of the World* has a zero tolerance approach to wrongdoing.'

Events now moved quickly. Scotland Yard's already ridiculous story was at breaking point. The previous February it had been forced to admit that thousands of people's names were in Glenn Mulcaire's notes; now lawyers were claiming one of them was a senior *News of the World* executive; and more civil cases looked likely to drag further details from the Mulcaire notes in its vaults in coming months. Also looming was the Max Mosley-backed judicial review, which would subject London's police force to a forensic examination of its treatment of victims. Two days after the news of Edmondson's suspension, on 7 January, Scotland Yard asked News International to hand over any new evidence about phone hacking.

On 14 January, Keir Starmer renewed his tougher approach by launching a 'comprehensive review' of the evidence in the Yard's possession by a highly regarded senior lawyer, Alison Levitt QC. In a letter to Starmer published the same day, John Yates welcomed the review, saying there remained 'outstanding public, legal and political concerns' surrounding phone hacking.

The following day a copy of the email chain sent to James Murdoch during the Gordon Taylor case in 2008 (suggesting phone hacking was 'rife' at Wapping) was deleted from his laptop by News International's IT department. The company later told the Commons Culture Committee that the deletion was part of an 'email stabilization policy and modernization programme which saw a number of users' accounts being prepared for the migration to a new email system'.[2] Coincidentally, on 8 March, the email chain was also deleted from Colin Myler's desktop computer due to 'a hardware failure'.[3]

Pressure built on Downing Street and Scotland Yard. After receiving information from a government source, Watson asserted in his Labour Uncut column of 12 January that 'the working assumption for Andy Coulson's departure announcement is now 25 January'. The Prime Minister's official spokesman dismissed Watson's claim as 'rubbish'. On 18 January, the comedian Steve Coogan and the football pundit Andy Gray lodged an application in the High Court demanding that Mulcaire disclose who had commissioned him. On 19 January, it was revealed that David Cameron had been a guest of Rebekah

Brooks at her home in the Cotswolds over Christmas. Downing Street did all it could to close down the story and refused to give any details of the meeting, which it justified on the basis that Brooks was a constituent of Cameron's – though that was undermined when it later came out that James Murdoch had also been present. Brooks and the Prime Minister had been socializing around the time David Cameron had stripped Vince Cable of the BSkyB decision. No one could say whether Brooks and Murdoch used their personal connection with the Prime Minister to lobby him but for the first time the relationship with News International had become an embarrassment to the government. The heat was now on the Prime Minister and his director of communications.

Andy Coulson could take no more. On 21 January, he resigned. In what would become a familiar refrain, he maintained he had done nothing wrong, but regretfully had become a part of the story. 'Unfortunately,' he said, 'continued coverage of events connected to my old job at the *News of the World* has made it difficult to give the 110 per cent needed in this role. I stand by what I've said about those events but when the spokesman needs a spokesman, it's time to move on.'

Denying that his judgement was called into question by his appointment of Coulson, the Prime Minister said:

> I am very sorry that Andy Coulson has decided to resign as my director of communications, although I understand that the continuing pressures on him and his family mean that he feels compelled to do so. Andy has told me that the focus on him was impeding his ability to do his job and was starting to prove a distraction for the government. During his time working for me, Andy has carried out his role with complete professionalism . . . He can be extremely proud of the role he has played, including for the last eight months in government.

Speaking to *Channel 4 News* later that day, Cameron said he felt Coulson had been 'punished for the same offence twice'. Given the very serious allegations made by the *New York Times* nearly four months earlier, it is unclear exactly when Cameron decided that Coulson would be right to resign.

The parliamentary lobby, the collective term for political reporters with special access to Downing Street, was shocked by Coulson's departure. Nearly every lobby correspondent had failed to report adequately the emerging problems for Coulson for fear of angering him. A senior BBC journalist claimed that they had to 'build a relationship' with the Prime Minister's spokesman. In admitting that, they gave the game away: lobby correspondents were spoon-fed stories and didn't want to jeopardize the servings.

Piers Morgan, who had highly praised Coulson on his appointment in 2007, tweeted: 'Very sad to hear news about Andy Coulson – good man, good friend. How many times does @guardian want people to quit over the same thing?' The Conservative blogger Tim Montgomerie suggested that Rupert Murdoch, currently visiting London, had ordered the resignation. Montgomerie explained later: 'A very senior cabinet minister who was in a position to know told me that Murdoch was an influence on Andy Coulson's decision to quit. Within minutes Andy Coulson rang to say the suggestion was rubbish.'[4]

If Murdoch had instigated the resignation in the hope that it would lance the boil, he was wrong; it only increased attention on it further. Until then, despite newspaper reports, TV bulletins, the launch of civil law suits and the protestations of a small number of parliamentarians, the affair had had little tangible impact. The campaigners had been heckling from the margins; now they had more credibility and it was harder for political correspondents to ignore them.

Gordon Brown, who had kept his own counsel on hacking despite growing concern, used the opportunity to go public with his concern that his own communications had been eavesdropped. On 23 January, the *Independent on Sunday*'s front page read: 'Exclusive: Brown asks Scotland Yard to investigate if he was hacked'. James Hanning, the paper's deputy editor, disclosed that the former Prime Minister had written to Scotland Yard asking if his messages had been targeted by the *News of the World*. Brown only occasionally used his mobile phone while in Number 10 for security reasons, but he asked whether his messages on other people's phones had been intercepted, or whether his phone had been hacked while he was Chancellor of the Exchequer.

Tom Watson believed that only if News Corp's directors and investors were affected would the cover-up at Wapping finally be smashed. He decided that one way of grabbing their attention was to explore the BSkyB takeover, since that was News Corp's biggest deal. Watson spent the afternoon of 24 January batting back and forth between his long-suffering assistant Paul Moore and Siôn Simon a draft of a letter to the Culture Secretary, Jeremy Hunt, asking him to expand Ofcom's consideration of News Corp's bid for the rest of BSkyB. Under the public interest provisions of the Enterprise Act, Watson pointed out, Ofcom's investigation was entitled to study 'whether the acquirer has shown evidence of bad practice in its other media companies'. Two individuals had already been imprisoned for phone hacking at the *News of the World*, he reminded Hunt, while another had been suspended as a result of civil actions against News Corp's British newspaper subsidiary. Watson added that he believed more evidence of wrongdoing would emerge.

Whatever the outcome of Hunt's current quasi-judicial deliberations, this was a new legal argument: that the systematically criminal activities of News Corp newspapers were a valid legal reason to oppose its tightening grip on British broadcasting. Jeremy Hunt eventually replied, on 8 February, that such an inquiry could not be mounted because only media plurality could be studied (he would later dramatically change that view). More interesting to Watson than the official response his letter prompted was what happened when it was published on Labour Uncut. A check on the server addresses revealed that those who viewed the story included Downing Street, the House of Commons, the Department of Culture, Media and Sport, the Department for Business, all the UK political parties, the White House, the US Congress, the Assemblée Nationale, the Italian Parliament, and what seemed like every major law firm and bank in London, Paris, New York and Hong Kong. Many people, apparently, were interested in the ambitions of News Corporation.

On 25 January, the day after Watson wrote to him, Jeremy Hunt announced his formal support for the BSkyB bid – despite the reservations of Ofcom. On the same day as he declared his provisional backing for the bid, the Cabinet minister published Ofcom's report to him of 31 December 2010, which suggested that the takeover could operate against the public interest because 'there may not be a sufficient plurality of persons with control of media enterprising providing news and current affairs to UK-wide cross-media audiences'; in other words, too few people would own the news. In its analysis, the regulator warned that the deal would increase News Corp's share of regular news consumers from 32 per cent to 51 per cent and recommended an inquiry by the Competition Commission. This would have taken at least six months and would have hurt Rupert Murdoch because by the time it reported – even if its findings were favourable – he would almost certainly have to pay a higher price because BSkyB's financial results were improving. Instead, Hunt told the Commons, he had paused the referral while he asked News Corp if it could provide safeguards that would render one unnecessary; specifically, News Corp would be asked to distance itself from the ownership of BSkyB's loss-making Sky News.

Rupert Murdoch had been buffeted by the steady revelations emerging from the hacking scandal ever since the publication of the *New York Times*'s damning story the previous September, but now, seemingly, he had weathered the storm and his friends in the Conservative-dominated government were being wonderfully supportive. Despite Andy Coulson's resignation and the suspension of Ian Edmondson, the fallout from hacking was not, crucially, cross-contaminating his wider business ambitions.

On 26 January 2011, Tom Watson decided he should increase further the pressure on the police and, in his Labour Uncut column, asked why Scotland Yard had been so reluctant in 2006 and subsequently to examine the Mulcaire files. He concluded:

> It may be that all the officers concerned acted in good faith and with consummate professionalism throughout. But, if I have understood [the criminal law guide] Archbold correctly, it is hard to conclude other than that the Metropolitan Police Service could itself be guilty of perverting the course of justice and/or misfeasance in public life and/or conspiracy [and this now] requires urgent investigation by an independent police force.

Later, at Prime Minister's Questions, watched live by 3 million TV viewers, Watson told David Cameron that the Met should be stripped of responsibility for investigating phone hacking: 'The former investigating officer is now on the payroll of News International and three senior editors have been identified in relation to phone hacking: is it not time that another police force took over the inquiry? You have the power to make it happen, Prime Minister, what are you afraid of?'

Cameron's anger rose. 'Let me be absolutely clear,' he said. 'Phone hacking is wrong and illegal, and it is quite right that the Director of Public Prosecutions is reviewing all the evidence.' He added that it was 'not necessarily fair' to say the police had not been active because there had been prosecutions, convictions 'and indeed imprisonments – but the law is quite clear and the prosecuting authorities should follow it wherever it leads'.

Back in his office in Portcullis House, a small TV set blared out a Sky News newsflash: four years after Goodman and Mulcaire had been jailed, the Metropolitan Police was launching a new inquiry into phone hacking. Watson stared at the screen in amazement. He flicked over to BBC 24, which was covering another story, then back to Sky News. Within ten minutes, he was inundated with requests for interviews from the likes of BBC News, Radio 4, Reuters and Bloomberg.

The new inquiry had been announced by the Met's Deputy Commissioner, Tim Godwin, while the Commissioner, Sir John Stephenson, was having an operation to remove a pre-cancerous tumour from his leg. Officially, at least, it had been prompted not by Watson's question in the Commons (although that had clearly embarrassed David Cameron), but by News International handing new evidence to police. This included internal emails culled from News International's under-investigation IT system concerning Ian Edmondson, the *News of the World*'s suspended news editor. Significantly, the Met said that the new inquiry would be carried out not by the counter-terrorism command (officially, because it was too busy) but by the Specialist Crime Directorate, which dealt with sophisticated organized crime: John Yates had been taken off the case. In his place was one of the Met's few senior women, Sue Akers, the Head of Organised Crime and Criminal Networks.

A tough woman with a bob of greying blonde hair, Akers had joined London's male-dominated police force as a twenty-year-old in 1976. She recalled in a rare newspaper interview in 2004: 'I had attracted unwarranted attention from my boss. There was no culture of whistleblowing then so you had to think of creative ways to protect yourself. I was very conscious that I was a woman.' She had risen steadily through the ranks, joining the Flying Squad, becoming a trained siege negotiator and tackling drug gangs. (She had been interviewed by the *Prime Suspect* actress Helen Mirren during her research for the role of DCI Jane Tennison.) Now aged fifty-five, she was, importantly, unsullied by any history of long lunches with Fleet Street editors.

Many newspapers that had ignored the hacking scandal were now forced to report the new inquiry. On 27 January, the *Guardian* and the *Independent* made the opening of Operation Weeting their splash and *The Times* and the *Telegraph* ran small pieces on their front pages. The mass market papers tucked the story inside, with the *Sun* running sixty-four words at the bottom of page 2. For the next six months among daily papers, only a few reporters, typically Nick Davies and James Robinson at the *Guardian*, Martin Hickman and Cahal Milmo at the *Independent*, and Ben Fenton at the *Financial Times* would actively pursue the story. Even the Press Association, the national news agency owned by the large newspaper groups, was unenthusiastic. One of its journalists later told Watson: 'You know we're partly owned by News International, don't you?'

The announcement of the inquiry emboldened previously silent victims to speak out. Nick Brown, Labour's former chief whip, revealed his residential landline had been tapped after he had been outed as gay by the *News of the World* ten years earlier: he had had a 'chilling' moment when he heard a recording of his conversation being replayed. A British Telecom engineer had found a manual recorder on the line, placed there, Brown assumed, by someone acting for a newspaper.[5] (As part of Operation Reproof, in 2005, Devon and Cornwall Police had contacted Brown to say they were prosecuting an individual for phone bugging and he had been one of the victims, 'but the case collapsed for legal reasons'.)

Aides to another senior Labour minister, David Blunkett, the former Home Secretary and a close personal friend of Rebekah Brooks, disclosed that he feared that his phone had been hacked around the time of his affair with the publisher of the right-wing *Spectator* magazine, Kimberly Quinn, in 2004. His voicemails had certainly been targeted because of his friendship in 2005 with a former estate agent, Sally King, who was informed by detectives from Operation Weeting that they had obtained eight recordings of phone messages left by Blunkett on her phone. According to the *Sunday Telegraph* in September 2011, at one stage a man (who may have been Glenn Mulcaire), could be heard saying on the recordings: 'Just say "I love you" and it's twenty-five thousand.'[6] Blunkett, who had been paid up to £150,000 a year for a weekly column in the *Sun*, did not sue. Whatever his attitude towards his own hacking, he was the fifth Labour cabinet minister to suspect or know that his phone had been tampered with by the tabloid press.

At the offices of the *Independent*, Martin Hickman dispatched a journalist on work experience, Louise Sheridan, to the newspaper library at Colindale in north London to comb through back copies of News International titles to identify stories that may have been derived from hacking. As she read through the rolls of microfiche, Sheridan found several potential victims of hacking. Among them were Jude Law and his former wife Sadie Frost, the state of whose relationship had been reported in the *News of the World*. When contacted, Law and Frost thanked the *Independent* but said they had no present intention of taking action.

Sheridan also found a story which suggested that phone hacking at Wapping might have extended beyond the *News of the World* – to the *Sun,* in the first week of Rebekah Brooks's editorship following her transfer from the *News of the World*. On 20 January 2003, while the Fire Brigade's Union was running a national strike against Tony Blair's government, the *Sun* had exposed an extra-marital affair by its leader Andy Gilchrist with a front-page story headlined: 'Fire strike leader is a love cheat'. A former firefighter in North Wales, Tracey Holland, had given the paper an account of the affair. Early that morning, someone anonymously pushed a copy of the *Sun* through Gilchrist's letterbox, presumably to ensure that he and his family saw the story.

The assumption, inevitably, was that Holland had approached the *Sun* and sold her story, but when Cahal Milmo tracked her down in 2011, she told him: 'When they first came to me it was clear that they knew all about it. They had lots of information about how long we'd been together.' By the time the *Independent* contacted him on 31 January, Gilchrist had already written to Scotland Yard demanding to know whether he was in Mulcaire's files. News International vigorously denied there was any substance to his claims, and the *Sun*'s managing editor, Graham Dudman, maintained the story had been legitimately obtained, though he could not remember exactly how. The *Independent*'s lawyers were nervous, but the paper ran the story on 9 February:

> Detectives are looking into allegations that a second newspaper at Rupert Murdoch's News International may have used hacked voicemails to publish stories about the private life of a prominent public figure. Andy Gilchrist, a former union leader, has asked Scotland Yard to investigate his belief that interception of his mobile phone messages led to negative stories about him appearing in the *Sun* at the height of an acrimonious national strike by the Fire Brigade's Union (FBU).

News International's solicitors Olswang dispatched a strongly worded letter complaining about the article, saying the allegations were 'completely false': 'No unauthorized and illegal access to telephone messages was employed in respect of the article concerning Mr Gilchrist and there is no evidence to suggest there was. Entirely legitimate means were used throughout.' The letter added the article was 'not consistent with the obligation on the part of your journalists to conduct themselves in accordance with the principles of responsible journalism'. News International appeared to be drawing a line: the phone hacking scandal must not infect the *Sun*. The *Independent* offered no correction or retraction. It would not be until November 2011 that the words 'the *Sun*' were revealed to be in Mulcaire's notes.

Despite considerable scepticism about the likely effectiveness of the new inquiry, Sue Akers had drafted forty-five officers to work on Operation Weeting, three times the number who investigated the MPs' expenses scandal. As they began ploughing through Mulcaire's paperwork, Akers's team quickly realized that the original investigation had failed. In its first public update on Operation Weeting on 9 February, Scotland Yard said it had identified a new group of victims previously told by the police that there was 'little or no evidence' about them. As part of 'urgent steps' to inform the misled victims, Akers personally visited John Prescott to tell him he had been targeted in April 2006, the month the *Daily Mirror* had revealed his affair with his diary secretary, Tracey Temple. Chris Bryant, party to the judicial review against the Met, remarked wryly: 'Until now, it has been the victims that have had to do the investigative work, so it's a welcome development that the police have finally taken on the responsibility.'[7]

While the police had previously handed over hacking evidence only under court order, detectives now started allowing some victims to view Glenn Mulcaire's notes. Under conditions of secrecy in a windowless room at Scotland Yard, victims could inspect the notes about them, though they were not allowed to photograph or copy them. As the actress Leslie Ash and her husband Lee Chapman read Mulcaire's references to them, they accidentally discovered the *News of the World* had targeted Leslie Chapman – who was not Leslie Ash using her husband's surname, but the father of one of the two children killed at Soham in 2002. For weeks in 2002, the disappearance of Holly Wells and Jessica Chapman (they were murdered by the local school caretaker, Ian Huntley) had horrified the public. Charlotte Harris, the couple's lawyer, recalled: 'Leslie Chapman's papers were in front of us and the police were saying of the address: "Yeah, well it's Fulham", but it wasn't a Fulham postcode and I was looking at it, and being so familiar with Glenn Mulcaire's handwriting, I said: "It doesn't say 'Fulham', it says 'Soham'."' Harris added: 'In my discussions with News International, I kept mentioning it. I told them: "What have you done? Do you know how serious this is? Do you know what's going to happen here?"'

Harris – who had been watched by the *News of the World* in April 2010 – was apparently put under surveillance again, by persons unknown, between January and April 2011. She discovered this only in May when she was handed a twenty-page document containing details about individuals in the scandal, including a section on the private lives of herself, Mark Lewis and Mark Thomson – the lawyers bringing most cases against News International. Harris told the Leveson Inquiry in December 2011:

There is a section in the report that is headed 'Report III' which contains material on the lawyers involved in the phone hacking cases including me and two others. The material is highly intrusive. The individual who gave me the documents told me that I should 'watch myself' because I was being followed. I read the report immediately. It was clear that an intrusive personal investigation had been conducted on me simply because I was a lawyer involved in the phone hacking cases. The purpose of the report was to obtain information which could be made public in the hope of putting pressure on me presumably to deter me (and my clients) from pursuing claims against the company.

One section of the document, which has not been released publicly in its entirety, read:

> The motivation of and association between the key civil lawyers opposing News International is becoming clear. Specifically, the main protagonists are politically motivated with a number being strong Labour supporters, their cases helping promote their professional advancement. The *News of the World* is planning to use these tensions and motivations as a way to force compromise and settlement.

Under the heading '*News of the World* strategy', the document continued: 'The *News of the World* is aware of these facts and is planning to put pressure back on the solicitors by revealing these facts and by linking their political affiliations and career benefits from the cases. They plan to do this publicly and through discreet lobbying.'

As the BBC, ITV and the liberal quality papers reported on Wapping's apparently widespread use of the dark arts, the number of individuals taking court action against News International, or inquiring about doing so, rose to 115. By now twelve cases were under way in the High Court, including those of Steve Coogan, Sienna Miller, her stepmother Kelly Hoppen and the TV presenter Chris Tarrant. The former Labour MP George Galloway – one of the few individuals warned by the police in 2006 of his appearance in the Mulcaire files – had also begun proceedings. (As the controversial founder of the far-left Respect Party, Galloway had in March 2006 been the target of a failed sting by the *News of the World*'s 'Fake Sheik' Mazher Mahmood, which had been thwarted when Galloway spotted one of the few tell-tale signs of Mahmood's operation – the metal teeth of his minder.) Given Glenn Mulcaire's former profession and the *News of the World*'s interest in footballers, many litigants came from that world: Gordon Taylor's deputy Mick McGuire, Sky Andrew, Andy Gray and Paul Gascoigne, the troubled former England star. Two other prominent football figures also asked police whether they had been targeted: the former England manager Sven-Göran Eriksson, and David Davies, the former executive director of the Football Association, whose flat had been broken into in a burglary in which nothing was stolen.

In February, the civil lawyers were methodically dismantling the rogue reporter defence, which Rupert Murdoch's company was still maintaining in court, despite the suspension of Ian Edmondson. On 1 February at the Court of Appeal, Sky Andrew's team, led by Charlotte Harris, made an important breakthrough when three judges agreed that Glenn Mulcaire should divulge who at the *News of the World* commissioned him to hack phones. In a statement to the High Court on 18 February, Mulcaire said: 'Information was supplied to the news desk at the *News of the World*. This was manned by different people . . .'*

For more than a year lawyers had been grinding out cases in the High Court to establish that Mulcaire worked for more than a single reporter. News International had spent millions trying to suppress that fact. The 'rogue reporter' line had now finally collapsed, but the company did not amend its defence in court. There was still a very big deal in progress – the takeover of BSkyB.

Despite the agitations of backbenchers, News International still enjoyed the support of all political parties. This was vital to the firm because while it was fighting off allegations about its newspapers, it was in the endgame of its bid to take over BSkyB – and still required Jeremy Hunt's sign-off. Provided it stepped over the regulatory hurdle set by the government – spinning off Sky News – the deal would be done. But News International still wanted opposition parties to acquiesce – or at least not make too much fuss, which might focus

---

* Mulcaire did later provide a list to the lawyers of the civil litigants, but it has not been publicly disclosed so as not to prejudice any possible criminal trials.

more attention on phone hacking and stir up further public and media opposition to the bid. On 27 January, Tom Baldwin, formerly a political reporter on *The Times* and now Labour's director of communications, had warned Labour shadow ministers against linking BSkyB with the phone hacking scandal. A Labour press officer distilled Baldwin's thoughts into a memo circulated to Labour frontbenchers (and subsequently leaked) which read:

> On phone hacking, we believe the police should thoroughly investigate all allegations. But this is not just an issue about News International. Almost every media organization in the country may end up becoming embroiled in these allegations ... Frontbench spokespeople who want to talk about their personal experiences of being tapped should make it clear they are doing just that – speaking from personal experience. We must guard against anything which appears to be attacking a particular newspaper group out of spite.

Meanwhile, inside News Corp there was concern about how deeply James Murdoch might become embroiled in the affair given his role in authorizing the Gordon Taylor pay-off three years earlier. On 21 February 2011, News Corp's chief executive and chairman, Rupert Murdoch, bought his daughter Elisabeth's TV production company Shine, maker of hits such as *Masterchef*, for $675 million, sixteen times its most recent annual profits. With James at risk, some critics thought Murdoch had overpaid for the company in order to bring Elisabeth back into the fold. In a statement on the deal, Rupert Murdoch said: 'I expect Liz Murdoch to join the board of News Corporation on completion of this transaction.'

On 1 March, News Corp finalized its undertakings to Jeremy Hunt over the BSkyB deal, offering to place Sky News into a new stock market-floated company, enshrine its editorial independence in articles of association and set up a corporate governance and editorial committee to guarantee its independence. News Corp was offering to amend the ownership structure of a £60 million-a-year business to tie up a £7.8 billion takeover.

With this happy arrangement in place, Hunt unsurprisingly signalled his intention to wave through the takeover. Announcing the deal to rowdy scenes in the Commons on 3 March, Hunt said that he was 'minded' to accept News Corp's takeover without a referral to the Competition Commission, because hiving off the rolling news channel into a new company, together with the assurances about editorial independence, satisfied concerns about media plurality. He put the plan out to public consultation until 21 March. Tom Watson used the debate as an opportunity to allege further widespread wrongdoing at News International which, he claimed, meant its owner was unfit to own the broadcaster. Watson said the BBC had been bullied into delaying its *Panorama* documentary, and that journalists on other News International titles had been involved in wrongdoing. That afternoon News International accused him of making unsubstantiated claims.

On 10 March, Chris Bryant raised the political temperature further by launching a scathing attack on John Yates and News International. In a Commons speech, Bryant disclosed that he had been threatened, indirectly, to deter him from speaking out. He said:

> This has been a many layered scandal, but at the heart of the issue is the rationale behind the whole *modus operandi* at the *News of the World* and other newspapers. As one police officer put it to me, the newspapers involved deliberately sought to harass, intimidate and bully people for their own commercial interests. In the pursuit of their victims they were reckless about the innocent bystanders whose personal messages were intercepted, transcribed and relayed to others.
>
> Almost as bad as the original activity – only the tip of which we have yet seen – has been the cover up. Other Members and former Members of the House have said they were warned off pushing the issue in the House and in select committees. When I raised the question of parliamentary privilege in the House last September, my friends were told by a senior figure allied to Rupert Murdoch and a former executive of News International to warn me that it would not be forgotten.

He said he believed that the *News of the World* had hacked phones in 2002, while it was being edited by Rebekah Brooks. In a rare public attack by an MP on a senior police officer, he accused John Yates of misleading the Commons by stating that the Crown Prosecution Service had advised police of a narrow interpretation of the law of hacking during the prosecution of Clive Goodman and Glenn Mulcaire, when, Bryant said, that was never the case.

Responding, the junior Home Office minister James Brokenshire read out a prepared speech, reassuring Bryant about the extensive action under way to tackle phone hacking, such as the inquiries by the Home Affairs Select Committee and the Metropolitan Police inquiry. For the box-tickers at the Home Office, there was nothing to be concerned about: the authorities were acting. News International declined to comment on Bryant's claims.

While the *Guardian* led its report the following day on Bryant's criticism of John Yates, the *Independent* focused on the threat made to the MP by Murdoch's allies:

> MPs were 'warned off' pursuing the phone hacking scandal in Parliament as part of a cover-up, a Labour frontbencher claimed last night during an incendiary speech in which he accused the country's biggest police force of misleading a Commons committee and its biggest newspaper group of engaging in the 'dark arts' of tapping, hacking and blagging.
>
> Damning the behaviour of the Metropolitan Police and Rupert Murdoch's News International, Chris Bryant claimed his friends had been told by an ally of Mr Murdoch that raising the issue 'would not be forgotten'.

No other newspapers reported Bryant's speech. Nonetheless, it provoked a response. On 17 March, Rupert Murdoch invited the new proprietors of the *Independent*, Alexander Lebedev and his son Evgeny, to a meeting at his flat in St James's, London. After a few minutes of pleasantries, Murdoch turned to the apparent reason for the meeting. Why, he asked, was the *Independent* pursuing the phone hacking story, when there had been no scandal: it was damaging not just to Murdoch but the whole industry. He appealed to his fellow proprietors to tone down the coverage, but the Lebedevs had dealt with far more menacing figures back in Russia. There was no diminution in coverage.

Separately, John Yates wrote to the *Independent* and the *Guardian* denying Bryant's 'very serious allegation' that he had misled Parliament. Yates complained that Keir Starmer's unequivocal advice in 2009 had been that, to establish a crime had taken place, the prosecution must prove that messages had not been heard before they were intercepted. Starmer, the Director of Public Prosecutions, then publicly complained that Yates had taken his evidence 'out of context'.[8] The country's top prosecutor and one of its most senior police chiefs were having a public spat over who was to blame for the faulty advice that, the police said, hampered their inquiries into phone hacking. Starmer was later asked by the Home Affairs Committee why he had made such a clear statement that it was only a crime to intercept heard messages when he later revised that opinion. He replied that he had been trying to reply quickly to a parliamentary inquiry and that 'nobody at that stage went through the documents in detail'.[9] The Director of Public Prosecutions was in effect admitting that the paperwork had not been properly read.

In what proved to be a miscalculation, Yates offered to give further evidence to the Commons Home Affairs and Culture Committees. At the Culture Committee on 24 March, Tom Watson asked how Scotland Yard had stored Glenn Mulcaire's notes. Yates replied they were in 'two or three' bin bags. This was the exchange that followed:

WATSON: Were they full?
YATES: I did not see them.
WATSON: Did you or your team examine all of the Mulcaire records?
YATES: At what point?
WATSON: When you were asked to establish the facts?
YATES: No.

Yates, by his own admission, had not bothered to look at the available evidence; he had only checked whether the 'For Neville' email represented 'new' or 'old' evidence. Watson pointed out that the Information Commissioner had discovered that Steve Whittamore had obtained phone numbers of the family of Milly Dowler, who was murdered in 2002 (see Chapter 15). Watson asked Yates: 'If it transpires from the review of the Mulcaire evidence that, when Sky News were broadcasting it round the clock, Glenn Mulcaire was instructed to hack the phones of the family members of children killed at Soham, would that warrant adequate use of police resources to investigate?'

Yates replied: 'I am sure that it would, but that is the first I have ever heard of that aspect.' As Leslie Ash and Lee Chapman had accidentally discovered the name of at least one of the Soham parents was indeed in the Glenn Mulcaire files, but John Yates, one of the most senior officers at Scotland Yard, did not know that – because he had not checked the evidence.

13

U-turn at Wapping

It is hurtful, but it is not that hurtful
– Michael Silverleaf QC, on the hacking of Sienna Miller

Away from phone hacking, Jonathan Rees's trial for murder collapsed on Friday 11 March 2011, when the Crown Prosecution finally abandoned the long attempt to bring Daniel Morgan's suspected killers to justice. Jonathan Rees and the Vian brothers – Gary and Glen – were acquitted at the Old Bailey. The acquittal allowed the revelation of another of the *News of the World*'s covert techniques: computer hacking.

For Scotland Yard, the collapse of the prosecution was another humiliating defeat in its attempts to right the corruption-riddled initial investigations into the murder of the South London private eye. Eighteen months of legal argument had ensued after Rees and his four co-accused had gone on trial in October 2009, as the defence picked away at the credibility of the prosecution case, particularly on the disclosure of evidence. Despite the Met's determination to bring Morgan's suspected killers to justice, there had been problems with the evidence. The murder squad had disclosed 250 crates of notes on the case dating back twenty-four years and the supergrasses it was relying upon to secure a conviction. But in 2010, eighteen crates of further evidence relating to a supergrass from the criminal world, James Ward, were discovered by chance in a disused building and presented to the trial. On 7 March 2011, the police handed over another four crates of evidence inexplicably missed by the exhibits officer. Although the evidence did not strike at the heart of the case, the Crown Prosecution Service felt that the Metropolitan Police's credibility had been fatally undermined. In February 2010, the case against Rees's business partner, Sid Fillery, was stayed and, in November 2010, the builder James Cook was acquitted, followed, in March 2011, by Rees and the Vian brothers.

After twenty-four years, five investigations, 750,000 documents and the expenditure of £50 million, Scotland Yard had again failed to jail anyone for the murder of Daniel Morgan. Detective Chief Superintendent Hamish Campbell said: 'This current investigation has identified ever more clearly how the initial inquiry failed the family and wider public. It is quite apparent that corruption was a debilitating factor.' Outside court, Jonathan Rees said that he should not have been prosecuted, claiming the police had failed to investigate up to forty other potential suspects.

He also sought to implicate the BBC in his activities, claiming that *Panorama* had paid the police. While *The Times* had been able to find little space to report the phone hacking scandal, despite the growing number of civil court cases, several parliamentary inquiries and a new police investigation, it reported Rees's claims. On 15 March, *The Times*'s crime reporter, Sean O'Neill, wrote a story headlined: 'Investigator accused by BBC reporter of "corrupt business" says he worked for *Panorama*.' *The Times* referred briefly to *Panorama*'s allegation about computer hacking at the *Screws*, before dealing at length with Rees's alleged work for the BBC, though it quoted 'friends of Mr Rees' as saying he 'had no documents or invoices to prove his claim'. *Panorama* later said it could find no evidence it had employed the private detective. The media commentator Roy Greenslade blogged: 'Note how the *Times*'s story is angled to fit two News International agendas. It throws mud at the BBC, yet again. It minimises the misbehaviour by the *News of the World*, yet again.'[1]

Though a devastating blow for Alastair Morgan and Scotland Yard, the end of the case meant newspapers no longer had to withhold their coverage of Rees's connections to the *News of the World* for fear of contempt of court. Newspapers could reveal Andy Coulson's employment of the private investigator and his links to corrupt detectives. The *Independent* ran a story in the following day's paper headlined: 'Private investigator cleared of murder was on Coulson payroll'. In the *Guardian*, Nick Davies's story, which referred to Rees commissioning burglaries, was headed: 'Jonathan Rees: private investigator who ran an empire of tabloid corruption'.

At the BBC, *Panorama*'s Glenn Campbell had already spent five months investigating Rees, with the help of police, Alastair Morgan and Nick Davies. By January 2011, he had gathered enough evidence to expose a further and even more serious development in the hacking story: as well as hacking phones and blagging bank and medical details, the *News of the World* had been hacking computers.

One especially sensitive target was Ian Hurst, a former intelligence officer in Northern Ireland. While in the British Army's Force Research Unit, Hurst had handled Britain's most valuable agent in the IRA – Freddie Scappaticci, codenamed 'Stakeknife' – who had infiltrated the IRA's notorious 'Nutting Squad', which hunted down, tortured and killed suspected informers. Hurst wanted to expose what he said was the dirty work done by the British in Northern Ireland. In 2004, he wrote a book with a former *Independent* journalist, Greg Harkin, *Stakeknife: Britain's Secret Agents in Ireland*, which alleged that in order to maintain Scappaticci's cover the British Army allowed him to commit murder. In 2006, *Panorama* discovered, Jonathan Rees had introduced the *News of the World*'s Alex Marunchak, now editing its Irish edition, to a computer hacker, who sent a Trojan virus to Hurst's computer. Once opened, Hurst's emails were faxed to Manchurak's office in Dublin.

Panorama filmed Hurst as he was shown faxed copies of the emails that had arrived at the *News of the World*. 'The hairs on the back of my head are up,' he said. Hurst subsequently secretly recorded a meeting with the alleged hacker, who explained: 'It weren't that hard. I sent you an email that you opened, and that's it . . . I sent it from a bogus address . . . Now it's gone. It shouldn't even remain on the hard drive. I think I programmed it to stay on for three months.' Questioned about who had asked him to do the hacking, he replied: 'The faxes would go to Dublin . . . . He was the editor of the *News of the World* for Ireland. A Slovak-type name. I can't remember his fucking name. Alex his name is. Marunchak.'

In the run-up to *Panorama*'s broadcast, News International complained about the programme, claiming it was part of an attempt by the BBC to damage News Corp's bid for BSkyB. In letters to the BBC on 10 and 11 March, Farrer & Co's Julian Pike – who the previous year had threatened to injunct Mark Lewis for representing phone hacking victims – accused the corporation of 'running a campaign' against the BSkyB bid. The corporation had 'an obligation to avoid embroiling itself in a political and commercial battle that it should have nothing to do with', he added, protesting that the programme was 'yet another attempt to undermine News Corp's bid for Sky'. The BBC faced down the complaints and *Panorama* was broadcast on 14 March, giving millions of viewers an insight into the range of covert techniques used by News International. Marunchak made no comment to *Panorama*, but later denied its allegations in a statement to *UK Press Gazette*.

News International records showed that the *News of the World* paid Rees more than £4,000 for research on Stakeknife in 2006.

Inside Wapping, someone was becoming concerned at what happened at News International during the early days of the cover-up. On 24 March 2011, an anonymous executive at News International (believed to be the ambitious general manager Will Lewis) asked Harbottle & Lewis for a copy of its work for NI in 2007. Harbottle & Lewis had carried out the review of *News of the World* emails for Clive Goodman's employment appeal, and had printed off some copies of the emails – which contained evidence that News International journalists had been bribing Metropolitan Police officers. The payments were not £50 for the occasional tip-off, but totalled more than £100,000, for handing over such sensitive data as the Queen's phone numbers. On 1 April, Harbottle & Lewis gave its file containing the print-outs to News International's lawyers Burton Copeland. One anonymous News International executive later told *The Sunday Times*: 'We were sitting on a ticking timebomb.'[2] Instead of immediately contacting the police, with whom it publicly said it was 'fully co-operating', News International sat on the documents for three months, while it was bidding for BSkyB. But its request for the Harbottle & Lewis file may have influenced what happened next. Six days after the emails were requested, on 30 March, Rupert Murdoch promoted his son James to the newly created post of deputy chief operating officer of News Corp. Although James would retain control of the company's Asian and European operations (and his chairmanship of BSkyB and News International), he would now be based at News Corp's headquarters in New York. He had been airlifted out of Wapping.

Less than a week later, on 5 April, the Metropolitan Police underlined the robustness of its new investigation by making the first arrests for phone hacking for five years: Ian Edmondson and Neville Thurlbeck were held at Kingston and Wimbledon police stations respectively after arriving for interview by appointment. The men, assistant editor and chief reporter, were central to the news operation at the *News of the World*. They were released on police bail, pending further inquiries.

By coincidence, the British Press Awards were being held that evening at the newly re-opened Savoy Hotel in the Strand. Despite the embarrassment of having its chief reporter Neville Thurlbeck make the wrong kind of headlines earlier in the day, it was a good night for the *News of the World*. The 'Fake Sheikh', Mazher Mahmood, won the award for News Reporter of the Year and the *News of the World* Scoop of the Year for his exposé of corruption in the Pakistani cricket team. *News of the World* staff rose alone to give him, and themselves, a standing ovation, whooping and hollering. As he accepted the scoop award, Colin Myler described the *Screws* as 'the greatest paper in the world'. The cricket sting was indeed the paper at its investigative best and later led to the jailing of three Pakistani cricketers and a sports agent. But, although this latest coup had been achieved without the use of phone hacking, the alleged extent of the paper's dark arts left many journalists shuffling uneasily in their seats.

On 6 April, Lord Fowler, a former Conservative cabinet minister and chairman of the Lords Communications Committee, rose from his seat in the House of Lords to challenge the government. 'My Lords, leaving aside the two arrests yesterday,' he said, 'is it not already clear that there has been a total abuse of power involving some parts of the press in this area? Have we not also seen a five-year delay in the investigation, a public dispute now taking place between the DPP and the Metropolitan Police and the utter failure of any system to prevent such wrongdoing?' He asked for an assurance that there would be an independent inquiry once criminal proceedings were complete. A government minister, Lord Wallace of Saltaire, hinted for the first time that the government might just look into the affair: 'He [Lord Fowler] raises some broad questions about the future relationship between the press and politics and it is fair to say that we will need to return to those questions once current investigations are complete.' Fowler was one of the senior figures of David Cameron's Conservative Party; his views could not be lightly dismissed.

As the public began to grasp the seriousness of the goings-on at Wapping, the Hollywood actor Hugh Grant, an implacable critic of the tabloid press, turned the tables on one of its defenders. Grant, who never gave interviews to the redtops, secretly taped a conversation with Paul McMullan, the former *News of the World* features executive who, in the mid-1990s, had stolen the picture from the woman who reputedly took John Major's virginity. Just before Christmas Grant's car had broken down in Kent and McMullan had happened to drive by in his van. Sensing the chance for a bit of freelance work, McMullan asked the actor to pose for pictures by his broken-down car, just for a personal memento. McMullan cheerily invited Grant to pop by his pub, then sold the breakdown pictures to the *Mail on Sunday*. Now Grant exacted his revenge by calling in at the Castle Inn in Dover and recording his conversation with McMullan for a feature, 'The bugger, bugged', in the *New Statesman*. During their encounter McMullan, who did not know he was being taped, claimed that Rebekah Brooks was so friendly with David Cameron that she went horseriding with him – and that every political leader since Margaret Thatcher in the 1970s had had to 'jump in bed with Murdoch'.[3]

Grant said later that the phone hacking scandal was confirmation of what he had been claiming to friends for years: that the popular press was out of control. 'I used to sue a lot and the libel lawyers would say: "By the way you should be careful of this or that" and "Do you realize that the *News of the World* have a white van that sits outside people's houses?" In the old days with listening devices, they could put things on your wall – and you would think: Can that really be true?'[4]

He had no complaint about the reporting of his arrest for lewd behaviour in Los Angeles in 1995 because that was a matter of public record, but once he had returned to London he suspected he had fallen victim to dirty tricks. There was a 'fishy event' when his flat was broken into. 'It was quite a violent break-in, they smashed the front door down, and nothing was taken; the only thing that happened was that the details of what the inside of my flat looked like and a few personal details appeared in the papers in the subsequent days. It became clearer and clearer in the mid to late 1990s, to me and who-ever else was in the public eye, that if you had a burglary, or you got mugged or your car was broken into, you had to think really hard about whether you were going to call the police – because the first person that came round was always a pap or a journalist, not a police-man.'[5] Grant developed 'permanent paranoia' and had his car and phone checked for listening devices: 'And then you get paranoid about every engineer that comes into the house – you look very carefully at their card and all that. When I would say this to people, normal people, they would slightly roll their eyes and think "fame's gone to his head", especially when I started to say: "You don't know how powerful they are, they've corrupted the police, and they've corrupted the government, successive governments, they're completely in their pockets." '[6]

Journalists on News International's four titles had long dismissed the hacking scandal as celebrities whinging about reporters eavesdropping on their gossip – and that the police response was disproportionate. 'With this whole story I just hear the shrill shriek of axes being ground,' Roger Alton, executive editor of *The Times*, complained to his former colleague, the *Independent*'s Archie Bland, for the May issue of the *Columbia Journalism Review*: 'People have gone to prison. Coulson's resigned twice. It's not as if any perceived wrongdoing hasn't been sufficiently addressed. For me it's roughly on a par with parking in a resident's parking bay in terms of interest.' On 7 April, the *Sun*'s columnist and former editor, Kelvin Mackenzie, protested that the allocation of forty-five Scotland Yard officers to the phone hacking inquiry was 'incredible', adding: 'Wouldn't it be nice if any of them might be spared from their piddly, politically motivated witch hunt to come round when your tools are nicked from the garden shed?'

Now in possession of the emails returned by Harbottle & Lewis, NI's executives on the tenth floor of Thomas More Square knew total denial was no longer an option. On Friday 8 April they put into action a plan they had been kicking around for weeks. Five years, nine months and eighteen days after Goodman and Mulcaire were jailed for phone hacking, Rupert Murdoch's News International admitted for the first time that the rogue reporter defence – advanced by its executives for years – was bogus. But it was still not ready to admit the full scale of the wrongdoing. In an anodyne press release, the company apologized for phone hacking, admitted its own inquiries had been flawed and announced it would settle civil cases brought by several claimants. The statement carefully limited wrongdoing at the *News of the World* to Andy Coulson's editorship between 2004 and 2006. It was headed: 'News International statement with regard to voicemail interception at the *News of the World* during 2004–2006':

> Following an extensive internal investigation and disclosures through civil cases, News International has decided to approach some civil litigants with an unreserved apology and an admission of liability in cases meeting specific criteria. We will, however, continue to contest cases that we believe are without merit or where we are not responsible. That said, past behaviour at the *News of the World* in relation to voicemail interception is a matter of genuine regret. It is now apparent that our previous inquiries failed to uncover important evidence and we acknowledge our actions then were not sufficiently robust.

At 4 p.m., the BBC's Robert Peston, again apparently using his close contacts at Wapping, named eight individuals whose cases the company intended to settle: Sienna Miller, her stepmother Kelly Hoppen, Sky Andrew, Andy Gray, Tessa Jowell and her estranged husband David Mills, Max Clifford's secretary Nicola Phillips, and Joan Hammell, John Prescott's chief of staff. In all, Wapping expected to settle up to ninety-one cases – the number of PINs recovered from Glenn Mulcaire. Peston was told that the company had set aside £20 million for the payouts.

In New York that day, James Murdoch explained to Bloomberg interviewer Charlie Rose that everything was going well despite the admission. 'The interesting thing about this one is,' Murdoch explained, 'you talk about a reputation crisis [but] actually the business is doing really well. It shows what we were able to do is really put this problem into a box. If you get everybody sucked into something like that, then the whole business will sputter, which you don't want.'[7]

On Sunday 10 April, Colin Myler, who told the Press Complaints Commission that Clive Goodman's hacking was 'aberrational', publicly apologized to his readers in a 159-word comment on page 2 of his newspaper: 'Voicemail interception: an apology': 'What happened to them [hacking victims] should not have happened. It was and remains unacceptable.' The *Screws* did not rescind its attacks on the Culture Committee and the *Guardian*, nor comment on their pioneering work in uncovering the scandal.

While News International had now withdrawn from the rogue reporter claim, it had merely retreated to a new line of defence – a few rogue reporters, at the *News of the World*, under Andy Coulson. *The Times*, *Sunday Times* and *Sun* continued largely to ignore the ongoing story. News International continued to behave firmly towards inquiring journalists: pursuing the scandal would 'not be forgotten'.

Despite its persistent claims to be fully cooperating with the police inquiry, News International, still chaired by James Murdoch, was still seeking to obstruct the police's efforts – as it had done so successfully in 2006 when it frustrated the police search of Wapping. On 14 April, detectives from Operation Weeting arrested the *News of the World* reporter James Weatherup at his home and then went to Wapping to seize his computer and other material. By the time they arrived, however, executives had bagged up Weatherup's belongings and sent them to the company's lawyers, Burton Copeland (though, strangely, Weatherup's computer – and a hard drive – remained on his desk). Furious, the Met flooded the *News of the World*'s newsroom with uniformed police. Burton Copeland returned Weatherup's belongings.

Shortly afterwards, Sue Akers, the leader of the new investigation, held a summit with the company's Will Lewis and Simon Greenberg 'to debate our very different interpretations of the expression "full co-operation"'.[8]

However, behind the scenes pressure remained on Scotland Yard. On 'several occasions' after Sir Paul Stephenson, the Commissioner, returned to work from his leg operation in April, Kit Malthouse, Mayor Boris Johnson's right-hand man, urged him to scale down Operation Weeting, telling Stephenson that he should not fall victim to the 'political media hysteria' surrounding phone hacking. Stephenson, whose force had disastrously shrugged off calls to reopen the inquiry for two years, resisted the overtures. Malthouse said he was only trying to ensure that policing was proportionate.

News International concentrated on what it could achieve: picking off the civil claimants. The company desperately wanted to settle to prevent executives testifying before a judge. It started with Sienna Miller. Rival newspapers often used her portrait to illustrate stories about the scandal and her claims were especially wide-ranging and damaging; among them that the *News of the World* hacked her computer in 2008, a year after the jailing of Goodman and Mulcaire. Despite the strength of her case and the size of the Gordon Taylor and Max Clifford settlements, Miller's lawyers had surprisingly requested only £100,000 damages. News International offered the full amount in a Part 36 offer.

At a High Court hearing on 12 May, NI's lawyer, Michael Silverleaf QC, played down the damage done to Miller, saying that most of the *News of the World*'s stories had been about her relationship with Jude Law. He told Justice Vos: 'It is hurtful, but it is not that hurtful. It does not belittle her in the public estimation.' What was more, he said, £100,000 was equivalent to the compensation payable for the loss of an eye – and compared favourably to the £60,000 damages awarded to Max Mosley for the *News of the World* story which had 'ruined' his life. Despite her desire to air her case in court, Miller was 'in a box' and accepted Wapping's admission of liability and the damages. News International had succeeded in killing off one of the most damaging cases, for an amount far lower than the earlier settlements –

and had set the bar relatively low for the cluster of civil cases, all being heard by Mr Justice Vos.

At Bindmans, Tamsin Allen had used her experience of public law to develop the judicial review on behalf of Chris Bryant, Brian Paddick, Brendan Montague and John Prescott. The essence of the case was that, despite their requests, Scotland Yard had breached their right to privacy by failing to inform them they were in Mulcaire's notes. At a preliminary hearing on 12 May, the Metropolitan Police's QC James Lewis tried to strike out the claim, denying there had been a conspiracy to avoid contacting the claimants. The police, he said, had been hampered by the untidiness and complexity of Glenn Mulcaire's scribblings. In Chris Bryant's case, for instance, Lewis explained, twenty-three numbers associated with him had been found not on the page with his details but on another page elsewhere in the notes. In court for the hearing, Bryant whispered to Nick Davies and Martin Hickman sitting in front of him: 'They were on the facing page.' Mr Justice Foskett ordered a full trial.

All the while, Operation Weeting was identifying likely new hacking victims and informing them that they were in Mulcaire's notes. Wayne Rooney, the Manchester United footballer whose manager, Paul Stretford, had been the target of covert surveillance, tweeted on 28 April: 'Looks like a newspaper have hacked into my phone. Big surprise.'

By May, Tom Watson had been cultivating a high-ranked and extremely sensitive source, Mr Y. During a meeting at a London apartment, Mr Y alleged that Jonathan Rees, the private investigator recently acquitted of murder, had – using a variety of methods including blagging, corruption and burglary – illegally acquired personal data about royalty, leading politicians and other senior members of the establishment on behalf of the *News of the World* and other red-top newspapers. For the first time Watson glimpsed the real picture of wrongdoing at Wapping, but the more he learned the more he realized that it involved the criminal underworld and some very dangerous characters. At the Birmingham home of his friend Siôn Simon that weekend, the MP was hugely animated as he relayed his discovery, then his tone changed. 'None of this stuff is written down – it's all just in my head.' However ridiculous or melodramatic, he contemplated that he might be killed.

On 11 May he stood up in the Commons and challenged David Cameron to call a judicial inquiry. Softly, he said:

> The Prime Minister told me that the hacking inquiry should go where the evidence leads. It leads to the parents of the Soham children and to rogue intelligence officers. He knows more sinister forms of cyber-crime. Lord Fowler is calling for a judicial inquiry. Will the Prime Minister please order one now, before the avalanche of new evidence forces him to do so?

Cameron replied there was a real problem of 'interfering' with the criminal investigations, adding: 'The most important thing is to allow the criminal investigation to take place'. The Prime Minister was opposed to a judicial inquiry. Yes, he seemed to be saying, some bad things have happened, but now they are being investigated.

Those following the scandal knew that, despite the thoroughness of the new phone hacking inquiry, Operation Weeting, Scotland Yard was not yet doing all it could to investigate Wapping's darkest arts. For some time the civil lawyers Mark Lewis, Charlotte Harris and Mark Thomson had been cooperating to concentrate their legal firepower; now reporters from competing media groups also began to cooperate. On 20 May, Tom Watson, the *Guardian*'s Nick Davies and BBC *Panorama*'s Glenn Campbell met at Watson's flat in south London, where they discussed News International's use of Jonathan Rees.

On 7 June, at a townhouse in Westminster, another meeting took place, this time between Tom Watson, Nick Davies and Martin Hickman (Glenn Campbell was on holiday). They discussed evidence held by Scotland Yard showing that Jonathan Rees, on behalf of News International, illegally targeted members of the royal family, senior politicians and high-level terrorist informers. The allegations were outside the remit of Operation Weeting, the Met's inquiry into phone hacking, and were not being investigated. Knowing that some of the media would not report the story if it appeared only in the two newspapers, the trio agreed that Watson would trail the allegations at Prime Minister's Questions the following day, making it almost impossible for broadcasters to ignore.

On the afternoon of 8 June, Watson said in the House of Commons:

> The Metropolitan Police are in possession of paperwork detailing the dealings of criminal private investigator Jonathan Rees. It strongly suggests that he was illegally targeting members of the Royal Family, senior politicians, and high-level terrorist informers yet the head of Operation Weeting has recently written to me to inform me that this evidence may be outside the inquiry's terms of reference. Prime Minister, I believe powerful forces are involved in a cover-up; please tell me what you intend to do to make sure that that does not happen.

As shock spread across the faces of his fellow frontbenchers George Osborne and Theresa May, David Cameron replied: 'The police are free to investigate the evidence and take that wherever it leads them, and then mount a prosecution if the Crown Prosecution Service supports that. In the case of phone hacking, which is illegal and wrong, there have been prosecutions and imprisonments, and if that is where the evidence takes them, that is what will happen in the future.' He added: 'There are no terms of reference as far as I am concerned; the police are able to look at any evidence and all evidence they can find.'

Broadcasters covered the speech, repeatedly running Watson's warning about 'powerful forces'. Characteristically, when the *Independent* put the list of Rees's targets to News International later that same day, its spokeswoman, Daisy Dunlop, warned the paper off writing the story, saying: 'Be very careful before linking those names to News International.' In a public statement, the company played down the seriousness of its role. It said: 'It is well documented that Jonathan Rees and Southern Investigations worked for a whole variety of newspaper groups. With regards to Tom Watson's specific allegations, we believe these are wholly inaccurate. The Met Police, with whom we are cooperating fully in Operation Weeting, have not asked us for any information regarding Jonathan Rees. We note again that Tom Watson made these allegations under parliamentary privilege.'

The *Guardian* and *Independent*'s stories disclosed a roll-call of Rees's political, royal, police and financial targets, on whom he had used a variety of techniques (some apparently illegal) to gain information.

Among them were Tony Blair and Kate Middleton, Prince William's fiancée. They also included Blair's director of communications, Alastair Campbell, his Home Secretary Jack Straw, and Peter Mandelson, then his Business Secretary. Several targets had been in charge of media policy: Gerald Kaufmann, the Labour chair of the Culture Committee between 1992 and 2005, and the Tory MP David Mellor, who threatened the press with tighter regulation in the early 1990s. Rees had even targeted the former Commissioner of the Metropolitan Police, Sir John Stevens, and John Yates, 'Yates of the Yard' himself.

While the royal family observed its usual diplomatic silence, politicians responded angrily to the news. Peter Mandelson said he was writing to Scotland Yard to ask what information had been held on him by Rees. Jack Straw suspected he may have been targeted by the *Daily Mirror* in 1997 (under the editorship of Piers Morgan) for its 'disgraceful sting' on his teenage son. David Mellor complained: 'Scotland Yard have been extremely tardy investigating these allegations, perhaps because senior officers were more concerned with protecting their own relationships with News International rather than doing their own duty.'[9]

By coincidence, the following day, 10 June, Tony Blair gave an interview to the *Times* about his hopes that there would be an elected EU President and had scheduled a TV interview with the BBC. Unlike his former cabinet colleagues, the former prime minister seemed reluctant to find out the extent to which he had been targeted. He said: 'I assume that if someone's got something they will get in touch with me.' In an interview with *Vogue* published in September 2011, Rupert Murdoch's wife, Wendi Deng, let slip that Tony Blair was godfather to her and Murdoch's nine-year-old daughter, Grace, and had been present at her baptism in early 2010 on the banks of the river Jordan. The Murdochs, Queen Rania of Jordan and Grace's official godparents, the Australian actors Nicole Kidman and Hugh Jackman, had all been pictured in *Hello!*'s coverage of the baptism, but Blair, described by Deng as one of the couple's 'closest friends', had been missing from the photocall. His role as godfather had remained a closely guarded secret until the interview. Blair's office refused to deny or confirm he was a godparent.

Irritated by Watson's implied criticism of her and her inquiry in the Commons, Sue Akers asked to see the MP. During a forty-minute meeting in her office in the upper floors of the Met's headquarters, she sought to assure Watson that the force would follow up his allegations about the targeting of senior public figures, but was working out who would take responsibility for different strands of the inquiry. They had a candid conversation which involved very sensitive evidence that Watson had seen showing that Jonathan Rees had a close business relationship with Alex Marunchak, the *Screws'* executive. Later that day, Scotland Yard disclosed that it had begun a 'formal assessment process', Operation Tuleta,* to consider potential prosecutions that fell outside the terms of Operation Weeting, such as computer hacking.

Police action against Rupert Murdoch's British news empire was growing rapidly: January had brought Operation Weeting; now June brought Operation Tuleta. Eight officers were working on the new inquiry. Overall more than fifty detectives at Scotland Yard were investigating the dark arts of Fleet Street.

At the same time, Watson was becoming anxious about the situation of Tommy Sheridan. On the day the new police inquiry into phone hacking was launched, 26 January, Tommy Sheridan was jailed for three years for perjury. Passing sentence, the judge, Lord Bracadale, told him: 'By pursuing, and persisting in the pursuit of, a defamation action against the proprietors of the *News of the World* you brought the walls of the temple crashing down not only on your head but also on the heads of your family and your political friends and foes alike.' Watson feared that Sheridan had gone to jail because of misleading evidence, and decided to make contact with him. On 26 May, he wrote to Sheridan in HMP Barlinnie. Watson began his letter: 'We've never met but I feel I know you . . . I think the hacking saga will continue for at least another year. It's going to get much worse before it gets better.' In a clear-sighted handwritten letter dated 29 May, Prisoner 32057 wrote back:

---

* That afternoon, Watson posted on Twitter and Facebook a letter dated 17 May 2011 from Sue Akers saying: 'The information regarding Mr Rees may be outside the Terms of Reference of my investigation but the MPS [Metropolitan Police Service] are assessing your allegation along with others we have received to consider a way forward.'

Dear Tom,

Many thanks for your warm, welcome and encouraging letter. As you say we haven't met personally yet throughout the News International hacking scandal and my three-month trial you have shown yourself to be a reliable and courageous ally with real backbone. Sadly you are the exception among your colleagues, far too many of whom are frightened of the power and influence wielded, unaccountably, by the Murdoch empire. I believe you share my opinion of that reactionary stable with their anti-trade union, sexist and racist agenda. They are bullies of the worst kind and as with any bully running away only invites them to become more aggressive. They have to be confronted not accommodated. The truth is criminality is at the heart of that beast and but for the complicity and sometimes collusion of the Met they would have been exposed before now. Several of their senior executives and former executives should face prosecution, including Coulson and Bird [Bob, editor of the Scottish edition of the News of the World*], but Murdoch himself must not be allowed to assume the role of Pontius Pilate in the whole sorry affair. I can only admire your commitment to expose [them] and encourage you to continue to do so.*

As for me in here I am fine. The staff and prisoners alike have treated me with nothing but support and respect since the day I was admitted. Their response and the support of my family, friends and the general public, has kept my head up and spirits high. My appeal is being processed and may bear fruit but whatever happens to me personally is less important than ensuring the Murdoch empire is exposed for its criminality and stripped of its billionaire-purchased authority.

I hope we can meet up personally when I am released Tom. I look forward to that. Take care comrade and stay strong.

In solidarity, Tommy

14

Summer's Lease

No other country in the world would allow somebody to
have so much power . . . apart, perhaps, from Italy
– Chris Bryant, House of Commons, 30 June 2011

Publicly, June was a quiet month in the phone hacking scandal: a summer's lull. Though events in the spring had lifted the lid, News International had started to weld it back on again. Wapping had made a public apology and concluded the civil cases of both Sienna Miller and Andy Gray (paying him a modest £20,000 damages and costs of £200,000). The talk in Westminster was that there was no significant opposition to the BSkyB takeover. News Corp enjoyed the solid support of the Conservative Party. Privately Will Lewis, Wapping's general manager, was saying that the company's three-year recovery plan was on track.

As usual, on Wednesday 15 June,* Rupert Murdoch hosted his annual summer party at the Orangery in the grounds of Kensington Palace in London. Traditionally the party attracted luminaries from the media, politics and showbusiness; so important was it in the political and media worlds that one former Wapping executive had it

---

* With Murdoch in town, earlier that day Sky News had broken the news that police had informed Rebekah Brooks that while she was editing the *Sun* in 2005 and 2006 her phone had been hacked twenty times. While ostensibly showing that the chief executive of News International was herself a victim of Glenn Mulcaire, the disclosure raised the possibility that Andy Coulson's *News of the World* had been spying on his close friend and colleague – or perhaps, as Sky's business editor Mark Kleinman helpfully suggested, Mulcaire had been working for another newspaper group.[1]

written into their redundancy package that they would receive an annual invitation to demonstrate that they were still part of the family. The previous summer, the new Conservative Prime Minister had walked hand in hand with his wife Samantha to the party – where the other guests included his Home Secretary, Theresa May, Richard Desmond, proprietor of the *Daily Express*, the TopShop tycoon Sir Philip Green and the comedian James Corden. With the allegations swirling around Murdoch's empire, gossip columnists speculated who would turn up in 2011. Downing Street had refused to say whether the Prime Minister would attend, but News Corp's chairman need not have worried – David Cameron arrived discreetly by car at a drop-off point sealed from the public, his brief emergence captured by a photographer's long lens. The shadow cabinet was present too – Ed Miliband, the Labour leader (who had called for an inquiry into phone hacking in April but did not mention phone hacking to the News Corp boss during their conversation), the shadow Chancellor Ed Balls and his wife, the shadow Home Secretary Yvette Cooper, and the shadow Foreign Secretary Douglas Alexander. The newly elected Labour MPs Gloria de Piero and Michael Dugher turned up. Guests drank Moët & Chandon champagne and Becks beer, and ate oysters.

On the surface, all was well. But increasingly, Brooks's position was being questioned by those inside as well as outside the company. In June, according to one well-placed News Corp source, security staff were ordered to record the times of Brooks's entry to and exit from Thomas More Square and cleaners were warned to avoid disturbing listening devices placed under her table and by her computer in her office. The chief executive herself was now being bugged.

On the tenth floor, News International's executives could hear the 'ticking timebomb' of police corruption. After being retrieved from storage in late March, Harbottle & Lewis's file on Clive Goodman's employment appeal had been handed to Burton Copeland, News International's solicitors, on 1 April. At some stage it was passed to News Corp's solicitors, Hickman & Rose. In May, Hickman & Rose arranged for several emails from the file to be reviewed by an eminent barrister. Now in private practice, Lord Macdonald had been the Director of Public Prosecutions at the time of the botched inquiry into phone hacking in 2006, when the Crown Prosecution Service had agreed to exclude high-profile witnesses from the prosecution. Examining the file was not a conflict of interest, Macdonald explained later, because the emails Hickman & Rose had placed before him contained not evidence of phone hacking, but of bribery of London's police force. Macdonald took around five minutes to realize they should be handed to the police. He told the Commons Home Affairs Committee later: 'I have to tell you that the material I saw was so blindingly obvious that anyone trying to argue that it shouldn't be given to the police would have had a very tough task.' The emails were not, however, immediately given to the police. Instead, Lord Macdonald presented his opinion to the News Corp board chaired by Rupert Murdoch. 'Reasonably shortly afterwards' – in fact on 20 June, eleven weeks after the emails had been retrieved from Harbottle & Lewis, during which time its bid for BSkyB was progressing – News Corp handed them to the police.[2] In secret, Sue Akers, already leading Operations Weeting into phone hacking and Tuleta into computer hacking, began a third inquiry, Operation Elveden, into police corruption. News International agreed to keep quiet about it so as not to prejudice the investigation.

Approaches were made to Tom Watson. By this stage, friends had been telling him: 'You've done a good job, it's time to move on'. But in an attempt to keep the issue to the fore, he had made an inflammatory speech at the GMB union's conference on 5 June, telling delegates his bins had been gone through during the Damian McBride affair and that the *News of the World* had targeted the parents of the Soham children. (He said: 'You probably didn't know they targeted the Soham parents. That's because it's hardly been written about in a British newspaper. Or ever mentioned by a British broadcaster.')

Two intermediaries close to News International offered a deal. One told Watson the company would 'give him' Andy Coulson, but Rebekah Brooks was 'sacred', which Watson took to mean that the company would hand over incriminating evidence on Coulson if he laid off Brooks. He had no idea what evidence that might have been. Over dinner, the other intermediary suggested to the West Bromwich MP that Rupert Murdoch might like to meet him. 'He's a charismatic man,' she said. 'He'd want to square off these difficulties and put matters right.' Watson was not interested in cutting a deal. The meeting was never formally offered.

News Corp was unsurprisingly nervous that it was now the subject of three major criminal inquiries by the Metropolitan Police. It did not, however, have to worry about its big upcoming deal. A fortnight after the party at the Orangery, in a written statement on Thursday 30 June, David Cameron's government announced its intention to wave through the BSkyB takeover.

Ofcom, which previously supported a referral to the Competition Commission, was now satisfied by News Corp's undertakings on Sky News. The Culture Secretary, Jeremy Hunt, said that although nothing had arisen out of the 40,000 responses to the public consultation to alter the acceptability of those undertakings, he had decided to insist upon some of the 'constructive changes' suggested: Sky News articles of association would define the role of independent directors and a monitoring trustee would oversee its independence. Hunt, apparently oblivious to Rupert Murdoch's string of broken promises in the past, said News Corp had 'offered serious undertakings and discussed them in good faith'. He added: 'Therefore, whilst the phone hacking allegations are very serious they were not material to my consideration.' Rupert Murdoch would win control of his big prize – total control of the UK's biggest broadcaster – after a further, brief eight-day consultation, ending on 8 July.

The government had backed the BSkyB deal despite the new allegations of criminality slowly engulfing Murdoch's powerful national newspapers. Avoiding a Commons debate by issuing a written statement irritated MPs from all parties, including Mark Pritchard, the independent-minded secretary of the Conservative backbench 1922 Committee. Watson put in a request for an urgent statement from the Culture Secretary, which was granted by the Speaker John Bercow. During a thirty-five-minute debate on 30 June Jeremy Hunt set out his case: he had proceeded carefully at all times, following and publishing the independent advice from Ofcom and the Office of Fair Trading; he believed News Corp's promises were serious and robust.

John Whittingdale, the Conservative chairman of the Culture

Committee, congratulated Hunt on the 'meticulous care' that he had taken in deciding the bid: could he confirm that every single concern of the regulatory authorities had been addressed? Hunt could. Opposition MPs were furious. Barry Gardiner said: 'He is propping up a crumbling empire. Murdoch is the Gaddafi of News Corporation.' Tom Watson pointed out that Rupert Murdoch had breached his assurances on *The Times*, *The Sunday Times*, the *Sun* and the *News of the World* and his company was now the subject of three police inquiries. Chris Bryant asked: 'How on earth did we – and I mean all of us, not just the minister – become so spineless as to allow a company whose directors not only failed in their fiduciary duties to prevent criminality at the *News of the World*, but actually participated in its cover-up, to hold dominion over such a vast swathe of the media in this country? No other country in the world would allow somebody to have so much power.' The Labour MP Kevin Brennan interjected: 'Apart from Italy', prompting Bryant to add reluctantly: 'Apart, perhaps, from Italy.'

The Murdochs had reason to celebrate. On Saturday 2 July, another of the dynasty's grand summer events was taking place, in the grandeur of Burford Priory, the Elizabethan home of Elisabeth Murdoch and her well-connected husband Matthew Freud in the Oxfordshire countryside. The Chipping Norton Set was out in force. The guests, according to a report in the *Mail on Sunday* later that month, included News International's chairman James Murdoch, chief executive Rebekah Brooks (though she reportedly circulated with diminished effervescence), and its general manager Will Lewis. A former *News of the World* editor, Piers Morgan – an old friend of Brooks and Andy Coulson – was there. The BBC was well represented by its director-general, Mark Thompson, business editor Robert Peston and creative director Alan Yentob. Among the political rainmakers were the Education Secretary Michael Gove, the Prime Minister's director of strategy, Steve Hilton, and his wife Rachel Whetstone, Google's European head of communications, the Culture Minister Ed Vaizey – a member of David Cameron's metropolitan Notting Hill Set, who had promised to abolish the BBC Trust – and four Blairite ex-ministers: Lord Mandelson, David Miliband, James Purnell and Tessa Jowell. The current Labour frontbench was represented by

Douglas Alexander. Some glamour was provided by the actress Helena Bonham Carter, the explorer Bear Grylls and the TV presenter Mariella Frostrup.[3] Andy Coulson himself, however, was absent.

The party continued into the next day. The phone hacking affair had fallen quiet – except that Nick Davies had found a new story.

15

A Missing Girl

*This is a watershed moment when, finally, the public starts to
see and feel, above all, just how low and disgusting this particular newspaper's methods were* – Hugh Grant, 6 July 2011

As Liz Murdoch and Matthew Freud's guests dispersed on Sunday,
3 July, the *Guardian* was about to break a story that would dominate
the headlines for weeks, send media, politics and police into panic,
cost tens of millions of pounds, and wreck multiple reputations. It
flashed up at 4.29 p.m. on Monday, 4 July on the *Guardian* website,
jointly bylined Nick Davies and Amelia Hill:

> The *News of the World* illegally targeted the missing schoolgirl
> Milly Dowler and her family in March 2002, interfering with police
> inquiries into her disappearance, an investigation by the *Guardian*
> has established.
>
> Scotland Yard is investigating the episode, which is likely to put
> new pressure on the then editor of the paper, Rebekah Brooks,
> now Rupert Murdoch's chief executive in the UK; and the then
> deputy editor, Andy Coulson, who resigned in January as the Prime
> Minister's media adviser.

The most incendiary detail was in the sixth and seventh paragraphs:
that not only had the tabloid hacked into the missing thirteen-year-
old's phone, it had deleted messages to make space for more – which
could then be mined for stories:

In the last four weeks the Met officers have approached Surrey Police and taken formal statements from some of those involved in the original inquiry, who were concerned about how *News of the World* journalists intercepted – and deleted – the voicemail messages of Milly Dowler. The messages were deleted by journalists in the first few days after Milly's disappearance in order to free up space for more messages. As a result friends and relatives of Milly concluded wrongly that she might still be alive.

Five months later, the *Guardian* would admit that it was unlikely the *News of the World* had caused this 'false hope' moment, which was more probably the result of an automatic deletion by the phone company. (See Chapter 23.) In July 2011, the Metropolitan Police, Surrey Police, News International and the Dowler family all believed that the *News of the World* had been responsible.

Ten minutes after the story had appeared on the *Guardian* website, Tom Watson (who had been given advance notice of it by Davies) stood up in the Commons chamber and relayed the news. 'In the last few minutes,' he said, 'it has just been revealed by the *Guardian* newspaper that Milly Dowler's phone was hacked by private investigators working for the *News of the World*. As well as being a despicable act . . . it also strongly suggests that Parliament was misled in the press standards inquiry held by the select committee in 2010.' MPs were stunned. David Heath, the Liberal Democrat Deputy Leader of the House, visibly shocked, followed Watson out of the chamber saying: 'Did you really say Milly Dowler's phone was hacked?', then ran off back to his office.

Mark Lewis, now representing the Dowler family, was interviewed by Sky News standing outside the Royal Courts of Justice. 'There are no words to describe how awful this is,' he said. 'The parents were getting through the most awful experience for any parent. It's unimaginable, and yet people in the *News of the World* had no compunction, no fear of anything; no sense of moral right.'

By any standards, Milly's parents, Bob and Sally Dowler, had been tormented enough. They had experienced nine awful years since their daughter had disappeared in the commuter town of Walton-on-Thames, Surrey, on her way home from school on 21 March 2002. In the weeks following her disappearance, despite a £100,000 reward offer from the *Sun*, detectives could not find her killer and even began to suspect her father, Bob. The Dowlers repeatedly fell victim to hoaxers who claimed to know what had happened to their daughter. Her body was found in woods twenty-five miles away in Yateley, Hampshire, in September 2002.

In 2008, police finally identified the prime suspect as Levi Bellfield, a nightclub bouncer jailed for murdering two young women. At his trial for Milly's murder in May and June 2011, Bellfield refused to testify but the Dowlers were subjected to a distressing cross-examination by Bellfield's barrister, Jeffrey Samuels, who explored Bob Dowler's private life and read out Milly's letters saying she was a disappointment to her family. During her cross-examination Sally Dowler collapsed in the witness box. On 23 June, Bellfield was convicted of murder, but prejudicial newspaper coverage led to the abandonment of his second trial for the attempted abduction of an eleven-year-old schoolgirl, Rachel Cowes. On Sunday 3 July, as Liz Murdoch and Matthew Freud's guests were waking up after their Cotswolds party, the *News of the World*'s leader column condemned the Dowlers' 'now-infamous courtroom torture'.

The reality was that within days of Milly Dowler's disappearance, the *News of the World* had put its electronic detectives on her trail, asking Steve Whittamore to trawl phone numbers registered to the Dowlers in Walton-on-Thames. His accomplice John Boyall had blagged two ex-directory numbers out of British Telecom, one for the Dowlers' home.

The Dowlers had clung to hope their daughter was alive partly because it looked as though she had been accessing the voicemail of her mobile phone. Soon after she went missing her inbox filled up with messages from anxious family members and friends and would accept no more, but on 24 March her voice could be heard again asking people to leave messages. (In November 2001 her mother explained her ecstatic reaction: 'She's picked up her voicemails, Bob. She's alive! I told my friends: "She's picked up her voicemails! She's picked up her voicemails!"')

Nine years later, detectives on the Met's Operation Weeting found evidence that the *News of the World* had hacked her phone; the reinstatement of her disembodied voice had seemingly been part of a calculated attempt to land stories for the *News of the World*, at a time when it was being edited by Rebekah Brooks, now chief executive of the UK's biggest newspaper group.*

News International said the *Guardian*'s 'allegations' were of 'great concern' and announced that it was launching an internal inquiry.

Radio and TV stations and press agencies picked up the story. At 6 p.m., it was the second item on the BBC news. By 10 p.m., it was top of the bulletin, a position it would retain for a fortnight. After the chimes of Big Ben on Radio 4, the *World Tonight*'s reporter Matt Prodger began his report: 'The allegations couldn't be worse.' On *Newsnight*, Tom Watson attacked the subservience of the three main political leaders towards the Murdochs: all of them had been informed of suspicions that victims of crime were also targets of phone hacking, he said. 'Politicians are frightened of News International. Ed Miliband is as guilty as David Cameron and Nick Clegg', he said. Jeremy Paxman checked with Watson whether he had just included his own leader in that list. He had.

In the *Independent*'s offices, Martin Hickman and Cahal Milmo confirmed Operation Weeting had visited the Dowlers and internally talked up the story's significance. The next morning, Tuesday 5 July, the *Guardian* and the *Independent* splashed the story; the *Daily Telegraph*, *Financial Times* and *Times* ran smaller pieces on the front pages, but despite the story leading the TV bulletins, the mass market papers tucked it inside – the *Daily Mirror* on page 6, the *Daily Star* on page 7, the *Daily Express* and *Daily Mail* on page 8. The *Sun* carried

---

* The *News of the World* had hacked into Milly's inbox by 12 April, three weeks after her disappearance, at the latest. On 4 April 2002, it had even published a story based on a hacked voicemail, about a recruitment agency leaving a message on her phone. The paper wrote: 'On March 27, six days after Milly went missing in Walton-on-Thames, Surrey, the employment agency appears to have phoned her mobile.' In the days before the story was published, the NoW had bullied the force, refusing to believe its explanation that the recruitment agency message was probably a hoax (it turned out to be a wrong number). The *News of the World* even played a voicemail recording from Milly's phone to Surrey Police. Despite knowing the paper had accessed the inbox – which could have triggered the automatic deletion of evidence (because murderers sometimes leave taunting messages on victims' phones) – Surrey took no action. Had it done so, it might have halted the *News of the World*'s phone hacking in its tracks.

a six-sentence account on page 2. Soon the blanket coverage on TV and radio made underplaying the story commercially and reputationally impossible.

Overnight in Wapping, News International executives devised a plan. On the morning of Tuesday 5 July, the story was still leading the bulletins, but with Wapping's spin: *News of the World* executives intended to meet the police to discuss the allegations. The BBC's business editor Robert Peston blogged that Brooks still enjoyed Rupert Murdoch's full support and would not be standing down, including supportive quotes from colleagues such as 'She is committed to finding out the truth of what happened here and leading the company through this difficult time.' (The right-wing commentator Toby Young complained on his *Telegraph* blog: 'It reads like a press release that's been handwritten by News International's chief executive.') John Whittingdale, chairman of the Culture Committee, said the *News of the World's* misconduct seemed to be 'a very separate question' from the BSkyB takeover.[1]

The story overshadowed a visit to Afghanistan by David Cameron. At a press conference, the Prime Minister spent fifty-five seconds condemning the hacking, while avoiding mentioning the *News of the World*, News International, Rebekah Brooks or Rupert Murdoch. Referring to 'the allegations', he said: 'If they are true, this is a truly dreadful act and a truly dreadful situation. What I've read in the papers is quite, quite shocking, that someone could do this knowing the police were trying to find this person and trying to find out what had happened.' The police should pursue the matter vigorously, he added.

At 10 a.m. the next day, as he drank black coffee at the Fire Station in Waterloo, Tom Watson was called by Ed Miliband's office, concerned that his comments on *Newsnight* made it look as if he was trying to 'bounce' the party leader into acting. Since winning the Labour leadership in September 2010, Miliband had been accused of being too low-profile. In a late-night phone call with Miliband in March, after watching tribute band the Whoo, Watson had mentioned the prospect of a public outcry arising from the *News of the World's* targeting of crime victims, shortly after which, on 19 April, Miliband had called for an inquiry: his office were perplexed at the charge of complacency.

At midday, Ed Miliband took the biggest gamble of his leadership to date: he called for Brooks to 'examine her conscience' and 'consider her position'. He described the hacking as 'truly immoral', adding: 'But this goes well beyond one individual. This is about the culture and practices that were going on at that newspaper over a sustained period. What I want from executives at News International is people to start taking responsibility for this . . .' Party leaders usually bent over backwards to accommodate News International; now Miliband was damning the company and effectively calling for its chief executive's resignation. Senior Murdoch journalists were furious. The parliamentary lobby was abuzz with rumours of a spat between the Labour Party spokesman Bob Roberts and Tom Newton Dunn, the *Sun*'s combative political editor. Roberts would not publicly discuss the row, but he reputedly told Newton Dunn not to take Miliband's comments personally, to which Newton Dunn replied: 'We do take it personally and we're going to make it personal to you. We won't forget.' 'They were very clear with us,' Miliband told the *New Statesman* later, 'that Rebekah Brooks and Rupert Murdoch would be the two people standing at News International when everyone else was gone.'[2]

News International now found itself under attack from all sides. While previous polling showed that the public disapproved of phone hacking, the best-known victims so far had been wealthy celebrities; the targeting of a missing schoolgirl was regarded as truly heinous. Irate readers berated journalists picking up phones in the *News of the World* newsroom; many were swearing. Reporters felt dreadful. Dave Wooding, the *News of the World*'s associate editor, woke up that morning and 'felt sick'. . .'And for the first time in my career – I've been in tabloid newspapers since I left local newspapers – I felt quite ashamed not only to work for the *News of the World,* but to work for a tabloid paper and actually started to think about changing career. [Readers] were all ringing in and Twitter was going into meltdown calling us scumbags . . .'[3] Subscribers complained about the lack of prominence given to the story by that morning's *Times*, which responded by making it its online lead. The *Sun* disabled the comment section of its website after it was deluged with complaints.

In an email to all News International staff, Brooks sought to steady nerves. The previous week she had warned that cost-cutting would lead to redundancies; now she had to confront the new 'allegations', which had left her 'sickened'. She wrote: 'Not just because I was editor of the *News of the World* at the time, but because if the allegations are true, the devastating effect on Milly Dowler's family is unforgivable.' She explained that NI's executives had no knowledge of the work of Mulcaire, whom she described as 'a freelance inquiry agent'. 'I am aware of the speculation about my position,' she added. 'Therefore it is important for you to know that as chief executive, I am determined to lead the company to ensure we do the right thing and resolve these serious issues.' At a lunch with advertisers in London, *The Times*' editor James Harding said that, 'if true', the 'allegations' – which no one had denied – were disgusting, and that his paper would report the story accurately.*[4]

Answers were demanded from individuals and institutions. Outside his home in Sutton, south London, Glenn Mulcaire made a statement. 'I want to apologize to anybody who was hurt or upset by what I have done,' he said. 'I've been to court, pleaded guilty. And I've gone to prison and been punished. I still face the possibility of further criminal prosecution. Working for the *News of the World* was never easy. There was relentless pressure. There was a constant demand for results. I knew what we did pushed the limits ethically. But, at the time, I didn't understand I'd broken the law at all.' To the incredulity of some, he appealed for the media to respect the privacy of his wife and children.

On the BBC TV show *Daily Politics* at midday on 5 July, presented by Andrew Neil, the Press Complaints Commission's chair, Peta Buscombe, finally grasped how seriously she had been misled by the

---

* *The Times* columnist David Aaranovitch would later admit: 'If we had been covering it in any other public body we would have been down on those people [News International executives] like a ton of bricks ... Our dark cousins in the tabloids are the people by and large the people who have subsidized [us] and that does create some really awkward problems for an editor at *The Times* if he wants to lam into his colleagues at the *News of the World*, when he knows that some of the money that the *News of the World* has made in profit actually funds the journalism at *The Times* ...'[5]

country's biggest newspaper group: she was furious. 'We personally, and the PCC, are so angry because clearly we were misled . . . There's only so much we can do when people are lying to us,' she said. The BBC's political editor and former Sky News journalist, Nick Robinson, who had seldom covered the controversy up to this point, suddenly decided it was worth reporting. He blogged that while the hacking story had previously united those hostile to the Murdoch empire and those angered by its switch to the Conservatives, 'now Murdoch, Brooks and Cameron will be aware that for the first time the hacking story may be engaging and horrifying readers'.

In the Commons, Labour MPs began agitating for action. Chris Bryant applied for an emergency Commons debate using Standing Order 24, an obscure parliamentary device. Labour MPs supported the move and the Speaker granted a three-hour debate for the following day into whether the government should hold a public inquiry. In the Lords, the government did not accede to one, but softened its opposition. (In a masterpiece of Whitehall speak, the Home Office minister Baroness Browning said: 'If the allegations were found to be true there will need to be new avenues to explore.') At Deputy Prime Minister's Questions, Nick Clegg described the hacking of Milly Dowler's phone as 'grotesque': 'If these allegations are true,' he said, 'they are simply beneath contempt.' He, too, rejected a public inquiry.

Events now crashed down upon each other every few minutes, panicking the institutions of national life. For years, Scotland Yard had stubbornly refused to inspect the evidence, dismissed any suggestion that its inquiry had failed and frustrated the attempts of individuals to discover whether they had been victims of crime. Now its Commissioner, Sir Paul Stephenson – who the previous week had said he would rather his officers were investigating burglaries than phone hacking – was shocked by the same evidence:

> My heart goes out to the Dowler family. Whose heart wouldn't with the additional distress this must have caused them? I have to be very careful to say nothing that could prejudice our live investigation but if it proved to be true, then irrespective of the legality or illegality of it, I'm not sure there is anyone who wouldn't be appalled and repulsed by such behaviour.[6]

Other equally ghastly 'new' cases began to be verified. Shortly after 4 p.m., Cambridgeshire Police confirmed what campaigners had known for months – that Glenn Mulcaire had targeted the parents of the Soham children.

Rupert Murdoch had failed to understand the dramatic arrival of new media; now his *News of the World*, one of Britain's oldest newspapers, was about to discover the protest power of an electronic age which could unite hitherto disparate individuals in a common cause, in a short space of time with devastating effect. Campaigners realized that hitting the tycoon in the pocket was likely to be the most effective tactic. At least five Facebook pages sprung up with titles such as 'Boycott the *News of the World*' and 'Dear NOTW, Millie Dowler is the Final Straw' and on Twitter, campaigners urged advertisers to shun the paper. Caitlin Moran, *The Times* columnist, advised her 100,000 followers to support a reader and advertiser boycott.

A media buying agency, Starcom MediaVest agency, advised clients to avoid that Sunday's *News of the World*, and hinted that the trouble could spread to the *Sun*. Ford, the US car giant responsible for about 10 per cent of the *News of the World*'s annual advertising revenue, pulled its advertisements from the title, saying it cared about the behaviour of its partners. Bombarded with protests following Ford's decision, Currys, Npower, Halifax, T-Mobile and Renault began to review their accounts. Tesco said that while the allegations were distressing, it would await the results of the police investigation before acting. Advertisers who failed to heed the public anger were warned; one disgruntled shopper who lived close to the Dowlers told Tesco: 'You will find that your sales in this area will be hit in the next couple of weeks.'[7]

One of the difficulties for Wapping was that Rebekah Brooks was heading the company's investigation into its behaviour towards Milly Dowler. Hugh Grant compared the situation to allowing Hitler 'to clean up the Nazi party'.[8] Wapping's spokesman, Simon Greenberg, struggled to explain the anomaly. On *Channel 4 News*, when Jon Snow asked: 'How can she investigate herself?', Greenberg responded: 'When we have got to the facts we will be able to establish exactly how that will be possible.' Alastair Campbell, Labour's former communications director, described Greenberg's media appearances as 'car crash interviews'.[9]

As the outlook for Brooks grew ever grimmer, the BBC's Robert Peston popped up again to pitch the news in a different direction. On the BBC *Ten O'Clock News* that night, 5 July, he disclosed that News International had passed evidence of police corruption at the *NoW* between 2003 and 2007 – during Andy Coulson's editorship – to Scotland Yard. Peston's story helped to deflect attention away from Rebekah Brooks and on to Coulson, but it failed to mention that the company had actually had the emails since retrieving them from Harbottle & Lewis on 1 April and had handed them to police two weeks beforehand, on 20 June.

Another BBC programme, *Newsnight*, devoted itself to phone hacking night after night. Paul McMullan, the former *News of the World* features executive, began to appear on the show regularly, wearing a crumpled cream suit and surprising viewers with his insouciance. That evening as presenter Jeremy Paxman looked on aghast, McMullan suggested that phone hacking was commonplace: 'When they first said it's just a rogue reporter, I thought that's so unfair, what about all the legitimate investigations that we've done, where we've had to go into these grey areas and do these things, surely you should be protecting us by saying: "Yes, sometimes we have to do these things" rather than "It's just one person and we didn't know anything about it."' The paper was ruthless, he explained: 'You're only as good as your next story, and they used to do a byline count every year and if you didn't have enough bylines in the paper it was goodbye.' Asked whether he could ever have imagined listening to Milly Dowler's voicemail messages, he replied:

> Yes. I thought about that today and initially the first time someone asked me, I thought: I've always been really proud to be a *News of the World* reporter, the biggest circulating English language newspaper in the world, but suddenly I felt a bit shamed because of what the parents had gone through. But in reality I've been thinking about it, taking a step back, and it's not such a big deal. I was talking to someone from Kenya earlier today who said: 'Well, you know, the journalists may have helped' if they had a little bit of extra information ... but I shouldn't be trying to defend the indefensible because it's not going to be a very popular position.

News International journalists became concerned that McMullan might not be representing their views very attractively.

Wednesday 6 July offered no respite for the Murdochs. Hacking stories dominated the newspapers, though Wapping's papers were still minimizing the story. *The Times* splashed on an item about judges being old and white, running a single column down its front page on police corruption: 'Hacking: Coulson authorized payments to police for stories'. The story stated that Rebekah Brooks was 'determined to stay in her job and steer the company through the scandal'. A *Times* leader described phone hacking as 'beyond reprehensible', adding: 'This is why it is so important that the truth be known.' The *Daily Mirror*, *Daily Mail* and *Daily Express* ran front-page pictures of the Soham girls. The *Guardian* and *Telegraph* splashed that detectives were urgently checking whether there was further evidence about high-profile murders and abductions in Mulcaire's notes and were contacting victims of the 7/7 terrorist attacks in London in 2005. Only the *Sun* left the story off the front, writing on page 6: 'Former *News of the World* editor Rebekah Brooks yesterday said she was "sickened" by allegations that a private eye hired by the paper hacked tragic Milly Dowler's phone.'*

As they raced to contact other victims of crimes, Scotland Yard had informed Graham Foulkes, whose 22-year-old son died in the Edgware Road bombing in July 2005, of evidence that his phone had been hacked. He told the *Today* programme's 7 million listeners: 'The thought that these guys may have been listening to that is just horrendous. It kind of fills you with horror really because we were in a very dark place, and you think that it's about as dark as it can get, and then you realize that there's somebody out there that can make it even darker.'

As public revulsion spread, 60,000 people signed a petition set up by the online campaigning organization Avaaz calling for a halt to the

---

* That morning, the BBC's Nick Robinson reported that News International executives believed they had uncovered which *News of the World* journalist had sanctioned the hacking of Milly Dowler's phone – and that it was not Rebekah Brooks. Although News International claimed to have had no sight of the Mulcaire material, its internal investigation had now apparently found evidence of wrongdoing which cleared its chief executive, who was leading the investigation.

BSkyB deal. Attention was now focused firmly not just on the *News of the World*, but on the wider commercial ambitions of News Corp. On the Liberal Conspiracy blog, Sunny Hundal called for readers to pressurize advertisers to pull out of the *NoW*. Halifax and Lloyds bank did so.

Shortly before midday the Metropolitan Police publicly announced the launch of Operation Elveden – which had actually been under way for two weeks already – to investigate police corruption. Confirming that the force had been passed emails by News International, the Commissioner, Sir Paul Stephenson, said: 'Our initial assessment shows that these documents include information relating to alleged inappropriate payments to a small number of MPS officers...' He assured the public that the inquiry would be as 'thorough and robust' as Operation Weeting.

At its daily briefing for political journalists, Downing Street said that David Cameron stood by his statement on Coulson's resignation in January when he had praised his director of communications. But he was about to do a U-turn on a public inquiry. In the Commons at midday, a hush descended as the Prime Minister told Ed Miliband: 'Yes, we do need to have an inquiry – possibly inquiries – into what has happened. We are no longer talking about politicians and celebrities; we are talking about murder victims – potentially terrorist victims – having their phones hacked into. What has taken place is absolutely disgusting...'

Cameron would not commit himself to a judge-led inquiry, nor say that it would be able to compel witnesses to give evidence on oath. He also resisted attempts to halt the BSkyB bid. Miliband, whose own communications director had insisted in March that the takeover was totally separate from phone hacking, pressed: 'The Prime Minister must realize that the public will react with disbelief if next week the decision is taken to go ahead with this deal at a time when News International is subject to a major criminal investigation and we do not yet know who charges will be laid against.' Cameron insisted that criminality in the newspaper group which had supported him and the commercial ambitions of its owner were separate: 'One is an issue about morality and ethics and a police investigation that needs to be carried out in the proper way, the other is an issue about plurality and competition which has to act within the law.' He declined to call for Rebekah Brooks's resignation.

Launching his emergency debate at 1.42 p.m. with references to the cases of Milly Dowler and 7/7 victims, Chris Bryant told MPs: 'These are not just the amoral actions of some lone private investigator tied to a rogue *News of the World* reporter; they are the immoral and almost certainly criminal deeds of an organization that was appallingly led and had completely lost sight of any idea of decency or shared humanity.' Frank Dobson, the former Health Secretary, remarked that News International's record of wrongdoing would bar it from getting a mini-cab licence. The Conservative MP Zac Goldsmith, whose sister Jemima Khan had been hacked by the *NoW*, said: 'Rupert Murdoch is clearly a very talented businessman and possibly even a genius, but his organization has grown too powerful and it has abused its power. It has systematically corrupted the police and in my view has gelded this Parliament, to our shame.'

Shortly after 2 p.m. that day, Ofcom, the organization which in his MacTaggart lecture in 2009 James Murdoch wanted to neuter, pointed out its duty to be satisfied that the holder of a broadcasting licence was 'fit and proper', adding that it was closely monitoring developments. In early trading in New York, News Corp shares fell by 3.3 per cent to $17.56. More advertisers fled: Aldi, Co-op, Renault, Vauxhall, Virgin Holidays and Mitsubishi (which that evening described the allegations as 'unbelievable, unspeakable and despicable'), all announced they would not advertise in the *Screws*. Other blue-chip advertisers including Procter & Gamble, Coca-Cola, Vodafone and the supermarkets Asda and Sainsbury were urgently reviewing their plans. It was turning into a commercial rout.

Soon after 3 p.m. on 6 July, inside Wapping, the *News of the World*'s editor, Colin Myler, told shell-shocked staff he was 'appalled' by the allegations, but assured them that their newspaper was not the same as the one in the headlines. Staff at all titles felt under attack. 'There were some people who were not just disgusted by the *News of the World* but wanted to express that anger in any way they could,' *The Times* editor James Harding said later. 'We saw small numbers of people cancelling their print subscriptions.' The *Times* was estimated to have lost 20,000. *The Times* journalist Giles Coren tweeted that he had been criticized in a butcher's shop, merely for working for News International.

At 4.30 p.m., as the public and businesses were swinging violently against the *NoW*, Rupert Murdoch made his first public statement since the story had broken forty-eight hours previously, saying that 'Recent allegations of phone hacking and making payments to police with respect to the *News of the World* are deplorable and unacceptable.' He announced that his faithful board member, Joel Klein, and an independent director, Viet Dinh, would manage its response. Worried about the damage to its reputation, and the possibility that the contagion could spread to its other businesses, News Corp had begun to take control of News International. Murdoch said: 'I have made clear that our company must fully and proactively cooperate with the police in all investigations and that is exactly what News International has been doing and will continue to do under Rebekah Brooks's leadership.' For now, therefore, Brooks remained in charge. The media commentator Roy Greenslade described the statement as further proof that his old boss Murdoch had 'lost his marbles', blogging: 'He has allowed himself to be seduced by Brooks's formidable charms. I cannot imagine him doing anything like this when at the height of his powers.'[10]

Another Wapping favourite, the mayor of London, Boris Johnson, demanded the Independent Police Complaints Commission oversee the Met's inquiry into the bribery allegations. Under Johnson's watch, Scotland Yard had failed to re-investigate hacking properly, and in September 2010 he had dismissed the scandal as 'codswallop'. Now, he said: 'If some police officers were indeed paid as part of this process, there is only one word for this, corruption. It doesn't matter that this happened many years ago, under a different commissioner and indeed mayoralty.'[11]

As detectives redoubled their efforts to inform prominent victims, they visited George Osborne, whose name and home phone number had appeared in Mulcaire's notes. The Chancellor of the Exchequer – who was thought to have been targeted around the time the *News of the World* was hacking 'Mistress Pain' Natalie Rowe's phone – did not wish to make a fuss about the news. His spokesman said there was no evidence to suggest his voicemail had actually been hacked, and that he was very grateful to the police: 'Frankly he thinks there are far more serious allegations surrounding the whole hacking affair and fully supports the police in their investigations.'

By coincidence, that evening had been scheduled for the launch in the House of Lords of a campaign for a public inquiry into the scandal, which was backed by John Pilger, the Australian journalist, Brian Cathcart, professor of journalism at Kingston University, the lawyer Charlotte Harris and Lord Fowler. Hugh Grant, the best-known supporter of 'Hacked Off', gave media interviews on College Green opposite Parliament denouncing Murdoch. In an interview earlier on Wednesday with the American broadcaster CBS, he said: 'This is a watershed moment when, finally, the public starts to see and feel, above all, just how low and disgusting this particular newspaper's methods were. And what will emerge shortly is that it wasn't just this newspaper.' BSkyB shares fell 18p to 827p, while in the US, News Corp stock tumbled by 3.6 per cent.

On Thursday 7 July, the *Independent* splashed on 'Murdoch empire in crisis' and the *Guardian* 'The day the prime minister was forced to act on phone hacking'. The *Daily Telegraph* and *Daily Mail* splashed on suspicions that the *NoW* had eavesdropped the phone messages of the families of soldiers killed in Iraq and Afghanistan. Rose Gentle, whose son Fusilier Gordon Gentle was killed in Iraq in 2004, described the possibility that her messages had been hacked as 'a living nightmare'. The potential targeting of soldiers' families was particularly embarrassing for News International, whose *Sun* vigorously supported the British Army and championed the cause of rank and file soldiers in award-winning campaigns. Wapping said in a statement: 'News International's record as a friend of the armed services and of our servicemen and servicewomen is impeccable. If these allegations are true, we are absolutely appalled and horrified.' The Royal British Legion dropped the *News of the World* as its partner for the 'Justice for the Brave' campaign, and began reviewing its advertising with News International, saying it had been 'shocked to the core' by the disclosures, which had affected hundreds of families.

The Times sought to focus attention on the police: 'Parliament puts press and police in the dock over hacking scandal'. The *Sun* found space on its front page for a twenty-three-word story by its political editor Tom Newton Dunn, which read: 'PM David Cameron ordered a public inquiry into newspaper phone hacking yesterday. He said illegal practices by ALL British media must be tackled.'

Despite Wapping's best efforts, the story was out of control – and becoming increasingly serious for David Cameron. His friendliness with Brooks and Murdoch was criticized by usually supportive figures. Douglas Carswell, the Tory MP for Clacton-on-Sea, tweeted: '"I don't think Maggie Thatcher would employ someone like that Andy Coulson", remarked my constituent. Me neither.' The *Telegraph*'s Peter Oborne, who had presented a Channel 4 *Dispatches* programme on phone hacking in October, said that like John Major in 1992 after Britain was forced to drop out of the Exchange Rate Mechanism, the Prime Minister faced a crisis from which he might never recover.

At 8.30 a.m., Ed Miliband described his disgust at the hacking of the families of dead soldiers, saying: 'It is grotesque beyond belief that these actions are alleged to have been committed on behalf of a news organization committed to the military covenant.' Politicians had 'lessons to learn' about their relationships with Rupert Murdoch, he added, renewing his call for Brooks to quit. 'The only people in the world who seem to think that Rebekah Brooks should carry on in her position are Rupert Murdoch and David Cameron.'

The government's enthusiasm for the BSkyB bid was waning. At 11.37 a.m., Labour's leader in the Lords, Lady Royall, demanded its suspension because of the loss of public and commercial confidence in News International. A government whip, Lady Rawlings, said that Jeremy Hunt was satisfied there were 'sufficient safeguards' to protect Sky News' independence, but added he would need time to respond to the public consultation. 'The Secretary of State will not be rushed, he will be fair,' she said, indicating for the first time that a judge would preside over the public inquiry. The government was not changing its mind about the BSkyB bid but was, seemingly, delaying the timetable.

A few newsagents stopped selling the *News of the World*. Nav Aggarwal, owner of five convenience stores in East Anglia, said he acted because one of his shops, at Ely station, was close to Soham. A Budgens franchise operator, Andrew Thornton, who banned the paper from his two stores in north London, said: 'Their actions have affected people in our community and communities around the country and there must be consequences for the complete lack of morality that seems to be part of the paper's culture.' In morning trading, BSkyB shares fell again, to 805p. Shortly before 11 a.m., the first of the big supermarkets, the lifeblood of national newspaper advertising, pulled out of the *Screws*: Sainsbury's would not advertise with the title until the end of the police investigation 'due to the rising concerns of our customers'. Asda and Boots shortly followed.*

Shortly before 2 p.m., the BBC's Robert Peston tweeted that the government had received 100,000 submissions to the consultation on News Corp's bid, adding – apparently with inside information from the Department of Culture, Media and Sport – 'Culture Sec won't give final decision on bid till Sept at earliest.'

Scotland Yard announced that to allay 'significant public and political concern', the Independent Police Complaints Commission would indeed oversee its corruption inquiry. Sue Akers explained why it was taking the Met so long to notify all the victims: there were simply so many of them. 'We are going through approximately 11,000 pages of material containing almost 4,000 names. In addition, we have been contacted by hundreds of people who believe that they may have been affected.'

---

* With the story at fever pitch and demands for interviews from newspapers in China and TV stations in India, Tom Watson travelled by train to Scotland for an afternoon press conference with Tommy Sheridan's lawyer Aamer Anwar. Before it took place, the Crown Office in Scotland announced: 'In light of emerging developments regarding the *News of the World*, the Crown has requested Strathclyde Police to investigate the evidence given by certain witnesses in the trial of Tommy Sheridan.' News International was now at the centre of four police inquiries: detectives were investigating whether its executives had perjured themselves. In Glasgow, Watson and Anwar announced they were handing a dossier of information to Strathclyde Police containing the *News of the World*'s orders to Steve Whittamore, extracts from Glenn Mulcaire's notes and transcripts of evidence from executives at his trial. Watson said the concealment of emails could have influenced the jury, and told reporters: 'Tommy Sheridan may be an innocent man.'

The *Evening Standard* hit London's streets with further details of News International's corruption of the city's police force. Officers in sensitive positions with access to confidential information had received more than £100,000 in bribes from journalists. One unidentified source was quoted as saying: 'They were running a criminal enterprise at the *News of the World*. Serious crimes have been found.' *News of the World* columnists began to notice the public mood. The comedian Dave Gorman quit his column and the personal finance writer Martin Lewis – the cousin of the lawyer Mark Lewis – cancelled his column that week. The *Match of the Day* presenter Gary Lineker privately considered whether to continue writing for the paper. One well-known *News of the World* journalist sought to calm the furore by repeating Colin Myler's point about the change of staff at the paper. While 'sickened' by the stories about the 'alleged hacking' of Milly Dowler, the showbiz editor Dan Wooton blogged to readers: 'What I have to stress to you is this: I do NOT work for the newspaper you are reading about.'

Shortly after 4 p.m., *News of the World* staff were called to a meeting with Rebekah Brooks. The last time such a big meeting had been called Andy Coulson had resigned: was Brooks about to go?

Staff on other titles were reading a 968-word email from James Murdoch. It started slowly. The *News of the World* was 168 years old, read by more people than any other English language newspaper and had a proud history of fighting crime, exposing wrongdoing and regularly setting the news agenda – but, sadly, it had failed to hold itself to account. Murdoch wrote:

> Wrongdoers turned a good newsroom bad and this was not fully understood or adequately pursued. As a result, the *News of the World* and News International wrongly maintained that these issues were confined to one reporter. We now have voluntarily given evidence to the police that I believe will prove that this was untrue and those who acted wrongly will have to face the consequences.
>
> This was not the only fault. The paper had made statements to Parliament without being in the full possession of the facts. This was wrong.

The company paid out-of-court settlements approved by me.
I now know that I did not have a complete picture when I did so.
This was wrong and is a matter of serious regret.

Humiliatingly, James Murdoch was finally admitting that the firm he chaired had misled Parliament. But he was careful to say that he had not known about the extent of the wrongdoing when he authorized the hush payments to Gordon Taylor (and unspecified others). At this stage, the internal documents detailing his involvement with the settlements had not been released.

Murdoch outlined the action he was taking to resolve the problems: NI was cooperating with the police, had admitted liability in civil cases, set up the Management and Standards Committee and a compensation scheme, and hired Olswang solicitors to examine past failings and recommend new systems and practices. Finally, he got to the big news. 'Having consulted senior colleagues, I have decided that we must take further decisive action with respect to the paper. This Sunday will be the last issue of the *News of the World*. Colin Myler will edit the final edition of the paper.'

This was a bombshell: the UK's top-selling Sunday newspaper was to close. All revenue from its final edition that Sunday would go to good causes. The company hoped to find jobs for many of the paper's 250 staff. Murdoch added: 'I can understand how unfair these decisions may feel. Particularly, for colleagues who will leave the company.'

One of the first journalists in *The Times* to get to the end of the email exclaimed: 'Fucking hell!'

In the *Screws* newsroom – where the IT department had disabled email and the Internet – staff were still listening to Rebekah Brooks. After rambling for several minutes, she suddenly announced the closure of the paper. She offered to take questions, but Colin Myler said: 'No, Rebekah, I think it's best if you leave the floor.'

The journalists were dazed. They headed for the pub, along with a contingent of *Sun* sub-editors. The *News of the World,* which was as British as fish and chips and which George Orwell had written about, was about to disappear.

As reporters left Wapping's gates, some were interviewed on live TV, their fate still hanging in the balance. Publicly, they seemed more disappointed than angry. Features editor Jules Stenson said staff showed 'quiet pride' when the announcement was made. 'There was shock, bewilderment, there were a few gasps, there were lots of tears from the staff. It's been reported that there was a lynch mob mentality which is completely untrue; there was none of that.'

Observers started to wonder whether the closure was a cosmetic move. Shortly before the Milly Dowler story had broken, News International had appointed a single managing editor to run both its redtops, increasing speculation that it would integrate the two papers. Would a *Sun on Sunday* soon roll off the presses? Speaking at the première of a new Harry Potter movie, the TV presenter Jonathan Ross said: 'Clearly this is a cynical move, clearly it is an excuse to carry on.' The National Union of Journalists described the decision as 'an act of damage limitation to salvage Murdoch's reputation and that of News International – both of which are now tarnished beyond repair'. On the BBC's *Question Time* that night, 7 July, Hugh Grant said:

> Clearly the *News of the World* was going out of business anyway. People were not going to buy it on Sunday, advertisers were falling out in their droves – and all credit to them . . . I think we should see this for what it is: it is a very cynical managerial manoeuvre which has put several hundred not evil people (there were certainly a lot of evil people), but certainly non-editorial staff, out of work and has kept in particular one person who was the editor when Milly Dowler was hacked in a highly paid job.

He was loudly applauded. Some weeks later, he said: 'That night a girlfriend of mine had a call, an anonymous call, first on her mobile and then on her home phone. She finally picked it up and it said: "Tell Hugh Grant to shut the fuck up".'[12]

The *NoW*'s closure made the front pages of *Le Monde* in France, *Bild* and *Die Welt* in Germany, *El País* in Spain and the *New York Times*. In Britain, the *Sun* splashed on 'World's End' and the *Daily Telegraph* 'Goodbye, Cruel World'. Quoting the words of an anonymous *News of the World* staffer, the *Independent* had: 'Newspaper "sacrificed to save one woman"'.

Rupert Murdoch's line had changed, again. For five years News

International had insisted there was only one rogue reporter, then only a few rogue reporters. Now it admitted it had been running a rogue newspaper. Murdoch was still not willing to concede, as many people believed, that News International had a rogue chief executive. Increasingly, the British public were beginning to wonder whether it was a rogue corporation.

16

Sky Plus

I'm not throwing innocent people under the bus
— Rupert Murdoch

If the world's wiliest newspaper proprietor thought changing the defence from one rogue reporter to one rogue newspaper would shut down the hacking scandal and salvage his reputation, he had failed to understand just how disarrayed News Corp and many British institutions had found themselves after the Milly Dowler story. The spasm of outrage that convulsed British public life at that moment had shaken an establishment previously too conflicted or too cowed to keep Murdoch and his newspapers in check. Politicians, media, police and prosecutors all knew they had failed to speak out or act when they should have done, and now, to assert themselves at last, they came to their own conclusion – rather than Rupert Murdoch's – as to what must be done.

Startlingly, a wave of openness spread over politics. On Friday 8 July, political leaders who had accepted Murdoch's power as a given began admitting he was too dominant. At a speech at Reuters' London headquarters that morning, Ed Miliband, the Labour leader, said: 'If one section of the media is allowed to grow so powerful that it becomes insulated from political criticism and scrutiny of its behaviour, the proper system of checks and balances breaks down and abuses of power are likely to follow. We must all bear responsibility for that.'

At a press conference in Downing Street an hour later, David Cameron agreed that politicians had become too close to media proprietors, adding: 'It is on my watch that the music has stopped.' Coolly and clinically, he cut his close friend Rebekah Brooks adrift, saying that if she had offered him her resignation he 'would have taken it'. The message to Rupert Murdoch was finally: Brooks must go. For the first time, Cameron confirmed that the public inquiry would be presided over by a judge and suggested the abolition of the Press Complaints Commission, for two decades the newspaper regulator. As to Andy Coulson, the Prime Minister said, no one had given him 'specific information' about his director of communications, but he would check if any warnings had been given to his staff. He declined to apologize for hiring Coulson – to whom his gratitude evidently ran deep: 'He became a friend and is a friend.' He said he had been in contact with Coulson but 'not in recent weeks'. The performance of the PR-executive-turned-PM had been assured; he had almost caught up with the public mood. His press conference concluded at 10.23 a.m.

By 10.30 a.m. his friend Andy Coulson was in police custody at Lewisham station in south London, held on suspicion of conspiring to hack phones and corrupting police. Plain-clothes detectives searched his home in Dulwich, south London, and seized a computer. Seven months before he had been the Prime Minister's most highly paid member of staff and helped him run the country.

Clive Goodman, too, had been arrested at his home in Surrey on suspicion of police corruption, four and a half years after his jailing for phone hacking. Police raided the offices of the newspaper where he had been working, Richard Desmond's *Daily Star Sunday*, leaving after two hours with a disc of Goodman's computer activity.

In the City, analysts began to downgrade the likelihood of the BSkyB deal going through. At the stockbrokers Panmure Gordon, Alex DeGroote told his clients there had previously been 90 per cent plus chance, but now it was no better than 50-50. BSkyB shares fell by 4.8 per cent. (They continued their slide throughout 8 July, closing down 8 per cent at 750p. Over the week, BSkyB shed 11.7 per cent of its value – £1.8 billion.)

Tony Blair, who had always maintained a close relationship with Rupert Murdoch, described phone hacking as 'beyond disgusting'. Addressing the centre-left Progress pressure group in London at lunchtime on 8 July, he sought to widen the scandal beyond Murdoch's newspaper group. He said: 'I think David Cameron and Ed Miliband are right to say this is not just about News International. It's not just about phone hacking.' He reminded the audience of his 'feral beasts' speech in 2007 when he criticized the demands of a 24-hour media ('a vast aspect of our jobs ... is coping with the media, its sheer scale, weight and constant hyperactivity') and its tendency to confuse news and comment – exemplified, he said, by the *Independent,* the only newspaper he singled out for criticism.

At 2.30 p.m. on the *Guardian* website, Nick Davies reported that police were investigating whether a News International executive had deleted emails from an internal archive in an apparent attempt to obstruct Scotland Yard's new inquiry. The unnamed executive had deleted 'massive quantities' of the archive on two occasions, most recently in late January – around the time the Metropolitan Police had opened its new investigation. There was now a fresh question mark over News International's assurance to the Information Commissioner that its data was fully intact.

At 4 p.m., *News of the World* journalists were called to another meeting with Rebekah Brooks. Speculation grew that, this time, she would resign. As News International's IT department again suspended internal email and the Internet, Brooks explained that the paper was closing because advertisers said it had become a 'toxic' brand. Ominously, she told staff: 'In a year's time it'll become apparent why we did this.' A journalist complained: 'We're all being contaminated by that toxicity by the way we're being treated,' adding – to applause – 'Do you think we'd want to work for you again?' Brooks soothed: 'There's not an arrogance about anyone wanting to work for us at all ... Sorry if that came across ... We haven't made the decision on any new publications or strengthening or expanding existing media, it's just too soon.' She revealed she was being removed from the internal Management and Standards Committee investigating the scandal. The MSC would now comprise Wapping's general manager Will Lewis, its director of communications Simon Greenberg and News Corp's general counsel in Europe Jeff Palker, reporting to Joel Klein in New York – who in turn reported to Viet Dinh, chairman of News Corp's Corporate Governance Committee. News Corp had taken complete charge of its wayward British subsidiary.

That night the comedian Steve Coogan came face to face with one of the tabloid journalists he despised during a studio discussion on *Newsnight*. He told Paul McMullan (still defending the *News of the World*): 'I think you are a walking PR disaster for the tabloids because you don't come across in a sympathetic way. You come across as a risible individual.' Coogan was thrilled at the closure of the *Screws*, which he described as 'an asylum-seeker hating newspaper'. The clip became a hit on YouTube.

On Saturday 9 July, most newspapers splashed on hacking. Throughout the day commentators sought to put the extraordinary events of the previous week into context. Like his former political master, Alastair Campbell sought to implicate other papers, saying the *Daily Mail*'s editor Paul Dacre could soon be under pressure. Campbell blogged:

> The *Mail* was the biggest user of Mr Whittamore.* When police investigating a murder trial involving Mr Rees raided his home, they found invoices totalling thousands and thousands of pounds relating to inquiries into many public figures for many different papers. The inquiries on me, for example, were made by my former paper, the *Mirror*. As for Glenn Mulcaire, well we know a lot about him, but there is a lot more to come. So Mr Dacre and his Mail Group, whose coverage of the phone hacking scandal has been minimal until recent days – wonder why? – will be an important part of any serious and rigorous inquiry.'[1]

In his later evidence at the Leveson Inquiry in February 2012, Paul Dacre denied that the Mail group had ever hacked phones. Writing for *Newsweek*, the Watergate journalist Carl Bernstein argued that the phone hacking scandal should have come as a surprise only to those who had ignored Murdoch's 'pernicious influence on journalism'. He wrote: 'Too many of us have winked in amusement at the salaciousness without considering the larger corruption of journalism and politics promulgated by Murdoch Culture on both sides of the Atlantic. As one of his former top executives – once a close aide – told me, "This scandal and all its implications could not have happened

---

* Although the Whittamore files reveal multiple breaches of data protection laws, there is no evidence that he hacked phones.

anywhere else. Only in Murdoch's orbit. The hacking at *News of the World* was done on an industrial scale. More than anyone, Murdoch invented and established this culture in the newsroom, where you do whatever it takes to get the story, take no prisoners, destroy the competition, and the end will justify the means".'[2]

Saturday was the last day of a conference for media magnates in Sun Valley, Idaho, which Rupert Murdoch had been reluctant to leave. He seemed oblivious to the anger in the country he had called home for many years and whose cash-generating newspapers funded his global expansion. Asked by reporters whether he would change his management team, he replied: 'Nothing's changed. We've been let down by people that we trusted, with the result the paper let down its readers.' Rebekah Brooks, his protégée, enjoyed his 'total' support: 'I'm not throwing innocent people under the bus.'[3]

As the *News of the World*'s staff prepared the final edition of the paper, Andy Coulson – released the previous day from eight hours in police custody – shared his view that it was 'a very sad day for the *News of the World*'. 'More importantly to the staff who, in my mind, are brilliant, professional people and I really feel for them.'

News International doubled the final print run to 5 million. While many readers would buy the *Screws*' swansong out of habit or curiosity, for others it had become so tarnished that they did not accept the offer of charity from its farewell. Oxfam, the RNLI, RSPCA, Action Aid, Salvation Army and many other charities refused. Paul McNamara, the paper's defence correspondent, had to make fifty calls before three would agree to take any money: Barnardos, the Forces Children's Trust and military projects at the Queen Elizabeth Hospital Birmingham Charity. He said: 'I had to beg.'[4]

Inside Wapping, according to one *NoW* journalist working his last day, a surreal atmosphere prevailed.

> People can't comprehend it and are still very angry with Rebekah. Staff were called together for a group photograph this morning and everyone was quite jovial, then someone called 'smile' and someone else said 'What have we got to smile about?' Someone shouted; 'Because we are the best'... The phones on the newsdesk have been ringing all week with people shouting the nastiest, most vile abuse, but today people are ringing up giving their support.[5]

Journalists were given framed front pages with the headline: 'Best in the World'. Once the paper was 'off stone', Colin Myler stood on top of a desk and addressed staff. He told them he could not imagine a more difficult day as a journalist, adding: 'It's not a place we wanted to be and absolutely not a place we deserve to be.' In line with Fleet Street tradition (when printers would whack their hammers against metal benches to mark the departure of a colleague), Myler 'banged out' each journalist, clattering a plastic ruler against a desk as they filed out. Shortly before 9 p.m., Myler emerged from the *Screws'* office block clutching its final front page, and – with his staff massed behind him – said to the bank of reporters, snappers and TV crews: 'We're going to do what we should do now and go and have a nice drink – or three.' The following week, News International said that most *News of the World* staff would be 'offered employment opportunities', and that thirty jobs at its colour magazine *Fabulous* would be saved by inserting it into Saturday's *Sun*.

The 8,674th edition of the *News of the World* was headlined: 'Thank You and Goodbye' and the strapline: 'After 168 years, we finally say a sad but very proud farewell to our 7.5 million loyal readers'. The paper was defiant, proud and a little remorseful, saying:

> We praised high standards, we demanded high standards but, as we are now only too painfully aware, for a period of a few years up to 2006 some who worked for us, or in our name, fell shamefully short of those standards.

It trumpeted its successful campaigns on the military covenant, toys for soldiers' children and compensation for 7/7 victims. Mazher Mahmood recalled how he had nailed 'scores of paedophiles, arms dealers, drug peddlers, people traffickers, bent doctors and lawyers'. A forty-eight page pullout celebrated the paper's front pages, including the sinking of the *Titanic*, the Profumo Affair, the Great Train Robbery, the death of Princess Diana and – in its more prurient modern incarnation – 'Chief of Defence Staff in Sex and Security Scandal' and 'Beckham's Secret Affair'. Missing from the pantheon were David Blunkett's affair and Max Mosley's 'Sick Nazi Orgy'.

News International was worried that the paper's departing journalists might insert rude messages into the final edition. Fleet

Street had a history of parting shots: on his last day at the *Daily Express* in 2001 before heading to *The Times*, the first letters of leader writer Stephen Pollard's final column spelled out: 'Fuck You Desmond'. Two *Sun* executives combed through the *NoW*'s last edition. They did a good job of checking the news stories, but less so with the crosswords, whose clues included: brook, stink, catastrophe, pest, less bright, woman stares wildly at calamity, criminal enterprise, string of recordings and mix in prison. Answers included disaster, stench, racket and tart. The answers to 1 across, 4 down, 10 across and 7 down were Tomorrow, We, Are, Sacked.

Roy Greenslade felt that the final *News of the World* had played down its 'villainy'. 'It's a bit rich to claim integrity while working for a paper that has engaged in the dark arts – entrapment, subterfuge, covert filming, the use of agents provocateurs and phone hacking – for the best part of twenty years.'[6]

On Sunday 10 July, the Murdoch empire was under attack unusually from its rivals. The *Mail on Sunday* carried a piece from an anonymous 'News International Insider' claiming that Rebekah Brooks had turned the *Sun* from an 'abrasive, aggressive paper known for breaking big stories' into a title afraid of upsetting politicians, whom she 'love-bombed'. 'She sold the soul of the *Sun* and the *News of the World* to PR snake-oil merchants.' Relationships with PR firms such as Freud Communications – run by Rupert Murdoch's son-in-law Matthew Freud – were so close that 'if they rang the newsdesk with a story, you had to run it'.[7]

Carrying a detailed report on the scandal for the first time, *The Sunday Times* revealed that an 'internal report' in 2007 had uncovered evidence of potential widespread phone hacking and police corruption. The 'report' had not been passed to police at the time, but had been found by Wapping executives in 2011. The *Sunday Times* carefully added that James Murdoch had not been told about the 'report'. In fact, the evidence was not a report but the Harbottle & Lewis file unearthed in March. As revealed by Robert Peston, the file had been passed to Scotland Yard in June, prompting its corruption inquiry.

At Scotland Yard, John Yates finally admitted that he had made a hash of the phone hacking affair. Ahead of a forthcoming appearance before the Home Affairs Committee, he told the *Sunday Telegraph*: 'I regrettably said the initial inquiry was a success. Clearly, now it looks different.' His decision not to reopen the case was a 'pretty crap one', he confessed, and he now wished he had looked at Glenn Mulcaire's notes. 'In hindsight, there is a shed load of stuff in there I wish I'd known. The Milly Dowler stuff is just shocking beyond anything. It's a tipping point and quite rightly so.'[8]

In Westminster, an anti-Murdoch coalition was cohering around a Labour motion in the Commons against the BSkyB bid. The Liberal Democrats, the Conservatives' smaller Coalition partners, were intending to support the symbolic vote the following Wednesday. On Sunday, the first signs emerged that the Conservatives were wobbling when Philip Hammond, the Transport Secretary, said: 'If the motion is sensibly formed that would be one thing, but if it called on the government to ignore the law that would not be possible.'

After five days in which his British news operation itself had dominated the headlines, Rupert Murdoch finally arrived in the UK at eleven that Sunday morning. After landing at Luton airport, he went straight to Wapping, carrying a copy of the final News of the World, then to his flat in St James's. At 5.35 p.m., Rebekah Brooks arrived and, surrounded by reporters and camera crews, they walked to a nearby hotel for a meal with James Murdoch. When asked for his priority, Rupert Murdoch gestured towards Brooks and said: 'This one.' The clip was repeatedly shown on the TV news that evening. Murdoch, the great reader of the public mood, was now clearly out of touch with it.

On Monday 11 July, amid pages devoted to the News of the World's demise, the cover-up and the prospects for the BSkyB bid, the Mirror reported a piece of potentially devastating news: the News of the World might have hacked the phones of victims of the 9/11 terrorist attacks in the US. Based on an anonymous police source, the claim, if true, would be highly damaging to Murdoch's New York-based empire, given the sensitivities of the American public to the worst terrorist attack on US soil.

The BSkyB bid was firing the scandal and focusing attention on the government's close links with the Murdoch empire. More than 300,000 people had now signed the Avaaz petition against the takeover. Finally, the government turned against it, when Jeremy Hunt asked Ofcom to assess whether the *News of the World*'s wrongdoing meant that News Corp's guarantees about the TV network's independence could not be trusted. In a text of the letter to Ofcom's executive director Clive Maxwell, released by the Department of Culture, Media and Sport that morning, Hunt wrote:

> As you are aware, my consultation on the revised undertakings in lieu offered by News Corporation closed on Friday at midday. I am now considering the responses to that consultation, but as I stated on Friday, I anticipate this taking some time.
>
> However, given the well-publicized matters involving the News of the World in the past week, and which have led to the closure of that paper, I should be grateful if you could let me know whether you consider those revelations and allegations cause you to reconsider any part of your previous advice to me, or otherwise give rise to concerns, on the credibility, sustainability and practicalities of the undertakings offered by News Corporation.
>
> Although I anticipate it taking some time in order to consider consultation responses, it would be of assistance if you could let me have your response as swiftly as possible as you are able in order that I can factor this into my thinking.

Hunt and the government had insisted since his letter to Tom Watson in February that Ofcom could not consider News Corp's criminal history when assessing its takeover bid for Britain's most profitable broadcaster. Political expediency had now changed that. Hunt's message to Ofcom was clear: 'Please now give me an excuse to block this takeover.'

After the text of the letter was released, BSkyB shares went into freefall, dropping 7 per cent. Conservative and Liberal Democrat politicians fell in behind the new position against the bid, which was still on the table. John Whittingdale, Tory chairman of the Culture Committee – who had deemed the bid to be an entirely separate issue the previous week – said: 'The best thing would be if it could be put on hold until we have a much clearer idea of who knew what, who was responsible.'[9] Shortly after an emotional fifty-minute meeting with Bob and Sally Dowler in Downing Street, Nick Clegg, the Deputy

Prime Minister, said: 'I would simply say to him [Murdoch]: look how people feel about this; look how the country has reacted with revulsion to the revelations. So do the decent thing and reconsider, think again, about your bid.'

Breaking off from a speech about public service reform in Canary Wharf, east London, at 3.30 p.m. David Cameron confirmed that the government wanted to kill the takeover. He said: 'All I would say is this: if I was running that company right now with all the problems and the difficulties and the mess frankly that there is, I think they should be focused on clearing those up rather than on the next corporate move.'

Murdoch finally got the message. Shortly before 4 p.m., faced with the prospect of an embarrassing Commons vote, News Corp withdrew its commitment to spin off Sky News, forcing the government to refer the bid to the Competition Commission. But though this looked like a major setback, News Corp had actually staged a tactical retreat. An investigation by the Competition Commission would take months, during which time the political row would probably cool. The company might then be able to proceed with the bid. It was still definitely on the table.

At 4.16 p.m. in a Commons statement, Jeremy Hunt duly confirmed he was referring the bid. The minister, who for months had vigorously defended the deal (once only days before the Milly Dowler story broke) explained his motivation:

> Protecting our tradition of a strong, free and independent media is the most sacred responsibility I have as Culture Secretary. Irresponsible, illegal and callous behaviour damages that freedom by weakening public support for the self-regulation on which it has thrived. By dealing decisively with the abuses of power we have seen, hopefully on a cross-party basis, the Government intend to strengthen and not diminish press freedom . . .

Angry MPs were in uproar at his audacity; the Speaker had to call for order.

Referring the bid, however, did not dull the clamour for its death. The Labour Party refused to withdraw its Commons motion, set for two days later, and support for it among Liberal Democrats – whose party had been ignored by Murdoch's newspapers for years – was hardening.

The opposition was bolstered by further reports of the alleged corruption at Wapping. In his latest bulletin from News International that morning, Robert Peston revealed that internal emails appeared to show payments of £1,000 to a royal protection squad officer for the phone numbers of senior members of the royal family, their friends and relatives. He quoted a 'source' inside Wapping as saying: 'There was clear evidence from the emails that the security of the royal family was being put at risk. I was profoundly shocked when I saw them . . .' In total, Peston said, the paper had paid Metropolitan Police officers £130,000 for information. The *Evening Standard* also leaked details of the payments, sending 1 million copies onto the streets of London with a front page reading: 'Queen's Police Sold Her Details to NoW'.

Scotland Yard responded angrily to the leaks, which appeared to come from Wapping. In a three-sentence statement personally authorized by Sir Paul Stephenson, the Met said it believed that information in media stories that day was 'part of a deliberate campaign to undermine the investigation into the alleged payments by corrupt journalists to corrupt police officers' – adding 'and divert attention from elsewhere'. The force said that News International had agreed to keep information confidential so the police could pursue the culprits without alerting them. 'However we are extremely concerned and disappointed that the continuous release of selected information – that is known only by a small number of people – could have a significant impact on the corruption investigation.'

On Tuesday 12 July, at the Home Affairs Committee, senior police officers had to account for their slow progress in bringing Murdoch's hackers to justice. Andy Hayman, the police chief who had joined *The Times*, denied that when he was at the Met there had been any impropriety in his social and professional contacts with NI's executives. Asked whether he had ever received any payment from a news organization while in the police, he cried: 'Good God, absolutely not.' Pulling an astonished face, he added: 'I cannot believe you suggested that.' Keith Vaz, the committee chairman, felt Hayman's performance had been 'more Clouseau than Columbo'. (Hayman later described the committee's treatment of him as 'appalling'. 'To be accused, as I was, of being a dodgy geezer, which is probably on the basis of my accent, I think that's a really poor show.')[10] Peter Clarke, the former Deputy Assistant Commissioner who led the 2006 investigation, accused News International of deliberately thwarting its inquiry. 'If there had been any meaningful cooperation at the time we would not be here today. It is as simple as that,' he said.

In a move unthinkable even a week before, the Culture, Media and Sport Committee called Rupert Murdoch, James Murdoch and Rebekah Brooks to give evidence, the following Tuesday, 19 July. Since buying the *News of the World* in 1969, Rupert Murdoch had appeared before a parliamentary committee only once, at the private session of the Lords Communications Committee in September 2007, when he had confirmed he exercised editorial control over his tabloid newspapers (see Chapter 5). John Whittingdale said that a figure like Murdoch being brought before a Commons select committee was 'unprecedented'. BBC political correspondent Laura Kuenssberg described it as 'something we simply could not have imagined seven days ago – even twenty-four hours ago'. News International declined to confirm that the Murdochs would turn up.

In the US, Rupert Murdoch moved to bolster his personal position, raising News Corp's share buyback programme from $1.8 billion to $5 billion dollars to support its share price.

On Wednesday 13 July, the Commons was braced for an historic day. The Liberal Democrats let it be known that they would vote for the motion against the BSkyB bid, tipping the voting arithmetic away from Murdoch. The Conservatives then announced they would vote with Labour and the Liberal Democrats. Extraordinarily, all three parties were planning to thwart the man who had frightened politicians for decades.

At Prime Minister's Questions, David Cameron acknowledged the scale of the crisis, telling MPs: 'There is a firestorm engulfing parts of our media, parts of our police and even our political system's ability to respond.' He called for 'root and branch change' at News International, adding crucially: 'It has now become increasingly clear that while everybody, to start with, wanted in some way to separate what was happening at News International and what is happening at BSkyB, that is simply not possible. What has happened at this company is disgraceful. It has got to be addressed at every level and they should stop thinking about mergers when they have to sort out the mess they have created.'

He had done a complete U-turn on Brooks, and now on BSkyB. He was pressed by Ed Miliband to explain what had happened to the warnings passed to his chief of staff about Andy Coulson. Cameron responded: 'All these questions relate to the fact that I hired a tabloid editor. I did so on the basis of assurances he gave me that he did not know about phone hacking and was not involved in criminality. He gave those self-same assurances to the police and to a select committee and under oath to a court of law.' Cameron – who only five days earlier had described Andy Coulson as a friend – added: 'If it turns out he lied, then it will not just be that he shouldn't have been in government, it will be that he should be prosecuted . . . . But I can say that I did not receive that information.' The Prime Minister was, in effect, blaming his staff for not passing on the *Guardian*'s warnings about Coulson's employment of Jonathan Rees.

Faced with the prospect of all three main parties voting, albeit symbolically, against the takeover, News Corp finally withdrew it. Rupert Murdoch left the announcement to his deputy, Chase Carey, who said: 'We believed that the proposed acquisition of BSkyB by News Corporation would benefit both companies, but it has become clear that it is too difficult to progress in this climate.' The aborted takeover had cost £40 million in fees alone. Quoting News Corp sources, Sky's business editor Mark Kleinman reported that on the conclusion of the phone hacking inquiries, the company could revive the bid. Under cover of the announcement, News International slipped out the news that Tom Crone, the *News of the World*'s director of legal affairs who in July 2009 had told the Culture Committee there was 'no evidence' that more than one journalist had used Glenn Mulcaire, had left the company.

The Commons debate still went ahead. Gordon Brown made a spectacularly angry contribution. Two days earlier, on Monday morning, the former Prime Minister had recorded an interview with the BBC's Glenn Campbell in which he had complained about two

News International stories. In 2000 *The Sunday Times* had used subterfuge to obtain an 'unfounded' story that he had bought a London flat from the administrators of a collapsed firm of the disgraced newspaper proprietor Robert Maxwell, for a 'knock-down price'. Criminals acting for *The Sunday Times*, Brown said, had successfully blagged details of his bank account from Abbey National, which had written to him to explain that it had been the target of 'a well-orchestrated campaign of deception'. Brown added that he and his wife Sarah had been 'in tears' in 2006 when he heard the *Sun* was going to publish a story revealing his son Fraser's cystic fibrosis, which was known only to a few people. 'I have not made any allegations about how it appeared. But the fact is, it did appear,' he said.

Murdoch's newspapers acted to rebut Brown's complaint. The day before the debate, Tuesday 12 July, *The Sunday Times* issued a statement that did not deny the subterfuge, but added: 'We believe no law was broken in the process of this investigation, and contrary to Mr Brown's assertion, no criminal was used and the story was published giving all sides a fair hearing.'[11] On Wednesday – the day of the BSkyB debate – the *Sun* ran the front page 'Brown Wrong' adding the strapline: 'We didn't probe son's medical records. Source was dad of cystic fibrosis child.'

Tom Watson had visited Brown in his room shortly before the Commons debate, and encountered him in a fierce mood. Rising to speak at 5.26 p.m., Brown vented a simmering rage that he had held inside himself for months. The phone hacking scandal involved many other forms of illicit and illegal behaviour, he said, including the sending of Trojan viruses to hack computers.

> It was not the misconduct of a few rogues or a few freelancers, but lawbreaking often on an industrial scale, at its worst dependent on links with the British criminal underworld.
>
> Others have said that in its behaviour towards those without a voice of their own, News International descended from the gutter to the sewers. The tragedy is that it let the rats out of the sewers.

His administration, he said, had angered News Corp by objecting to its demands to cut the BBC's budget and by ordering it to sell a 16.8 per cent stake in ITV accumulated in order to frustrate a takeover by Richard Branson's Virgin Media (Operation Weeting had informed Branson in 2011 that his phone might have been hacked by the *News of the World*). By a 'strange coincidence' News International and the Conservative Party had come to share almost exactly the same media policy, Brown said:

> It was so close that it was often expressed in almost exactly the same words. On the future of the licence fee; on BBC online; on the right of the public to see free of charge the maximum possible number of national sporting events; on the future of the BBC's commercial arm; and on the integrity of Ofcom, we stood up for what we believed to be the public interest, but that was made difficult when the opposition invariably reclassified the public interest as the News International interest.

Brown said that James Murdoch's 2009 MacTaggart lecture 'underpinned an ever more aggressive News International and BSkyB agenda adding: 'I rejected those policies.'

The end of the BSkyB bid made the top of all the TV bulletins and the front pages of Thursday morning's newspapers. The focus was now on whether the Murdochs would attend the select committee the following Tuesday. Rebekah Brooks, a UK citizen, agreed to give evidence, while James Murdoch, a joint UK–US citizen, wrote that 'unfortunately' he was not available to attend on 19 July but would be pleased to give evidence in August. Rupert Murdoch, an American citizen, said he was unable to make the hearing. 'Dear John,' he wrote to John Whittingdale. 'Thank you for your letter of 12 July, on behalf of the committee, inviting me to give evidence to you on 19 July. Unfortunately, I am not available to attend the session you have planned next Tuesday . . .'

Downing Street issued a statement saying the Murdochs should appear, while Nick Clegg said that if they had 'any shred of sense of responsibility or accountability' they would do so. The Culture Committee met to determine its response. While it was still in session, its decision to compel the Murdochs to attend their hearing was silently communicated to the Commons authorities, who quickly dispatched the Deputy Serjeant-at-Arms to News International's headquarters. Travelling on the London Underground dressed in an ordinary suit, the ancient-office holder of the Commons slipped past the reporters

milling outside Wapping and arrived unannounced, causing conster-
nation among senior NI executives. After refusing to hand over the
summons to a security guard he was asked to sit in a waiting room
where he watched Sky News break the news of his visit on giant flat-
screen TVs. The Murdochs were not available to accept the documents
in person, which were given to their lawyers. Had they refused to
attend, the Commons could have arrested them for contempt of the
authority of Parliament.

Faced with a crisis spinning ever more dangerously out of control,
News Corp called in the PR and lobbying specialists Edelman. With
Edelman in charge, News Corp became slicker. Shortly before 5 p.m.,
the Murdochs agreed they would give evidence after all, and Rupert
Murdoch called one of his own newspapers, the *Wall Street Journal*,
to defend his handling of the scandal, explaining that News Corp had
dealt with it 'extremely well in every way possible', making just 'minor
mistakes'. He rejected criticism that James Murdoch had been too
slow to clean up the stables. His father said: 'I think he acted as fast
as he could, the moment he could.'

While the Murdochs had been wondering whether to attend the
committee, another drama was playing out in Scotland Yard. At ten
that morning officers had arrested a long-standing friend of Commissioner Sir Paul Stephenson – Neil 'Wolfman' Wallis – on suspicion of
phone hacking. When the Yard's top brass dined with the *News of the
World*, it was most often with Wallis, who had left the paper in August
2009 to found his own company, Chamy Media. Extraordinarily,
between October 2009 and September 2010, the Metropolitan Police
had taken on Wallis as a £1,000-a-day consultant to the director of
public affairs, Dick Fedorcio. Wallis had been giving media advice to
Scotland Yard for two days a month at the time it was refusing
to reopen the inquiry and complaining to the *Guardian* about its
coverage.

At 4.30 p.m., the Met issued a statement owning up to the mis-
judgement, explaining that Chamy Media had supplied 'strategic
communications advice' after tendering the lowest fee. During his
time advising Scotland Yard, it seemed, Wallis had been selling stories
about its investigations to his old friends in the tabloids. Overall, he

received more than £25,000 from the press – more than the value of his police contract. News International reportedly paid him £10,000 for one story. Among the scoops were details of a suspected assassination attempt on the Pope.[12]

News of Wallis's work for the Yard was met with astonishment. The government, which had been in the spotlight for its contacts with Wapping, was particularly angry. The Home Secretary Theresa May wrote to Sir Paul Stephenson to get 'the full picture' of the contract. The Mayor, Boris Johnson, still playing catch-up on his 'codswallop', told journalists he had 'a very frank' hour-long discussion with Stephenson, who assured him that Operation Weeting was proceeding swiftly.

Scotland Yard's former Assistant Commissioner, Andy Hayman, also came under attack. The family of Jean-Charles de Menezes, the Brazilian electrician killed by police on the London Underground in 2005 after being mistaken for a suicide bomber, disclosed that day that police had informed his cousin, Alex Pereira, that he was in Mulcaire's files. In a statement, the Menezes family pointed out that the Independent Police Complaints Commission had criticized Hayman for having deliberately 'misled the public' over claims that Menezes had been one of four men being hunted for attempted bombings in London the previous day. They wrote: 'We are conscious that the newspapers owned by News International provided some of the most virulent and often misleading coverage around Jean's death and its aftermath.' Michael Mansfield, the Menezes family lawyer, revealed that his phone might have been hacked by the *News of the World*. In London, Bindmans announced that two new claimants would join Tamsin Allen's judicial review against the police: Jude Law's personal assistant Ben Jackson, and 'HJK', the friend of a politician whose messages had been intercepted.

That day in the US, Eliot Spitzer, the former New York Attorney General, called for News Corp to be investigated by the US Department of Justice over allegations of 'bribery, illegal wiretapping, interference in a murder investigation, political blackmail, and rampant disregard for both the truth and basic decency'. Spitzer, who had brought a series of prosecutions against investment banks, said that the company could be in breach of the Foreign Corrupt Practices Act, which bars American companies from bribing foreign officials. After receiving a formal complaint from the US Congressman Peter King, the FBI began an investigation into the corrosive allegations that the *News of the World* hacked into the phones of 9/11 victims. The phone hacking scandal was now going global.

News Corp's second biggest investor was also becoming increasingly concerned. Tracked down by *Newsnight* to his yacht in the Mediterranean, Saudi Prince Al-Waleed bin Talal Al-saud said Rebekah Brooks should resign if she was found to have been involved in wrongdoing. Sitting on the deck of his yacht, he said: 'If the indications are that her involvement in this matter is explicit, for sure she has to go, you bet she has to go. I will not accept . . . to deal with a company that has a lady or a man that has any sliver of doubts on her or his integrity.'

The Business Secretary Vince Cable, who had wanted to bring down the Murdoch empire when others were still kow-towing, but who had spoken too early, ruefully reflected on a turbulent ten days in an interview with the BBC Radio 4's *PM* programme that afternoon: 'It is a little bit like the end of a dictatorship when everybody suddenly discovers they were against the dictator.'

17

'We Are Sorry'

We are sorry that we have been caught

– Private Eye, 22 July 2011

On Friday 15 July, Rupert Murdoch made a sacrifice he had been resisting stubbornly. He had clung to his chief executive, Rebekah Brooks, despite having to close a best-selling newspaper and abandoning his £7 billion bid for BSkyB, but in four days' time, he was facing a parliamentary inquisition at which her continued presence would be a major line of questioning. Even his most supportive investor, Saudi Prince Al-Waleed bin Talal Al-saud, whose stake he needed in the boardroom, was questioning her record.

At 9.57 a.m., after eleven days at the centre of David Cameron's 'firestorm', Brooks's extraordinary twenty-year rise from secretary to chief executive ended with her resignation. During her two years in charge, News International had repeatedly denied any wrongdoing and in a valedictory email to staff, she again denied that she had done anything wrong. But, she explained, her desire to 'remain on the bridge' was 'detracting attention from all our honest endeavours to fix the problems of the past'. Brooks lavished praise on Rupert Murdoch's wisdom, kindness and advice, James Murdoch's loyalty and friendship and News International's staff, who she said were talented, professional and honourable. She wrote: 'I am proud to have been part of the team and lucky to know so many brilliant journalists and media executives. I leave with the happiest of memories and an abundance of friends.' She also left with a reported pay-off of £1.7 million, a free office and a car.[1]

Politicians welcomed her departure, but it failed to end questions about the company's conduct and the extent of Rupert Murdoch's power. Indeed the fact that Brooks had stayed in post so long had weakened his position. In her remarks to *News of the World* staff, Brooks had cryptically referred to being 'a conductor' for the scandal. Now the Murdochs were left to feel the heat alone.

Ed Miliband had taken a gamble in rising up against Murdoch; now, enjoying a poll boost and, perhaps, fearing that a wounded but intact News International could try to bring him down, he fired directly at Rupert Murdoch. In a personal attack unthinkable a fortnight beforehand, he issued a statement saying: 'Rupert Murdoch says that News Corp has handled these allegations "extremely well". He still hasn't apologized to the innocent victims of hacking. He clearly still doesn't get it.' At the Downing Street lobby briefing, David Cameron's spokesman would not say whether Cameron still considered Brooks to be a friend, but replied that the Prime Minister did think that the relationship between politicians and the media had been 'too cosy'. In the Lords, the Tory grandee Lord Fowler said that one of the lessons of the affair was that political parties had been fearful of Murdoch:

> The aim of both main parties has been to get his support. Mr Blair famously flew to Australia in search of his support and Lady Thatcher also had the same goal, although at least she expected him to come to her . . . It is one of the extraordinary features of the whole phone hacking scandal just how long it has taken to agree that a public inquiry was necessary. Since January I have asked questions on the floor of this House. And on five occasions I've been told more or less politely to jump in the Thames.

Brooks's successor was not Will Lewis, the general manager, but a low-key figure who had been heading Sky Italia's tussle against Silvio Berlusconi, the 56-year-old New Zealander Tom Mockridge. With Brooks gone and Mockridge not yet in charge, the public relations professionals took over. News Corp had failed to grasp the scale or the significance of its difficulty, and now, instead of denial, it offered apology. Over the coming days, the Murdochs and News International would be a picture of contrition, humility and hurt feelings. James

Murdoch emailed staff displaying the new emollient tone. 'The company has made mistakes. It is not only receiving appropriate scrutiny, but is also responding to unfair attacks by setting the record straight.'[2]

News International ran full-page advertisements in national newspapers apologizing for its behaviour and wrote to advertisers outlining its remedial action. Mark Borkowski, an entertainment PR specialist, described the adverts as 'classic damage limitation mode'.[3]

The text of the News International apology read:

We are sorry.

The *News of the World* was in the business of holding others to account. It failed when it came to itself.

We are sorry for the serious wrongdoing that occurred.

We are deeply sorry for the hurt suffered by the individuals affected.

We regret not acting faster to sort things out.

I realize that simply apologizing is not enough.

Our business was founded on the idea that a free and open press should be a positive force in society. We need to live up to this.

In the coming days, as we take further concrete steps to resolve these issues and make amends for the damage they have caused, you will hear more from us.

Sincerely,

Rupert Murdoch.

Private Eye parodied the ad thus:

We are sorry.

We are sorry that we have been caught.

We are sorry that we had to close down the *News of the World*.

We are sorry that we can't take over BSkyB.

We deeply regret that our share price has gone down as a result of previous wrongdoing by some individuals in our employ.

I was personally shocked and appalled to find out the kind of thing that had been going on in my business.

Another act of contrition took place on Friday afternoon when Rupert Murdoch met Milly Dowler's parents, Bob and Sally, at a central London hotel, One Aldwych. As photographers and reporters waited outside, Murdoch apologized abjectly to the Dowlers. Mark Lewis – the lawyer who had taken on the Gordon Taylor case four years earlier – emerged shortly before 6 p.m. to tell reporters that Murdoch was 'very humbled and very shaken and very sincere'. Lewis said: 'I think this was something that had hit him on a very personal level and was something that shouldn't have happened, I don't think somebody could have held their head in their hands so many times and say that they were sorry.'

News Corp exploited Brooks's resignation and Murdoch's meeting with the Dowlers to dump more bad news. Of all the Fridays in the phone hacking scandal, 15 July was the biggest of what PRs term 'put out the trash day'. For days the *Independent* and ITN's Keir Simmons had been chasing Wapping for confirmation that Jude Law had launched a phone hacking lawsuit against the *Sun*. News International desperately wanted to contain hacking to the now closed *News of the World*, but Law, a major Hollywood star, was dragging Murdoch's daily redtop into the mire. At 7 p.m., News International leaked the story to Sky News, giving the Murdoch outlet an exclusive and helpfully burying the story under the bigger corporate meltdown.

Shortly after 9 p.m. UK time, another News Corp star disintegrated. Les Hinton, loyal servant of Rupert Murdoch for fifty years, resigned as chief executive of Dow Jones. Hinton – who had apparently remembered almost nothing of critical events at News International when questioned by Parliament two years before – apologized while also distancing himself from any wrongdoing. He had seen hundreds of news reports about misconduct, he said, and had watched events unfold at the *News of the World* with sorrow. 'That I was ignorant of what apparently happened is irrelevant,' he added, 'and in the circumstances I feel it is proper for me to resign from News Corp and apologize to those hurt by the actions of the *News of the World*.' News International also disclosed that its legal affairs director Jon Chapman had left the company. Chapman had told the company he was leaving on 23 June, three days after NI passed to police the corruption emails that he had reviewed four years earlier.

On Saturday 16 July, journalists and politicians who had dismissed the scandal finally began to grasp the scale of the original wrongdoing and the cover-up, which raised much broader questions about the probity of national institutions and the dominance of the Murdochs. Seeking to explain the disclosures of the past twelve days, the *Daily Telegraph* pointed out in a leader: 'Large swathes of the British establishment have been implicated in this scandal. And the shady characters who have been exposed – policemen, politicians and News International executives – have so far revealed only one aim. That is, to avoid giving a straight answer to the public. The suspicion is that they are living in fear of what might be revealed.'[4]

The Murdochs' resilience was nevertheless on display on Sunday 17 July, both through the agenda-setting power of their papers and from fresh evidence of the spread of the family's tentacles into the power-making elite. The *Independent on Sunday* disclosed that the man who would lead the Commons inquisition two days hence, John Whittingdale, was friendly with Les Hinton and Liz Murdoch. On Facebook, among Hinton's ninety-three friends and Elisabeth Murdoch's 386, the only MP was Whittingdale (who in 2007 had received £3,000 for his local cricket club from BSkyB). Committee members felt that Whittingdale's chairmanship had been decent and he had turned down an invitation to Hinton's wedding in 2009 – the year his committee was investigating hacking. Nonetheless the reach of the Murdochs was apparent. 'I wouldn't say they are close friends,' Whittingdale said, 'but you can't do the job I've done for six years without having them as acquaintances.'[5]

Murdoch's *Sunday Times* carried two exclusives which helped relieve the pressure on his embattled business. Its front page directed attention towards the police, revealing that while recuperating from his leg operation in early 2011, Sir Paul Stephenson and his wife had accepted a twenty-day free stay at the £598-a-night Champneys health spa in Hertfordshire as a guest of its owner, Stephen Purdew, his friend of Sir Paul's. While the commissioner's acceptance of thousands of pounds of free hospitality might have raised eyebrows in its own right, what made the story explosive was that Champneys' part-time publicist was the Outside Organisation, whose managing director was – Neil Wallis. *The Sunday Times* did not mention that among Purdew's many acquaintances were Rebekah and Charlie Brooks.

In his column, Jeremy Clarkson disclosed what had been discussed between David Cameron, James Murdoch and Brooks at her home in the Cotswolds on 23 December, hours after the Conservative leader had stripped Vince Cable of the BSkyB decision: sausage rolls. They had all been planning to go for a walk, Clarkson wrote, and Brooks had wondered what they would eat: the Prime Minister had suggested sausage rolls. 'In other words, it was like a million other Christmas-time dinners being held in a million other houses all over the world that day. BSkyB was not mentioned. Nor was phone hacking.'

Within hours of the latest revelations, Scotland Yard robustly demonstrated its independence by arresting Brooks. On Friday morning, she had been running the most powerful media organization in the country; at noon on Sunday she was in police custody, detained on suspicion of phone hacking and corruption. Brooks was shocked because she had turned up by appointment to a London police station expecting only to be interviewed. The BBC's Robert Peston put out that when News International had been discussing her resignation it had 'no inkling' of her imminent arrest.

Stephenson, the police chief whose force had carried out the arrest, found himself facing questions of his own. He said he had not known of Wallis's connection to Champneys, but his position came under pressure from Coalition ministers, whose own links to Rupert Murdoch had been under intense scrutiny. Nick Clegg, the Liberal Democrat leader, said he was 'incredibly worried' about the impact of the hacking scandal on London's police force and offered Stephenson less than full support. The Home Secretary who had repeatedly rejected calls for a public inquiry, Theresa May, announced that she would make a statement to Parliament the following day about Scotland Yard's relationship with Wallis. By the evening, Stephenson – still recovering from his operation – could take no more. At 7.30 p.m., reporters were summoned to a hastily called press conference. At Scotland Yard, Stephenson, the shoe salesman who had risen to become the country's top police officer, announced he was quitting.

In the space of a fortnight, the scandal had horrified the public, closed the country's best-selling Sunday paper, sunk a £7.8 billion takeover, forced out Rupert Murdoch's favourite bosses in Britain and the United States and now cost London's police chief his job. Senior officers felt Stephenson was carrying the can for the Yard's close relationship with the press forged during Sir John Stevens's tenure from 2000 to 2005. Sir Hugh Orde, the head of the Association of Chief Police Officers, described Stephenson as 'one of the finest officers I have worked with.'[6]

In his resignation statement, Stephenson insisted he had done nothing wrong, but said that the speculation about the links between senior officers and News International was distracting him from his job. He had known Neil Wallis since 2006, but had 'no reason' to suspect he might have been involved in phone hacking. 'I do not occupy a position in the world of journalism,' Stephenson said. 'I had no knowledge of the extent of this disgraceful practice and the repugnant nature of the selection of victims that is now emerging; nor of its apparent reach into senior levels.' He pointed out that while his force had employed a *News of the World* executive who had not resigned over phone hacking, David Cameron had personally employed a man who had done so, Andy Coulson. The country's most senior police officer had not informed the Prime Minister he was about to resign.

Saying he understood Stephenson's decision, Cameron – on a tour of Africa which he abruptly cut short to return to the UK – stressed the importance of ensuring the police investigations proceeded with full confidence and 'all the necessary leadership and resources'.

On Monday 18 July, politicians were content to let the spotlight fall on Assistant Commissioner John Yates. Boris Johnson, who had failed to challenge the Met over phone hacking when it mattered, said that questions would now be asked about Yates's relationship with Neil Wallis. Brian Coleman, a fellow Conservative member of the London Assembly, said: 'The Commissioner has done the right thing by resigning and accepting the error of judgement in employing Neil Wallis. Yates, who has shown that his stewardship of the original hacking inquiry was to put it bluntly, inept, should go – and go now.'[7]

Yates tried to cling to his post, telling Sky News at 11.30 a.m.: 'I've done nothing wrong.' But his position became untenable. The BBC's political editor Nick Robinson reported that Yates had been in charge of carrying out 'due diligence' on Wallis before he was hired by Scotland Yard (though this was not technically correct); the Home Affairs Committee announced that it was recalling Yates to give evidence; and the Metropolitan Police Authority began examining his decision not to reopen the investigation after the Gordon Taylor story in July 2009.

Shortly after 2 p.m., John Yates bowed to the inevitable and resigned. He expressed some regret that victims of phone hacking had not been dealt with appropriately by the Met, but added: 'Sadly, there continues to be a huge amount of inaccurate, ill-informed and on occasion downright malicious gossip published about me personally. This has the potential to be a significant distraction in my current role as the national lead for counter-terrorism.' The Independent Police Complaints Commission opened an investigation into all the senior Scotland Yard officers whose conduct had been questioned: Sir Paul Stephenson, John Yates, Andy Hayman and Peter Clarke.

Scotland Yard's links with News International were shown to be even deeper, when it disclosed that Alex Marunchak, the *News of the World* executive who had handled Jonathan Rees's stories from corrupt police, had for the twenty years between 1980 and 2000 – while a crime reporter and news editor at the *Screws* – worked for the Met as an interpreter for Ukrainian victims and suspects, giving him inside information on police investigations. With a degree of under-statement, Scotland Yard said: 'We recognize that this may cause concern and that some professions may be incompatible with the role of an interpreter.'[8] A few days later the Yard revealed that no fewer than ten of the staff in Dick Fedorcio's Directorate of Public Affairs had previously worked for News International.

A series of personal and professional relationships had connected Britain's biggest news group and its biggest police force. The chief reporter of its Sunday newspapers, Neville Thurlbeck, was being slipped criminal records by the police, while its news editor inter-preted for criminal inquiries. Its quality daily, *The Times*, had employed Andy Hayman after he headed the failed hacking inquiry in 2006 (where he voiced his opinion that there had been only a 'handful' of victims). And one of NI's most senior executives, Neil 'Wolfman' Wallis, had long been friends with Dick Fedorcio, who ran the media unit, John Yates, who reviewed the failed inquiry, and the Commis-sioner, Sir Paul Stephenson – who had all complained to the *Guardian* about its coverage. Wallis had then been employed by Scotland Yard at exactly the same time it was maintaining that the original inquiry had been a success. All the while, NI's journalists had been bribing Met officers for tips, leaks and telephone numbers.

Confidence in the integrity of the police had been badly shaken. In the House of Commons, Theresa May announced three inquiries: Elizabeth Filkin, the former Parliamentary Commissioner for Standards, would investigate Scotland Yard's relationship with the media; Her Majesty's Inspectorate of Constabulary would investigate police corruption; and a body yet to be announced would investigate the powers and effectiveness of the Independent Police Complaints Commission.

After many years of denial when no one in authority took responsibility for wrongdoing at News International, there were now no fewer than twelve inquiries under way: Lord Leveson's public inquiry; the Press Complaints Commission review; News International's Management and Standards Committee; the inquiries by the Commons Culture and Home Affairs Committees; the three new ones into policing; and four criminal inquiries: Scotland Yard's Weeting, Elveden and Tuleta, and Strathclyde's Operation Rubicon into phone hacking and perjury.

As the clock ticked down to the Murdochs' appearance before the Commons Culture Committee, the first journalist to speak out about phone hacking was found dead at his house in Langley Road, Watford, twenty miles from central London. More than any other former *News of the World* reporter, Sean Hoare had exposed the paper's dark arts, and now he had paid the price. He had been spurned by former colleagues who had been friends – one ex-*News of the World* executive slammed down the phone on him, saying: 'Don't ever call me on this number again' – and he had been treated as a suspect rather than a witness by the police. A day before Hoare was about to see his old boss account to Parliament for his conduct, Hertfordshire police began investigating the whistleblower's death. His inquest later ruled that he had died of liver failure, seven months after he started drinking again because of stress.

Shortly after news of Hoare's death, the *Guardian*'s Amelia Hill, who had co-authored the Milly Dowler story, revealed that the Metropolitan Police were examining a laptop computer found in a

19. The Golden Lion pub in Sydenham, east London, in whose car park Daniel Morgan was murdered in 1987.

20. Jonathan Rees, whose office was bugged by the Metropolitan Police, said: 'No one pays like the *News of the World* do.' Andy Coulson's *News of the World* re-employed Rees after he was jailed for conspiracy to pervert the course of justice.

21. At the time of his murder, Morgan was increasingly concerned about the links between Rees, his business partner at Southern Investigations and corrupt police.

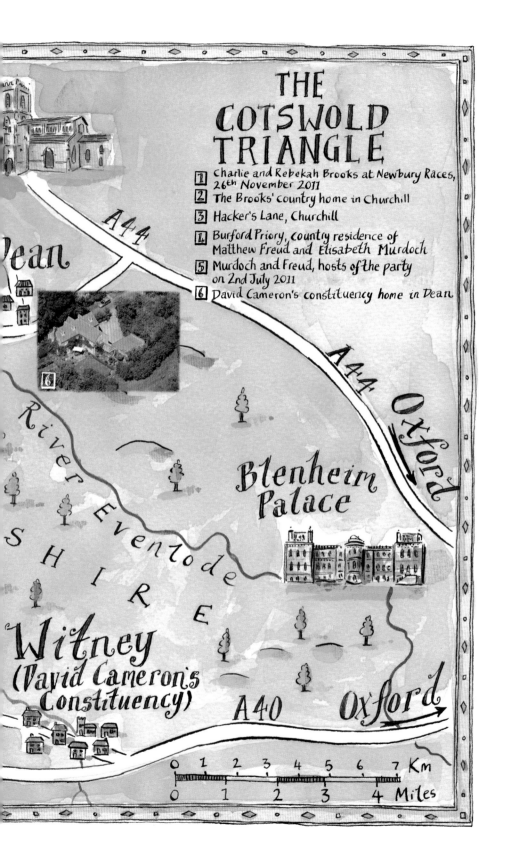

THE COTSWOLD TRIANGLE

1. Charlie and Rebekah Brooks at Newbury Races, 26th November 2011
2. The Brooks' country home in Churchill
3. Hacker's Lane, Churchill
4. Burford Priory, country residence of Matthew Freud and Elisabeth Murdoch
5. Murdoch and Freud, hosts of the party on 2nd July 2011
6. David Cameron's constituency home in Dean

Dean

A44

River Eventode

SHIRE

Witney
(David Cameron's Constituency)

Blenheim Palace

A44 Oxford

A40   Oxford

0 1 2 3 4 5 6 7 Km
0 1 2 3 4 Miles

22. Flanked by *News of the World* staff outside Thomas More Square, Wapping, on 9 July 2011, Colin Myler holds its 8,674th edition bearing the legend, 'The world's greatest newspaper 1843–2011'.

23. Britain's top policeman, Sir Paul Stephenson, resigned as Commissioner of the Metropolitan Police after accepting an £11,000 free stay at Champneys health spa – whose PR advisor was Neil Wallis.

24. Hours after the *News of the World*'s presses rolled for the last time, Murdoch shrugged off demands for Rebekah Brooks to resign. Asked for his priority, he pointed at her and said: 'This one.' Brooks went five days later.

25. Scotland Yard detectives search Andy Coulson's home in south London following his arrest on 8 July 2011 on suspicion of phone hacking and corruption. In January 2012, Coulson put the five-bedroom house on the market for £1.6m.

26. In the House of Commons on 20 July, the Prime Minister said that 'in hindsight' he wished he had not appointed Coulson as his director of communications: 'You live and you learn – and believe me, I have learnt.'

27. Protesters gathered outside the Houses of Parliament as Rupert and James Murdoch appeared before MPs on 19 July 2011. Millions around the world watched the hearing live on television.

28. 'Before you get to that, I would just like to say one sentence ... This is the most humble day of my life.'

29. A comedian, a film star and the former head of world motorsport– Steve Coogan, Hugh Grant and Max Mosley– railed against tabloid tactics at Parliament's joint committee on privacy on 5 December 2011.

30. J. K. Rowling felt like she was being 'blackmailed' by the *Sun* in 2003 over a leak of her new book, *Harry Potter and the Order of the Phoenix*.

31. In exchange for singing at Rupert Murdoch's and Wendi Deng's wedding in 1999, Charlotte Church was promised 'good press': it didn't happen. After settling her case in February 2012, she said: 'In my opinion, they are not truly sorry, only sorry they got caught.'

32. Sienna Miller could not understand how reporters and photographers knew about her life. 'I felt like I was in a video game.' Her legal case against News International uncovered a crucial weakness in the company's story.

33. Milly Dowler's parents, Bob and Sally, arrive at the Leveson Inquiry at the Royal Courts of Justice in London, with the combative Mark Lewis (in the orange coat). Lewis and Charlotte Harris (plate 12) were the first lawyers to challenge News International over phone hacking.

bin at London's Chelsea Harbour, the riverside apartment complex where Rebekah and Charlie Brooks lived. At around 3 p.m. that day, the day after Rebekah Brooks had been released from twelve hours' questioning, the computer had been handed to a security guard. Charlie Brooks had tried to reclaim it but had been unable to prove it was his and the guard had called the police. Within half an hour, two marked police cars and an unmarked forensics vehicle had arrived at the scene.

18

Democracy Day

I do not have direct knowledge of what they knew and at what time, but I can tell you that the critical new facts, as I saw them and as the company saw them, really emerged in the production of documentary information or evidence in the civil trials at the end of 2010

– James Murdoch, 19 July 2011

On the morning of 19 July, all eyes were on the showdown between Rupert Murdoch and his son and the Commons Culture Committee. Since taking over the *News of the World* and the *Sun* in 1969, forty-two years previously, Rupert had dominated the media and politics in Britain but he had never appeared before a parliamentary inquiry in public.

As he arrived at Westminster shortly before midday, he had reason to fear not just for his reputation but for his business. Investors were now as concerned about his company as the public were about his ethics. Two big business deals had gone sour. In February 2009 News Corp had to write off $2.8 billion from its top-of-the-market $5.7 billion acquisition of the *Wall Street Journal*-owned Dow Jones in 2007. MySpace, too, had been a disaster: Murdoch had paid $580 million for it in 2005 but had been outwitted by Facebook's 24-year-old computer programmer, Mark Zuckerberg. In June, News Corp had disposed of the loss-making MySpace for $35 million, while analysts valued Facebook at $100 billion.

Rupert Murdoch's faltering instincts were forgiven, at least by the board, because he packed it with associates and family members, including his sons Lachlan and James, and because the family owned 40 per cent of the voting shares. With the support of his close ally Prince Al-Waleed bin Talal Al-saud, who owned a further 7 per cent, the Murdochs had effective control, even though they actually owned only 12 per cent of the share capital. Investors undervalued News Corp by billions of dollars because of the imbalance. For eight years on the trot between 2003 and 2010 the business ratings company Governance Metrics International had given News Corp's corporate governance its lowest F grade, complaining: 'This isn't a dysfunctional board, it's a nonfunctional board.'[1] In March 2011, two small US shareholders, the Amalgamated Bank of New York and the Central Laborer's Pension Fund, had filed a lawsuit accusing Murdoch of running the company like 'a family owned candy store'.[2]

There were also signs of disharmony within the Murdoch clan. At a book party hosted by Matthew Freud and the *Times* editor James Harding, on 9 July, Elisabeth Murdoch was reported to have said Rebekah Brooks had 'fucked the company'.*

In the days running up to the meeting, James and Rupert Murdoch were coached by public relations professionals. Rebekah Brooks – who was due to appear at the committee after the Murdochs – was seen in a 'distressed state' visiting the offices of the former Met Commissioner, Sir John Stevens.

Over the weekend, Tom Watson had also been working through lines of questioning. At the offices of Max Mosley's solicitors Collyer Bristow on Monday, the day before the hearing, he had spent four hours role-playing the questions with Mosley and others. He expected News Corp's advisers to the Murdochs would try to protect Rupert by getting James to answer most of the technical questions. Watson believed the way to keep the focus on Rupert was to concentrate on questions of corporate governance. Watson hoped that Murdoch

---

* According to Murdoch's biographer Michael Wolff those reports were incomplete: 'She said: "James and Rebekah fucked the company".'[3] Wolff had conducted fifty hours of interviews with an initially cooperative Murdoch for *The Man Who Owns the News*, but his biography had not been favourable; subsequently the *New York Post*'s page 6 gossip column delved into his private life, exposing an extra-marital affair. Wolff continued to be an outspoken critic.

would either have to admit that he had known about the criminality at the *News of the World* or that he hadn't known about it at a corporate level – either way he was arguably unfit to run the company. Watson assumed the Murdochs would try to begin by reading out an opening statement, which would almost certainly apologize for the wrongdoing, express regret and outline measures to ensure it never happened again. Just like the attempt to remove Watson from the committee in 2009, this opening gambit, an apology, would then become the main story for the rolling news channels and divert attention away from the examination of who was culpable for the wrongdoing. Committee members determined not to let this happen. At midday, Watson shut the door of his office in Portcullis House, put on the Doors album *LA Woman* at full blast and paced around rehearsing questions.

At 14.34 in the Wilson Room of Portcullis House, James Murdoch led his father to his chair, which Rupert's wife Wendi Deng pulled out for him. She whispered something in his ear and poured him a glass of water.

James Murdoch could be impetuous, aggressive and arrogant, the multimillionaire son of a billionaire. Rupert Murdoch could humiliate his editors, shouting and swearing at them. At the committee, the well-coached Murdochs were not brash or arrogant, but contrite and respectful. James Murdoch – as expected – took the lead. He began with a note of disappointment, even anger. In his British-American accent, he said: 'Our understanding was that we would be afforded the opportunity to make an opening statement, and we prepared on that basis.' Appealing to the chairman, John Whittingdale, he said: 'We would like the opportunity to make that statement. Would you allow us?' Whittingdale explained that the members had discussed that and the answer was no: 'We feel that we have a lot of questions.'

Whittingdale started by pointing out that the Culture Committee's last report in February 2010 had found it 'inconceivable' that phone hacking had been down to a single rogue reporter, pointing out that it was now obvious that Parliament had been misled. He turned to James Murdoch and referred to his email to staff announcing the closure of the *News of the World*: 'You made a statement on 7 July in which you stated that the paper had made statements to Parliament without being in full possession of the facts, and that was wrong. You essentially admitted that Parliament had been misled in what we had been told. Can you tell us to what extent we were misled, and when you became aware of that?'

James Murdoch started reciting what sounded like the statement he had planned to make, referring not to phone hacking (too pithy) but 'illegal voicemail interceptions'. 'First, I would like to say as well just how sorry I am,' James said, 'and how sorry we are, to particularly the victims of illegal voicemail interceptions and to their families. It is a matter of great regret to me, my father and everyone at News Corporation . . .'

Rupert Murdoch stretched out his right hand and placed it on his son's forearm. 'Before you get to that,' he told his son, 'I would just like to say one sentence. This is the most humble day of my life.'* The statement flashed up on the rolling news channels.

With his fierce eyes, politeness and strained management-speak voice (which the following day prompted an unkind suggestion that he was 'half Harry Potter, half Hannibal Lecter'),[4] James responded to Whittingdale's question: 'I do not have direct knowledge of what they knew [Wapping's executives] and at what time, but I can tell you that the critical new facts, as I saw them and as the company saw them, really emerged in the production of documentary information or evidence in the civil trials at the end of 2010 . . . It is a matter of real regret that the facts could not emerge and could not be gotten to my understanding faster.'

This, then, was the Murdoch's defence: they had only realized the previous year that hacking had been widespread at Wapping. Alas, the company's external lawyers, the Metropolitan Police and the Press Complaints Commission had all failed to detect the wrongdoing.

The questioning passed to Tom Watson, who, as he had planned, concentrated on Rupert. 'Mr Murdoch senior, good afternoon, sir,' he said breezily. 'You have repeatedly stated that News Corp has zero tolerance to wrongdoing by employees. Is that right?'

* The US satirist Jon Stewart later joked: 'Not so humble you couldn't wait for your turn to talk!'

'Yes,' replied Rupert.

'In October 2010, did you still believe it to be true when you made your Thatcher speech and you said, "Let me be clear: we will vigorously pursue the truth – and we will not tolerate wrongdoing"?'

'Yes,' replied Rupert again, apparently coached to answer economically.

'So if you were not lying then,' Watson said, 'somebody lied to you. Who was it?'

'I don't know,' Murdoch said grumpily. 'That is what the police are investigating, and we are helping them with.'

'But you acknowledge that you were misled.'

'Clearly.'

Watson took him back to 2003, when Rebekah Brooks had admitted the company had paid police for information in the past. Did anyone in News Corp or News International investigate that at the time?

Rupert paused. 'No.'

'Can you explain why?'

'I didn't know of it,' he replied. 'I'm sorry,' the tycoon added tetchily. 'Allow me to say something?' He started slapping the table with his hand, which he had a habit of doing when he wanted to emphasize his exasperation. 'And this is not [slap] an excuse [slap]. Maybe it is an explanation of my laxity [slap]. The *News of the World* is [slap] less than [slap] 1 per cent of our company. I employ 53,000 [slap] people around the world [slap] who are proud and great and ethical [slap] and distinguished people – professionals in their line. And [slap] perhaps I am spread [too thin] watching and appointing [slap] people whom I trust [slap] to run those divisions.'

Watson continued: 'If I can take you forward to 2006: when Clive Goodman was arrested and subsequently convicted of intercepting voicemails, were you made aware of that?'

Rupert replied: 'We worked with the police on further investigations, and eventually we appointed – very quickly appointed – a very leading firm of lawyers in the City to investigate it further . . .'

This was unwelcome detail. James jumped in: 'Perhaps I can help here – ?'

'I will come to you in a minute, sir. Just let me finish my line of questioning and then I will come to you.' He turned to Rupert: 'What did you personally do to investigate that after Mr Goodman went to prison? You were obviously concerned about it.'

'I spoke to Mr Hinton who told me about it.'

Watson paused. 'Okay.' He said: 'In 2008, another two years, why did you not dismiss *News of the World* chief reporter Neville Thurlbeck, following the Mosley case?'

'I had never heard of him.'

Watson queried: 'Despite a judge making clear that Thurlbeck set out to blame two of the women involved?'

'I didn't hear that.'

'A judge made it clear Thurlbeck set out to blackmail two of the women involved in the case.'

To the surprise of those who had followed the *News of the World*'s recent history, News Corp's chief executive replied: 'That is the first I have heard of that.'

Watson continued: 'Do you agree with Mr Justice Eady when he said that the lack of action discloses a remarkable state of affairs at News International?'

'No.'

Turning to the corruption of the Metropolitan Police, Watson asked whether Lord Macdonald had found 'evidence of indirect hacking, breaches of national security and evidence of serious crime in the Harbottle & Lewis file'.

'He did indeed.'

James, growing ever more concerned, interjected: 'Mr Watson, please, I can address these in some detail, if you will allow me.'

'I will come to you, Mr Murdoch, but it is your father who is responsible for corporate governance . . .'

Had Murdoch senior been informed about the payments to Gordon Taylor and Max Clifford?

'No.'

At what point had News Corp's chairman and chief executive discovered that criminality was endemic at the *News of the World*?

'Endemic is a very hard, wide-ranging word,' Murdoch protested. '. . . I became aware as it became apparent.'

Hadn't the Culture Committee's last report referred to the

'collective amnesia' of his executives? 'I haven't heard that,' Rupert replied. 'I don't know who made that particular charge.'

Watson reminded him: 'We found your executives guilty of collective amnesia,' adding: 'I would have thought that someone would like to bring that to your attention; that it would concern you. Did they forget?'

'No.'

Jim Sheridan, the veteran Labour MP, asked Rupert to confirm that he had entered Downing Street by a back door to visit David Cameron days after the election, asking if it was at Cameron's request.

'I was asked would I please come in through the back door,' Rupert replied, avoiding giving the precise answer sought.

Sheridan remarked: 'It is strange, given that heads of state manage to go in the front door.'

He asked: 'Have you ever imposed any preconditions on a party leader in the UK before giving them the support of your newspapers?'

'I never guaranteed anyone the support of my newspapers,' News Corp's chief executive replied, becoming more loquacious. 'We had been supporting the Thatcher government and the Conservative government that followed. We thought it had got tired and we changed and supported the Labour Party thirteen years ago, or whenever it was, with the direct loss of 200,000 circulation.'

'Did you ever impose any preconditions on either the Labour or Conservative Party?'

'No.'

Who, wondered Sheridan, did Murdoch blame for the scandal, the closure of the *News of the World* and the loss of the BSkyB bid?

'A lot of people had different agendas, I think, in trying to build this hysteria,' Rupert replied, his accent still heavily Australian despite three decades in the US. 'All our competitors in this country formally announced a consortium to try and stop us. They caught us with dirty hands and they built the hysteria around it.'

Did he accept that he was ultimately 'responsible for this whole fiasco'?

'No.'

Sheridan pressed: 'Who is responsible?'

'The people that I trusted to run it, and then maybe the people they trusted. I worked with Mr Hinton for fifty-two years and I would trust him with my life.'

Why hadn't Wapping disclosed emails in the Tommy Sheridan perjury case?

James said: 'I do not have direct knowledge of that, Mr Sheridan. I apologize, but certainly if you have additional questions on that in the future, I am happy to supply written answers, but I do not have direct knowledge and I am not in a position to answer those questions.'

He explained that he had settled the Taylor case after receiving legal advice about the cost of fighting it: 'It was advised that, with legal expenses and damages, it could be between £500,000 and £1 million or thereabouts. I do not recall the exact number of the advice. I think that it was £250,000 plus expenses, plus litigation costs, something like that.'

Adrian Sanders, a Liberal Democrat and one of the committee's most assiduous questioners, asked: 'Was part of the advice that a high payment would ensure the matter was kept confidential?'

'No, not at all. Out-of-court settlements are normally confidential,' replied James who – at that time unbeknownst to the committee – had been copied into an email chain saying hacking was 'rife'.

Sanders pressed on: 'The *New Statesman* carried a story last week that News International subsidized Andy Coulson's wages after he left your employ. Can you shed any light on that?'

'I have no knowledge of Andy Coulson's wages after he left the company's employment.'

Sanders asked: 'Finally, are you familiar with the term "wilful blindness"?'

'Mr Sanders,' James said wearily, 'would you care to elaborate?'

Sanders explained: 'It is a term that came up in the Enron scandal. "Wilful blindness" is a legal term. It states that if there is knowledge that you could have had and should have had, but chose not to have, you are still responsible.'

Seemingly perplexed, James responded: 'Mr Sanders, do you have a question? Respectfully, I just do not know what you would like me to say.'

'The question was whether you were aware –'

James snapped: 'I am not aware of that particular phrase.'

Sanders: 'But now you are familiar with the term, because I have explained it to you.'

Deadpan, with his eyes still glinting, James replied: 'Thank you, Mr Sanders.'

'I have heard the phrase before,' chipped in his father, 'and we were not ever guilty of that.'

Asked about the frequency of his contact with editors, Rupert said he occasionally rang the editor of the *News of the World* on a Saturday night to ask: 'Have you got any news tonight?' 'I ring the editor of *The Sunday Times* [John Witherow] nearly every Saturday,' he added, 'not to influence what he has to say at all. I am very careful always to premise any remark I made to him by saying, "I'm just inquiring".'

'I'm not really in touch,' added the proprietor.* 'I have got to tell you that, if there is an editor that I spend most time with, it is the editor of the *Wall Street Journal*, because I am in the same building. But to say that we are hands-off is wrong; I work a ten or twelve-hour day, and I cannot tell you the multitude of issues that I have to handle every day. The *News of the World*, perhaps I lost sight of, maybe because it was so small in the general frame of our company, but we are doing a lot of other things too.'

Philip Davies, the Conservative MP who the previous year had complained Labour MPs had hijacked the committee's last report on NI, now displayed a more robust touch. He asked: 'Surely in your weekly conversations with the editor of the *News of the World*, with something as big . . . as paying someone £1 million or £700,000, you would have expected the editor just to drop it into the conversation at some point during your weekly chat?'

Rupert replied simply: 'No.'

Davies pressed: 'You wouldn't have expected them to say that to you?'

---

* Rupert Murdoch's troublesome biographer Michael Wolff claimed the proprietor had misled the MPs over the extent of his involvement in his British newspapers. Wolff said the tycoon would spend up to half his day speaking to his newspaper editors in London: 'His involvement with the papers is total. Rupert sat up there [at the committee] and they [his advisers] said, "You have got to say you are not involved with the newspapers." And that's what he said and that's a lie.'[5]

'No . . . He might say, "We've got a great story exposing X or Y" or, more likely, he would say, "Nothing special". He might refer to the fact that however many extra pages were dedicated to the football that week.'

'But he wouldn't tell you about a £1 million pay-off?'

'No.'

To the suggestion that the *News of the World* had been shut to protect Rebekah Brooks, Rupert answered: 'The two decisions were absolutely and totally unrelated.'

'So when you came into the UK and said that your priority was Rebekah Brooks, what did you mean?' asked Davies.

Looking confused, Rupert replied: 'I am not sure I did say that; I was quoted as saying that. I walked outside my flat and had about twenty microphones stuck at my mouth, so I'm not sure what I said.'

'You were misquoted, so to speak?'

Perhaps knowing that the remark had been captured by TV crews, he replied: 'I am not saying that. I just don't remember.'

The Murdochs were clearly struggling to give straightforward answers.

Paul Farrelly MP asked whether News Corp had been paying Glenn Mulcaire's legal fees.

James started: 'As I said earlier in answer to a question from Mr Davies . . .'

Farrelly interrupted: 'Let's keep it short. Yes or no? It is a yes or no question.'

James responded blankly: 'I do not know the current status of this. You asked the question have I paid all Mr Mulcaire's legal fees.'

Farrelly: 'Have you been paying legal fees for Glenn Mulcaire during the course of the civil actions?'

'I don't know the details of the civil actions,' James added, 'but I do know that certain legal fees were paid for Mr Mulcaire by the company.' He added: 'I was as surprised and shocked to learn that as you are.'

Farrelly said: 'Can you understand that people might ask why a company might wish to pay the legal fees of a convicted felon, who has been intimately involved in the destruction of your reputation, if it were not to buy his cooperation and silence?'

'No, it is not,' James protested. 'I can understand that, and that is exactly why I asked the question – when the allegations came out, I said: "How can we? Are we doing this? Is this what the company is doing?"... I am not a lawyer, but these are serious litigations and it is important for all of the evidence from all of the defendants to get to court at the right time. The strong advice was that from time to time it is important, and customary even, to pay a co-defendant's legal fees. I have to rest on counsel's advice on some of these serious litigation matters.'

Farrelly tried again: 'Is the organization still contributing to Glenn Mulcaire's legal fees?'

'As I said earlier, Mr Farrelly,' James replied deadpan, 'I do not know the precise status of that now, but I do know that I asked for the company to find a way for those things to cease with respect to these things.'

'Will you let us know?'

'I am happy to follow up with the committee on the status of those legal fees.'

Farrelly would not give in. Turning to Rupert, he said: 'Is it not time for the organization to say: "Enough is enough"? This man allegedly hacked the phone of the murdered schoolgirl Milly Dowler. Is it not time for your organization to say: "Do your worst. You behaved disgracefully. We are not going to pay any more of your costs"?'

Rupert responded: 'I would like to do that. I do not know the status of what we are doing, or indeed what his contract was and whether it still has any force.'

'If the organization is still paying his fees, will you give the instruction now that that should stop?'

'Provided that it is not in breach of a legal contract, yes,' Rupert replied.

Farrelly turned to the unfair dismissal claims by Goodman and Mulcaire: 'Do you know what sorts of allegations they were making? We can only imagine that they were saying that such-and-such a person knew and such-and-such a person knew. Have you satisfied yourself about what allegations they were making?'

'As to Glenn Mulcaire,' James replied, 'I am not aware of allegations at the time and other things. As to Goodman – again, this was in 2007, before I was there – it is my understanding that that is what Harbottle & Lewis were helping to deal with, and that that opinion did satisfy the company at the time and we, the company, rested on that [Harbottle & Lewis's] opinion for a period of time.'

James had skipped out of trouble, but Farrelly asked if he would give the committee the instructions given to Harbottle & Lewis in 2007.

'If additional detail is required around those legal instructions,' James responded, 'we will consult and come back to the chairman with a way to satisfy you with the information that you'd like to have.'

Asked whether it was 'remotely possible' that the *News of the World*'s editors had not known about illegality at the paper, Rupert replied: 'I can't say that, because of the police inquiries and, I presume, coming judicial proceedings. That is all I can tell you, except it was my understanding . . . that Mr Myler was appointed there by Mr Hinton to find out what the hell was going on, and that he commissioned that Harbottle & Lewis inquiry.'

Simple questions elicited bland, or uninformative replies; for instance, this from Farrelly: 'Can you tell us why Jon Chapman has left the organization?'

James: 'Jon Chapman and the organization decided it was in mutual interest to part ways. I think one of the pieces here as well is for the company to move forward – I think this is important – and even if there is no evidence of wrongdoing or anything like that and no evidence of impropriety, many individuals have chosen that it is time to part ways. I was not involved with the discussions with Mr Chapman.'

Asked about his relationship with prime ministers and presidents, Rupert joked: 'I wish they would leave me alone.' He was disappointed that his relationship with Gordon Brown had foundered, he said. 'His wife and my wife struck up quite a friendship, and our children played together on many occasions. I am very sorry that I am no longer – I thought he had great values, which I shared with him, and I am sorry that we have come apart.' He added: 'I hope one day that we'll be able to put it together again.'

At 4.54 p.m., two hours and twenty minutes into the session, Jonathan May-Bowles rose from his chair and shoved a shaving foam plate into the face of News Corp's octogenarian chief executive. Leaping from her chair with quicker reactions than anyone else (including his karate black belt son James) Wendi Deng slapped the attacker and threw his plate back at him, smearing him with his own shaving cream.*

The proceedings were called to a halt for ten minutes. Tom Watson strolled over to the Murdochs and passed the time of day with them, pouring a drink of water for James. At 5.08 p.m. the hearing resumed.

The Conservative MP Louise Mensch, better known as the chick-lit author Louise Bagshawe, focused on other newspaper groups and read out a passage from Piers Morgan's book *The Insider* (actually it was not a passage from the book, but an extract from a newspaper article by Morgan), apparently referring to phone hacking at the *Daily Mirror*. Mensch added: 'Yesterday, Paul Dacre of Associated Newspapers said to a committee of Parliament, in my view risibly, that the *Daily Mail* has never in its history run a story based on phone hacking or blagging in any way.' The Murdochs did not want to be drawn on the misbehaviour of other newspaper groups, though they may have been grateful for the reference.

As the session came to a close, after two long, sometimes extraordinary and sometimes dull hours, Whittingdale allowed Watson a final question. 'James – sorry, if I may call you James, to differentiate,' he began. 'When you signed off the Taylor payment, did you see or were you made aware of the "For Neville" email, the transcript of the hacked voicemail messages?'

James replied: 'No, I was not aware of that at the time.' It was an important answer.

The session finished at 5.31 p.m., after two hours and forty-three minutes of questioning. The committee had failed to land any killer blows. Rupert Murdoch seemed to be a doddery, proud old man and

---

* Deng was later the subject of admiring newspaper profiles about Murdoch's 'Tiger wife'. Rupert did not want to press charges but 'Jonnie Marbles' was sentenced to six weeks for assault, reduced to four weeks on appeal. On the steps of the court, mockingly contrite, he said: 'I would just like to say this has been the most humble day of my life.'

his son had intelligently evaded making any serious admissions. But the answers they gave had stored up trouble for the future. First, they had admitted that they were still paying Glenn Mulcaire's fees despite publicly decrying his behaviour, and secondly they had suggested Harbottle & Lewis had failed to identify the wrongdoing. Thirdly, and most importantly, James Murdoch said he did not know about the 'For Neville' email, the document which indicated widespread wrongdoing at the company years before the truth was admitted.

At 5.43 p.m. the same day, Rebekah Brooks made her first appearance before the Culture Committee since 2003, this time accompanied by her solicitor, Stephen Parkinson of Kingsley Napley. Unnoticed by most of the public, Alison Clark, the former public affairs director of News International, slipped into a seat at the back of the room.

John Whittingdale started off by referring to News International's statement in July 2009 which denied point-blank that *News of the World* reporters had hacked the phones of anybody apart from the eight victims named in court and Gordon Taylor, or that there 'was systemic corporate illegality by News International'. Whittingdale asked Brooks: 'Would you accept now that that is not correct?'

Brooks sang the Murdochs' song: the documentation from the Sienna Miller case was 'the first time that we, the senior management of the company at the time, had actually seen some documentary evidence actually relating to a current employee'. She added: 'I think that we acted quickly and decisively then, when we had that information.'

Taking his turn to interrogate NI's recently departed chief executive – who had threatened to pursue him – Watson looked directly at her and said slowly: 'There are many questions I would like to ask you, but I will not be able to do so today because you are facing criminal proceedings, so I am going to be narrow in my questioning . . . Why did you sack Tom Crone?'

The company had not sacked Tom Crone, she said; the closure of the *News of the World* had deprived him of a job.

'As a journalist and editor of *News of the World* and the *Sun*,' Watson asked, 'how extensively did you work with private detectives?'

Not at all on the *Sun*, Brooks replied, but there had been questions at the *News of the World* about Steve Whittamore. Among his customers, she continued: 'Certainly in the top five were the *Observer*, the *Guardian, News of the World, Daily Mail* –'*

So, she had worked with private detectives?

What she had said, she corrected Watson, was that the use of private detectives in the late 1990s and 2000s 'was a practice of Fleet Street'.

The MP asked: 'For the third time, how extensively did you work with private detectives?'

'The *News of the World* employed private detectives, like most newspapers in Fleet Street.'

She could not remember authorizing payments; they would have gone through Stuart Kuttner's office.

'You can't remember whether Kuttner ever discussed it with you?'

Brooks: 'Sorry. What?'

'You can't remember whether Kuttner ever discussed it with you?'

'I can't remember if we ever discussed an individual payment, no,' she said.

Had she ever met Glenn Mulcaire?

No.

Would he claim that he had met her?

She replied: 'I am sure he would, although – yes it's the truth [that she had not met him].'

'One last question,' Watson said. 'Do you have any regrets?'

'Of course I have regrets,' Brooks replied. 'The idea that Milly Dowler's phone was accessed by someone being paid by the *News of the World* – or even worse, authorized by someone at the *News of the World* – is as abhorrent to me as it is to everyone in this room.'

Louise Mensch again raised Paul Dacre's evidence to Parliament that the *Daily Mail* had never published a story based on hacking or blagging despite Associated Newspapers requesting 1,387 searches from Steve Whittamore.

'I am not here in a position to comment on other newspaper groups,' Brooks replied. 'Like I said at the beginning, things went badly wrong

---

* The *Observer* was ninth; the *Guardian* not on the list at all.

at the *News of the World*, and we are doing our best now to sort it out.'

Regarding the Culture Committee's withering report in 2010, Brooks sounded contrite. 'Everyone at News International has great respect for Parliament and for this Committee,' she said, sounding pained. 'Of course, to be criticized by your report was something that we responded to. We looked at the report. It was only when we had the information in December 2010 that we did something about it. But I think you heard today from Rupert Murdoch, who said that this was, you know, the most humble day. We come before this committee to try and explain, openly and honestly, what happened. Of course we were very unhappy with the criticisms that this committee found against the company.' In her mind still working for the company, she added: 'We aspire daily to have a great company, and your criticisms were felt.'

She denied that she had a particularly close relationship with David Cameron: 'I have read many, many allegations about my current relationship with the Prime Minister, with David Cameron, including my extensive horseriding with him every weekend up in Oxfordshire. I have never been horseriding with the Prime Minister . . . The truth is that he is a neighbour and a friend, but I deem the relationship to be wholly appropriate, and at no time have I ever had any conversation with the Prime Minister that you in the room would disapprove of.' George Osborne had suggested that Cameron hire Andy Coulson as his communications director.

Adrian Sanders pressed the point: 'So you had no conversation with David Cameron about Andy Coulson being suitable for that position?'

'No.'

'None whatsoever?'

'No.'

Sanders changed tack: 'Did you approve the subsidizing of Andy Coulson's salary after he left the *News of the World*?'

'Again, that's not true,' Brooks replied, 'so I didn't approve it.'

Sanders double-checked: 'So the *New Statesman* report is inaccurate? His salary is not being subsidized by News International.'

'That is correct. They are incorrect.'

The session ended at 7.20 p.m. Brooks had been questioned for one hour and thirty-seven minutes. Like the Murdochs, she had not made any embarrassing disclosures, but the committee had been relatively gentle: she had been arrested and was in enough trouble already.

Watson was inundated with requests for media interviews, but he was exhausted from a fortnight with no more than four hours' sleep a night, and wanted to decompress. He jumped into a cab with his researcher Katie Murphy, the general secretary of the Unite union, Len McClusky, and another Unite official, Jim Mowatt, to Claridge's, where he ordered a bottle of pink champagne.

19

Assault on the Establishment

*If it turns out that he knew about hacking, he will have lied to
a select committee, he will have lied to the police, he will
have lied to a court of law and he will have lied to me*

– David Cameron, 20 July 2011

The Home Affairs Committee worked through the night of the Murdochs' appearance to publish its report, 'Unauthorised Tapping or Hacking of Mobile Communications' at 5 a.m. on 20 July. The committee knew that it could not give a definitive account of affairs, but it was highly critical of News International and the Metropolitan Police. Even without knowing that NI staff had obstructed the police during their search of the building in 2006, the MPs concluded:

> We deplore the response of News International to the original investigation into hacking. It is almost impossible to escape the conclusion voiced by [Deputy Assistant Commissioner] Mr Clarke that they were deliberately trying to thwart a criminal investigation. We are astounded at the length of time it has taken News International to cooperate with the police but we are appalled that this is advanced as a reason for failing to mount a robust investigation.

Even taking into account the large number of anti-terrorist operations under way in 2006, the police's failure to investigate the Mulcaire evidence properly had led to 'serious wrongdoing'. Andy Hayman, the officer who had dined with the *News of the World* while formally overseeing the inquiry, had an 'apparently lackadaisical attitude' towards contacts with those under investigation and the committee was 'appalled' at Scotland Yard's employment of Neil Wallis. Dick Fedorcio, its director of public affairs, had apparently failed to carry out due diligence on Wallis and had 'attempted to deflect all blame on to [Assistant Commissioner] Mr Yates when he himself was responsible for letting the contract'. At a broader level, the MPs wrote:

> We are concerned about the level of social interaction which took place between senior Metropolitan Police Officers and executives at News International while investigations were or should have been being undertaken into the allegations of phone hacking carried out by the *News of the World.*

Intriguingly, the committee also wondered why the Crown Prosecution Service had not in its early consultations with the police placed more emphasis on Section 2 of RIPA, which stated that it was a crime to hack messages even if they had already been listened to by their intended recipient and were merely being stored. The committee concluded: 'Section 2 (7) of the Regulation of Investigatory Powers Act 2000 is particularly important and not enough attention has been paid to its significance.'

From March 2011, Tom Watson had been using Freedom of Information requests to obtain more details about the relationship between those in power and the country's biggest newspaper group. One link was between News International and Ken Macdonald, the Director of Public Prosecutions at the time of Operation Caryatid in 2006. The trail started with a reference in the *Guardian*'s media diary on 18 October 2005 to the Society of Editors conference – at a time when the *News of the World* was regularly hacking phones. Headed 'No Sleep to Bowness', it reported: 'News International arrived in the Lake District mob handed. They tried to leave that way too. The twin tabloid editors Rebekah Wade and Andy Coulson were last seen at the gala dinner with the Director of Public Prosecutions Ken Macdonald threatening to take him to a nightclub in Bowness.' Watson's FoI requests to the Crown Prosecution Service revealed Macdonald had visited the Society of Editors conference as a guest of Les Hinton, then News International's chief executive. Among meetings with other journalists, Macdonald had several meetings with News International's editors. On 17 January 2006, a month after Caryatid began – but before the CPS became involved in March – Macdonald was treated to dinner at Gordon Ramsay's Maze by the *News of the World*'s editor, Andy Coulson. On 10 April 2006, while the police and CPS were discussing what charges might be brought, but before he became aware of the investigation, Macdonald lunched with Rebekah Wade and Trevor Kavanagh at the RAC Club in Pall Mall. His diary contained a reference to a News Corporation reception with Rupert Murdoch at Burlington Gardens on 19 June, but Macdonald later said that he did not attend. On 20 February 2007, a month after the jailing of Goodman and Mulcaire, he again lunched with Rebekah Wade at the RAC Club.

Discreetly, the Crown Prosecution Service had agreed in late April 2006 to exclude sensitive (and thus embarrassingly newsworthy) witnesses from any prosecution. A month later, Macdonald had been informed by the prosecutors in the case that there was 'a vast array' of potential victims in Glenn Mulcaire's notes. In a letter to the Home Affairs Committee, the then Attorney General Lord Goldsmith, who also received the memo, said that legal convention dictated he himself could not contact the police about the inquiry, but, he pointed out, Macdonald, the Director of Public Prosecutions, could have done so. In a letter to the Home Affairs Committee, Macdonald said that had the CPS been shown evidence that victims of crime, such as Milly Dowler, had been hacked, he was sure that 'firm . . . action would have followed'. There was no evidence that Macdonald acted improperly during his meetings with News International (which subsequently employed him to assess the emails showing evidence of police bribery), but it was clear that the CPS had first been run by a director who was friendly with executives at Wapping and who continued to meet them while the organization was under investigation – and then by a man, Keir Starmer, who had not fully read the paperwork but who, when he did a year later, totally reversed the narrow interpretation of the law which the police claimed had hindered their inquiry.

David Cameron had refused to confirm the number and timings of his meetings with the Murdochs and their executives when asked to do so by Tom Watson in June 2010 but on Friday 15 July 2011 – the evening of Rebekah Brooks's resignation – he had published a list of his contacts with media figures which laid bare his closeness to the Murdochs. In the fourteen months since entering Number 10 in May 2010 – while News Corp was seeking to take over BSkyB – he had met News Corp's editors or executives fifteen times and attended five events and three parties organized by the company. Twice, Rebekah Brooks had been a guest at his official country residence, Chequers. Most surprisingly of all, perhaps, in March, two months after his resignation, Andy Coulson had also visited Chequers. By comparison Cameron had met the *Daily Mail*'s publishers four times, the *Independent* and *Evening Standard* three times and the *Guardian* twice. He had had no meetings with the BBC's director general, Mark Thompson. For the first time, rival Fleet Street editors could see exactly how relatively unimportant they were to Downing Street compared with Rupert Murdoch's empire.

Cameron's ministers also met News Corp or News International executives more than any other organization. Since the 2010 general election, cabinet ministers had had 107 meetings with Murdoch or his executives. Two ministers were particularly close to the Murdochs – George Osborne and Michael Gove. Osborne, the Chancellor of the Exchequer, had sixteen separate meetings with News International. Gove, the Education Secretary and former assistant editor of *The Times*, whose wife Sarah Vine still worked for the paper, had met Rupert Murdoch for breakfast, lunch or dinner six times, and had had six other meetings with Murdoch executives*. The Defence Secretary, Liam Fox, twice gave confidential defence briefings on Afghanistan and Britain's strategic defence review to Rebekah Brooks.[1]

A spokesman for Gove said: 'He did not discuss the BSkyB deal with the Murdochs and isn't at all embarrassed about his meetings, most of which have been about education, which is his job.' Osborne pointed out that the proportion of meetings he had had with Murdoch or his executives matched the record of Ed Miliband, eleven of

---

* In 2004, before he became a minister, Gove was paid an unspecified advance by HarperCollins, Murdoch's publishing arm, for a biography of the eighteenth-century politician Viscount Bolingbroke. The biography has not yet been delivered to the publishers. Between 2005 and 2009, Gove was paid £60,000 to £65,000 a year for assorted articles in *The Times*.

whose thirty-one media meetings had been with News Corp. In total, almost one quarter of all hospitality provided to Number 10 staff in the first seven months of the Coalition government came from News International. David Cameron's press aide Gabby Bertin had been wined and dined nine times, and also generously taken to Wimbledon. Of 111 events on the Downing Street hospitality register, twenty-six were Murdoch-related in one way or another.

The Foreign Secretary, William Hague, who, while in opposition, had received £195,000-a-year for a column in the *News of the World* and around £300,000 from Murdoch's HarperCollins between 2002 and 2006 for his biographies of William Pitt the Younger and William Wilberforce, defended the government's relationship with News International. 'Personally I'm not embarrassed by it in any way, but there is something wrong here in this country and it must be put right. It's been acknowledged by the Prime Minister and I think that's the right attitude to take,' he said.

On Wednesday 20 July, David Cameron faced his last Commons showdown before Parliament went into summer recess. Very unusually, Parliament's sitting had been extended by a day so there could be a debate on the scandal. At 11.36 a.m., Cameron began his statement on public confidence in the media and the police with the words: 'Over the past two weeks, a torrent of revelations and allegations has engulfed some of this country's most important institutions.' He outlined the action he had taken, ensuring a 'well led' police investigation, publishing his meetings with the media and establishing the Leveson Inquiry. By expressing so clearly its revulsion at the phone hacking allegations, he added, Parliament had helped end News Corp's bid for BSkyB. Labour MPs groaned at the irony of it.

In a little-noticed aside, Cameron conceded that Andy Coulson's deputy at the *News of the World*, Neil 'Wolfman' Wallis – who had subsequently been arrested on suspicion of intercepting communications – might have provided Coulson 'with some informal advice on a voluntary basis before the election'. The Prime Minister added: 'To the best of my knowledge, I did not know anything about this until Sunday night.'

Cameron also distanced himself further from Andy Coulson, his recent guest at Chequers, and who only a week earlier had been his friend. He told the Commons that if it turned out that he had been misled, he would have to offer a 'profound apology'. He said: 'With 20:20 hindsight and all that has followed, I would not have offered him the job , and I expect that he would not have taken it. But you do not make decisions in hindsight; you make them in the present. You live and you learn and, believe me, I have learnt.'

Ed Miliband responded:

> Given the New York Times's evidence, the public will rightly have expected very loud alarm bells to ring in the Prime Minister's mind, yet apparently he did nothing. Then in October the Prime Minister's chief of staff was approached again by the Guardian about the serious evidence it had about Mr Coulson's behaviour. Once more nothing was done. This cannot be put down to gross incompetence. It was a deliberate attempt to hide from the facts about Mr Coulson . . . He now says that in hindsight he made a mistake by hiring Mr Coulson. He says that if Mr Coulson lied to him, he would apologize. That is not good enough. It is not about hindsight or whether Mr Coulson lied to him; it is about all the information and warnings that he ignored. He was warned, but he preferred to ignore the warnings.

Miliband and Labour MPs asked Cameron thirteen times during the debate whether he had discussed the BSkyB bid with Murdoch's executives and each time the Prime Minister declined to say, merely repeating that he did not have any 'inappropriate conversations.'

Before it was over, Cameron had answered 136 questions. Many Conservative MPs pointed out that Labour had not tackled the influence of powerful media groups while in power, and that its leader was employing a former Times journalist, Tom Baldwin.

Cameron maintained that he had been open about the meeting with Rupert Murdoch in May 2010, though he had not divulged it to Tom Watson in June 2010, doing so only the previous week. He said: 'In relation to the meeting I held with Rupert Murdoch, the question is not whether he came in through the back door or front door but whether it was declared in the proper way, and yes, it was.'

The former Labour Home Secretary Alan Johnson asked: 'When the Prime Minister read of the extensive investigation in the New

York Times on 1 September last year, what was his reaction and what did he do?'

Cameron replied: 'The question I ask myself all the way through is: "Is there new information that Andy Coulson knew about phone hacking at the *News of the World*?" I could not be clearer about this: if it turns out that he knew about hacking, he will have lied to a select committee, he will have lied to the police, he will have lied to a court of law and he will have lied to me. I made the decision to employ him in good faith, because of the assurances he gave me. There was no information in that article that would lead me to change my mind about those assurances . . .'

Chris Bryant raised News International's refusal to release Harbottle & Lewis from client confidentiality. He asked the Prime Minister: 'Is this not clear evidence that News International, contrary to the pretend humility yesterday, is still refusing to cooperate fully with the investigation?'

Cameron responded: 'The point I would make is that that information, if it's germane to the police inquiry, needs to be given to the police and indeed to the Leveson inquiry.' (The message to Wapping was clear: release Harbottle & Lewis from confidentiality.)*

Asked whether the *Mail on Sunday* was correct to report that he had hired Andy Coulson at Rebekah Brooks's suggestion instead of the ex-BBC journalist Guto Harri, Cameron offered another non-answer. He replied: 'She specifically rejected that point yesterday. Guto now works

---

* In a letter to the Culture Committee that same day, July 20, Harbottle & Lewis issued a coded threat to Wapping: 'Notwithstanding News International's position to date, we are considering whether we can, consistently with our professional obligations and the constraints currently imposed on us by News International, assist the committee by providing substantive comments on yesterday's evidence. If we take the view that we can properly assist the committee, we will do so within whatever timeframe assists the committee.'

John Whittingdale, the committee chairman, stepped up the pressure, telling the Commons: 'I hope that in the light of the assurance that Rupert and James Murdoch gave us of their wish to cooperate as much as possible, the firm will review that decision and perhaps release Harbottle & Lewis from the arrangement, so that we can see the correspondence.'

for my good friend and colleague the Mayor of London, and he does a brilliant job.'

While the debate was continuing, the *Guardian*'s political editor, Patrick Wintour, wrote: 'Government officials said during the statement that the Prime Minister did not recall any specific conversations with News International about the BSkyB bid, but said he could not stop News Corporation officials from lobbying him about the bid during meetings. The officials stressed that the decision was for the Culture Secretary, Jeremy Hunt, on his own, and he at no point discussed the bid with Cameron. The spokesman said the conversations were "completely appropriate".'[2] So it was the case that they had discussed the BSkyB bid.

Shortly afterwards, the Labour backbencher John Mann published the response of the Cabinet Secretary, Gus O'Donnell, to his complaint on 18 July that Cameron's meeting with James Murdoch and Rebekah Brooks at Christmas 2010 had broken the rules on conflicts of interest. Unsurprisingly, O'Donnell cleared the Prime Minister of any interference.

When he finally sat down at 2.28 p.m., Cameron had evaded the gravest threat yet to his reputation, and at the backbench 1922 Committee that afternoon he received from his MPs forty seconds of desk banging, the traditional seal of approval. He reportedly told his backbenchers that his action over the phone hacking scandal had been 'decisive, frank and transparent'. After a tumultuous fortnight in which his close relationship with News International had imperilled his position, the Prime Minister had made it through to the summer holidays.

Rupert Murdoch flew out of the UK on his private Gulfstream jet that afternoon, 20 July, and editors now sought to move the news agenda on to other issues. On 21 July, a cartoon in *The Times* by Peter Brookes titled 'Priorities' showed starving African children with grotesquely swollen stomachs saying 'I've had a bellyful of phone hacking.' (The website Political Scrapbook said it was 'tasteless' to suggest that talking about phone hacking had prolonged Somalia's starvation: 'No one is stopping *The Times* covering both stories.'). On the same day, the *Sun* centred its coverage on a story about a Unicef official urging the media to focus on the drought in Africa, headlined:

'UN: forget hacking, kids are starving'. The *Sun* also ran a poll that day: YouGov asked 1,800 people online whether phone hacking was the most important story. Under the headline: 'Is phone hacking getting too much coverage?' the paper disclosed the results: Yes, 59 per cent; No 28 per cent, Not sure 13 per cent.

Aware that the company was potentially facing corruption charges in the US for bribing police in Britain, News Corp's directors began to take ever tougher action to identify and isolate the scandal. On the afternoon of 20 July, Wapping's Management and Standards Committee terminated News International's agreement to pay Glenn Mulcaire's legal fees and in the evening, under pressure from Cameron's comments earlier in the day, finally released Harbottle & Lewis from client confidentiality. Previously News International had always looked after fallen members of the family, as it had when Clive Goodman was jailed.

On 21 July the two former *News of the World* executives, Colin Myer and Tom Crone, struck back. Myler and Crone had defended the company to the Culture Committee but had, in effect, been accused by James Murdoch of failing to inform him of the full background to the Gordon Taylor settlement. On 19 July James Murdoch had told the Culture Committee that he had not known about the 'For Neville' email when authorizing the pay-off for Gordon Taylor. Now, two days later in a joint statement, the *News of the World*'s last editor and lawyer said:

> Just by way of clarification relating to Tuesday's Select Committee hearing, we would like to point out that James Murdoch's recollection of what he was told when agreeing to settle the Gordon Taylor litigation was mistaken. In fact, we did inform him of the 'For Neville' email which had been produced to us by Gordon Taylor's lawyers.

This was not the only challenge to James Murdoch's assertion that he had had only a minimal role in approving the settlement. The lawyer Mark Lewis claimed that during negotiations with Farrer's Julian Pike, over the Gordon Taylor case, Pike had told him that he was negotiating 'with Murdoch'. According to a company official with direct knowledge of the settlement who spoke to the *New York Times*,

News International's chief financial officer, Clive Milner, who made the financial arrangements, was told the case was very sensitive and 'the cheque is for James Murdoch'.[3] In a statement News Corp said: 'James Murdoch stands by his testimony to the committee.'

As the Culture Committee decided how to respond to this clash of evidence, Robert Peston again intervened to send the news in a different direction: he reported that the *Sun* had abruptly sacked its features editor and former *News of the World* features executive, Matt Nixson, whose computer was seized, over allegations of serious misconduct while at the *Screws*. Nixson said he had not been told the reason for his dismissal.*

On Twitter, Watson complained to Robert Peston: 'Why Sun story now Peston? More spin to deflect Myler/Crone statement? Where's your dignity?', to which Peston responded: 'Tom, this is an outrageous and untrue allegation.' As the spat played out in front of tens of thousands of computer users, Watson shot back: 'I'm sorry Peston but you are being spoonfed stories. The Myler statement creates a crisis at NI. You have form. Stop being a patsy.' Peston responded: 'That is not worthy of a response.'

On Friday 22 July, the Crown Office and Procurator Fiscal Service confirmed that Strathclyde Police had begun a full investigation into claims of phone hacking and breaches of data protection in Scotland. The investigation would cover allegations that witnesses gave perjured evidence in the trial of Tommy Sheridan, and that there were breaches of data protection legislation, phone hacking and police corruption.

Meanwhile another newspaper group – Trinity Mirror – and its most famous former editor, Piers Morgan, who had become a prime-time chatshow host on CNN, were dragged into the contro-

---

* In November 2011 Nixson launched a claim against News International for £100,000 damages for unfair dismissal. News International said it had sacked him for authorizing the bribery of a prison officer guarding the Soham murderer Ian Huntley. In his claim, Nixson said bribery of public officials was routine at the paper and that, under its rules, banned only payments to criminals or witnesses in criminal trials: the *News of the World* 'frequently sanctioned payments to civil servants, members of the armed forces and prison officers' of between £750 and £1,000 for tips and exclusives. The police informed Nixson that he was of no interest to their inquiries.

versy. Following a slump in its share price, the Mirror Group launched its own review of editorial practices. Trinity Mirror said: 'In the light of recent events, we thought it was timely to look at our controls and procedures,' though its inquiry was focused on current procedures rather than identifying previous wrongdoing. Taking to Twitter, Piers Morgan responded to suggestions that he had known of phone hacking while at the *Mirror* by denouncing his detractors as 'liars, druggie ex-bankrupts and conmen'. Huffpost UK had reprinted a transcript of Morgan's appearance on the BBC's *Desert Island Discs* in 2009 when he defended the dark arts by saying: 'A lot of it was done by third parties. That's not to defend it, because obviously you were running the results of their work. I'm quite happy to have to sit here defending all these things I used to get up to.' In the *Daily Mail* in 2006, Morgan had written: 'I was played a message of a tape Paul [McCartney] had left for Heather on her mobile phone. It was heartbreaking.'[4] Now Morgan said: 'I have never hacked a phone, told anyone to hack a phone, nor to my knowledge published any story obtained from the hacking of a phone.'[5]

Following a gunman's tragic rampage in Norway, phone hacking moved off the front pages, where it had been for eighteen days. Inside the *Guardian* on Saturday 23 July, the Commons Speaker, John Bercow, said that the scandal had re-energized a Parliament laid low by the row over MPs' expenses scandal: 'Parliament has started to reassert itself. We have rediscovered our collective balls. I would not want to be smug or complacent. We are now out of intensive care, but we are still in the recovery unit.' After a frantic fortnight, Parliament was in recess and the scandal was again receding, but one more particularly unwelcome victim of phone hacking was about to emerge.

The *News of the World* had long considered that it had a special relationship with Sara Payne, whose eight-year-old daughter Sarah had been abducted yards from her home in West Sussex in 2000, prompting Rebekah Brooks's 'For Sarah' campaign. Within hours of the news that the paper had hacked Milly Dowler, rumours spread that the paper had also eavesdropped on Sara Payne, who, to much relief at Wapping, issued a statement on 7 July saying that she had not been contacted by police.

Despite her concern about the eavesdropping of other grieving parents, Payne still thought warmly of the *News of the World*, which had supported her so steadfastly, and for its final edition she had contributed a column mourning 'the passing of an old friend', recalling that its managing editor, Stuart Kuttner, and spokeswoman, Hayley Barlow, had spent hours at her bedside in 2009 as she recovered from a stroke. She wrote: 'God only knows why the *News of the World* has stuck by me for so long and for that you'd have to ask them but the reason I have stayed with them is that they have always been a paper that cares and a voice for the people.'

At 5 p.m. on 28 July, Nick Davies and Amelia Hill at the *Guardian* disclosed that while championing her cause, the *News of the World* had been hacking into her messages to profit from her ongoing grief.

Payne was hit hard by the betrayal. Phoenix Chief Advocates, the charity she ran for victims of paedophilia, said she was 'absolutely devastated'. Like the Milly Dowler case, the story could hardly have been more damaging for News International and it put the company back in the spotlight just as it was fading from the news after almost three weeks. The 'Hacked Off' campaign said the Payne allegations indicated 'breathtaking hypocrisy and a complete lack of moral sense'.

News International's spin machine whirred into operation. In a statement issued by her new PR firm, Bell Pottinger (which specialized in representing regimes with reputational issues), Brooks said it was 'unthinkable' that the *News of the World* had hacked Payne. 'The idea of her being targeted is beyond my comprehension,' Brooks said. 'It is imperative for Sara and the other victims of crime that these allegations are investigated and those culpable brought to justice.'*

News International said it was 'deeply concerned' by the story.

---

* The following day, 29 July, Glenn Mulcaire said any suggestion that he had acted 'unilaterally' was untrue. In a statement, his solicitors said: 'As an employee he acted on the instructions of others.' Intriguingly, they added: 'There were also occasions when he understood his instructions were from those who genuinely wished to assist in solving crimes.'

On the evening of 28 July, Watson told Sky News he would ask the Culture Committee to recall the younger Murdoch; instead, the committee decided the following morning to write to James Murdoch, Colin Myler and Tom Crone asking them to clear up whether Murdoch had been told about the 'For Neville' email or not.

As News International continued to battle to restore its reputation, the police operation into its activities daily grew more serious. The day after the Sara Payne story broke, Scotland Yard confirmed it was expanding Operation Tuleta into a full-blown inquiry. Senior officers had been reluctant to take action against computer hacking while they devoted such substantial resources to phone hacking. Now, however, the evidence was too strong to ignore: detectives said that it was clear that computer hacking had been happening for much longer than the three months reported by the BBC's *Panorama* in March. Ian Hurst, whose computer had been hacked by the *News of the World* trawling for the whereabouts of the IRA informer Stakeknife, expressed concern that the Met had been so slow to act, despite having the evidence from the Daniel Morgan trial. The former army intelligence officer said: 'Officers do not appear to have investigated these crimes, which, given everything else that has happened, reinforces my belief that the Met is institutionally corrupt.'

On 1 August, further evidence emerged about a possible data clean-up at Wapping. In a letter to the Home Affairs Committee an IT firm used by News international, HCL Technologies, disclosed that, on nine occasions between April 2010 and July 2011, its help had been requested in deleting emails from Wapping's systems. HCL Technologies had 'answered in negative' to one of the requests, in January 2011 – the month Scotland Yard launched its new inquiry. News International, in effect, admitted important data had been deleted, saying in a statement: 'News International keeps backups of its core systems and, in close cooperation with the Operation Weeting team, has been working to restore these backups.'

The following day, Operation Weeting's detectives arrested one of the most important figures at the *News of the World*: Stuart Kuttner, its managing editor since 1987. Nicknamed 'Kuttie' by reporters for his questioning and trimming of expenses, Kuttner had been the public face of the paper, defending the Sarah's Law campaign and the secret videotaping of a sting on the Countess of Wessex. When he appeared before the Culture Committee in 2009, Kuttner had denied any knowledge of wrongdoing. He was detained on suspicion of phone hacking and police corruption, and released on bail. The police operation had now arrested all but a few of the senior editorial executives at the *News of the World* between 2000 and 2007.

20

The Ghosts of Wapping

There was no ambiguity about the significance of that document
– Colin Myler

News International had staggered into high summer. Its best-selling Sunday newspaper had hacked into the voicemails of a missing schoolgirl, victims of terrorist bombings and the mother of a murdered child in whose name it had campaigned. The disclosures had revolted readers and advertisers, forcing its closure. At least sixty detectives were investigating phone hacking, computer hacking and the corruption of police officers, and they had arrested most of the *News of the World*'s senior staff. Most worryingly of all for Rupert Murdoch personally, his reputation had been under its greatest assault in his sixty-year career.

Faced with this barrage, on 5 August, News Corp announced that Elisabeth Murdoch – whose TV company it had expensively acquired in February – would not take up her seat on the board. Presenting News Corp's full year results on 10 August, Rupert Murdoch stressed that he always acted in partnership with his deputy, Chase Carey. 'Make no mistake – Chase Carey and I run this company as a team,' he told investors, saying that if he fell under a bus, Carey would take over 'immediately'. Bolstered by a strong performance from its television interests, full-year profits were up 9 per cent to $982 million and the remuneration committee awarded Rupert Murdoch a $12.5 million bonus, Chase Carey $10 million and James Murdoch $6 million, though James forewent his bonus as contrition for 'the current controversy'.

While News Corp sought to slough off its autocratic image, problems mounted at its troubled British newspapers. The day Rupert Murdoch was announcing bumper profits, officers from Operation Weeting arrested Greg Miskiw, one of the *Screws* newsdesk's two veteran Ukrainians, on his return from Florida, where he had been working for the *National Enquirer*.

The following week, on 16 August, the Commons Culture Committee published Clive Goodman's withering 2007 letter appealing against his dismissal.* In 2009, after the Gordon Taylor story broke, MPs had wondered why Goodman had been paid off after being jailed for committing crimes which had damaged his employers; the suggestion that he had a strong case in employment law seemed far-fetched. Now the public learned what News International's executives had known all along: after his sacking Goodman had written to Daniel Cloke, Wapping's human resources director, claiming that phone hacking had been so routine at the *News of the World* that journalists openly discussed it at editorial conferences (see page 55).

Dated 2 March 2007, the letter preceded all the evidence given by Wapping's editors maintaining that Clive Goodman was a lone 'rogue reporter'. If Goodman's claims were true, Wapping had mounted a cover-up and its executives had told lie after lie to politicians, journalists and the public. Even if they were false, executives were clearly wrong to tell the Culture Committee that there was 'no evidence' of more widespread wrongdoing. This time, News International – employing Edelman PR – did not deny there had been a cover-up, saying: 'We recognize the seriousness of materials disclosed to the police and parliament and are committed to working in a constructive way and open way with all the relevant authorities.'

Publication of the letter at 3 p.m. on the Culture Committee website dominated the TV news bulletins and front pages. (The *Guardian* headline was: 'Explosive letter lifts the lid on four-year hacking

---

* The Culture Committee had received two copies of Goodman's letter, one from Harbottle & Lewis and one from News International. The News International version blanked out Goodman's allegations that phone hacking had been openly discussed, that Tom Crone and Andy Coulson had promised he could return to his job if he did not implicate the paper in court, and that the company had continued to pay him after he pleaded guilty to stealing the secrets of the Royal Household. The version of the letter in Chapter 5 is Harbottle & Lewis's.

cover-up'; the *Independent*'s: 'Phone hacking: the smoking gun'.) While the letter itself was deeply embarrassing, it was published alongside a politely worded but venomous attack on News International from Harbottle & Lewis. Evidently, the law firm had been storing up its anger for two years since December 2009, when in answer to a question about Wapping's internal inquiries, Rebekah Brooks had released its letter of 29 May 2007 (see p. 60) about Goodman's employment case to the Culture Committee.

At that time News International had used Harbottle's letter to suggest that outside lawyers had carried out a thorough review of wrongdoing at the *News of the World*. As the Murdochs came under pressure in July 2011 for their failure to investigate the criminality, they again reinforced that impression. In his interview with the *Wall Street Journal* on 14 July Rupert Murdoch blamed the lawyers for making a 'major mistake' in underestimating the problem, and on 19 July James Murdoch had told the Culture Committee: 'That opinion was something that the company rested on.'

Released from client confidentiality, Harbottle & Lewis now revealed that it had never been asked to launch an internal investigation at Wapping:* News International had asked it to check some emails to see if Goodman had a valid claim for unfair dismissal. Harbottle & Lewis had simply reviewed and agreed with Wapping that it could not find 'reasonable' evidence in them that executives knew about Goodman's behaviour, yet its letter had been presented to the Culture Committee as evidence of an inquiry. In its letter to the MPs dated 11 August, Harbottle & Lewis revealed that its bill was £10,294 plus VAT, which hardly indicated that it had been commissioned to carry out a forensic examination of the goings-on at Britain's biggest newspaper group. And if News International really had 'rested on' its letter from 2007, it pointed out, it would not have paid out nearly a quarter of a million pounds to Goodman – since its review had not supported his claim that phone hacking was widespread (though there was evidence of police corruption).

---

* In a letter to the Culture Committee on 16 August, Burton Copeland said: 'BCL was not instructed to carry out an investigation into "phone hacking" at the News of the World.'

The letter left committee members in no doubt that News International had deliberately exaggerated its role in Wapping's supposed internal investigation. Even more damningly, Harbottle & Lewis delicately indicated that crucial evidence about corruption in the emails had been destroyed. It carefully explained that in 2007, after its lawyers had been given remote access to Goodman's emails, they had printed out some for further study and, because they were unable to open others, obtained hard copies from the IT department. On concluding its review, Harbottle had filed all its work on the case, together with the printouts, in its archives for four years (during which time News International was denying all wrongdoing) until 24 March 2011, when News International asked for the file. Harbottle & Lewis told the Culture Committee that what was of 'principal interest' in the file was not confirmation of its remit or Goodman's letter – but the printouts of the emails themselves. Without mentioning the deletion of emails, Harbottle & Lewis wrote: 'It seems that the firm's copies of these documents from News International's own records are now the only remaining copies (on paper or in electronic form) still in existence.' In an understated but umistakable way, it was suggesting there had been a data clean-up at Wapping.

News International's defences were rapidly being overwhelmed. James Murdoch had said the company had been relying upon evidence provided by the police, the PCC and Harbottle & Lewis. But the police were now saying Wapping had frustrated its inquiry; the Press Complaints Commission was complaining it had been misled; and Harbottle & Lewis insisted it had never been asked to conduct a widespread inquiry. Most worryingly of all, there now appeared to be evidence of the deliberate destruction of data, apparently in an attempt to prevent the truth ever becoming known about what happened at the *News of the World*.

At the same time the career of another executive embroiled in the scandal, Andy Coulson, was being cast in an ever less flattering light. At the end of August the BBC's Robert Peston divulged that David Cameron's friend had received large payments from News International after leaving the *News of the World*. Few nights were better to slip out embarrassing news than 22 August, when TV bulletins were reporting the triumphant entry into Tripoli of Colonel Gaddafi's opponents. At 9.50 p.m. on his BBC blog, Peston disclosed that News International had paid Coulson six-figure sums while working for the Conservatives:

> As I understand it, after Mr Coulson resigned News International said it would pay him his full [leaving] entitlement under his two-year contract as editor of the *News of the World* – although the money would be paid in instalments. I am also told that Mr Coulson also continued to receive his News International work benefits, such as healthcare, for three years, and he kept his company car.

Coulson had been receiving large sums of money from Britain's most powerful media group while occupying a senior position in Her Majesty's Loyal Opposition, in direct contradiction of his testimony to the Culture and Media Committee on 21 July 2009 (see page 93). The Conservative Party, which had denied that Coulson had any other source of income,* issued a statement saying it had been unaware of the payments until the night of Peston's story. While he was at Number 10, Wapping also reimbursed Andy Coulson's legal bills for his evidence at the perjury trial of Tommy Sheridan. The following day, 23 August, News International's new chief executive, Tom Mockridge, informed Coulson that it would no longer pay his legal fees in any litigation arising from phone hacking. Coulson appealed to the courts to force News International to pay. He lost, and is appealing once more.

Scotland Yard was experiencing its own problems, despite receiving some good news. On 17 August, after just twenty-two working days, the Independent Police Complaints Commission's inquiry had cleared Sir Paul Stephenson, John Yates, Andy Hayman and Peter Clarke of any misconduct in their handling of the phone hacking investigations. However, the IPCC added the public would 'make its own judgements' about the wisdom of Stephenson's acceptance of a free stay at

---

* In July, a senior Conservative Party official said: 'We can give categorical assurances that he wasn't paid by any other source. Andy Coulson's only salary, his only form of income, came from the party during the years he worked for the party and in government.'[1]

Champneys. It also began an investigation into possible misconduct by Dick Fedorcio, the director of public affairs who had arranged the lunch and dinners with *News of the World* executives.*

At the same time the Met was worried that some officers were still too friendly with the press. In August it had arrested an unnamed 51-year-old male detective on suspicion of making 'unauthorized disclosures' from Operation Weeting. Shortly afterwards, in the week beginning 29 August, officers questioned Amelia Hill, the *Guardian* reporter who had co-written the Milly Dowler story and who had broken news of several arrests and the recovery of the bag found outside Rebekah and Charlie Brooks's home (which was still being held by police).

On 16 September, four days after Merseyside's police chief Bernard Hogan-Howe became the Met's new Commissioner, Scotland Yard announced its intention to use the Police and Criminal Evidence Act, and possibly also the Official Secrets Act, to force Hill and the *Guardian* to hand over her notes on the Dowler story and others. The Met said: 'We recognize the important public interest of whistleblowing and investigative reporting, however neither is apparent in this case. This is an investigation into the alleged gratuitous release of information that is not in the public interest.'

The suggestion that the Milly Dowler story had not been in the public interest staggered journalists, lawyers and MPs – it had prompted the furore which had exposed the full extent of Wapping's wrongdoing, led to the establishment of the Leveson Inquiry (yet to start) and sank Rupert Murdoch's attempts to seize full control of BSkyB. Index on Censorship and the National Union of Journalists condemned the move – which irritated all Fleet Street papers, including those owned by News International, to which heavy-handed action by a police force said to have been in its pocket was unwelcome. *The Sunday Times* urged the Met to 'call off its legal dogs'. The Met briefed that a superintendent in its Professional Standards Directorate had fired the legal salvo without the knowledge of Hogan-Howe, and the Attorney General, Dominic Grieve, and the Director of Public Prosecutions, Keir Starmer, made it known that

---

* At the time of writing, this report has yet to be published.

they had not been consulted either. Three days before the planned hearing on 23 September, Scotland Yard backed down, maintaining it had not intended to target journalists or disregard their duty to protect sources. The decision was welcomed but the Met had once again demonstrated that it was susceptible to political and media pressure.

In Britain the police investigation and the number of civil cases were growing, but News Corp's greatest problem lay in the United States, where amid the flurry of news in July, the Department of Justice had ordered an FBI investigation into whether the company had breached the Foreign Corrupt Practices Act. Under the Act News Corp's directors could be jailed for five years if they had authorized or known about bribery in the UK but had failed to stop it. By now the American directors had become thoroughly disenchanted with the British newspapers. The *Sun* and the *News of the World* had thrown off cash from the 1980s onwards, but now profits were dwindling and they were causing serious reputational and shareholder damage: in 2010 globally newspapers contributed only $6 billion of revenue while TV and film made $22 billion.

The company decided on a three-track approach. Firstly, it would cooperate fully with the police. In the past it had paid lip service to helping the police while deliberately obstructing their inquiries; that strategy was no longer working because the company was no longer the toast of policemen and politicians and a humiliated Scotland Yard was mounting a proper investigation. News Corp's Management and Standards Committee called in lawyers from the City firm Linklaters to root out criminality at all NI titles, including the *Sun*, *The Times* and *Sunday Times*. Up to 100 lawyers began interviewing staff on the three titles and combing through old expenses claims, invoices and emails dating back years. Up to twenty police officers from Operation Elveden were embedded with the lawyers and asked them to search the company's computer database, which had been forensically recovered, including all the deletions. They were also able to begin examining all the emails on the second server which the IT whistleblower had alerted Tom Watson to in 2010 and about which Watson had subsequently informed Sue Akers.

Secondly, the company stepped up its efforts to settle the rising number of phone hacking cases in the civil courts. On 18 August, it paid Leslie Ash and Lee Chapman a 'healthy six-figure sum' and, on 19 September, it struck a deal to settle the most embarrassing case of all – that of the Dowlers. Mark Lewis had negotiated a vast settlement – £2 million from the company for the Dowlers and £1 million directly from Rupert Murdoch for a charity of their choice. The settlement – fifty times the *News of the World*'s record non-hacking privacy payout to Max Mosley – suggested that the £20 million Wapping had notionally set aside in April for dealing with the scandal would fall well short of what was needed. The company also decisively cut its ties with those it deemed had acted wrongly. Previously, during the cover-up, Wapping had helped erring members of its family, paying off Goodman and Mulcaire and remunerating Andy Coulson while he was working for the Conservatives, but now it said it would 'vigorously contest' employment tribunal claims from the *News of the World*'s former news editor Ian Edmondson, who had launched an unfair dismissal claim in April, and its chief reporter Neville Thurlbeck. In his first public statement since his arrest, on 30 September Thurlbeck indicated that the blame for hacking lay with others: 'I say this most emphatically and with certainty and confidence that the allegation which led to my dismissal will eventually be shown to be false. And those responsible for the action, for which I have been unfairly dismissed, will eventually be revealed.' Ominously, he added: 'There is much I could have said publicly to the detriment of News International but so far have chosen not to do so.'

Thirdly, while seeking to cooperate with the police in their inquiries, the company stuck by its chief executive, James Murdoch, despite growing questions about his role arising from the evidence of two of Wapping's recently departed executives, Colin Myler and Tom Crone. Appearing before the Culture Committee on 7 September, Myler and Crone (in line for large pay-offs) appeared reluctant to launch a full-frontal attack on News International, but equally they did not wish to be held culpable for the cover-up. They were adamant that James Murdoch had known about the 'For Neville' email when he signed off the payment to Gordon Taylor. 'Mr Murdoch is the chief executive of the company,' Myler said. 'He is experienced, I am experienced, Mr Crone is experienced. I think everyone perfectly understood the seriousness and significance of what we were discussing. There was no ambiguity about the significance of that document.' Looking every part the urbane lawyer with his silvery hair and sharply cut suit, Tom Crone stated laconically: 'We went to see Mr Murdoch and it was explained to him what this document was and what it meant.' Within hours, News Corp released a statement from James Murdoch saying bluntly: 'Neither Mr Myler nor Mr Crone told me that wrongdoing extended beyond Mr Goodman or Mr Mulcaire.' The Culture Committee decided to recall News Corp's deputy Chief Operating Officer, meaning that he would face another showdown with MPs and undergo hours of questioning about his recollection of events.

With Rebekah Brooks gone and its British empire under serious attack from almost all sides, News International adjusted to its new humility in public life. In previous years, ministers and MPs had hob-nobbed with the Murdochs and their executives at lavish champagne receptions at the party conferences but in 2011 it was possible no one would turn up and the events were cancelled. At a special debate on phone hacking on 27 September at the Labour Party conference in Liverpool, Chris Bryant remarked on the company's sharp reversal of fortune: 'This time last year I was thrown out of the party – the News International party. I'm glad to say that at this conference there isn't a News International party to be thrown out of.' Tom Watson, who had been the target of a whispering campaign the previous year, suggested that The *Sun* had also been hacking phones. Delegates unanimously passed a motion calling for James Murdoch to resign as chairman of BSkyB.

Nonetheless News International still had some supporters. At the Conservative Party conference in Manchester on 4 October, Michael Gove, the Education Secretary, expressed his ardent admiration for Rupert Murdoch at a fringe meeting. 'I think he is a force of nature and a phenomenon. I think he is a great man,' Gove said.

What is alleged to have happened breaches every journalist's rule in the book. However, I don't think you can look at this episode and all the questions that it has raised, without looking into the context of all of Rupert Murdoch's career. The investment he has made in quality journalism has meant that as a result we have a flourishing collection of broadsheets, and we also have vigorous tabloids, which hold people like me to account.

The Times accurately headlined the story: 'Murdoch's a phenomenon and I admire him, says minister'. Gove's experience as Education Secretary might be useful if, as has been suggested, News Corporation makes a move into the educational publishing business.

Despite the support of one of the Coalition's leading ministers, News Corp could not stem the increasing evidence that its heir, James Murdoch, had seen or known about the 'For Neville' email – which indicated widespread wrongdoing at the *Screws* – before he signed off the £425,000 settlement to Gordon Taylor.

In early October 2011, Tom Watson's phone rang. In a soft and precise Wearside accent, the caller said: 'I've got some information for you.' A rendezvous was arranged for the following Monday, 10 October, at a 1930s semi-detached house in the south London suburbs. For the first time in months, its occupant was wearing a suit. After he brewed some coffee, Neville Thurlbeck told his story.

For two years, much of the media had suspected he was a phone hacker, that he was the Neville in the 'For Neville' email. But although he was, he wanted it to be known that he had never hacked any phones or ordered any phones to be hacked, and he wanted Watson to help clear his name.

Thurlbeck was furious with his former employers. In April, he had been arrested and in September, after twenty-one years' service at the *News of the World*, he had been sacked without a pay-off. On the basis of his £96,000-a-year salary as chief reporter, he calculated he should have received a redundancy payment of £245,000.

Coolly and precisely, he gave his account of what happened inside the *News of the World*. In early 2005, seeking to become a freelance seller of stories as well as a researcher, Glenn Mulcaire had offered the executive news editor, Greg Miskiw, a story about the PFA's chief executive, Gordon Taylor, which he said he had picked up at a PFA dinner. In February 2005, Miskiw had agreed to buy the story, signing the contract with Mulcaire later found at his house by police, but Miskiw had shortly thereafter left the paper, in July 2005. Sensing that he would not get paid, Mulcaire had contacted Thurlbeck, but Thurlbeck was not interested. He told Watson: 'It's about an F-list personality that nobody's ever heard of unless you closely follow football. It's overpriced at £12,000 . . . I think it's never going to get into the paper because it's a poor celebrity, it's too expensive and the editor will say "no".' So he recommended Mulcaire contact another, more senior, *NoW* journalist – who was interested and dispatched Thurlbeck to 'doorstep' Taylor's colleague, Jo Armstrong in Blackburn. The email containing extracts of Taylor's hacked messages was 'For Neville', Thurlbeck said, only in the sense that the gist of its contents were to be relayed to him.

When in early 2008, the police disclosed the 'For Neville' email to Mark Lewis, the paper was deeply worried. According to Thurlbeck, Tom Crone had confronted him about the email, saying: 'Neville, we've got a problem because of this, what's this all about?'

'I looked at it [and said]: "I don't know, Tom, I never received it. Tom, this had nothing to do with me . . ." He said: "However, this shows that this had gone through the office . . . so clearly News International are culpable and we're going to have to settle. And I'm going to have to show this to James Murdoch."'

Thurlbeck went on: 'The reason I can remember him saying that was because I said to him: "Please, do you have to show him this? Because he's going to assume the worst of me and he's going to think it's all to do with me. Is there any way we can get around this?" And he said to me: "Nev, I'm sorry but I'm going to have to show him this because it is the only reason why we're having to settle. I've got to show him this."'

Thurlbeck stressed: 'This is not some vague memory. I was absolutely on a knife edge. He [Crone] was going to show this to James Murdoch. There's only going to be one conclusion he's going to jump to which is: "Get rid of Thurlbeck." Tom took it to him. The following week I said to him: "Did you show him the email?" and he said: "Yes, I did." Now Tom can't remember if he showed him it or spoke to him about it, but he said: "Yes I did."'

Thurlbeck kept his job, but so did the journalist he claimed had been responsible.

When Nick Davies's story about the Taylor settlements broke on

8 July 2009, Thurlbeck recalled: 'There was a big outcry' in Wapping and executives again came up with the same solution: redundancy for Neville. Thurlbeck said: 'Tom [Crone], who I've always got on well with, very kindly said to me, very privately: "You're going to be called into the editor's office and you're going to be made an offer. . ." And I was completely shell-shocked and I said to him: "What do you mean?". And he said: "The transcript for Neville." And I said: "Tom, I've already explained to you what all that was about." And he said: "I know." So I went in and explained to the boss: "But I didn't do this. I've explained to Tom the sequence of events. Have you spoken to [the other journalist] about this?" The reply he gave me was: "Yes, he can't even remember anything about the story."'

He added: 'There was a telephone call, a conference call, between Tom, Colin and [the other journalist] . . . and Tom screamed [at the other journalist]: "You fucking liar". And the company was aware at this point that I had been telling the truth and that [the other journalist] had been lying.'

Despite warning the management and supplying internal emails from the journalist he blamed, Thurlbeck believed that it had been convenient for the management – which stuck by its rogue reporter defence – to allow 'the iron filings of suspicion' to stick to him rather than the other, more senior journalist, whose naming would suggest a wider problem at the paper. Neither Crone nor Myler mentioned the conversation described by Thurlbeck in their evidence to the Commons Culture committee on 21 July 2009.

Watson asked: 'So they effectively misled the committee. They knew?'

Thurlbeck replied: 'They did. I don't know why. The only reason I can suggest is that it wouldn't be to their corporate benefit to say: "Oh, no, it wasn't "Neville – it was [the other journalist]." There's no corporate brownie points to be won for that. All you're doing is spreading the flame-thrower further and further over your company at the time it was still desperately clinging to the rogue reporter defence. So they sat on this for two years, knowing that he was a hacker.'

He suggested it was not the only time the management had hidden the truth. He said he had not wanted to threaten the women in the

Max Mosley case to cooperate with the paper, and only did so because the news editor, Ian Edmondson, was standing over him. 'The black-mail emails were the most awful – the most cynical emails to the Max Mosley prostitutes – when I say: "Look, we know who you are, come on board and tell us your story and we won't name you". Those emails were dictated to me by Ian Edmondson . . . "Write this, write this to them". He dictated these emails to me and I had to stand there and face this barrage of assault about these [emails] from Mosley's QC in the High Court. I can understand why. It's just that I wasn't able to stand up and say: "It wasn't me", even in court. The advice was don't start throwing flame-throwers around.' Later, Ian Edmond-son told the Leveson Inquiry that he could not remember whether he had dictated the email.[2]

Traditionally, Thurlbeck said, hacking had not been a tactic of the *News of the World*. 'I was aware of somebody who did hacking in the nineties . . . he was juggling two mobile phones and I said: "What are you doing there?" and he told me what he was doing – and he went on to do great things on Fleet Street – but anyway, I said to him: "What do you do that for?" And he said: "Well, you can get good stuff."'

But by the early 2000s phone hacking had become much more common at the paper, after the influx of journalists from the *People*. 'At the *People*, one of our competitors, they couldn't rival us for money, they couldn't compete with the buy-ups but the way they could get stories was by stealing them, by hacking.' While Thurlbeck had been on secret assignments for the *News of the World*, he recalled his surprise at finding reporters from the *People* turning up at the same job: they had been hacking his phone.

Referring to Rebekah Brooks, Thurlbeck told Watson: 'She didn't like you at all. She took an absolute pathological dislike to you . . . She saw you as the person that was really threatening. She tried to smear you as being mad. She was briefing. She was saying to Blair: "We've got to call this man off, he's mad."' He also told Watson of the smear operation against the Culture Committee in 2009 (see chapter 7).

Before he finished, Thurlbeck had something to say about James Murdoch, who was due to reappear before the Culture Committee within days – that he could not possibly admit he had seen the 'For Neville' email:

> It would be absolute suicide for him to admit that he knew it, to say: 'I knew that hacking went further than a rogue reporter and allowed the company to provide the rogue reporter defence for so long and not do anything about it,' and now the paper's had to close and the company's been tarred and feathered, then it's suicide for him. He can't.

The Management and Standards Committee finally released its former lawyer Julian Pike of Farrer & Co* from client confidentiality in early October. On 19 October, giving evidence to the Culture Committee, Pike freely admitted that the 'For Neville' email and the Greg Miskiw contract with Mulcaire suggested several *News of the World* journalists had been involved in phone hacking and that the one rogue reporter defence advanced to Parliament was false. Asked by Paul Farrelly: 'So it was quite clear to you at the time that the "one rogue reporter" defence the company was still maintaining, including in front of this committee, was not true?', he replied: 'That is correct.'

Farrelly probed: 'You have told us that you were aware from the moment that News International came in front of Parliament that it was not telling the truth and did nothing. Does that make you uncomfortable?' Pike replied: 'Not especially, no.'

Farrelly: 'Do you have any scruples?' Pike: 'Yes.'

Although client confidentiality prevented Farrer & Co from informing police of the wrongdoing, it could have declined to act for News International, but it did not: Rupert Murdoch's newspaper company was its biggest client.

Most important of all, Farrer's disclosed the legal opinion James Murdoch had referred to in July when he explained to the MPs why he had authorized such a large payment to Gordon Taylor. Michael Silverleaf's advice in June 2008 (see page 71) clearly indicated that

---

* It is not known why News Corp released Farrer's from the restrictions of client confidentiality. It may be that Farrer's (cf. Harbottle & Lewis, page 261), considering its reputation had been unfairly tarnished by its recent activities on behalf of News International, had threatened to stretch confidentiality to its limits, or it may be that the move was part of the MSC's attempt to distance the company from its former executives and lawyers.

there had been a culture of wrongdoing in the newsroom of the *News of the World* which extended beyond a rogue reporter.

On 21 October, Rupert Murdoch faced two problems at the highlight of News Corp's calendar, its annual meeting: personal criticism of his handling of phone hacking and a vote to oust James and Lachlan from the board, which threatened his dynasty's grip on the company. News Corp switched the meeting from New York, its usual venue, where most investors and business journalists were based, to its 20th Century Fox film studios on the outskirts of Los Angeles. Investors were bused to the meeting and frisked before entering. Outside, protestors held up placards saying 'Fire the Murdoch Mafia' and 'Rupert Isn't Above the Law'.

At the meeting, Murdoch appeared to be sharper than he had been at the Culture Committee in July, though he several times forgot the rules of the meeting he was chairing. He stressed the 'legend' of News Corp's transformation from a single newspaper in Australia to a multibillion-dollar digital giant headquartered in New York. Some of its newspaper journalists in the UK had hacked voicemails but he said: 'We could not be taking this more seriously or listening more intently to criticisms,' before limiting contributions from investors to one minute.

The Californian pension fund Calpers, the Australian Shareholders' Association and other shareholders assailed Murdoch about the company's governance and its handling of the scandal. At the beginning of a contribution from Edward Mason, representing the Church of England Commissioners, Murdoch mocked: 'Your investments haven't been that great, but go ahead.' Shrugging off the comment, Mason said the commissioners were deeply concerned at the company's management: 'There need to be radical changes to corporate governance. The voting rights of the Murdoch family should be more proportionate to their economic interests in the company and there must be more genuinely independent voices on the board.'

Nominated as a proxy shareholder by the US trade union group American Federation of Labor and Congress of Industrial Organizations, Tom Watson had flown to LA for the meeting. Determined to make the most of his minute, he stressed the scale of the allegations facing News Corp: 200 British police were investigating not just

Glenn Mulcaire but Daniel Morgan's former business partner Jonathan Rees, and the allegations involved not just phone hacking but computer hacking, perjury and conspiracy to pervert the course of justice. News Corp was facing a 'Mulcaire Two' [Jonathan Rees] as victims of computer hacking sued for invasion of privacy. He said: 'You haven't told any of your investors about what is to come, and I have to say Mr Murdoch, if I know about this, then with all the resources you're putting in to clearing up the scandal, then you must know about this too.'

'What happened a few years ago was absolutely wrong,' Murdoch replied, 'and I have said so and I've said that we are all ashamed of it. But these recent rumours you speak about have all been worked by us with the police. In fact 90 per cent of what the police know comes from all the searches of emails and tens of thousands of things we are supplying them with.'

The Murdochs survived the rebellion but outside the family's holding, 67 per cent of non-aligned shareholders had voted to depose James Murdoch and 64 per cent his brother Lachlan. Non-family shareholders also opposed (unsuccessfully) Rupert Murdoch's $33 million pay. Following the meeting, a senior analyst from Invesco, Kevin Holt, estimated that News Corp was trading at a 40 per cent discount to its true value because of its recent failures, including a 20 per cent 'Rupert discount' – 'because of the acquisitions and the risk of capital destruction'.[3]

In the countdown to James Murdoch's second appearance before the Commons Culture Committee, News Corp's policy of dumping former supporters stirred further trouble. Derek Webb of Silent Shadow revealed on 7 November that the *News of the World* had ordered him to follow more than 100 high-profile individuals over eight years – right up to the paper's closure in July. He was disclosing his covert work, he said, because News International had refused to give him the 'loyalty' payment received by other freelancers after the *NoW*'s demise. Among his targets were Boris Johnson and his friend Anna Fazackerley; the former Liberal Democrat leader Charles Kennedy, and Lord Goldsmith, the Attorney General, whom he had tailed in early 2005. Others included the Chelsea manager José Mourinho; Simon Cowell; Elle Macpherson; Prince Harry's ex-girlfriend Chelsy Davy, whom he monitored after she arrived at Heathrow Airport; and Prince William, whom he claimed he had followed for days without attracting the attention of Royal Protection Squad officers.

In an interview with *Newsnight*, Webb said: 'Ninety-five per cent of the job, I was never rumbled, even following them for weeks on end. Basically I would write down what they were wearing at the time, what car they were in, who they met, the location they met, the times . . . I don't feel ashamed. I know to a certain extent people's lives have been ruined with front page stories but . . . if I wasn't doing it, somebody else would have been.'[4]

Days before James Murdoch's reappearance before the Culture Committee, News International experienced another problem. As part of News Corp's checks at Wapping, News International had passed to police information about the *Sun*'s Thames Valley reporter Jamie Pyatt, whose scoops included Prince Harry dressing in Nazi regalia for a fancy dress party. On 7 November, officers from Operation Elveden arrested Pyatt on suspicion of bribing police officers. The arrest caused serious concern among *Sun* journalists because it suggested that the management was now actively seeking to turn over reporters to the police. One colleague commented: 'They have opened up a Pandora's box.'[5] At a meeting with staff, the *Sun*'s editor Dominic Mohan, a former showbusiness reporter who had once mockingly thanked Vodafone for its help on stories,* reassured staff that Rupert Murdoch had committed himself to the paper's future.

On 10 November, members of the public began queuing at 7 a.m. for a place at James Murdoch's hearing. At 11 a.m., Murdoch took his seat in front of the Culture Committee. In place of the passive-aggressive technocrat who had given evidence in July came a more confident,

---

* When editing the *Sun*'s showbusiness column 'Bizarre', Mohan had mentioned mobile phone security at a party for the most bogus showbusiness stories, the Shaftas. On 1 May 2002, the *Guardian*'s media diary reported a snippet headlined: 'Ring, a ring a story': 'How appropriate that the most glamorous event in the showbusiness calendar should be sponsored by a phone company. Mohan went on to thank "Vodafone's lack of security" for the *Mirror*'s showbusiness exclusives. Whatever does he mean?' Mohan later told the Leveson Inquiry that he could not be 100 per cent sure that stories which had appeared in the *Sun*'s 'Bizarre' column had not been derived from phone hacking.

assured witness, but he still answered questions in an anodyne and obfuscatory manner: he did not want to make good television.

Murdoch's greatest difficulty was how to explain that he had no knowledge that wrongdoing had spread beyond Clive Goodman when he authorized the Taylor pay-off. In the closing moments of the hearing, he had told Tom Watson he had neither seen nor been aware of the 'For Neville' email. Now, he admitted he had been made aware of the email's existence, but insisted he had not been shown it; nor told it indicated wrongdoing was rife at the *Screws*. He also denied seeing the advice from Michael Silverleaf QC. Committee members were understandably surprised at his claim that he had not read Silverleaf's opinion, because it was the basis on which he subsequently approved the largest privacy settlement in British legal history.

Tom Watson started his questions by pointing out that last time the Murdochs and their senior staff had appeared before the committee he had had to be careful in his questioning of Rebekah Brooks because she had been arrested and he wanted to be sure he was free to ask Murdoch anything: could he say whether he had been arrested? Keeping his calm, Murdoch replied wearily: 'I have not been arrested, and I am not currently on bail. I am free to answer questions, and I would like to.' Murdoch insisted that he was correct to say in July that the company had only learned of more widespread wrongdoing at the end of 2010. 'The facts did not emerge in 2008,' he said. 'Certain individuals were aware. The leading counsel's opinion was there. The "For Neville email", so called, was there. None of those things were made available or discussed with me and I was not aware of those things.' Murdoch's insistence that he had not misled the committee logically meant he thought that Myler and Crone had done so, but he was reluctant to say so:

> WATSON: Mr Murdoch, let me just ask you again: did you mislead this committee in your original testimony?
> MURDOCH: No, I did not.
> WATSON: So if you did not, who did?
> MURDOCH: As I have written to you and said publicly, I believe this committee was given evidence by individuals either without full possession of the facts or, now, it appears – in the process of my own discovery

in trying to understand as best I can what actually happened here – it was economical. I think my own testimony has been consistent. I have testified to this committee with as much clarity and transparency as I possibly can, and where I have not had direct knowledge in the past, since I testified to you last time, I have gone and tried to seek answers and find out what happened, and where the evidence is and what is there; and that is what I am here to do.

WATSON: So was it Mr Crone, a respected and in-house legal adviser for many years?

MURDOCH: As I said to you, as I wrote to you, and I issued a public statement, certainly, in the evidence that they gave to you in 2011, with respect to my knowledge, I thought it was inconsistent and not right, and I dispute it vigorously.

WATSON: So you think Mr Crone misled us?

MURDOCH: It follows that I do, yes.

WATSON: And so do you think Mr Myler misled us as well?

MURDOCH: I believe their testimony was misleading, and I dispute it.

WATSON: There are allegations of phone hacking, computer hacking, conspiring to pervert the course of justice and perjury facing this company and all this happened without your knowledge?

MURDOCH: As I have said to you, Mr Watson, and to this committee on a number of occasions, it is a matter of great regret that things went wrong at the *News of the World* in 2006. The company didn't come to grips with those issues fast enough . . .

With an eye on media coverage of the hearing, Watson countered: 'Mr Murdoch, you must be the first mafia boss in history who didn't know he was running a criminal enterprise.'

'Mr Watson, please,' Murdoch replied disdainfully. 'I think that's inappropriate.'

To Murdoch's claim that he had not checked the QC's opinion before authorizing the Taylor settlement, the Conservative MP Damian Collins remarked: 'Honestly, it may not be the mafia, but it is not *Management Today*.' Philip Davies MP found it 'absolutely incredible' that Murdoch would not have checked the QC's opinion before settling.

Murdoch said News International's surveillance of the lawyers

Mark Lewis and Charlotte Harris was 'just not acceptable'. Asked about surveillance of members of the Culture Committee, he said: 'I am aware of the case of the surveillance of Mr Watson; again, under the circumstances, I apologize unreservedly for that. It is not something that I would condone, it is not something that I had knowledge of and it is not something that has a place in the way we operate.'

The Liverpudlian MP Steve Rotherham, a campaigner for victims of the Hillsborough disaster (fans had been slurred by the *Sun*), asked Murdoch whether, if the *Sun* had been hacking phones too, he would close that paper too? To the shock of committee members, the media and the paper's journalists, Murdoch replied: 'I don't think we can rule, and I shouldn't rule, any corporate reaction to behaviour of wrongdoing out.'

By sticking to his defence, no matter how questionable, Murdoch had successfully avoided incriminating himself but in doing so had been forced to plead gross ignorance of the working of his company and that he had not bothered to read crucial documents. This was not good for the reputation of the deputy chief operating officer of a multibillion-dollar media conglomerate.

In its leading article the next day, *The Times* nonetheless rallied to the corporate flag:

> James Murdoch yesterday came to Parliament to answer two sets of questions. The first were about his personal integrity. The second were about the culture of the company in which he is a senior executive. Mr Murdoch was recalled by the MPs to answer allegations that, when he had last appeared as a witness, he misled them. On this, as on other questions that touched on the integrity of his personal conduct, he was clear, consistent and convincing.

Opinion was divided as to whether Tom Watson was right to liken him to a mafia boss.

21

The Press on Trial

Are these all real headlines?
— Lord Leveson, 29 November 2011

For decades reporters had been drawn through the imposing Victorian stone archway of the Royal Courts of Justice in London by the prospect of scandal-packed cases. In its light and modern Court 73 on 14 November, a judge began a hearing with a sensational mix of celebrity, sex, power and crime; this time the press itself was on trial. The inquiry was launched in July under pressure by the Prime Minister, who tasked Lord Leveson to inquire, not specifically into News International, but into the 'culture, practice and ethics' of the whole industry, with a view to establishing a better system of regulation which would banish once and for all phone and computer hacking, blagging and bribery, and the associated issues of intrusion, exaggeration and fabrication. Although the scandal had begun with a single Wapping title, the Prime Minister had put all newspapers in the dock. Lord Leveson said his task was to answer the question: 'Who guards the guardians?'

On 14 November, Robert Jay QC, the inquiry's counsel, outlined its concerns about the press and the failure of the police, politicians and the Press Complaints Commission to control its sometimes overweening and destructive power. He made plain the chasm which separated the suspected scale of News International's phone hacking and the charges brought during the original investigation in 2006. There were twenty-eight 'corner names' in Glenn Mulcaire's notes (one referring to the *Mirror*). Some were more prolific than others. Of the 2,266 'taskings', 2,143 of them, 95 per cent, were by four prolific individuals: 1,453 for 'A'; 303 for 'B', 252 for 'C' and 135 for 'D'. According to the Metropolitan Police, the *Screws*' hacking operation had begun by 2002, Milly Dowler being the first named victim. 'We, however, have recently seen a document which emanates from May 2001. The police believe it continued until 2009,' Jay said: 'It is clear that Goodman was not a rogue reporter. Ignoring the private corner name and the illegibles, we have at least twenty-seven other News International employees. This fact alone suggests wide-ranging illegal activity within the organization at the relevant time . . .'

One of the tasks before the inquiry, he explained, was to consider the regulation of the press. The Press Complaints Commission had failed – and the press had been given second chances before, a long time ago. In 1991, the cabinet minister David Mellor had warned newspapers were 'drinking in the last chance saloon'. The PCC, Jay pointed out, lacked the power to fine newspapers or make them print apologies on the same page as the offending story: 'All of this gives the impression that the PCC is operating largely without teeth and that in the ruthless world in which it is forced to operate, something sharper is required.'

He had searching questions about the power of newspapers over politicians.

> The press have sway over politicians to the extent that it is within their power to endorse particular political parties or causes and certain newspaper groups are seen as floating voters . . .
>
> On one level, it might simply be said that press proprietors and editors enjoy the wielding of an unaccountable power and that this enjoyment is enough to constitute the price for the bestowing of favour. On the other hand, it may be said that for some the quid pro quo is a higher price, namely the bestowing of commercial favours by government. The unaccountable power of the press, or of certain parts of it, is a consistent theme here, and if that power is concentrated in a limited number of individuals the problem is capable of being visualized as all the more menacing.[1]

Slandered, impugned and damaged, the targets of newspapers appearing before the inquiry could now tell their stories direct to the public. The proprietors, editors and reporters would have to account publicly for their actions.

Appropriately the first witnesses were Bob and Sally Dowler. They relived the moment they believed that their daughter was still alive in 2002 (see chapter 15). They also suspected that their own phones had been hacked at the time because a photographer had been stalking them as they walked along the route their daughter had taken on the day of her disappearance – culminating in a story in that Sunday's *News of the World*: 'Mile of Grief'.

On 23 November, Kate and Gerry McCann explained that soon after their daughter Madeleine had disappeared on a family holiday to the village of Praia da Luz on 3 May 2007, a British press desperate for new angles recycled reports from the Portuguese press stating that the McCanns themselves were under suspicion. Gerry McCann said: 'I do not know whether they [Portuguese police] were speaking directly the British media, but what we clearly saw were snippets of information which as far as I was concerned the British media could not tell whether it was true or not, which was then reported, often exaggerated and blown up into many tens, in fact hundreds of front-page headlines.' A meeting with newspaper editors stating there was no evidence to support the suggestion that they were involved in their daughter's disappearance had 'very little effect'. Photographers would spring out from behind hedges to give Kate McCann a fright; newspapers would then carry those pictures saying she looked 'frail' or 'fragile'. From September 2007 to January 2008, many UK newspapers, but particularly those in the stable of Richard Desmond – the *Daily Star, Daily Star Sunday* and *Daily* and *Sunday Express* (Express Newspapers) – initially fought the couple's resulting libel claim. Gerry McCann recalled: '. . . they couldn't agree to our complaint, but they did suggest that we did an interview with [Desmond's] *OK!* magazine, which we found rather breathtaking.'

Express Newspapers eventually paid £550,000 to Madeleine's Fund and apologized on the front page of the *Daily Star* and *Daily Express* on 19 March 2008:

> . . . there is no evidence whatsoever to suggest that Mr and Mrs McCann were responsible for the death of their daughter, that they were involved in any sort of cover-up and there was no basis for Express Newspapers to allege otherwise. Equally, the allegations that

Mr and Mrs McCann may have sold Madeleine or were involved in swinging or wife swapping were entirely baseless. Naturally the repeated publication of these utterly false and defamatory allegations has caused untold distress to Mr and Mrs McCann. Indeed, it is difficult to conceive of a more serious allegation.

Although the McCanns had treated all publications equally for fear of alienating their rivals, they did give an interview to *Hello!* on 29 April 2008, the first anniversary of Madeleine's disappearance, to publicize a new European alert system for missing children. At the *News of the World*, which had put up a £250,000 reward for Madeleine's safe return, editor Colin Myler was furious and straight on the phone to the McCanns. Gerry McCann said:

> I think it would be fair to say that Mr Myler was irate ... and was berating us for not doing an interview with the *News of the World* and told us how supportive the newspaper had been, the news and rewards. And at a time of stress for us on the first anniversary – where we were actually launching a new campaign ... he basically beat us into submission, verbally, and we agreed to do an interview the day after.

This cooperation was not repaid as the McCanns might have expected: without warning, on 14 September 2008 Myler's *News of the World* published extracts from Kate McCann's personal diary in which she had recorded her intimate thoughts about Madeleine. The Portuguese police had seized the diary and a copy had fallen into the hands of a Portuguese journalist, who had sold it for €20,000 to Rupert Murdoch's newspaper. The *Screws* printed extracts of 'Kate's Diary: In Her Own Words'.

Kate McCann said: 'I felt totally violated. I'd written those words and thoughts at the most desperate time in my life, most people won't have to experience that, and it was my only way of communicating with Madeleine, and for me, you know, there was absolutely no respect shown for me as a grieving mother or as a human being or for my daughter, and it made me feel very vulnerable and small and I just couldn't believe it.'

Stars who for years had felt frustrated or intimidated or harrassed – or all three – by photographers and reporters gave evidence. Several made the point that, while their jobs put them on the public stage, they had not courted tabloid interest, nor did they believe that it should open the gates to their private life. Hugh Grant said 'hundreds' of people in the public eye would willingly never be mentioned in newspapers again. He singled out several articles, including an 'interview' with him in the *Sunday Express,* explaining: 'I had not even spoken to a journalist. It was completely, as far I could see, either made up or patched and pasted from previous quotations I might have given in an interview.'

He suggested that an article in the *Mail on Sunday* in February 2007 about his relationship with Jemima Khan being on the rocks because he had been receiving late-night calls from a plummy-sounding woman, might have come from hacking his phone. He had indeed been receiving calls from a plummy-sounding studio executive's PA while he was in Los Angeles – late at night British time. He had not been having an affair with her, sued for libel and won. 'But thinking about how they could possibly have come up with such a bizarre left-field story . . . I cannot for the life of me think of any conceivable source for this story in the *Mail on Sunday* except those voice messages on my mobile telephone.' That evening the *Mail on Sunday* accused him of spreading 'mendacious smears'.

He said misreporting and invasions of privacy were still happening. He suspected that a story in the *Sun* and the *Daily Express* in March 2011, about his visit to Chelsea and Westminster Hospital, recording that he was 'dizzy and short of breath', had come from someone at the hospital being on a retainer from a tabloid newspaper or picture agency. 'You know: "If anyone famous comes in, tell us and here's 50 quid or 500 quid."'

The police had told him that the paparazzi were increasingly recruited 'from the criminal classes' – who would 'show no mercy, no ethics, because the bounty on some of these pictures is very high'.

In his written evidence, Grant made the case for press reform, but added: 'I don't want to see the end of popular print journalism. And I certainly wouldn't want a country that was fawning to power or success. I like, admire and would always want to protect the British instinct to be sceptical, irreverent, difficult, and to take the piss.'

Dressed in black with little make-up, Sienna Miller explained that as a 21-year-old woman she had been regularly chased down the street by packs of ten to fifteen big male photographers. She had been spat at. The *Daily Mirror* had printed a picture of her at a charity ball suggesting she was drunk. In fact she had been playing dead in a game with a very sick child, who had been edited out of the picture, making it look as though she was indeed drunk. She sued, won her case and the paper subsequently printed an apology:

> Sorry, Sienna. On Saturday 12 March, we printed pictures of Sienna Miller, who is an ambassador for the Starlight Children's Foundation charity, at the Starlight Children's Foundation charity for terminally ill children. We said that Sienna's boozy antics had shocked guests at the event and thereby suggested that she had behaved in an unprofessional manner. We are happy to make clear that Sienna was not drunk and did not behave unprofessionally. In fact in the pictures Sienna was on the floor playing with a seriously ill six-year-old child. We have apologized to Sienna.

She believed that the paper had calculated the cost in money and reputation of printing an apology before misreporting the story.

But Miller's most significant evidence, given on 24 November, was on the hacking by News International. She could not understand how photographers and reporters kept popping up wherever she went:

> I think what was more baffling was the fact that people found out before I'd even arrived where I was going. I did feel constantly very scared and intensely paranoid . . . Every area of my life was under constant surveillance and instinctively I felt that and felt very violated and very paranoid and anxious . . . I felt I was living in some kind of video game.

JK Rowling, the author of the Harry Potter novels, found a reporter had slipped a note into her daughter's school satchel: 'It's very difficult to say how angry I felt that my five-year-old's school was no longer a place of complete security from journalists.' In 2003, she felt she was being blackmailed when the *Sun* allegedly offered to return a stolen copy of her fifth Harry Potter book – yet to be published – in exchange for a photo opportunity.

She attacked newspapers for picturing her children. When she asked why a photographer from a Scottish tabloid was outside her home, she was told: 'It's a boring day at the office.' Giving evidence on 24 November, she said: 'There wasn't even a sense there was a story. So my family and I were literally under surveillance for their amusement ... It's a very unnerving feeling to know that you're being watched.'

The singer Charlotte Church recalled that as a teenager she was constantly chased by reporters and photographers, some of whom tried to take pictures up her skirt. Between the ages of sixteen and eighteen, she was followed by up to eight photographers a day.

She had had particular problems with News International newspapers, and recounted a strange encounter with Rupert Murdoch. When the 'voice of an angel' was thirteen, she said, Murdoch's office approached her to sing at his wedding to Wendi Deng in 1999. According to Church, she was given a choice of rewards – £100,000 or positive coverage in Murdoch's papers. (News International denies that this offer was made.) Church said: 'I remember being told that Rupert Murdoch had asked me to sing at his wedding to entertain and it would take place on his yacht in New York, and ... I remember being thirteen and thinking: "Why on earth would anybody take a favour or £100,000?" and me and my mother being quite resolute on this point that £100,000 was definitely the best option – but being advised by management and by members of the record company to take the latter option, that he was a very powerful man, I was in the early stages of my career and could absolutely do with a favour of this magnitude.'

Murdoch wanted her to sing 'Pie Jesu'. She pointed out that it was a funeral song. 'He said he didn't care whether it was a funeral song, he liked that song and he wanted me to sing it, which I did.'

If Murdoch's staff did promise favourable press coverage, it did not arrive. Church said that *The Sunday Times* had fabricated 'horrific' comments by her that New York firefighters after the attack on the Twin Towers in 2001 did not deserve their heroic status, when what she had actually said was that TV producers had demeaned them by getting them to present the Best Soap category at the National Television Awards. Unusually, no one from her management or Sony had sat in on or taped the interview. 'I was only fifteen and to be exposed by a newspaper of this type to ridicule and derision upon such a sensitive subject was a terrible experience. That article then went over to the *New York Post*, which was also owned by Mr Murdoch's company and the headline was: "Voice of an angel spews venom". And of course because of the massively sensitive nature of this subject, there was a massive backlash against me in America . . .'

The *News of the World* published the most grievous story, on 11 December 2005, about her father having an affair, headlined: 'Church's three in a bed cocaine shock'. The first line was: 'Superstar Charlotte Church's mum tried to kill herself because her husband is a love rat hooked on cocaine and three-in-a-bed orgies.'

Church said:

> I just really hated the fact that my parents, who had never been in this industry apart apart from in looking after me, were being exposed and vilified in this fashion. It had a massive impact on my family life, on my mother's health, which the *News of the World* had reported on before then, on her mental state and her hospital treatment. We also think the only way they could have known about that hospital treatment was either through the hacking or possibly through the bribing of hospital staff. So they knew how vulnerable she was and still printed this story, which was horrific.

Another star, the TV presenter Anne Diamond, also had a brush with Murdoch. Testifying on the same grim day for News Corp as Church, 28 November, Diamond recalled that in the 1980s she had told Murdoch that his newspapers seemed intent on ruining people's lives. Earlier in 2011, Murdoch's former butler, Phillip Townsend, had explained to a Channel 4 documentary that Murdoch had called together a number of his newspaper editors and 'possibly indicated to his editors that I was a person from that point on to be targeted'. Diamond said: 'When you look back now in the knowledge of what Mr Townsend had said . . . well, it would suggest it becomes evident from that point onwards there were consistent negative stories about me in Mr Murdoch's newspapers.'

Hours after visiting a private clinic in 1986 fearing that she was losing her first baby at the eight-week stage, she explained, a *Sun* reporter called asking if she was pregnant. Not having told her parents, and not being sure that the baby would actually survive a potential miscarriage, she denied she was pregnant. 'They ran the story anyway . . .' Then the labour: 'I was actually in labour in the hospital and at one point an administrator came in and said: "Very sorry to interrupt, we don't really want to alarm you but you do need to know that we have just caught somebody who was a reporter for the *Sun* who was impersonating a doctor and we've had to eject him from the hospital, but we do feel you ought to know."' The *Sun* subsequently obtained a story from her first nanny – offering her £30,000 – about life with the Diamonds. Although the nanny later wanted to ditch the deal, the paper ran her comments from a lunchtime interview with a journalist – and didn't pay her the £30,000. In December 1987, *Today* (Rupert Murdoch's now closed fifth national newspaper) printed the details of Diamond's new home: 'It wasn't just a dreadful invasion of privacy of my new home, it was a burglar's charter.'

The most shocking episode came in 1991, when Diamond lost her new baby, Sebastian, to cot death. Diamond and her then husband wrote to every newspaper editor asking them not to cover Sebastian's funeral in a small family church. All journalists stayed away apart from a freelance photographer, who took pictures from the road. Diamond recounted:

> Within a few hours of the funeral, the editor of the *Sun* [Kelvin Mackenzie] rang my husband and said: 'We have a picture. It's an incredibly strong picture. We would like to use it.' And my husband said: 'No, we've asked all of you to stay away. No.' And the editor said: 'Well, we're going to use it anyway. We'll use it without your permission.'

The next day the paper put the story on the front page and rang to say that it had received such an enormous response that it wanted Diamond to launch a fundraising campaign. She felt 'emotionally blackmailed' but relented, because she knew 'the power of the press'.*

---

* She was right. Within days, the *Sun* – which also backed the campaign with its own money – had raised £100,000 for cot death research. In the twenty years since Diamond fronted the 'Back to Sleep' campaign urging parents to make sure babies slept on their backs, the number of cot deaths in the UK fell from 2,500 to 300 a year.

The tricks of the redtops continued to be laid bare. Steve Coogan recalled:

In August 2002 I received a phone call from Rav Singh, a reporter with Andy Coulson's 'Bizarre' column in the *Sun*. He tipped me off that I was about to be the target of a sting from Coulson's office. He told me I would receive a call from a girl with whom I had spent some time and that she would try to lure me into talking about intimate details of my life. The call would be recorded and Andy Coulson would be listening. When the call came I deadpanned it and nothing was printed.

Naturally I felt grateful for this tip-off, but this episode was probably a ruse to gain my trust or a sense of debt to Rav Singh, presumably on the basis that the story they actually had did not appear to be very much and wanted a 'better' story in the future.

In April 2004, Rav Singh, who now had his own gossip column in the *News of the World*, phoned me. He wanted to 'negotiate' about an article that was to be printed the next day about a relationship I had had. Singh said that if I were to admit certain parts of the story the paper would omit other details that I felt would be embarrassing to my family. I trusted him, partly as a result of the earlier tip-off, so I had a conversation with him on what I thought was a confidential basis. Afterwards, Coulson, by then the editor of the *News of the World*, called my publicist and told him they had recorded the whole phone conversation and would publish all the details including those they had agreed not to. The promises had been a sham to get me on the phone and get more details in my own words. I was in a vulnerable state at that time in any event and they knew it and used my vulnerability to their advantage.

Coogan added: 'Strangely I don't think it was a malicious personal vendetta against me. My feeling is that it was a dispassionate sociopathic act by those who operate in an amoral universe where they are never accountable.'

At the Leveson Inquiry, the newspaper industry was finally held to account. Almost all the titles had some explaining to do. One of the greatest twists was the *Guardian*'s handling of the Milly Dowler story in July 2011. In a story on 10 December 2011, the paper explained that the *News of the World* might not, after all, have been responsible for the Dowlers' 'false hope' moment.* News International and former *News of the World* journalists leapt on this. On 13 December, the *Sun*'s managing editor, Richard Caseby, accused the *Guardian* of 'sexing up' its coverage of the Milly Dowler story.[2] After the paper's columnist Marina Hyde wrongly reported that the the *Sun* had doorstepped one of the Leveson Inquiry's junior counsel, a couriered parcel arrived from Wapping for Alan Rusbridger, containing a toilet roll and a note which read: 'I hear Marina Hyde's turd landed on your desk. Well, you can use this to wipe her arse.'

For the newspaper industry, the witnesses broadly divided into those who admitted they had taken part in wrongdoing and those who did not. Among the innocent was Kelvin Mackenzie, the former *Sun* editor. On 9 January, Mackenzie agreed that his policy while editing the *Sun* was that if something sounded right he would 'lob it in'. 'I didn't spend too much time pondering the ethics of how a story was gained nor over-worry about whether to publish or not,' he explained. 'If we believed the story to be true and we felt *Sun* readers should know the facts, we published it and we left it to them to decide if we had done the right thing.' He denied Murdoch had ever urged his editors to go after Anne Diamond: 'I have had the advantage as distinct from Ms Diamond of working with Rupert Murdoch for thirteen years closely. And I have never heard him say: "Go after anybody" under any circumstances, whether it is a prime minister, a failing breakfast show host, or anybody.'

On 12 January 2012, the proprietor of the *Daily Star* and *Daily Express*, Richard Desmond, appeared to be bemused at the fuss being made. Asked what interest he took in the ethical conduct of his papers, he replied: 'Well, ethical, I don't quite know what the word means.' He said that his newspapers had been 'scapegoated' over their coverage of Madeleine McCann. He apologized for their treatment of the McCanns, but added: 'If there were 102 articles on the McCanns, and thirty-eight bad ones ... you could argue there were sixty-eight or

---

* At the time of going to press, it was still unclear why messages on Milly Dowler's phone were deleted. It may have been as a result of the *NoW*'s hacking, or it may have been done automatically by the phone company.

seventy good ones.' He suggested the McCanns had been 'quite happy to have articles about their daughter' on the front page. Robert Jay, the Inquiry's counsel, described that as a 'grotesque characterization'.

In stark contrast to Desmond was one of his former reporters, Richard Peppiatt, who repented of his role in the bias, exaggerations and fabrications of the *Daily Star*, where he freelanced full-time for two years, on £118 a day, until March 2011. Spilling the secrets of the *Daily Star* in spectacular fashion on 29 November, he said its reporters wrote to its 'ideological perspective on certain issues, say immigration or national security or policing':

> And so whatever a story may be, you must try and adhere to their ideological perspective. Say there is a government report giving out statistics. Well, you know, any statistics which don't fit within that framework you ignore or sort of decontextualize and pick maybe the one statistic which does. If there's something that comes out saying crime has gone down, you then go and look for the statistic which says knife crime has gone up 20 per cent . . .

Some stories were 'dictated more from the accounts and advertising departments than the newsroom floor', such as one he wrote about Marks & Spencer's skinny pants.* To the amusement (and horror) of the inquiry, he read out the headlines of false *Daily Star* stories: ' "Chile mine to open as theme park"; "Angelina Jolie to play Susan Boyle in film"; "Bubbles to give evidence at Jacko trial" (Bubbles was Michael Jackson's monkey); "Jade's back in *Big Brother*" (she was dead at the time). Obviously we have the likes of "Maddie's body stored in freezer", which we've heard already; "Grand theft Rothbury". That was the Raoul Moat killing, there was going to be a computer game based around it – completely untrue. "Brittany Murphy killed by swine flu"; wasn't the case; "Macca versus Mucca on ice", which was that Paul McCartney and his ex-wife were apparently going to showdown on *Dancing On Ice*, never transpired. Then we have the likes of "Muslim-only public loos". . . completely untrue as well.'

* Published on 23 July 2010, it read: 'All the girls are talking about vampire hunk R-Patz – now us fellas have our own R-Pantz. Marks & Spencer are launching a range of slim-fitting undies with blokes who wear skinny jeans in mind.'

Lord Leveson, apparently not a *Daily Star* reader, interrupted: 'Are these all real headlines?' Peppiatt replied: 'These are real headlines.'

Among those giving evidence were those who had written raucous accounts of backstabbing and misbehaviour in tabloid newspapers, but who were now testifying about those accounts in a wholly new context suggesting that what they had written previously about tabloid life was little more than gossip.

Giving evidence via videolink from New York, Piers Morgan was asked about *The Insider*, the account of his tabloid days editing the *News of the World* and the *Mirror*. The inquiry wanted to know about the time that Rupert Murdoch rang up and suggested he drop the Kray story (see page 15). In his statement, Morgan wrote: 'This is my recollection of the gist of our conversation, almost ten years later on. I did not make a contemporaneous note. Mr Murdoch's recollections and impressions may well differ from mine.' He added: 'I would note that my books were not intended to provide a historical record.'

He said he did not believe that phone hacking took place during his editorship of the *Daily Mirror* between 1995 and 2004. He said he could not explain how he came to hear a tape recording Paul McCartney had left for his wife Heather Mills after a row. Suddenly the insider seemed not to know much at all.

Sharon Marshall, who had delved into the devious ways of hacks in *Tabloid Girl: A True Story*, suggested her account had been based on personal recollections and chats with old hacks in the pub. In her foreword to the book, published in 2010, she had written: 'This is what happened when I worked in the tabloid press. Look back through the newspaper archives and you'll see my name on these stories. I wrote them. They're true. I'm not proud of everything we did, but I loved the tabloid journalists I worked with. Every single double-crossing, devious, scheming, ruthless, messed up, brilliantly evil one of them.' Now, she explained when she said 'devious' she was referring to nothing more than probably apocryphal examples of hacks trying to claim camels on expenses and that 'accordingly, no reliance can be placed upon those stories as providing a statement or an indication of general practice in the journalism industry'.

*

The *News of the World*'s former executives, of course, had to account for their cover-up. Out of a job and with their paper closed, they no longer had to lie.

Tom Crone, the paper's lawyer who had stuck doggedly to the rogue reporter defence, now recanted. Giving evidence on 14 December, and still playing the part of the respectable lawyer, he explained languidly: 'I can't remember when and by whom the rogue reporter explanation was first put out, but I was of the view that it was erroneous from the start.'

Did that ever cause him concern? 'Yes,' he replied. 'My feeling is I thought it would probably come back to bite the people who were saying it, which was the company, sure.'

At the meeting on 10 June 2008 at which James Murdoch authorized the Gordon Taylor payment, he said he had taken in a copy of Michael Silverleaf QC's damning opinion on a culture of illegal newsgathering at the organization, as well as spare copies of the 'For Neville' email. Jay asked: 'Did you supply any of those documents to Mr Murdoch?' Laconically, Crone replied: 'I can't remember whether they were passed across the table to him, but I'm pretty sure I held up the front page of the email .... I'm also pretty sure that he already knew about it. What was certainly discussed was the email. Not described as 'For Neville', but the damning email and what it meant in terms of further involvement beyond – further involvement in phone hacking beyond Goodman and Mulcaire. And what was relayed to Mr Murdoch was that this document clearly was direct and hard evidence of that being the case.'

On 15 December, Colin Myler – who was shortly to accept a new job as editor of the New York *Daily News*, rival to Murdoch's *Post* – disputed that there had been a cover-up. 'I don't think there was a cover-up,' said the editor who two years previously had told a parliamentary inquiry that there was 'no evidence' phone hacking extended beyond Clive Goodman. Lord Leveson inquired: 'It might be slightly semantic, mightn't it, Mr Myler? What one person might describe as a cover-up another person would describe as an attempt to limit reputational damage?'

Myler replied: 'Absolutely, sir.'

On 29 November, Paul McMullan, the former *News of the World* features editor, painted a hilarious world: car chases, at least when Princess Diana was alive, were 'great fun'. He blamed executives for making scapegoats of Clive Goodman and other reporters. But he was unrepentant about the tabloid world, or his role in it. He suggested the hacking of Milly Dowler's phone was 'not a bad thing' because reporters 'were trying to find the little girl'.

McMullan clearly reckoned the best method of defence was attack: 'I have a huge amount of cynicism for both Hugh Grant and Steve Coogan who have really done quite well by banging on about their privacy. All you have to do is jump off the stage for five minutes and people lose interest every quickly. Privacy is for paedos.'

Giving evidence, Stuart Hoare said his late brother Sean's sole motivation in speaking out about phone hacking was 'trying to put wrongs right'. Stuart Hoare said in his statement:

> The reality was that phone hacking was endemic within the News International group (specifically Sean identified that this process was initiated at the *Sun* and later transferred to the *News of the World*) . . . undoubtedly, one of the major issues during Sean's employment with the *News of the World* was that the news desk was out of control and that stories were obtained with very little or no ethics because of the pressure put on journalists to deliver.

In his written testimony on 19 December, Matt Driscoll, the sacked sports reporter, agreed:

> It seemed to me that any methods that could stand a story up were fair game. It was also clear that there was massive pressure from the top to break stories. It was largely accepted that this pressure came from the proprietors and editors on the basis that big, sensational stories sell papers and therefore make more money.
>
> There were times when I would return from interviewing a prominent Premier League football manager only to find the paper using material from a months old interview in order to obtain a better headline.

He added:

> I feel that for many years some newspapers have been on course for destruction. Editors were handed far too much power and their egos

were allowed to run wild. Some that I worked for often became pampered peacocks who only wanted to hear the word 'yes' and would shout and scream if they heard anything else. An example was when one editor I worked for sent his chauffeur fifty miles back to his home to pick up a bow tie he had left behind. No doubt the power and lucrative lifestyle that gives them front-row seats and free holidays helped to corrupt them – so that some editors totally lost sight of reality . . . As a result of this aggressive and grotesque arrogance, those in charge – the proprietors and the editors – came to believe that they could do and say whatever they wanted and remain untouchable.

In my years at News International, I came to believe – along with other journalists – that the newspaper group were indeed confident that they were untouchable because they were sure they had the government and police fighting their corner. Thus, they felt that they were almost beyond the reach of the law. These powerful contacts were the reason why some on the *News of the World* felt they could leave their morals and their respect for ethics at the door when they clocked in each morning. The next front page was all that mattered, however it was obtained.

22

Darker and Darker

Hugely in the national interest

– Mr Justice Vos

As the Leveson Inquiry swept into 2012, News International's problems deepened – and spread to its other titles. Confronted with overwhelming evidence of the wrongdoing of its parent company, *The Times* could no longer avoid confronting its failings – though it still maintained that those failings were not the fault of the Murdochs. In an 1,800-word leader on 17 January arguing against stronger regulation, *The Times* paid a back-handed compliment to the investigative journalism which unpicked the deceit:

> As the evidence of wrongdoing came to light, News International, Rupert Murdoch's company that also owns *The Times*, was unable or unwilling to police itself. This was a disgrace. It was, of course, the press that put Fleet Street in the dock. The dogged investigative reporting that unearthed the phone hacking scandal deserves respect, even if the story was exaggerated and key details misreported.

In his evidence to Lord Leveson that day, *The Times*'s editor James Harding said: 'I certainly wish we had got on the story harder, earlier.' He disagreed with the views of the paper's star columnist David Aaranovitch (see page 195) that the failure was linked to the Murdochs' ownership. A failure to understand the significance of the story rather than proprietorial influence was to blame, Harding explained.

In the courts, News International strove to avoid a show trial that would put its executives in the witness box and publicly disclose countless incriminating documents, settling thirty-seven cases on a single day, 19 January. John Prescott received £40,000, Chris Bryant £30,000 and Sara Payne undisclosed damages. In an accompanying statement of brazen doublethink, News Group Newspapers said: 'Today NGN agreed settlements in respect of a number of claims against the company. NGN made no admission as part of these settlements that directors or senior employees knew about the wrongdoing by NGN or sought to conceal it. However, for the purpose of reaching these settlements only, NGN agreed that the damages to be paid to claimants should be assessed as if this was the case.' News Group was in essence admitting responsibility for its actions, but at the same time maintaining the legal fiction that it was not.

Claimants settled for two main reasons: the Part 36 offers they had received were unlikely to be bettered in court and pressing ahead to hearings would leave them facing substantial legal costs; and the Metropolitan Police and the Leveson Inquiry were now properly investigating what News International had done to them. Many, however, were still disgusted by their treatment. In a statement after his case was settled for £130,000 on 19 January, Jude Law's anger was palpable:

> For several years leading up to 2006, I was suspicious about how information concerning my private life was coming out in the press. I changed my phones, I had my house swept for bugs but still the information kept being published. I started to become distrustful of people close to me. I was truly appalled by what I was shown by the police and by what my lawyers have discovered. It is clear that I, along with many others, was kept under constant surveillance for a number of years.
>
> No aspect of my private life was safe from intrusion by News Group newspapers, including the lives of my children and the people who work for me. It was not just that my phone messages were listened to. News Group also paid people to watch me and my house for days at a time and to follow me and those close to me both in this country and abroad.
>
> I believe in a free press but . . . they were prepared to do anything to sell their newspapers and to make money, irrespective of the impact it had on people's lives.

At the same hearing, News International sought to halt a search requested by litigants of three desktop computers and six laptops belonging to former employees. Wapping's lawyer, Dinah Rose, said the searches were a waste of time since the company was settling civil cases, telling the judge, Mr Justice Vos: 'We accept we are the villains. We have the horns and the tails.' Vos – who had presided over phone hacking cases for a year – rejected her arguments and replied that News International should be regarded as 'deliberate destroyers of evidence'. Documents he had seen, he said, might lead a court to conclude that it 'deliberately concealed and told lies and deleted documents and effectively tried to get off scot-free'. He rejected News International's case, telling Rose:

> I am rather hesitant, as you probably notice, about acceding to the 'Oh, it is all very expensive and difficult and time consuming and the trial is only around the corner,' because if I had acceded to that last year none of us would be sitting here in the present situation and you just seem a little over-sensitive about these laptops, and they look to me to cover a period when things were going on in your client's offices . . .

He said that finding out what had happened at News International was 'hugely in the national interest'.

On 9 February, another batch of cases was settled: Steve Coogan received £40,000, Simon Hughes £45,000 and Sky Andrew £75,000. An undisclosed payment was made to Sheila Henry, the mother of 7/7 terrorist victim Christian Small. A £110,000 payment was made to Sally King, a friend of the former Home Secretary David Blunkett.*

Michael Silverleaf QC – still working for News International – expressed its 'sincere apologies' for the damage and distress. Charlotte Church – who had wanted her case to be heard in court until NI made it clear that it would seek to cross-examine her mentally fragile mother, Maria – questioned that sincerity. Outside court, the singer, whose family had received £600,000 in costs and damages, said:

---

* In the House of Commons register of interests, Blunkett disclosed that in July 2011 News International paid his family an undisclosed fee for 'intrusion'. He did not seem to bear grudges. In January 2012, he was on a rolling six-month contract worth £49,500 a year advising News International on 'corporate social responsibility'.

I have discovered that, despite the apology which the newspaper has just given in court today, these people were prepared to go to any lengths to prevent me exposing their behaviour, not just in the deliberate destruction of documents over a number of years but also by trying to make this investigation into the industrial scale of their illegal activity into an interrogation of my mother's medical condition, forcing her to relive the enormous emotional distress they caused her back in 2005. It seems they have learned nothing . . . In my opinion they are not truly sorry, only sorry they got caught.

Scotland Yard had by now given up any pretence that its original investigation was adequate. On 7 February, it finally abandoned its defence against the Max Mosley-funded judicial review and admitted it had behaved unlawfully towards the claimants John Prescott, Chris Bryant, Brian Paddick, Ben Jackson and HJK by failing to inform them they were victims of Glenn Mulcaire. It apologized and agreed to pay all costs.

Lord Prescott said: 'Time and again I was told by the Metropolitan Police that I had not been targeted by Rupert Murdoch's *News of the World*.' Chris Bryant said:

> As I have always maintained, this was a three-headed scandal. First there was the mass criminality, then there was the massive cover-up and then, from 2007, the inexplicable failure of the Met properly to investigate the *News of the World* or even interrogate the material that they had gathered from Glenn Mulcaire.

As the FBI stepped up its investigations under the Foreign Corrupt Practices Act,* News Corporation became ever more desperate to distance itself from its increasingly troublesome newspapers. In a special unit at Wapping sealed off from News International's remaining journalists, legal and support staff working for News Corp's Management and Standards Committee were scouring through invoices, expenses claims and emails for evidence of corruption. Detectives embedded with them uncovered the payment of tens of thousands of pounds of

---

* 'The FBI made it perfectly clear that if the British police drop the ball on this they will pick it up and run with it,' said one legal source familiar with the US investigation – *Independent on Sunday*, 18 March 2012

bribes to police and public officials, not from the now-closed *News of the World* but from journalists on the *Sun*.[1]

At dawn on Saturday 28 January, around forty police officers arrested the *Sun*'s executive editor, Fergus Shanahan (who during the Damien McBride affair in 2009 had described Tom Watson as an 'unsavoury creature lurking in the shadows'); the news editor, Chris Pharo; the former managing editor, Graham Dudman; the crime editor, Mike Sullivan; and a Metropolitan Police officer. To the fury of *Sun* journalists, an anonymous member of News Corp's Management and Standards Committee described the arrests as part of a process of 'draining the swamp'.[1]

On Saturday 11 February, the Metropolitan Police staged a bigger raid, arresting on suspicion of bribing public officials: the *Sun*'s deputy editor, Geoff Webster; long-serving chief reporter, John Kay; chief foreign correspondent, Nick Parker; the picture editor, John Edwards; and the deputy news editor John Sturgis. Also arrested were a member of the armed forces, a Surrey Police officer and a Ministry of Defence employee.

Writing in the *Sun* the following Monday, 13 February, the paper's long-time political pundit Trevor Kavanagh turned on the police (whom the *Sun* usually lauded) in an article headed 'Witch-hunt has put us behind ex-Soviet states on Press freedom'. Outraged, he complained that the arrests had infringed the journalists' privacy:

> Wives and children have been humiliated as up to twenty officers at a time rip up floorboards and sift through intimate possessions, love letters and entirely private documents . . . .
>
> Their alleged crimes? To act as journalists have acted on all newspapers through the ages, unearthing stories that shape our lives, often obstructed by those who prefer to operate behind closed doors.
>
> A huge operation driven by politicians threatens the very foundations of a free Press. Before it is too late, should we not be asking where all this is likely to lead?

At the same time, *The Times* was becoming embroiled in its own long-buried scandal: the hushed-up hacking of the emails of the police blogger 'Nightjack', DC Richard Horton (see page 86). Confronted with a standard question from the Leveson Inquiry about computer hacking, *The Times*'s editor, James Harding, told the law lord in his first statement on 14 October: '*The Times* has never used or commissioned anyone who used computer hacking to source stories. There was an incident where the newsroom was concerned that a reporter had gained unauthorized access to an email account. When it was brought to my attention, the journalist faced disciplinary action.' That statement was disingenuous since Harding knew that the paper's reporter, Patrick Foster, *had* used computer hacking on the Nightjack story. Over the coming weeks the truth was slowly dragged out of *The Times*. Its legal director, Alastair Brett, and its managing editor, David Chappell, had known by 4 June 2009 that Foster had used hacking, but the paper had published his story days later regardless after seeing off a legal attempt by Horton to prevent its publication. In that High Court case, *The Times* had made no mention of the hacking to the judge, Mr Justice Eady, who was told that Foster had identified Horton by painstaking detective work. At the Leveson Inquiry on 7 February 2012, Harding said he did not think the paper's testimony to the High Court had been truthful, but he insisted that he had not personally known about the hacking until several days after publication of the story – despite being alerted to it in an email prior to publication (which he claimed he had been too busy to read). Harding disciplined Foster over the incident, but promoted him a year later to media editor. Cheeks flushed, Harding told Lord Leveson: 'When you look back at all of this, sir – I really hope you understand – it's terrible. I really hope you appreciate that. I know that as keenly as you do.' Operation Tuleta, the Metropolitan Police's inquiry into computer hacking, began investigating the Nightjack affair.

Battered on all sides, morale among journalists at Wapping sank. On 16 February, however, Rupert Murdoch jetted into London to reaffirm his faith in the papers that built his empire. With Lachlan Murdoch by his side, he toured the newsroom, revoked the suspensions of the arrested staff and announced the imminent launch of a Sunday edition of the *Sun*. On 20 February, the *Sun* ran a 484-word story proclaiming that it would rise the following Sunday, without mentioning the *News of the World*. (The *News of the World* had been written out of the past, just as James Murdoch was being written out of the future.)

But Murdoch, the grand manipulator, could no longer control events. On 27 February, the police chief Sue Akers – irritated by criticism that her officers were arresting journalists merely for trivial offers of hospitality to the police – responded by explaining that the paper was being investigated for paying tens of thousands of pounds of bribes to staff across a swath of public life, including the police, military, prisons and health service. Lest anyone be in doubt, she added the officials were being bribed not for public interest stories but for 'salacious gossip' and that the *Sun* had tried to cover its tracks by paying cash and channelling the payments to friends and relatives of public servants. In her witness statement she said:

> The payments have been made not only to police officers but to a wide range of public officials. There are other categories as well as police: military, health, government, prison and others. This suggests that payments were being made to public officials who were in all areas of public life. I have said that the current assessment is that it reveals a network of corrupted officials. When I say 'network' I don't necessarily mean that the officials are in contact with each other; more that the journalists had a network upon which to call at various strategic places across public life.
>
> There also appears to have been a culture at the *Sun* of illegal payments, and systems have been created to facilitate those payments, whilst hiding the identity of the officials receiving the money.

At the end of February, News Corp announced that James Murdoch, once the heir, was standing down from the chairmanship of News International. On 3 April he gave up the even more powerful position of chairman of BSkyB, saying optimistically: 'I believe that my resignation will help to ensure that there is no false conflation with events at a separate organisation.' At the time this book went to press, he was still a director of News Corporation.

On 13 March, his friend Rebekah Brooks and her husband Charlie, and four other individuals, including Mark Hanna, News International's head of security, were arrested on suspicion of conspiracy to pervert the course of justice. The following day, Neville Thurlbeck, the *News of the World*'s former chief reporter, was arrested on suspicion of intimidating a witness. He had written a report on his website that News International had upgraded the home security of Will Lewis, now overseeing the efforts of the Management and Standards Committee to distance the company from corruption, in which he had identified the street Lewis lived on.

By now, News Corp was surrounded in every direction and facing investigations from regulators and the police on both sides of the Atlantic. In secrecy in January, Ofcom – the regulator the Murdochs had hoped to hobble – had begun 'Project Apple', an inquiry into whether the stream of disclosures from the Metropolitan Police and the Leveson Inquiry rendered News Corp unfit to own its 39 per cent controlling stake in BSkyB, the broadcaster it had been on the verge of taking over the previous July. In February, the Independent Police Complaints Commission launched an inquiry into whether a police officer had in 2006 inappropriately passed Rebekah Brooks details of Operation Caryatid, the original police investigation into phone hacking (see page 46). Lord Leveson's inquiry was publicly delving into the relationship between Murdoch's organization and senior police officers and politicians; dozens of new victims were launching phone hacking cases; and the Commons Culture Committee was preparing a report which would make clear the extent to which News International had misled Parliament. The FBI was intensifying its investigations into bribery, which could result in corporate prosecutions under the Foreign Corrupt Practices Act.

At Scotland Yard, in March, 169 detectives and support staff were working on the linked Operations Weeting, Tuleta and Elveden, making them together the biggest criminal inquiry in the country. Weeting had discovered the names and phone numbers of 4,375 individuals in Glenn Mulcaire's notes, of which 829 were likely to have been victims. Elveden was investigating the corruption of a network of police and public officials by the *Sun*. Tuleta was examining more than fifty computers and other electronic devices, including those of the former Prime Minister, Gordon Brown, the former Secretary of State for Northern Ireland, Peter Hain – who may have had his emails hacked while occupying one of the most sensitive posts in government – and the former Labour aide Derek Draper. Ironically, it was Draper who had received the rumour-mongering emails sent by Damien McBride in 2009 which so damaged Brown's administration, months before News International decisively switched to the Conservatives – the party which was prepared to grant its parent company complete control of BSkyB.

What began with the battle of Prince William's wounded knee had turned into the worst scandal in British public life in decades, touching almost every pillar of British life: the royal family, the government, the civil service, the courts, the police, the Crown Prosecution Service and, of course, the media.

All News International's titles and many others on Fleet Street had been tainted, but two facts separated Rupert Murdoch's newspapers from others: the hard evidence and the cover-up. When detectives raided Glenn Mulcaire's home on 8 August 2006 they found 11,000 pages of notes clearly indicating that the *News of the World* had been systematically engaged in a campaign of illegal phone hacking. The Metropolitan Police failed to tackle that properly for five years, until 2011. Rather than a fearless, impartial investigator, it was meek and malleable. Its senior officers were lunched by the newspaper executives they should have been investigating and, both before and after leaving office, eagerly accepted their largesse. Less senior officers have now been arrested for directly accepting corrupt payments for the supply of stories. Scotland Yard's reputation for competence and probity has been so badly damaged it will take years to repair. Urgent questions remain about the murder of Daniel Morgan (and in Scotland about the conviction of Tommy Sheridan, which looks increasingly unsafe).

But Scotland Yard was not the only force or regulator to fail. If Devon and Cornwall's inquiry in 2002 had succeeded, if Surrey Police had prosecuted the blatant phone hacking identified that same year, or if, the following year, the Information Commissioner's Office had prosecuted the most prolific law-breaking journalists, thousands of people might have been saved from the illegal intrusions into their lives – intrusions which were seldom in the public interest and which often carried a high personal price. Deliberately denuded of the power to levy fines or seize documents, the Press Complaints Commission proved itself inadequate to its task. Under its new chairman the

Conservative politician Lord Hunt, it is reinventing itself as a tougher body, but that may not be enough to satisfy Lord Leveson, whose inquiry is likely to end the system of self-regulation which has creaked for decades.

Many institutions failed – but there were individual failures too. The holders of high office failed in their duty to protect the public:

- the Scotland Yard detectives who ignored the bulk of the wrongdoing
- the PCC chairwoman who did not understand how the press actually operated
- the Assistant Commissioner who did not open the bags of evidence
- the Director of Public Prosecutions who did not read all the paperwork
- the London mayor who did not demand action from his police force
- the Queen's solicitors who knowingly continued to act for a lying corporation
- the national newspaper editors who persistently avoided the story
- the BBC executives who failed to devote resources to a national scandal
- the cabinet minister who did not take into account a history of broken promises when supporting a £7 billion takeover
- the Prime Minister who did not listen to warnings about his new director of communications, and whose government prostrated itself in front of a foreign tycoon

Incompetence alone cannot explain all of these failures. Fear allowed the phone hacking scandal to happen – fear of public humiliation for an indiscretion, fear of not winning that glowing endorsement. Politically, given the fixed opinions of much of the press – to the left the *Mirror*, the middle the *Independent* and *Guardian*, and the right the *Daily Mail*, *Express* and *Telegraph* – Rupert Murdoch held the balance of power. He was the ultimate floating voter and five successive governments courted his support. All prime ministers from Margaret Thatcher to David Cameron turned a blind eye when they should have intervened and allowed his dominance to rise, deal by deal, election by election.

From the start of his career in 1950s Australia, Murdoch manipulated politicians and broke rules and promises to accumulate money and power. It may not be possible to prove beyond reasonable doubt that he knew about the wrongdoing in Britain. Many, including the authors, think he is, at best, guilty of wilful blindness. As the head of the company, he shaped its culture. While he depicted phone hacking as an *anomaly*, something set apart from an otherwise virtuous organization, seasoned Murdoch-watchers identified the wrongdoing as part of a *pattern* – the greatest manifestation of a win-at-all-costs diktat which bent and broke the rules at will, as the former *Sunday Times* editor Andrew Neil pointed out:

> You create a climate in which people think it's alright to do certain things. And I would argue that Rupert Murdoch with his take-no-prisoners attitude to journalism – the end will justify the means, do whatever it takes – created the kind of newsroom climate in which hacking and other things were done with impunity on an industrial scale.[2]

In a sense, what is most revealing is not that his newspaper company was breaking the law at will and paying off police and officials, but how it responded when it was caught. In 2006 its representatives blocked and intimidated police trying to execute a search warrant and failed to hand over important evidence to detectives. In 2007, Murdoch's chief lieutenant Les Hinton failed to tell the Commons Culture Committee about Goodman's claims that hacking was routine, and failed to call in the police to investigate those claims; instead he sanctioned hush payments for Goodman and Mulcaire. When given evidence of more widespread wrongdoing in 2008, Murdoch's son and heir, James, did not correct Hinton's testimony, nor inform the police. Instead, he authorized another massive hush payment, to Gordon Taylor. In 2009, under James Murdoch's chairmanship, News International impugned the reputation of an honest journalist, repeatedly misled Parliament, surveilled an MP, began a smear exercise and intimidated and lied. In 2010, still with James Murdoch in charge, executives ordered the systematic destruction of evidence to cover up its illegal handiwork, ordered surveillance on lawyers challenging the company, and secretly paid off another high-profile victim. Under Murdoch and Rebekah Brooks, News International fought civil claimants all the way, denying everything they possibly could at every stage. Even if the Murdochs did only learn of the extent of their employees' previous criminality at the end of 2010, as they claim, they did not then inform the police, nor correct four years of misleading evidence to MPs, nor apologize to journalists and the public. Only journalistic, parliamentary, police and judicial inquiries prised out the truth. At all times until very recently – and then arguably only under the pressing need to avoid its directors being jailed – News Corp acted to cover up rather than uncover its past.

By dogmatically sticking to the lie of the rogue reporter defence for five years, the Murdochs paid a far higher price than the one payable if they had come clean straight away. The cost can be counted in the shredded reputations of many senior executives; the closure of a best-selling newspaper and the loss of 150 loyal journalists; the failure to take over the whole of Britain's biggest television network; at least $195 million (and counting) in compensation, legal fees, internal investigations and redundancy payments; some of the worst publicity imaginable for a global corporation; and shareholder revolts which threaten the family's grip on News Corp. Perhaps worst of all, they have lost most of their lucrative power to influence British politics and policing. Everyone who kow-towed before, who pushed for a place at their side, is going to be wary even of being seen in their company from now on. Like the paper they closed, the Murdochs have become toxic.

And it is going to get worse. There are investigations into media practices in the US and Australia, an increasing number of investigative journalists and parliamentarians looking at other forms of intrusive surveillance techniques, former contracted private investigators and disgruntled former staff members speaking out, civil cases pointing to wrongdoing at other newspapers. In the margins of the scandal, whispered voices speak about the involvement of rogue intelligence officers, secret political campaigns and commercial espionage. Almost certainly there will be several criminal trials, leading to fresh bursts of bad publicity, further disclosures and, possibly, lengthy custodial sentences for former employees. News Corp may not be strong enough to withstand it. 'What's happening in Britain is eating News Corp up – its slow, agonizing pace may even be more corrosive than the prospect of trials and even potential convictions,' Michael Wolff observed in February. 'An extraordinary corporate death is taking place.'[3]

In the end, this story is about corruption by power. Some of Murdoch's enforcers departed from the company line (it's all about business) and pursued personal agendas and vendettas, even against minor politicians. Their arrogance was so stratospheric they discussed their crimes even though they knew they were being recorded. They thought they could destroy the evidence, threaten and cover up. They thought they were cleverer than everyone else; they thought they were untouchable. From the criminal underworld to the headquarters of London's police force, from the decks of yachts in the Mediterranean to farmhouses in the Cotswolds and the deep-carpeted rooms of Downing Street, they had spun an invisible web of connections and corruption. They had privileged access to government ministers, state secrets, tax, health and vehicle data, to the records of phone companies and banks, to the intimate personal information of members of the public. They listened to phone messages, of course, but they also blagged, bribed, spied and bullied, and imposed their will through blackmail, corruption and intimidation. The names of their agents spoke of the darkness: Silent Shadow, Shadowmenuk. Rupert Murdoch was not running a normal business, but a shadow state. Now exposed by the daylight, it has been publicly humbled, its apparatus partially dismantled and its executives in retreat, at least for the moment. It stands shaken and ostensibly apologetic but it is still there, and Rupert Murdoch is still in charge.

Appendix 1 – Individuals in Glenn Mulcaire's Notes

NAME/RELEVANCE AT TIME OF HACKING

Prince William
Prince Harry
Jamie Lowther-Pinkerton, royal aide
Paddy Harverson, royal aide
Helen Asprey, royal aide
Sarah Ferguson, ex-royal
James Hewitt, former boyfriend of Princess Diana
Paul Burrell, butler to Princess Diana
Guy Pelly, friend of Prince Harry
Tracey Temple, girlfriend of John Prescott
Cherie Blair, wife of Prime Minister Tony Blair
Alastair Campbell, communications director to Tony Blair
Carole Caplin, fitness adviser to Cherie Blair
John Prescott, Labour Deputy Prime Minister
Joan Hammell, chief of staff to John Prescott
David Blunkett, Labour Home Secretary
Sally King, friend of David Blunkett
Andrew King, husband of Sally King
John Anderson, father of Sally King
Tessa Jowell, Labour Culture Secretary
David Mills, lawyer and Tessa Jowell's husband
Denis MacShane, Labour minister
Joan Smith, girlfriend of Denis MacShane
Elliot Morley, Labour minister
Boris Johnson, Conservative MP
Chris Bryant, Labour MP
Mark Oaten, Liberal Democrat MP

George Osborne, Conservative MP
Natalie Rowe, former friend of George Osborne
Simon Hughes, Liberal Democrat MP
George Galloway, Labour MP
Tommy Sheridan, Scottish Socialist MP
Claire Ward, Labour MP
Nigel Farrage, Leader of UK Independence Party
Ian Blair, Commissioner, Metropolitan Police
John Yates, Assistant Commissioner, Metropolitan Police
Andy Hayman, Assistant Commissioner, Metropolitan Police
Brian Paddick, Deputy Assistant Commissioner, Metropolitan Police
Ali Dizaei, Commander, Metropolitan Police
Mike Fuller, Commander, Metropolitan Police
David Cook, Detective Chief Superintendent, Metropolitan Police
Jacqui Hames, wife of David Cook
Andy Gilchrist, trade union leader
Gordon Taylor, trade union leader
Jo Armstrong, lawyer
John Hewison, lawyer
Michael Mansfield, lawyer
Graham Shear, lawyer
Sir Richard Branson, entrepreneur
Jude Law, actor
Sadie Frost, former wife of Jude Law
Ciara Parkes, publicist to Jude Law
Ben Jackson, personal assistant to Jude Law
Sienna Miller, actress
Hugh Grant, actor
Jemima Khan, girlfriend of Hugh Grant
Cornelia Crisan, friend of actor Ralph Fiennes
Steve Coogan, comedian
Lisa Gower, former partner of Steve Coogan
Dan Lichters, friend of comedian Michael Barrymore
Charlotte Church, singer
Maria Church, mother of Charlotte Church
James Church, father of Charlotte Church
James Blunt, singer
Pete Doherty, singer
Meg Matthews, ex-wife of singer Noel Gallagher
Kelly Hoppen, interior designer
Elle Macpherson, model

Mary-Ellen Field, representative of Elle Macpherson
Abi Titmuss, model
Laura Rooney, dancer
Max Clifford, publicist
Nicola Phillips, PA to Max Clifford
Michelle Milburn, theatre agent
Alan McGee, record label manager
Jeff Brazier, boyfriend of Jade Goody
Chris Tarrant, TV presenter
Ulrika Jonsson, TV presenter
Lance Gerrard-Wright, husband of Ulrika Jonsson
Dannii Minogue, TV presenter
Brendan Minogue, brother of Dannii Minogue
Leslie Ash, TV presenter
Lee Chapman, husband of Leslie Ash
Jamie Theakston, TV presenter
Duncan Foster, TV director
Rebekah Brooks, newspaper editor
Brendan Montague, freelance journalist
Kelvin Mackenzie, journalist, the *Sun*
Ted Hynds, journalist
Tom Rowland, freelance journalist
Dennis Rice, journalist, *Mail on Sunday*
Amanda Hobbs, wife of Dennis Rice
Louise Artimati, sister of Dennis Rice
David Davies, football executive
Sven-Göran Eriksson, football manager
Wayne Rooney, footballer
Ryan Giggs, footballer
Ashley Cole, footballer
Peter Crouch, footballer
Abbey Clancy, wife of Peter Crouch
Kieron Dyer, footballer
Paul Gascoigne, footballer
Jimmy Gardner, friend of Paul Gascoigne
Michael McGuire, football agent
Andy Gray, football commentator
Phil Hughes, agent for footballer George Best
Calum Best, son of George Best
Paul Stretford, football agent
Sky Andrew, football agent

Gavin Henson, rugby player
Samantha Wallin, racing trainer
Kieren Fallon, jockey
Chris Eubank, boxer
Karron Stephen-Martin, ex-wife of Chris Eubank
Eimer Cook, wife of golfer Colin Montgomerie
Colette Bos, unknown
HSK, friend of politician
Miss X, alleged victim of rape by celebrity
Colin Stagg, exonerated murder suspect
Robert Thompson, child murderer
Harold Shipman, son of murderer Harold Shipman
Alex Pereira, cousin of police shooting victim
Sheila Henry, mother of terrorist victim
Graham Foulkes, father of terrorist victim
Sean Cassidy, father of terrorist victim
Paul Dadge, survivor of terrorist attack
Shaun Russell, father of murder victim
Sara Payne, mother of murder victim
Sharon Chapman, mother of murder victim
Leslie Chapman, father of murder victim
Milly Dowler, missing schoolgirl
There are another 698 likely victims, yet to be named.

Appendix 2 – Arrests*

2006

Clive Goodman, royal editor, *News of the World* – 8 August, on suspicion of phone hacking

Glenn Mulcaire, private investigator, *News of the World* – 8 August, on suspicion of phone hacking

2011

Ian Edmondson, news editor, *News of the World* – 5 April, on suspicion of phone hacking

Neville Thurlbeck, chief reporter, *News of the World* – 5 April, on suspicion of phone hacking

James Weatherup, news editor/reporter, *News of the World* – 14 April, on suspicion of phone hacking

Taras Terenia, freelance contributor, *News of the World* – 23 June, on suspicion of phone hacking

†Laura Elston, royal correspondent, Press Association – 27 June, on suspicion of phone hacking

Andy Coulson, editor, *News of the World* – 8 July, on suspicion of phone hacking

Clive Goodman, royal editor, *News of the World* – 8 July, on suspicion of police corruption

Unidentified 63-year-old man – 8 July, on suspicion of corruption

* Some staff have left or changed jobs; most relevant position stated. It does not follow that anyone arrested will be charged with criminal offences.
† Police later said these individuals were of no interest to their inquiries

323

Neil Wallis, executive editor, *News of the World* – 14 July, on suspicion of phone hacking

Rebekah Brooks, editor, *News of the World* and the *Sun* – 17 July, on suspicion of phone hacking and corrupting police

Stuart Kuttner, managing editor, *News of the World* – 2 August, on suspicion of phone hacking and corrupting police

Greg Miskiw, news editor, *News of the World* – 10 August, on suspicion of phone hacking

†James Desborough, showbusiness reporter, *News of the World* – 18 August, on suspicion of phone hacking

Dan Evans, reporter, *News of the World* – 19 August, on suspicion of phone hacking

Ross Hall, reporter, *News of the World* – 2 September, on suspicion of phone hacking and perverting the course of justice

Raoul Simmons, deputy football editor, *The Times* – 7 September, on suspicion of phone hacking

Jamie Pyatt, news editor/reporter, the *Sun* – 4 November, on suspicion of bribing police

52-year-old member of the public – 24 November, on suspicion of computer hacking

†Bethany Usher, reporter, *News of the World* – 30 November, on suspicion of phone hacking

Glenn Mulcaire, private investigator, *News of the World* – 7 December, on suspicion of phone hacking and perverting the course of justice

Lucy Panton, crime editor, *News of the World* – 15 December, on suspicion of bribing police

2012

Cheryl Carter, beauty editor, the *Sun* and Rebekah Brooks's former PA – 7 January, on suspicion of attempting to pervert the course of justice

Unidentified police officer – 10 January, on suspicion of making unauthorized disclosures to the press

Graham Dudman, managing editor, the *Sun* – 28 January, on suspicion of corrupting public officials

Mike Sullivan, crime editor, the *Sun* – 28 January, on suspicion of corrupting public officials

Chris Pharo, news editor, the *Sun* – 28 January, on suspicion of corrupting public officials

Fergus Shanahan, executive editor, the *Sun* – 28 January, on suspicion of corrupting public officials

Unidentified policeman, 28 January, on suspicion of corruption

Geoff Webster, deputy editor, the *Sun* – 11 February, on suspicion of corrupting public officials

John Kay, chief reporter, the *Sun* – 11 February, on suspicion of corrupting public officials

Nick Parker, chief foreign correspondent, the *Sun* – 11 February, on suspicion of corrupting public officials

John Edwards, picture editor, the *Sun* – 11 February, on suspicion of corrupting police/public officials

John Sturgis, deputy news editor, the *Sun* – 11 February, on suspicion of corrupting police/public officials

Unidentified Surrey police officer – 11 February, on suspicion of corruption

Unidentified Ministry of Defence employee – 11 February, on suspicion of corruption

Unidentified member of the armed forces – 11 February, on suspicion of corruption

Virginia Wheeler, defence editor, the *Sun* – 1 March, on suspicion of corrupting public officials

Rebekah Brooks, Chief Executive, News International – 13 March, on suspicion of conspiracy to pervert the course of justice

Charlie Brooks, husband of Rebekah Brooks – 13 March, on suspicion of conspiracy to pervert the course of justice

Mark Hanna, head of security, News International – 13 March, on suspicion of conspiracy to pervert the course of justice

Unidentified male employee, News International – 13 March, on suspicion of conspiracy to pervert the course of justice

Unidentified man – 13 March, on suspicion of conspiracy to pervert the course of justice

Unidentified man – 13 March, on suspicion of conspiracy to pervert the course of justice

Neville Thurlbeck, chief reporter, *News of the World* – 14 March, on suspicion of intimidating a witness

Acknowledgements

The authors together

Many of the central figures in this story were interviewed for or otherwise helped us with this book, including Jo Becker, Chris Bryant, Glenn Campbell, Steve Coogan, David Davies, Nick Davies (one of the great exemplars of good journalism), Paul Farrelly, Hugh Grant, Jacqui Hames, Amelia Hill, Sienna Miller, Alastair Morgan, Max Mosley, Don van Natta Jr, Peter Oborne, Alec Owens, Alan Rusbridger and 'Miss X'. Their bravery gave us confidence and hope, and we thank them.

The lawyers Tamsin Allen, Charlotte Harris, Mark Lewis, Mark Thompson and Dominic Crossley brilliantly uncovered the cover-up. Without them, this shameful business might still be concealed.

We thank our literary agent, Clare Alexander of Aitken Alexander Associates, Toby Mundy of Atlantic Books, and agent David Luxton for their help at different stages. Had Judith Attar not put us together at Hull University, we would never have reconnected in 2010.

We are grateful to all at Penguin, but especially to our editor Stuart Proffitt, whose long experience informed its writing; his efficient and ever-cheerful assistant Shan Vahidy, the editorial managers Richard Duguid and Rebecca Lee, publicity manager Thi Dinh, and Bela Cunha, our expertly thorough copy-editor.

Tom Watson

I couldn't have survived the events this book describes without the team who have put up with the maelstrom around me: Kim Frazer,

Sophie Goodchild, Gareth Illmann-Walker, Paul Moore, Karie Murphy and Raeesa Patel. Many have shown me friendship and solidarity in tough times: Diane Abbott, Dave Anderson, Luciana Berger, Billy Bragg, Kevin Brennan, Gordon Brown, Richard Burden, Shami Chakrabarti, Darren Cooper, Paul and Karen Corby, John Cryer, Geoffrey Goodman, Simon Hackett, David Hamilton, Harriet Harman, George Hickman, Lyndsay Hoyle, Mahboob Hussain, Amy Jackson, Tessa Jowell, Fraser Kemp, Paul Kenny, Peter Kilfoyle, Tarsem King, Neil Kinnock, Ian Lavery, Ian Lucas, Kevin Maguire, Len McCluskey, Iain McNicol, Michael Meacher, Ed Miliband, Vincent Moss, Jim Mowatt, Stephanie Peacock, Tom Powdrill, Lucy Powell, Mark Pritchard, Ian Reilly, Peter Rhodes, James Robinson, Steve Rotherham, Martin Rowson, Adrian Sanders, Jim Sheridan, Tommy Sheridan, Dennis Skinner, Nicholas Soames, John Spellar, Mark and Sally Tami, Steve Torrance, Keith Vaz, Iain Wright, Peter Hooton, Pete Wylie and the extraordinary people of the city of Liverpool.

Above all, I thank my family for their love and understanding: Linda and Barry Halliwell, Meg and Will Tremayne, Dan and Jo Watson, Tony, Jan and Anna Watson, and Amy Watson. My children, Malachy and Saoirse, remain the centre of my universe and I thank them for sharing the keyboard with me.

One friend in particular helped me through some very dark times. I will always be indebted to Siôn Simon for being there when it counted.

Martin Hickman

Any journalistic career needs the help of good bosses, and I thank Paul Durrant, Nick Small and Trevor Mason.

At the *Independent*, my gratitude runs deep to Cahal Milmo, a prince among journalists; Chris Blackhurst for willingly (though – gratifyingly – not too readily) allowing me to take unpaid leave at very short notice; Oliver Duff, Chris Green and the other newsdesk stalwarts; reporters Jim Cusick and Ian Burrell, who chipped away at the official version; Mike McCarthy for his extraordinary enthusiasm; at the *i* paper its editor Stefano Hatfield; at the *Independent on Sunday*, James Hanning, one of the first journalists to recognize the story's importance, and Matthew Bell, both of whom who helped promptly and generously.

Over the past year friends and relatives have put up with absences, cancellations and my single topic of conversation. I thank them all, but especially Liz Hickman and Simon Hickman. To my lovely, patient children, Kate and Finlay, come the welcome words: 'The book is finished', and to my long-suffering wife Rachel, whose job-home-family juggling equalled that of a circus act and whose support stretched astonishingly beyond the reasonable, the message: 'It couldn't have been done without you.'

Notes

1. THE WRONG HEADLINES

1. *The Man Who Owns the News*, Michael Wolff, Vintage Books, 2010
2. *Good Times, Bad Times*, Harold Evans, Coronet, 1983, pp. 489–90
3. *Where Power Lies*, Lance Price, Simon & Schuster, 2010, p. 333
4. *The Insider: The Private Diaries of a Scandalous Decade*, Piers Morgan, Ebury Press, 2005, p. 147
5. 'Untangling Rebekah Brooks', Suzanna Andrews, *Vanity Fair*, February 2012
6. *The Insider*, p. 382
7. Interview with Siôn Simon, November 2011

2. WAPPING'S NEWS FACTORY

1. *Murdoch*, William Shawcross, Simon & Schuster, 1992, p. 116
2. 'Tabloid's Dirty Secrets,' *Dispatches*, Channel 4, 7 February 2011
3. *Full Disclosure*, Andrew Neil, Macmillan, 1996, p. 160
4. Ibid., p. 172
5. *The Insider: The Private Diaries of a Scandalous Decade*, Piers Morgan, Ebury Press, 2005, p. 82
6. Ibid., p. 103
7. Ibid., p. 95
8. Paul McMullan, oral evidence, Leveson Inquiry, 29 November 2011
9. Ibid.
10. Interview with anonymous News International executive, October 2011
11. *Confessions of a Fake Sheikh*, Mazher Mahmood, HarperCollins, 2008, p. 74
12. Interview with anonymous News International executive, March 2011
13. 'Stephen Glover on the press', Stephen Glover, *Independent*, 21 March 2005

14. Interview: Andy Coulson, David Rowan, *Evening Standard*, 16 March 2005
15. 'How the Screws screwed its rivals', Tim Luckhurst, *Independent*, 19 February 2006
16. Matt Driscoll, oral evidence, Leveson Inquiry, 19 December 2011
17. Matt Driscoll, written evidence, Leveson Inquiry, 12 December 2011
18. Matt Driscoll, oral evidence, Leveson Inquiry, 19 December 2011
19. 'Former NoW sports reporter in £792k tribunal payout', Dominic Ponsford, *Press Gazette*, 24 November 2009

3. THE DARK ARTS

1. Interview with Alec Owens, January 2012
2. Ibid.
3. Alec Owens, written evidence, Leveson Inquiry, 17 November 2011
4. Ibid.
5. Richard Thomas, written evidence, Leveson Inquiry, 6 September 2011
6. Stephen Whittamore, BBC Radio 4 *PM* programme, 21 September 2010
7. Alec Owens, oral evidence, Leveson Inquiry, 30 November 2011
8. 'Exposed after eight years: a private eye's dirty work for Fleet Street', Ian Burrell, *Independent*, 6 September 2011
9. Tom Bradby, http://blog.itv.com/news/tombradby/2011/11/phone-hacking-the-movie/, 10 November 2011

4. FIRST HEADS ROLL

1. 'Fury after he ogled lapdancer's boobs', Clive Goodman and Neville Thurlbeck, *News of the World*, 9 April 2006
2. Document written by Detective Superintendent Philip Williams, Leveson Inquiry, 29 February 2012
3. Alec Owens, written evidence, Leveson Inquiry, 17 November 2011
4. Carine Patry Hoskins, counsel to the Leveson Inquiry, during Matt Driscoll's oral evidence, Leveson Inquiry, 19 December 2011
5. Sheridan Victory Speech in Full, BBC News Online, http://news.bbc.co.uk/1/hi/scotland/glasgow_and_west/5246764.stm, 4 August 2006
6. 'Met failed to pursue data on tabloid phone taps', Nick Davies, *Guardian*, 5 April 2010
7. Statement by Detective Chief Inspector Keith Surtees, Judicial Review by Lord Prescott, Chris Bryant, Brian Paddick, Ben Jackson and HJK against Metropolitan Police, High Court, 30 September 2011

8. Detective Chief Inspector Keith Surtees, oral evidence, Leveson Inquiry, 29 February 2012

9. Detective Superintendent Philip Williams, oral evidence, Leveson Inquiry, 29 February 2012

10. Robert Jay QC, Leveson Inquiry, 29 February 2012

11. Document, Leveson Inquiry, 29 February 2012

12. Deputy Assistant Commissioner Peter Clarke, oral evidence, Leveson Inquiry, 1 March 2012

13. Lawrence Abramson, oral evidence, Leveson Inquiry, 13 December 2011

14. Richard Thomas, written evidence, Leveson Inquiry, 6 September 2011

5. ROGUE DEFENCE

1. Interview with Mark Lewis, June 2011

2. Harbottle & Lewis, written evidence, Commons Culture, Media and Sport Select Committee, August 2011

3. Interview with George Eustice, September 2011

4. Ibid.

5. 'The World according to Rupert', Nicholas Wapshott, *Independent*, 23 July 2006

6. Ibid.

7. Interview with George Eustice, September 2011

8. 'Rebekah vetoed BBC man and told Cameron he should give No 10 job to Andy Coulson', Simon Walters, *Mail on Sunday*, 16 July 2011

9. ' Cameron fires up the faithful', Brian Whelan, BBC News Online, http://news.bbc.co.uk/1/hi/uk_politics/7025958.stm, 3 October 2007

10. 'Police Cameron Action', George Pascoe-Watson, *Sun*, 30 January 2008

6. THE MANCHESTER LAWYERS

1. Interview with Charlotte Harris, August 2011

2. Email from Tom Crone to Colin Myler headed: 'Strictly private and confidential and legally privileged', 6.10 p.m., 24 May 2008, disclosed by Farrer & Co to the House of Commons Culture, Media and Sport Committee on 31 October 2011

3. Legal Opinion by Michael Silverleaf QC, to News Group Newspapers [the News International subsidiary which owned the *News of the World*], 3 June 2008, disclosed by Farrer & Co to the House of Commons Culture, Media and Sport Committee on 31 October 2011

4. Email from Colin Myler to James Murdoch, 2.31 p.m., 7 June

2008, disclosed by Linklaters to the House of Commons Culture, Media and Sport Committee on 12 December 2011.

5. Email from Julian Pike to Tom Crone, 5.16 p.m., 6 June 2008, disclosed by Linklaters to the House of Commons Culture, Media and Sport Committee on 12 December 2011

6. James Murdoch's reply at 2.34 p.m.

7. Richard Thomas, written evidence, Leveson Inquiry, 6 September 2011

8. Ibid.

9. 'Bloated BBC out of touch with the viewers', David Cameron, *Sun*, 3 November 2008

10. 'Tory government "would force BBC to reveal stars' salaries"', Leigh Holmwood, Guardian online, http://www.guardian.co.uk/media/2009/jan/22/tory-government-bbc-pay, 22 January 2009

11. 'Tories would cut Ofcom powers, says David Cameron', Jason Deans, Guardian online, http://www.guardian.co.uk/media/2009/jul/06/tories-cut-ofcom-powers-david-cameron

12. 'We'd abolish BBC Trust, says Tory culture spokesman Jeremy Hunt', John Plunkett and Tara Conlan, Guardian online, http://www.guardian.co.uk/media/2009/oct/19/wed-abolish-bbc-trust-hunt, 19 October 2009

7. ONE DETERMINED REPORTER

1. Interview with Nick Davies, February 2012

2. Ibid.

3. Ibid.

4. Interview with Alan Rusbridger, August 2011

5. 'Revealed: Murdoch's £1m bill for hiding dirty tricks', Nick Davies, *Guardian*, 9 July 2009

6. Minutes of Gold Meeting, Scotland Yard, 9 July, disclosed at Leveson Inquiry, 29 February 2012

7. Ibid.

8. Interview with Chris Bryant, June 2011

9. 'Sienna Miller: hacking's heroine', Jemima Khan, *Independent*, 23 September 2011

10. Tom Crone, oral evidence, House of Commons Culture, Media and Sport Committee, 21 July 2009

11. Phone conversation between Neville Thurlbeck and Tom Watson, October 2011

12. 'Tony Blair accused of trying to silence Rupert Murdoch critic', Martin Hickman, *Independent*, 11 July 2011

13. Alastair Campbell, draft statement to Leveson Inquiry, November 2011. This passage was included in Campbell's draft statement to the Leveson Inquiry but was omitted after he consulted 'close friends'

8. INTIMIDATING PARLIAMENT

1. Mark Lewis, oral evidence, House of Commons, Culture, Media and Sport Committee, 2 September 2009
2. Ibid.
3. 'News of the World faces £800,000 payout in bullying case', Hugh Muir and Chris Tryhorn, *Guardian*, 23 November 2009
4. Matt Driscoll, written evidence, Leveson Inquiry, 12 December 2011
5. 'Tabloids, Tories and Telephone Hacking', *Dispatches*, Channel 4, 4 October 2010
6. Letter from the *Guardian* to Dick Fedorcio, Guardian online, http://www.guardian.co.uk/media/interactive/2011/jul/15/letter-from-the-guardian-to-dick-fedorcio, July 15 2011
7. 'We must hold the powerful to account', Philip Davies, *News of the World*, 28 February 2010
8. News International Statement on Phone Hacking, *Press Gazette*, 24 February 2010

9. A MURDER

1. Tom Watson, adjournment debate on murder of Daniel Morgan, House of Commons, 29 February 2012
2. 'Fraudster Squad', Graeme McLagan, *Guardian*, 21 September 2002
3. Ibid.
4. Jacqui Hames, written evidence, Leveson Inquiry, 22 February 2012
5. Lord Stevens, oral evidence, Leveson Inquiry, 6 March 2012
6. Jacqui Hames, written evidence, Leveson Inquiry, 22 February 2012
7. 'Collapse of long-running inquiry leaves unanswered questions and accusations', Sandra Laville, *Guardian*, 12 March 2011
8. Interview with Charlotte Harris, August 2011
9. Ibid.
10. Max Clifford, oral evidence, Leveson Inquiry, 9 February 2012
11. Interview with Charlotte Harris, August 2011
12. Julian Pike, written evidence, Leveson Inquiry, 14 November 2011
13. Tom Crone, oral evidence, Leveson Inquiry, 14 December 2011
14. Charlotte Harris, written evidence, Leveson Inquiry, 5 December 2011

15. Mark Lewis, written evidence, Leveson Inquiry, 21 November 2011
16. Email from Nick Davies to Martin Hickman, August 2011
17. Interview with Alan Rusbridger, August 2011

10. OUR MAN IN DOWNING STREET

1. 'Ashdown: I warned Cameron about the huge danger of hiring Coulson', Toby Helm and Daniel Boffey, *Observer*, 10 July 2011
2. Ibid.
3. 'Takeover of BSkyB must be blocked, says media analyst', James Robinson, *Guardian*, 14 September 2010
4. Email from Steve Coogan to Tom Watson, October 2011
5. Generic Particulars of Claim, [anonymized] Voicemail Claimant versus News Group Newspapers and Glenn Mulcaire, High Court, December 2011
6. Email from Don van Natta Jr to Tom Watson, November 2011
7. 'Phone hacking: Andy Coulson offers to talk to police', Haroon Siddique, Andrew Sparrow, Patrick Wintour and Nick Davies, Guardian online, http://www.guardian.co.uk/media/2010/sep/06/phone-hacking-met-now-case, 6 September 2011
8. 'Police chief: NYT refused to help phone-hack probe', *Press Gazette*, http://www.pressgazette.co.uk/story.asp?storycode=45967, 7 September 2010
9. London Assembly (Plenary) Transcript, w.london.gov.uk/.../20100915/.../MQT%20Transcript%20RTF.rtf, 15 September 2010

11. LOSING A BATTLE

1. Interview with Max Mosley, May 2011
2. 'NI "tried to bully LibDems into backing bid for BskyB"', Henry Porter and Toby Helm, *Observer*, 24 July 2011
3. 'Exclusive: News Corp exec suspected in leak', Mark Hosenball, Reuters, http://uk.reuters.com/article/2011/07/22/uk-newscorp-lewis-idUKTRE76L30S20110722, 22 July 2011
4. 'Phone hacking: "News of the World" emails "lost" on the way to India', James Hanning and Paul Bignell, *Independent on Sunday*, 19 December 2010
5. 'Andy Coulson denies knowledge of criminal activity at News of the World', Nick Davies and Severin Carrell, Guardian online, http://www.

guardian.co.uk/media/2010/dec/10/andy-coulson-tommy-sheridan-trial, 10 December 2010

6. Interview with Tommy Sheridan, March 2011
7. 'Culture Secretary "has not prejudged" BSkyB takeover', Hélène Mulholland, Patrick Wintour and Matthew Weaver, http://www.guardian.co.uk/politics/2010/dec/22/more-lib-dem-ministers-recorded, 22 December 2010

12. OUT OF CONTROL

1. 'Sienna Miller: hacking's heroine', Jemima Khan, *Independent*, 23 September 2011
2. Generic Particulars of Claim, [anonymized] Voicemail Claimant versus News Group Newspapers and Glenn Mulcaire, High Court, December 2011
3. Letter from Linklaters to House of Commons Culture, Media and Sport Committee, 25 January 2012
4. Email from Tim Montgomerie to Martin Hickman, February 2012
5. 'Nick Brown says his phone was bugged', Joe Murphy, *Evening Standard*, 28 January 2011
6. 'Blunkett voicemails hacked', Robert Mendick, *Sunday Telegraph*, 11 September 2011
7. 'Phone hacking: police uncover more evidence', Cahal Milmo and Martin Hickman, *Independent*, 10 February 2011
8. 'RIPA and the phone hacking investigation', Letters, *Guardian*, 14 March 2011
9. Keir Starmer, oral evidence, House of Commons Home Affairs Committee, 5 April 2011

13. U-TURN AT WAPPING

1. 'The Times discovers hacking scandal – but bashes the BBC again', Roy Greenslade, Guardian online, http://www.guardian.co.uk/media/greenslade/2011/mar/16/thetimes-phone-hacking, 16 March 2011
2. 'Twelve face jail over hacking', David Leppard and Jon Ungoed-Thomas, *Sunday Times*, 10 July 2011
3. 'The bugger bugged', Hugh Grant, *New Statesman*, 12 April 2011
4. Interview with Hugh Grant, September 2011
5. Ibid.
6. Ibid.

7. 'James Murdoch: no reputation crisis at News Corp', The Holmes Report, http://www.holmesreport.com/news-info/10100/James-Murdoch-No-Reputation-Crisis-At-News-Corp.aspx, 8 April 2011

8. Sue Akers, oral evidence, House of Commons, Home Affairs Select Committee, 12 July 2011

9. 'Straw and Mandelson demand police answers', Oliver Wright and Martin Hickman, *Independent*, 10 June 2011

14. SUMMER'S LEASE

1. 'Exclusive: Brooks "among most-hacked victims"', Mark Kleinman, *Sky News*, http://blogs.news.sky.com/kleinman/Post:18500ee9-77c2-4370-8d7d-8b6ce17d5194, 15 June 2011

2. Lord Macdonald, oral evidence, House of Commons Home Affairs Select Committee, 19 July 2011

3. 'Mandelson (dancing wildly), a "giddy" Steve Hilton, Mark Thompson of the BBC (and, of course, Robert Peston) ... how a leather-trousered Matthew Freud hosted the decadent last hurrah of the Chipping Norton Set', Simon Walters and Glen Owen, *Mail on Sunday*, 17 July 2011

15. A MISSING GIRL

1. John Whittingdale interview, BBC Radio 4 *Today* programme, 5 July 2011

2. 'I'm ripping up the rule book', Mehdi Hasan, *New Statesman*, 26 September 2011

3. *What the Papers Say*, BBC Radio 4, 31 December 2011

4. 'News of the World's alleged actions "indefensible" says Times' Harding', Arif Durrani, *Brand Republic*, 5 July 2011

5. *What the Papers Say*, BBC Radio 4, 31 December 2011

6. 'Milly Dowler phone hacking: the reaction', Raf Sanchez, Telegraph online, http://www.telegraph.co.uk/news/uknews/crime/8617579/Milly-Dowler-phone-hacking-the-reaction.html, 5 July 2011

7. ' News of the World loses adverts over Milly Dowler scandal', Tim Ross, Amanda Andrews and Katherine Rushton, Telegraph online, http://www.telegraph.co.uk/news/uknews/crime/8619123/News-of-the-World-loses-adverts-over-Milly-Dowler-scandal.html, 5 July 2011

8. Interview with Hugh Grant on BBC Radio 5 Live, 5 July 2011

9. Interview with Alastair Campbell on BBC *Newsnight*, 5 July 2011

10. ' Phone hacking: reading between the lines of Murdoch's statement', Roy Greenslade, Guardian online, http://www.guardian.co.uk/media/green-state/2011/jul/06/rupert-murdoch-phone-hacking, 6 July 2011

11. Statement from London Mayor on phone hacking, http://www.london. gov.uk/media/press_releases_mayoral/statement-mayor-london-phone-hacking-0, 6 July 2011

12. Interview with Hugh Grant, September 2011

16. SKY PLUS

1. http://www.alastaircampbell.org/blog/2011/07/09/steve-coogan-spot-on-in-asking-where-paul-dacre-is-in-all-this-but-his-time-is-surely-coming, 9 July 2011

2. 'Murdoch's Watergate', Carl Bernstein, *Newsweek*, 18 July 2011

3. 'Murdoch says current News Corp. management stands: embattled former editor Brooks has his "total support"', Sarah McBride, Reuters, 9 July 2011

4. 'News of the World's desperate final hours', Paul McNamara, *New York Times*, 25 July 2011

5. 'News of the World phone hacking', Guardian online, Scandal, http://www.guardian.co.uk/media/blog/2011/jul/09/phone-hacking-newsoftheworld, 9 July 2011

6. 'News of the World's last breath: put the handkerchiefs aside', Roy Greenslade, Guardian online, http://www.guardian.co.uk/media/2011/jul/10/news-of-the-world-last-edition, 10 July 2011

7. 'Insider reveals: "PR men would think up a Story and Rebekah's Sun and News of the World would run it, word for word. Some were complete fiction"', *Mail on Sunday*, 9 July 2011

8. 'Police chief: I failed victims of hacking', Robert Mendick, Alasdair Palmer and Patrick Hennessy, *Sunday Telegraph*, 10 July 2011

9. 'Politics live blog', Andrew Sparrow, Guardian online, http://www.guardian.co.uk/politics/blog/2011/jul/11/politics-live-blog, 11 July 2011

10. Hayman hits out at MPs after 'appalling' hacking treatment, LBC, http://www.lbc.co.uk/hayman-hits-out-at-mps-after-appalling-hacking-treatment-42292, 13 July 2011

11. 'Sunday Times reject Gordon Brown "criminal claims"', BBC News Online, 13 July 2011

12. 'Phone hacking: News International paid Neil Wallis while he was at Scotland Yard', Robert Winnett and Mark Hughes, http://www.

telegraph.co.uk/news/uknews/phone-hacking/8785470/Phone-hacking-News-International-paid-Neil-Wallis-while-he-was-at-Scotland-Yard.html, 23 September 2011

17. 'WE ARE SORRY'

1. *Guardian*, 5 November 2011
2. Full James Murdoch statement on Rebekah Brooks, *New Statesman*, 15 July 2011
3. 'Rupert Murdoch Says "Sorry" in ad campaign', Guardian online, http://www.guardian.co.uk/media/2011/jul/15/rupert-murdoch-sorry-ad-campaign, 15 July 2011
4. 'A scandal that has diminished Britain', *Daily Telegraph*, 16 July 2011
5. 'Murdoch's Commons inquisitor has close ties to mogul's family', Jane Merrick, Brian Brady, James Hanning and Andy McCorkell, *Independent on Sunday*, 17 July 2011
6. Sir Hugh Orde, ACPO statement on the resignation of Sir Paul Stephenson, http://www.acpo.presscentre.com, 17 July 2011
7. 'Phone hacking: John Yates "to be suspended" over Neil Wallis links', Mark Hughes, Andrew Hough and Robert Winnett, Telegraph.co.uk, 17 July 2011
8. 'NoW phone-hacking whistle-blower Sean Hoare found dead', BBC News Online, http://www.bbc.co.uk/news/uk-14194623, 19 July 2011

18. DEMOCRACY DAY

1. 'Rupert Murdoch: can he survive a coup?', Neil Tweedie and Matthew Holehouse, Telegraph.co.uk, http://www.telegraph.co.uk/news/uknews/phone-hacking/8655490/Rupert-Murdoch-can-he-survive-a-coup.html, 23 July 2011
2. ' Shareholders sue Rupert Murdoch, News Corp. over Shine acquisition', Dawn Chmielewski, *Los Angeles Times*, 16 March 2011
3. 'Murdochs in "family fall-out" over crisis,' Jamie Doward and Lisa O'Carroll, Guardian online, http://www.guardian.co.uk/media/2011/jul/16/elisabeth-james-murdoch-family-crisis, 16 July 2011
4. 'Lots of questions but very few answers', Jemima Khan, *i*, 20 July 2011
5. 'Biographer: Murdoch talks to his editor more than he admits', Oliver Wright, *Independent*, 23 July 2011

19. ASSAULT ON THE ESTABLISHMENT

1. 'Murdochs were given secret defence briefings', Oliver Wright, *Independent*, 27 July 2011
2. 'Phone hacking scandal: Wednesday 20 July', Guardian online, http:// www.guardian.co.uk/media/blog/2011/jul/20/phone-hacking-scandal-live-coverage, 20 July 2011
3. 'Ex-executives dispute testimony of Murdoch son', Jo Becker and Don van Natta Jr, New York Times online, http://www.nytimes.com/2011/07/22/world/europe/22murdoch.html?pagewanted=all, 21 July 2011
4. 'I'm sorry, Macca, for introducing you to this monster', Piers Morgan, *Daily Mail*, 19 October 2006 (Morgan wrote: 'Stories soon emerged that the marriage was in trouble – at one stage I was played a tape of a message Paul had left for Heather on her mobile phone. It was heartbreaking. The couple had clearly had a tiff, Heather had fled to India, and Paul was pleading with her to come back. He sounded lonely, miserable and desperate, and even sang "We Can Work It Out" into the answerphone'.)
5. ' Morgan defiant as enemies try to implicate him in hacking scandal', Ian Burrell, *Independent*, 28 July 2011

20. THE GHOSTS OF WAPPING

1. 'Andy Coulson reportedly paid by News International when hired by Tories', James Robinson and Polly Curtis, Guardian online, http://www .guardian.co.uk/media/2011/aug/23/andy-coulson-news-international-tories, 23 August 2011
2. Ian Edmondson, oral evidence, Leveson Inquiry, 27 February. He said: 'I don't recall these emails being sent at all . . . I can't remember anything about these emails being sent.'
3. 'Rupert Murdoch urged to sell off newspaper by top News Corp shareholder', Richard Blackden, Telegraph online, http://www.telegraph. co.uk/finance/newsbysector/mediatechnologyandtelecoms/8843215/Rupert-Murdoch-urged-to-sell-off-newspapers-by-top-News-Corp-shareholder .html, 23 October 2011
4. BBC *Newsnight,* 9 November 2011
5. 'Unrest at Wapping spreads to the Sun after arrest', Ian Burrell, *Independent*, 9 November 2011

21. THE PRESS ON TRIAL

1. Robert Jay, counsel to the Leveson Inquiry, opening statement, Leveson Inquiry, 14 November 2011
2. Richard Caseby, oral evidence, Parliamentary Joint Committee on Privacy Injunctions, 13 December 2011

22. DARKER AND DARKER

1. 'Operation Elveden: five bailed in police payments probe', BBC Online, http://www.bbc.co.uk/news/uk-16771809, 29 January 2012
2. Andrew Neil interview, CNN, 16 February 2012
3. 'Rupert Murdoch should sell the Sun', Michael Wolff, Guardian online, http://www.guardian.co.uk/commentisfree/2012/feb/12/rupert-murdoch-should-sell-the-sun, 12 February 2012

Index

Note: The following abbreviations are used in the index: ICO = Information Commissioner's Office; *NoW* = *News of the World*; NI = News International. *n* attached to a page number denotes a footnote.

Aaranovitch, David 195*n*, 305
Abramson, Lawrence 49, 59–60, 103
Aggarwal, Nav 204–5
Akers, Sue
  background 155–6
  and John Prescott 159
  and *NoW* cooperation 176
  Operation Elveden (2011) 185
  and Operation Weeting 155, 158
  Sun bribery investigation 311
  and Tom Watson 180, 275
  victim notification 205
Aldhouse, Francis 30
Alexander, Douglas 188
Allen, Tamsin 124, 135, 136,
    177, 226
  see also judicial review
Alton, Roger 119, 173
Anderson, Janet 104
Andrew, Sky 51, 58, 116, 161, 174,
    307
Anwar, Aamer 205*n*
armed forces, phone
    hacking 203, 204

Armstrong, Jo 58, 69, 73, 116
arrests 43–4, 171, 211, 225, 267–8,
    270, 309, 311–12, 323–5
Ash, Leslie 159, 276
Ashdown, Paddy 121
Asprey, Helen 37, 39, 51
Austin, Ian 12
Australia 5

Baker, Andrew 111
Baldwin, Tom 162, 260
Balls, Ed 12, 184
Barlow, Hayley 266
BBC 79, 138, 223–4
  Andrew Marr Show 130
  Crimewatch 109, 110
  and Milly Dowler 195–6
  Newsnight 198
  Panorama 141–2, 163, 168,
    169–70
  Today programme 81–2, 130
Becker, Jo 115
Beckham, David 23, 51, 113
Begley, Charles 18–19

Bellfield, Levi 191
Bercow, John 131, 186, 265
Berlusconi, Silvio 7
Bernstein, Carl 213
Bertin, Gaby 259
Bindmans, judicial review 124, 135,
    136, 150, 177, 226, 308
Bird, Bob 141
Blair, Sir Ian 45
Blair, Tony
  departure date 9–10
  godfather to Rupert Murdoch's
    daughter 180
  and the media 211–12
  phone hacking target 180
  and Tom Watson 9, 94
  visit to Rupert Murdoch in
    Australia 7
Bland, Archie 173
Blunkett, David 23, 44–5, 156–7, 307
Boateng, Paul 18
Bonham Carter, Helena 188
Bovey, Grant 117
Bowley, Graham
Boyall, John 28, 32, 191
Bracadale, Lord 181
Bradby, Tom 34–5
Bradshaw, Ben 100
Bragge, Nicholas 69
Brennan, Kevin 187
Brett, Alastair 310
British Army, phone
  hacking 203, 204
Brokenshire, James 164
Brooks, Charlie 78, 80, 237, 311
Brooks, Rebekah
  Andy Gilchrist story 157–8
  anti-paedophile campaign
    17–18, 265
  arrest 311
  background 7–8

calls for resignation of 211, 227
Christmas meeting 150–51, 233
criticism of 216
Culture Committee evidence
  251–4
and David Cameron 63–4, 78, 80,
  150–51, 253
declines to give evidence to
  Culture Committee 103–4
early career 15
and Ed Vaizey 145
Hames and Cook surveillance 111
illegal data request 29, 70
Independent's election coverage
  119–20
and Ken Macdonald 256, 257
laptop computer 237, 274
management style 18–19, 216
and Milly Dowler 193,
  195, 197
NI chief executive 79
no knowledge of Mulcaire's
  work 195
NoW closure 206, 207, 212
and Operation Caryatid details
  46–8, 312
and pay-offs 103
police bribery comments 8,
  40, 242
potential phone hacking victim
  46–7, 312
resignation 228–9
and Sara Payne 17–18, 266
summer party 187
support from Rupert Murdoch
  202, 214, 217, 247
surveillance of 183*n*, 184
and Tom Watson 11, 281
and Tony Blair 8, 10
Brown, Gordon
  attacked by *Sun* 99

and the BBC 223–4
and Damian-gate plot 10–12
data checks on 33
and data theft 75
flat purchase 223
on phone hacking 83
phone hacking victim 100,
    152, 312
and the press 62
and Rebekah Brooks 80
and Rupert Murdoch 249
son's medical records 223
and Tom Watson 94
Brown, Nick 12, 33, 156
Browning, Baroness 196
Bruni, Carla 16
Bryant, Chris
    Blair's departure date 9–10
    BSkyB deal 187
    Commons debates 131, 132,
        163–4, 196, 201
    damages payment 306
    and Harbottle & Lewis 261
    and News International 87–8, 277
    and police bribery 8n
    and Scotland Yard judicial review
        124, 136, 177, 308
    and Tom Watson 100
BSkyB
    Ashes coverage 100
    government approval 186–7
    News Corp bid for 2, 122–3,
        138–40, 144–6, 161–3, 170
    News Corp withdraws bid
        for 2, 222
    opposition to bid 200–201,
        218–20
    Project Apple 312
    shares 203, 205, 211
Burton Copeland 45, 170, 175
Buscombe, Baroness 101, 195–6

Cable, Vince 138–9, 227
Cameron, David
    and Andy Coulson 83, 127, 151,
        211, 222, 259–60, 261
    Andy Coulson as communications
        director 62–3, 100–101,
        121–2, 253
    Andy Coulson's resignation 151
    and BSkyB 200–201, 219,
        222, 260
    Commons debates 221–2, 259–62
    Damian-gate plot 10
    and Harbottle & Lewis 261
    and the media 229, 257–8
    and Milly Dowler 193
    and MPs' expenses 100
    and the Murdochs 78–80, 184,
        204, 257–8
    and phone hacking 179
    and the press 61–2
    and public inquiry 2, 178,
        200, 211
    and Rebekah Brooks 78, 80,
        150–51, 211, 253, 258
    Rupert Murdoch post-election
        meeting 122, 244, 260
    and Scotland Yard 154–5
Campbell, Alastair 95, 197, 213
Campbell, Glenn 142, 178
Campbell, Hamish 168, 169
Campbell, Naomi 16
Campbell, Sol 51
Carey, Chase 222, 269
Carling, Will 15–16
Carswell, Douglas 204
Caseby, Richard 299
Cathcart, Brian 203
Chapman, Jessica 159, 178,
    197
Chapman, Jonathan (Jon) 57,
    59–60, 103, 231, 249

Chapman, Lee 159, 166, 276
Chapman, Leslie 159
Chappell, David 310
Charles, Prince 51
Chorley, Matt 130
Christensen, Helena 16
Church, Charlotte 31, 295–6, 307–8
Church of England
    Commissioners 283
Clark, Alison 8, 251
Clarke, Peter 47–8, 221, 273
Clarkson, Jeremy 23–4, 78, 80,
    232–3
Clegg, Nick 121, 196, 218–19
Clifford, Max
    decision to sue 87
    and George Osborne story 62
    hacking victim 51, 58
    NoW and Kerry Katona 39–40
    privacy claim and settlement
        113–14
Cloke, Daniel 54–5, 57
Coleman, Brian 234
Collins, Damian 287
computer hacking 86n,
    169–70, 181, 267, 307,
    309–10, 312
Coogan, Steve 123–4, 150, 160,
    213, 298, 307
Cook, David 110–12
Cook, James 112, 168
Cooper, Yvette 184
Copeland, David 109
Corden, James 184
Coren, Giles 202
Coulson, Andy
    apologizes to Prince Charles 51
    arrest 211
    background 22
    and Cameron 211, 222,
        259–60, 261
    Cameron's communications
        director 62–3, 83, 100–101,
        121–2, 127, 253
    and Clive Goodman 49
    denies knowledge of phone
        hacking 93, 141
    and George Osborne story 62–3
    and Jonathan Rees 107, 112,
        168–9
    and Ken Macdonald 256, 257
    and Matt Driscoll 26, 42, 101
    and Neil Wallis 259
    and New York Times
        article 127
    and Nick Robinson 137
    NoW awards 22–4, 41
    NoW final edition 214
    NoW income while working for
        Conservatives 93, 245, 253,
        272–3
    phone hacking email 46–7
    phone hacking knowledge 59–60,
        60, 125–6
    and police corruption 93, 198, 199
    resigns as communications
        director 150, 151–2
    resigns as NoW editor 53
    Scotland Yard interview 142–3
    Scotland Yard links 39
    security clearance 122
    staff sackings 26, 42
    and Steve Coogan 298
    and Tommy Sheridan 42, 141
    visit to Chequers 258
Cowell, Simon 284
Cowes, Rachel 191
cricket corruption 171
Crone, Tom
    and Clive Goodman 49, 55–6
    Culture Committee evidence
        89–93, 280, 286–7

departure from *NoW* 222, 251
'For Neville' email 73, 90,
    279, 280
'For Neville' email and James
    Murdoch 263, 276–7, 302
Gordon Taylor case 59, 70, 72–3,
    263
Harris/Lewis surveillance
    116–18
Max Clifford case 113–14
phone hacking admitted 302
phone hacking email 46–7
Will Carling interview 15–16
Crow, Bob 32
Crown Prosecution Service (CPS)
    advice on saved messages 38, 165,
        256, 257
    failings 256–7
    limited scope of Operation
        Caryatid 42
    and phone hacking allegations
        84, 87
    and saved messages 38
    Scotland Yard evidence 129
    Scotland Yard review (2011)
        150, 155
    see also Macdonald, Lord (Ken);
        Starmer, Keir
Culture, Media and Sport
    Committee
    Coulson and Kuttner evidence
        93–4
    Goodman appeal letter 270–72
    Hinton evidence 56–7, 97–8
    James Murdoch second appear-
        ance 285–8
    members' personal lives 94, 104
    Murdochs' appearance 3–5,
        240–51
    Myler and Crone evidence 89–93
    NoW inquiry 89–95

press standards investigation
    56–7, 65–6, 97–8, 104–6
Rebekah Brooks evidence 251–4
requires Murdochs to attend
    221, 224–5
shaving foam incident 4, 250
Yates evidence 97, 165–6

Dacre, Paul 75*n*, 213, 250, 252
Daily Express 192, 199, 291–2, 293
Daily Mail 74, 105, 192, 199, 213,
    250, 265
Daily Mirror 74, 108, 110, 180,
    199, 294
Daily Star 192, 291–2, 300–301
Daily Star Sunday 211
Daily Telegraph 85, 139–40, 192,
    199, 232
Dale, Iain 10
Dando, Jill 109
Darlow, Judge Paul 33
Darroch, Jeremy 144, 145
Data Protection Act (1998) 30, 31,
    32, 40, 49–50, 74–5, 141
Data Research Ltd 28
Davies, David 161
Davies, Nick
    claims questioned 102
    discloses potential hacking
        victims 116
    email deletions 212
    Flat Earth News 81–2, 119
    Max Clifford settlement 114
    and Milly Dowler 189–90
    phone hacking stories 82–3,
        104, 132
    and public figures 178
    and Sara Payne 266
    surveillance fears 118–19
Davies, Philip 91, 106, 131,
    246–7, 287

Davy, Chelsy 284–5
de Niro, Robert 16
de Piero, Gloria 184
Deng, Wendi (Murdoch's wife) 4,
    180, 240, 250, 295
Denham, John 144, 145
Desmond, Richard 184, 299
Devon and Cornwall Police,
    Operation Reproof 27–8,
    33–4, 156
Diamond, Anne 296–7
Dinh, Viet 202, 212
Diss, Philip 28, 33
Dobson, Frank 201
Dow Jones 64, 66, 67, 238
Dowler, Bob and Sally 190–91, 218,
    230–31, 276, 291
Dowler, Milly
    deleted messages 298–9
    Guardian sources 274–5
    NoW investigates
        disappearance 18
    phone hacking media coverage
        192–3
    phone hacking revealed 189–95
    reaction to revelations 192, 193,
        194–5, 196, 197, 252
Draper, Derek 10, 312–13
Driscoll, Matt 25–6, 41–2, 57, 101,
    125, 303
Dudman, Graham 158, 309
Dugher, Michael 11, 184
Dunlop, Daisy 179

Eady, Justice 77, 243, 310
Edelman PR 225, 270
Edmondson, Ian
    arrest 171
    joins *NoW* 23
    knowledge of phone hacking 60
    lawyers' surveillance 117

    and Max Mosley 281
    suspension from *NoW* 149–50,
        155
    unfair dismissal claim 276
Edwards, John 309
Enders, Claire 123
Eriksson, Sven-Göran 161
Eustice, George 61, 62
Evans, Rob 114
Evening Standard 24, 206, 220
Express Newspapers 291–2,
    299–300

Farmer, Richard 20
Farrelly, Paul 91, 97, 247–9, 282
Farrer & Co 43, 70–71, 96,
    113–14, 170, 282–3
Fazackerley, Anna 284
Federal Bureau of Investigation
    (FBI) 2, 227, 275, 308, 312
Fedorcio, Dick
    and the *Guardian* 102, 104
    investigation into 274
    and Neil Wallis 225, 235, 256
    and *NoW* surveillance 111, 126
    and press contacts 38–9, 235
Fenton, Ben 156
Ferguson, Sir Alex 25
Filkin, Elizabeth 236
Fillery, Sid 108, 110, 112, 168
Financial Times 156, 192
Firth, Sue and Bob 17
Flat Earth News (Davies) 81–2, 119
'For Neville' email
    contents and significance 69–70
    deletions 150
    employees named Neville 103
    Guardian story 82–3
    and James Murdoch 5, 73,
        251, 263, 276–7, 279,
        281–2, 302

and Neville Thurlbeck 90, 97, 279, 280
and Scotland Yard 85, 165–6
Foreign Corrupt Practices Act (US) 227, 275, 308, 312
Fortier, Kimberly 44
Foster, Patrick 86n, 310
Foulkes, Graham 199
Fowler, Lord 171–2, 203, 229
Freud, Matthew 65, 78, 123, 187–8
Frost, Sadie 157
Frostrup, Mariella 188
Fuller, Michael 128

Galloway, George 45, 160–61
Gardiner, Barry 187
Gascoigne, Paul 161
Geldof, Sir Bob 23–4
Gentle, Rose 203
Gilchrist, Andy 157–8
Glover, Stephen 24, 87
Godwin, Tim 155
Goldsmith, Lord 257, 284
Goldsmith, Zac 201
Goodman, Clive
  arrests 43–4, 211
  employment appeal letter 55–6, 270–72
  employment tribunal appeal 55–6, 57, 59–60, 103, 248–9
  employment tribunal payment 66, 91
  freelance career 66
  Harbottle & Lewis email review 59–60, 103, 170, 249, 271
  NoW royal editor 36–7
  NoW support and salary 49
  phone hacking 37–8
  phone hacking widely known 55–6, 59–60, 270
  prison sentence 51–2

and Rupert Murdoch 242–3
  sacked by NoW 54
  see also Harbottle & Lewis
Gorman, Dave 206
Gove, Michael 130, 187, 258, 277–8
Graham, Christopher 141
Grant, Hugh
  'Hacked Off' campaign 203
  Leveson Inquiry evidence 293
  and McMullan encounter 172
  and Milly Dowler 197
  NoW closure 208
  phone hacking victim 31, 41
  surveillance fears 173
Gray, Andy 150, 161, 174, 183
Green, Sir Philip 184
Greenberg, Simon 176, 197, 212
Greenslade, Roy 168, 202, 216
Grieve, Dominic 274–5
Gross, Justice 52
Grylls, Bear 188
Guardian
  and Culture Committee report 105
  Davies phone hacking stories 82–3, 104, 132
  and Jonathan Rees 107, 108, 112, 179–80
  Max Clifford settlement 114
  Milly Dowler story 189–90, 192, 199, 274–5, 298–9
  and New York Times 115, 130
  NoW stories 169
  Operation Weeting 156
  phone hacking crisis 203
  phone hacking story reaction 83–7, 102
  potential hacking victims 116
  on Scotland Yard 131–2
Guido Fawkes blog 10
Gunning, John 33, 110

'Hacked Off' campaign 203, 266
Hague, William 22–3, 259
Hain, Peter 312
Hall, Phil 17, 125
Hames, Jacqui 110–12
Hammell, Joan 44, 174
Hammond, Philip 217
Hanna, Mark 311
Hanning, James 141, 152
Hanrahan, Daniel 109
Harbottle & Lewis
    client confidentiality 261, 263
    email deletions 272
    file handed to NI lawyers 170
    internal review never requested
        271–2
    review of Goodman emails
        59–60, 103, 170, 249, 271
Harding, James 78, 86n, 195, 201,
    305, 310
Harkin, Greg 169
Harri, Guto 261–2
Harris, Charlotte
    'Hacked Off' campaign 203
    Max Clifford claim 87, 113–14
    Mulcaire files 68–9
    NoW surveillance 116–18,
        159–60, 288
    and public figures 178
    and Soham victims 159
    and Tom Watson 100
Harry, Prince 34, 36–7, 51, 285
Harverson, Paddy 39, 51
Hayman, Andy
    cleared of misconduct 273–4
    denies impropriety 220–21
    expenses inquiry 86n
    Home Affairs criticism 255–6
    and Menezes shooting 226
    Mulcaire details on 45
    and NoW links 38–9

personal conduct 136–7
    Times columnist 86–7, 235
Heat 22
Heath, David 190
Hello! 71, 73, 292
Henry, Sheila 307
Hewison, John 73, 116
Hickman & Rose 184–5
Hickman, Martin xviii–xix, 120,
    156, 157, 177, 178, 192
Hill, Amelia 189–90, 236, 266, 274
Hilton, Steve 107, 187
Hindley, Ross 69, 90, 132
Hinton, Les
    appointed to Dow Jones 67
    Clive Goodman pay-off 56–7, 98
    Clive Goodman sacked 54
    Culture Committee evidence
        56–7, 90
    and Data Protection Act reform
        49–50
    failures 315
    and John Whittingdale 232
    no evidence of widespread phone
        hacking 57, 90, 126
    resignation 231
HJK 40, 226, 308
Hoare, Sean 26, 125, 127, 130,
    133, 142, 143, 236
Hoare, Stuart 303
Holland, Tracey 157–8
Holt, Kevin 284
Home Affairs Committee 131,
    220–21, 255–6
Hoon, Geoff 83
Hoppen, Kelly 160, 174
Horton, Richard (Nightjack
    blogger) 86n, 310
House of Commons
    debates 131, 132–3, 163–4, 201,
        221–4, 259–62

Deputy Serjeant-at-Arms 3, 224–5
see also Culture, Media and Sport
    Committee; Home Affairs
    Committee
House of Lords, Murdoch evidence
    to Communications Committee
    66–7, 221
Hughes, Simon 51, 58, 260, 307
Hundall, Sunny 200
Hunt, Jeremy
    background 139–40
    and BBC Trust 79
    and BSkyB 153–4, 162–3, 186–7,
        217–18, 219
    links with News Corp 144–6
    public consultation 204
Hurst, Ian 169, 267
Hyde, Marina 299

Independent
    Andy Gilchrist story 157–8
    and Culture Committee report
        105
    and Jonathan Rees targets
        179–80
    and Milly Dowler 192
    News International intimidation
        164
    NoW stories 168–9
    phone hacking 156, 203
    Rupert Murdoch's approach to
        164
Independent Police Complaints
    Commission (IPCC) 205, 226,
    235, 236, 273–4, 312
Independent on Sunday 130, 141,
    152, 232
Information Commissioner's
    Office (ICO)
    infringements for Taylor case
        69, 70

Operation Motorman 28–33,
    40–41
What Price Privacy? 40, 41,
    50, 74

Jackson, Ben 149, 226, 308
James, Kim and Simon 110
Jay, Robert, QC 289–90,
    300, 302
John, Elton 23
Johnson, Alan 131–2, 260–61
Johnson, Boris 45, 133–4, 202, 226,
    234, 284
Jones, Kevan 137
Jones, Taff 33
Jowell, Tessa 44, 130, 174, 187
judicial review of Metropolitan
    Police 124, 135, 136, 150, 177,
    226, 308

Katona, Kerry 40, 51
Katz, Ian 107, 112, 122*n*
Kaufmann, Gerald 180
Kavanagh, Trevor 11, 257, 309
Kay, John 309
Keeler, Christine 13
Keller, Bill 115, 133
Kelner, Simon 119–20
Kelsey-Fry, John 51–2
Kemp, Ross 8
Kennedy, Charles 284
Keswick, Archie 149
Khan, Jemima 41, 201, 293
Kilfoyle, Peter 130
King, Alan 32
King, Peter 275
King, Sally 157, 307
Kirby, Ian 98
Klein, Joel 202, 212
Kleinman, Mark 222
Kray, Ronnie 15, 301

Kuenssberg, Laura 221
Kuttner, Stuart 60, 81–2, 93–4, 252, 266, 267–8

Law, Jude 88, 149, 157, 226, 231, 306–7
   see also Jackson, Ben
Lawson, Glen 33
Lebedev, Alexander 119, 164
Lennon, Kevin 108
Leveson Inquiry
   announcement and terms of reference 32n, 289–90
   evidence 290–304
   members 32n
Leveson, Lord Justice 302
Levitt, Alison 150
Lewis, James 177
Lewis, Mark
   Gordon Taylor case 58–9, 71–2, 73, 263
   injunction threat 96
   Milly Dowler case 190, 231, 276
   NoW surveillance 116–18, 159–60, 288
   and public figures 178
   and Scotland Yard 136–7
   Scotland Yard's Mulcaire files 68–9
   and Whittamore searches 69
Lewis, Martin 206
Lewis, Will 80, 140, 170, 176, 187, 212, 312
Linehan, Graham 137
Lineker, Gary 206
Llewellyn, Ed 122, 122n
London terrorist attacks 199, 226, 307
Loos, Rebecca 23, 51, 113
Lowther-Pinkerton, Jamie 37, 51
Luckhurst, Tim 24

Maberly, Mark 69
McBride, Damian 10–11, 12, 312
McCann, Gerry and Kate 291–2, 299–300
McCartney, Paul 265, 301
McCluskey, Len 254
Macdonald, Lord (Ken) 184–5, 243, 256–7
McGuire, Mick 161
McKenna, Rosemary 104
Mackenzie, Kelvin 6, 173–4, 297, 299
McKinnon, Justice Colin 20
McLagan, Graham 109
McMullan, Paul 16, 132, 143, 198–9, 213, 302–3
Macpherson, Elle 51, 58, 284
MacTaggart lecture 79, 224
Maguire, Kevin 98
Mahmood, Mazher 19–20, 160–61, 171, 215
Mail on Sunday 15–16, 74, 187, 216, 293
Malthouse, Kit 176
Man Who Owns the News, The (Wolff) 5, 239n
Management and Standards Committee (MSC) 207, 212, 263, 275, 282, 308–9, 312
Mandelson, Peter 130, 180, 187
Mann, John 262
Mansfield, Michael 226
Marshall, Paul 31, 32
Marshall, Sharon 126
   Tabloid Girl 21, 301
Marunchak, Alex 110, 111, 169, 170, 181, 235
Mason, Edward 283
May, Theresa 131, 184, 226, 233, 236
May-Bowles, Jonathan 4, 250
Mellor, David 180, 290

Menezes, Jean-Charles de 226
Mensch, Louise 250, 252
Metropolitan Police *see*
    Scotland Yard
Meyer, Sir Christopher 31, 54
Michael, George 137
Middleton, Kate 54, 180
Miliband, David 187
Miliband, Ed
    and Andy Coulson 260
    and the media 210
    and Rebekah Brooks 194, 204
    and Rupert Murdoch 229
    social contacts 184
Miller, Sienna
    decision to sue 124, 149, 160
    Leveson Inquiry evidence 293–4
    NI settlement 174, 176
    press publicity 88–9
Mills, David 44, 174
Mills, Heather 265, 301
Milmo, Cahal 156, 157–8, 192
Milner, Clive 264
Miskiw, Greg
    arrest 270
    illegal data request 29
    and Mulcaire's contract 69, 71,
        105, 278–9
    NoW executive news editor 17, 19
mobile phone companies 48, 104
Mockridge, Tom 229, 273
Mohan, Dominic 285
Montague, Brendan 130*n*, 136, 177
Montgomerie, Tim 152
Moran, Caitlin 197
Morgan, Alastair 108, 168
Morgan, Daniel 107–9, 110–12,
    167–9, 313
Morgan, Piers
    Blair and Murdoch 7
    on Coulson's resignation 152

and Kray story 15, 301
NoW editor 15
and Paul McCartney 265, 301
and phone hacking 264–5
and police bribery 8*n*
social contacts 187
The Insider 15, 301
Mosley, Alexander 135–6
Mosley, Max
    financial support for judicial
        review 135–6, 150, 308
    NoW story 75–8, 281
    and Tom Watson 239
    see also judicial review
Moss, Vincent 98
Mourinho, José 284
Mowatt, Jim 254
Mulcaire, Glenn
    contract 69, 71, 105, 278–9
    employment tribunal 66, 91,
        248–9
    employment tribunal
        payment 66
    and Gordon Taylor 68–70,
        278–9
    Hames and Cook data 110–11
    illegal activities 1–2
    legal fees 66, 91, 247, 251,
        263
    and Milly Dowler 195
    no unilateral action 267*n*
    notes *see* Mulcaire files
    NoW contacts 161
    offices raided 44
    phone hacking for *NoW* 39–40,
        104, 132
    PIN codes 104
    prison sentence 2, 51
    security adviser 66
    volume of material seized 44, 82,
        116, 289–90

Mulcaire files
  failure to inform individuals
    85, 129
  on Gordon Taylor 68–9
  individuals informed 130, 177
  individuals named in notes 312,
    319–22
  judicial review (Bindmans) 124,
    135, 136, 150, 177
  on Max Clifford 113
  redacted 113
  requests for access to 88, 89
  Soham parents 159, 166
  storage 165
  volume of material 44, 82,
    116, 289–90
  see also 'For Neville email'
Murdoch, Elisabeth (Liz) 65, 78,
  162, 187–8, 232, 239, 269
Murdoch, James
  apologies 229–30, 288
  bonus forgone 269
  Culture Committee appearances
    3–5, 221, 241–51, 285–8
  email deletion 150
  failings 315–16
  'For Neville' email 5, 73,
    251, 263, 276–7, 279,
    281–2, 302
  Gordon Taylor pay-off 71, 72–3,
    92–3, 162, 207, 245, 282–3,
    286, 287–8
  Independent's election coverage
    119–20
  MacTaggart lecture 79, 224
  News Corp career 65, 67,
    170–71, 311
  NoW closure 206–7
  reputation crisis 175
  resigns as BSkyB chairman 311
  summer party 187

Murdoch, Lachlan 64–5, 239, 283,
  284, 310
Murdoch, Rupert
  arrival in UK 217
  BSkyB see BSkyB
  and Charlotte Church 295
  and Clive Goodman 242–3
  Culture Committee appearance 1,
    3–5, 221, 241–51
  Culture Committee attendance
    declined 224
  and David Cameron 61–2, 122,
    244, 260
  denies wrongdoing 138
  and Dowler parents 230–31
  editorial style 6, 14–15, 66–7,
    221, 246–7
  and Gordon Brown 249
  and Gordon Taylor pay-off 246–7
  humble statement 3, 241
  and Independent proprietors 164
  Lords Committee evidence
    66–7, 221
  market dominance 5–6
  and MySpace 64, 238
  and Neville Thurlbeck 243
  News Corp annual meeting 283–4
  newsroom climate 5–6, 13–14,
    315
  political endorsements 6–7, 62,
    121, 244, 249, 314
  and Rebekah Brooks 202, 214,
    217, 247
  reliance on Harbottle & Lewis
    material 249, 271
  salary and bonus 269, 284
  statement on phone hacking
    scandal 202
  summer party 183–4
  Sun Sunday edition 310–11
  and Tom Watson 94

and Tony Blair 7
and *Wall Street Journal* 64, 66
Murphy, Katie 254
Myler, Colin
  apologies 175
  appointed *NoW* editor 53
  and Clive Goodman 54
  Culture Committee evidence
    89–93, 280, 286–7
  email deletion 150
  and Gordon Taylor case 70, 71,
    72–3, 263
  James Murdoch and 'For Neville'
    email 263, 276–7, 280
  and the McCanns 292
  and Milly Dowler 201
  no cover-up 302–3
  NoW award 171
  NoW final edition 214
  and phone interception 96–7
  and resignation from BSkyB 311
MySpace 64, 238

Neil, Andrew 14, 87
New Statesman 245, 253
New York Times 115, 125–7, 133
News Corporation
  and BSkyB bid 2, 122–3, 138–40,
    153–4, 170
  Dow Jones acquisition 64, 66,
    67, 238
  future of 316
  governance 67, 239, 269, 283, 284
  Management and Standards
    Committee (MSC) 207, 212,
    263, 275, 282, 308–9, 312
  market dominance 5–6
  and MySpace 64, 238
  profits 269
  salaries and bonuses 269, 284
  share price 2, 67, 201, 203, 221

and Shine 162
US investigations 2, 226–7, 275,
  308, 312
News International (NI)
  Andy Coulson payments 93,
    245–6, 253, 272–3
  apologies 230
  and Cameron government 257–9
  civil court actions 160–61, 174–5,
    276, 306, 307–8
  computer hacking 86*n*, 169–70,
    267, 307
  Culture Committee criticism 105
  denies *Guardian* story 85
  and Director of Public
    Prosecutions 256–7
  email deletions 96, 124–5, 133,
    150, 212, 267, 272
  email storage 141, 147–8
  employment tribunals 55–6, 57,
    59–60, 66, 91, 103, 248–9, 276
  inquiries 236
  intimidation 163–4
  James Murdoch resignation 311
  knowledge of phone hacking
    55–6, 57, 59–60,
    174–5, 251–2
  links with Scotland Yard 235–6
  and Milly Dowler 192, 193,
    195, 252
  pay-offs 92–3, 102–3
  police corruption evidence 57, 60,
    170, 184–5, 216
  Rebekah Brooks named chief
    executive 79
  and senior public figures 178–81
News of the World
  advertiser boycott 197, 200,
    201, 205
  armed forces 203, 204
  awards 23–4, 41, 171

News of the World – cont.
 and celebrity 22
 and Charlotte Church 296
 closure 206–9, 212
 computer hacking 169–70, 267
 and confidential data 108
 and Culture Committee members
  89, 94, 104
 Culture Committee report 105–6
 final edition 214–16
 and George Osborne 62–3
 Gordon Taylor case 68, 69–74
 Guardian breaks phone hacking
  story 82–3, 86–7
 Guardian's Milly Dowler story
  189–95, 197, 198, 201, 206,
  252, 299
 history 13
 illegal activities 1–2, 24–6, 71–3,
  109–10, 126–7, 177
 and Madeleine McCann 292
 and Max Clifford 112–14
 and Max Mosley 75–8
 Murdoch's editorial control 6, 15,
  66–7, 221, 246–7
 newsroom culture 14–17, 21
 and police corruption 93, 198,
  199, 206
 police obstruction 43–4, 175–6
 and private detectives 107, 112,
  168–9, 252, 284–5
 and Sara Payne 17–18, 266–7
 and Steve Coogan 298
 surveillance 110–12, 116–18,
  159–60
Newton Dunn, Tom 105, 194, 204
Nightjack blogger 86*n*, 310
9/11 victims 217, 227
Nixson, Matt 264
Northern Ireland 169

NoW magazine 22
Noye, Kenneth 109

Oborne, Peter 204
Observer 130
O'Donnell, Sir Gus 144–6, 262
Ofcom 79, 139, 153–4, 186,
  201, 312
O'Neill, Sean 168
Operation Caryatid (2006) 35–40,
  42–8, 85, 90, 126, 136–7, 312
Operation Elveden (police
  corruption) 185, 200, 205,
  275, 285, 312
Operation Glade (2004) 31–3
Operation Motorman (2003)
  28–33, 40–41
Operation Reproof (2002) 27–8,
  33–4, 156
Operation Tuleta (computer
  hacking) 181, 267, 310, 312
Operation Weeting (2011) 155–6,
  158, 175–6, 177, 179, 192,
  202, 224, 226, 267–8, 312
Opik, Lembit 100
Orde, Sir Hugh 234
Osborne, George
 and Andy Coulson 253
 and the BBC 138
 and NI 258
 NoW drugs story 10, 62–3
 social contacts 80
 victim of phone hacking 202–3
Owens, Alec 28–31, 32, 40–41, 74

Paddick, Brian 124, 128, 136,
  177, 308
Palker, Jeff 212
Panton, Lucy 39
Parker, Nick 309

Parkes, Ciara 149
Parkinson, Stephen 251
Pascoe-Watson, George 10, 11, 64
Paxman, Jeremy 198
Payne, Sara 265–7, 306
Payne, Sarah 17–18, 265
PCC *see* Press Complaints
    Commission (PCC)
People 281
Peppiatt, Richard 300–301
Pereira, Alex 226
Peston, Robert
    and BSkyB 139, 205
    and Coulson 272–3
    and Edmondson 149
    Nixson sacking 264
    NoW payouts 174–5
    and Rebekah Brooks 193, 233
    royal family security 220
    social contacts 187
    and Watson 264
Pharo, Chris 309
Phillips, Nicola 116, 174
Pike, Julian
    and BSkyB 170
    Gordon Taylor case 70–71,
      71–2, 263
    Harris/Lewis surveillance
      116–18
    Max Clifford case 113–14
    and phone hacking 282
    Scotland Yard office search 43
Pilger, John 203
Pinochet, Augusto 109
police *see* Devon and Cornwall
    Police; Scotland Yard; Strath-
    clyde Police
Police and Criminal Evidence Act
    (1984) 45–6, 274
Pound, Stephen 137

Prescott, John
    and Andy Coulson 83
    damages payment 306
    phone interception 44, 48, 84,
      130, 131, 159
    Scotland Yard judicial review
      136, 177, 308
    and Tom Watson 100
Press Complaints Commission (PCC)
    Code of Practice 31
    and covert newsgathering 59
    exonerates *NoW* 101–2, 104–5
    failings 211, 290
    future of 313–14
    and Milly Dowler 195–6
    new inquiry 83, 97
    NoW investigation 54
    and Victoria Spencer 15
Price, Adam 93, 104
Price, Lance 7
Pritchard, Mark 186
Private Eye 6, 230
Prodi, Romano 7
Project Apple 312
Purdew, Stephen 232
Purnell, James 187
Pyatt, Jamie 285

Quinn, Kimberly 156

Rawlings, Baroness 204
Red Rag website 11–12
Reed, Jeremy 68, 69, 113–14
Rees, Jonathan 107–10, 122n,
    167–9, 170, 178–80, 181
Regulation of Investigatory Powers
    Act (2000) (RIPA) 38, 51, 87,
    131, 142, 256
Rimmer, Stephen 131–2
Roberts, Bob 194

Robinson, James 156
Robinson, Nick 137, 196, 234
Rooney, Wayne 177
Rose, Dinah 307
Ross, Jonathan 137, 208
Rotherham, Steve 288
Rowe, Natalie 62
Rowling, J.K. 294–5
Royal British Legion 203
Royal family 51, 220, 268
    see also Harry, Prince; William,
        Prince
Royall, Baroness 204
Rusbridger, Alan
    and Andy Coulson 121
    and Gordon Taylor 82
    and Milly Dowler 299
    and New York Times 115
    and phone hacking 102
    and Scotland Yard 104
    surveillance fears 119

Sabbagh, Dan 86
Sabey, Ryan 37
Salter, Martin 33
Samuels, Judge John, 32, 191
Samuels, Judge John, QC 32
Sanders, Adrian 245–6, 253
Scappaticci, Freddie (Stakeknife)
    169, 170
Scotland Yard
    advice on saved messages 38, 165,
        256, 257
    Andy Coulson interviewed 142–3
    arrests 43–4, 171, 211, 225, 267–8,
        270, 309, 311–12, 323–5
    Chamy media contract 225–6
    corruption 8, 93, 198, 199,
        206, 225–6
    corruption evidence 57, 60, 170,
        184–5, 216
    corruption inquiry see Operation
        Elveden (below)
    counter-terrorism responsibilities
        36
    CPS review (2011) 150, 155
    Culture Committee criticism 105
    Daniel Morgan murder enquiries
        108–9, 110–12, 167–8
    failures 45–6, 47–8, 313, 314
    and Guardian 102, 274–5
    inquiries 236
    judicial review (Bindmans) 124,
        135, 136, 150, 177, 226, 308
    links with News International
        235–6
    and NoW stories 20
    and NoW surveillance 110–12
    Operation Caryatid (2006)
        35–40, 42–8, 85, 90, 126,
        136–7, 312
    Operation Elveden (police
        corruption) 185, 200, 205,
        275, 285, 312
    Operation Glade (2004) 31–3
    Operation Tuleta (computer
        hacking) 181, 267, 310, 312
    Operation Weeting (2011)
        155–6, 158, 175–6, 177, 179,
        192, 202, 224, 226, 237,
        267–8, 312
    Rebekah Brooks's comments on
        police bribery 8, 40, 242
    review of phone hacking alleg-
        ations 83–5
    and victims of phone hacking 85,
        115–16, 128–9, 130, 205
    Watson's letter 128–9
    see also Hayman, Andy; Mulcaire
        files; Stephenson, Sir Paul
7/7 London attacks 199, 226, 307
Shanahan, Fergus 11, 309

Sheridan, Jim 4, 244–5
Sheridan, Louise 157
Sheridan, Tommy 23, 42, 140–41,
    181–2, 205n, 245, 265, 273, 313
Shine 162
Silverleaf, Michael, QC 71,
    176, 282–3, 286, 287–8,
    302, 307
Simon, Siôn 9, 12, 128, 147, 177
Singh, Rav 298
Small, Christian 307
Smith, Adam 145
Snow, Jon 197
Soham children 159, 166, 178, 197,
    199, 205
Spencer, Victoria 15
Spitzer, Eliot 226–7
Staines, Paul 10
Stakeknife: Britain's Secret
    Agents in Ireland (Hurst
    and Harkin) 169
Starmer, Keir 84, 87, 142, 150, 165,
    257, 274–5
Stenson, Jules 60, 208
Stephenson, Sir Paul
    and Guardian 102
    health issues 155
    hospitality 232, 274
    and Milly Dowling 196
    and Neil Wallis 225, 263
    and Operation Weeting 176
    phone hacking inquiry 83,
        273–4
    and police corruption 200
    resignation 233–4
Stevens, Sir John 20, 66, 180
Stidwell, Alan 28, 33
Strathclyde Police 205n, 264
Straw, Jack 74, 180
Stretford, Paul 177
Sturgis, John 309

Sullivan, Michael 309
Sun
    and Anne Diamond 296–7, 299
    and armed forces 203
    arrests of staff 309
    bribery investigation 311
    Culture Committee report 105
    and David Cameron 63–4, 121
    false stories 6
    and Gordon Brown 99, 223
    and Hugh Grant 293
    and J.K. Rowling 294
    and Max Mosley 77
    and Milly Dowler 192–3, 199
    Murdoch's editorial control 6,
        66–7, 221
    Neil Wallis editorship 23
    and phone hacking 157–8, 262–3,
        277
    and Steve Coogan 298
    sued by Jude Law 231
    sued by Tom Watson 89
    Sunday edition 310–11
    Tom Watson and Damian-gate
        10, 11–12
Sunday Express 293
Sunday Mirror 108, 110
Sunday Telegraph 157
Sunday Times, The
    and Charlotte Church 295–6
    and data protection reform 50
    and Gordon Brown 223
    Murdoch's editorial control 6, 14,
        66–7
    and Paul Stephenson 232
    and police corruption 216
Surtees, Keith 43, 44
Sutcliffe, Peter 109

Tabloid Girl (Marshall) 21, 301
Tarrant, Chris 31, 160

Taylor, Gordon
  damages request 58–9
  and Jo Armstrong 58
  NoW reaction 69–74
  payout request 58–9, 71–4
  Scotland Yard files 68–9
  settlement 73, 82–3, 92–3, 162,
    207, 245, 246–7, 263, 286
  see also 'For Neville' email
terrorism
  7/7 London attacks 199, 226, 307
  9/11 victims 217, 227
Thatcher, Margaret 6
Thomas, Richard 30–31, 32–3, 40,
    49–50, 74–5
Thompson, Mark 187
Thomson, Mark 88–9, 124, 149,
    159–60, 178
Thornton, Andrew 205
Thurlbeck, Neville
  arrest 171, 311–12
  Clive Goodman story 37
  contests hacking allegations 276,
    278–80
  corruption trial 20
  and Culture Committee
    members 94
  and Dorset guesthouse 17
  'For Neville' email *see* 'For
    Neville' email
  and Jo Armstrong 58
  and Max Mosley 75–7
  meeting with Tom Watson
    278–82
  promoted to news editor 17
  and Rupert Murdoch 243
  and Scotland Yard 235
Times, The
  attacks *Guardian* story 86–7
  computer hacking 86n, 309–10
  Culture Committee report 105

  and data protection reform 50
  and investigative journalism 305
  and Milly Dowler 192, 195, 201–2
  priorities 262
  Rees and BBC 168
  Rupert Murdoch's influence 6,
    66–7
  Wapping dispute 6
Today 287
Townsend, Phillip 296
Trinity Mirror 264–5
Turner, Anthea 117

United States
  9/11 attacks 217, 227
  News Corp investigations 2,
    226–7, 275, 308, 312
  Rupert Murdoch's influence 5

Vaizey, Ed 79, 145, 187
Van Natta Jr, Don 125, 126
Vian, Glenn and Gary 112, 167,
    168
Vos, Justice 113, 176, 177, 307

Wade, Rebekah *see* Brooks,
    Rebekah
Al-Waleed bin Talal Al-saud 227,
    228, 239
Wall Street Journal 64, 66, 225, 271
Wallace of Saltaire, Lord 172
Wallis, Neil (Wolfman)
  arrest 225
  background 23
  knowledge of phone hacking 60
  and Matt Driscoll 42
  and Scotland Yard 39, 102,
    225–6, 232, 234, 235
Warby, Mark 76
Ward, James 167
Warnes, Austin 110

Watson, Tom
  and Andy Coulson 122
  and BSkyB 144–6, 153, 186, 187
  Commons debates 131, 132–3, 163
  Culture Committee sessions 4, 89,
    92–4, 241–4, 250, 252, 254,
    286–7
  and 'Damian-gate' 10–12
  and David Cameron 178
  effect on personal life xviii, 3–4,
    146–7
  and email storage 141
  GMB conference speech 185
  and Gordon Taylor pay-off 92–3
  letter to Metropolitan Police
    128–9
  and Milly Dowler 190
  Neville Thurlbeck's story 278–82
  News Corp annual meeting
    283–4
  News International deal offered
    185–6
  NoW requests removal from
    Committee hearing 89
  NoW surveillance 98, 137, 147
  and Rebekah Brooks 281
  and Robert Peston 264
  and Rupert Murdoch's influence
    8–9
  and Scotland Yard 154–5
  and senior public figures 178–9,
    181
  social media use 137
  and the Sun 89, 277
  and Tommy Sheridan 181–2, 205n
Weatherup, James 23, 175
Webb, Derek 98, 117–18, 146–7,
    284–5
Webster, Geoff 309
Wells, Holly 29, 159, 166, 178, 197
Welsh, David 27

Wessex, Countess of 268
Westlake, Richard 132
'What Price Privacy?' 40, 41, 50, 74
Wheelan, Charlie 12
Wheeler, Brian 63
Where Power Lies (Price) 7
Whetstone, Rachel 187
White, James 18
Whittamore, Steve
  customers 252
  and Daily Mail 213
  detailed records 28–30, 40, 74
  ICO prosecution 32–3
  and Milly Dowler 191
  NI requests 69–70, 83
Whittingdale, John
  BSkyB bid 186–7, 218
  Culture Committee chairman
    56–7, 89, 240–41, 250, 251
  NoW misconduct 193
  social connections 232
Wild, David 147
William, Prince 34, 36–7, 51,
    54, 285
Williams, Paul 39
  see also Mulcaire, Glenn
Williams, Philip 38, 45, 84
Wintour, Patrick 262
Wolff, Michael 239n, 246n, 316–17
Wooton, Dan 206

Yates, John
  accused of misleading Parliament
    163, 164–6
  admits failings 216–17
  at Home Affairs Committee 131
  and CPS review 150
  Culture Committee evidence 97,
    165–6
  and Guardian story 102, 104
  media duties 83–4

Mulcaire target 45
and *New York Times* article
130–31, 133
personal conduct 136–7
phone hacking inquiry 83–5,
273–4

phone hacking target 180
resignation 234–5
response to Watson
letter 130*n*
Yentob, Alan 187
Young, Toby 193